Rogue Empires

CONTRACTS AND CONMEN IN EUROPE'S SCRAMBLE FOR AFRICA

Steven Press

Harvard University Press
Cambridge, Massachusetts
London, England
2017

Second printing

Library of Congress Cataloging-in-Publication Data

Names: Press, Steven, author.
Title: Rogue empires : contracts and conmen in Europe's scramble for Africa / Steven Press.
Description: Cambridge, Massachusetts : Harvard University Press, 2017. | Includes bibliographical references and index.
Identifiers: LCCN 2016044726 | ISBN 9780674971851 (cloth)
Subjects: LCSH: Africa—Colonization—History. | Berlin West Africa Conference (1884–1885 : Berlin, Germany) | Europe—Colonies—Administration—History. | Bismarck, Otto, Fürst von, 1815–1898. | Gladstone, W. E. (William Ewart), 1809–1898.
Classification: LCC JV246 .P74 2017 | DDC 325.6—dc23
LC record available at https://lccn.loc.gov/2016044726

To my parents, Michael, Deborah, and David

Contents

Rogue Empires

Introduction

IN OCTOBER 1890, George Washington Williams wrote to President Benjamin Harrison about what he called "one of the foulest crimes of modern diplomatic history."[1] Williams, an African American historian in his forties, had just spent several months in the heart of Central Africa. On behalf of several newspapers, he was investigating some five hundred treaties by which indigenous leaders had allegedly sold their sovereignty—a European concept usually associated with supreme rulership over a place's land and people.[2] The buyer of this unusual bounty, located along the Congo River, was the Independent State of the Congo. Yet this was no ordinary state. It was, to quote one diplomat, "an anomaly and a monstrosity": "a curious case of abnormal birth" that Europeans and Africans alike struggled to explain.[3] Before the Independent State had become the world's newest government, Williams told Harrison, it had begun in the 1870s as a modest private association run not from the Congo, or even from another part of Africa, but from the Château de Laeken, a royal palace outside of Brussels, Belgium. Incredibly, this same organization now claimed that purchases it had made in the Congo region gave it political control over a territory estimated at more than one million square miles in dimension.[4] The territory amounted to an area eighty-three times the size of Belgium, or almost four times the size of France.[5] It also, Williams added, rested on a gigantic lie.

Williams made for an unlikely whistleblower. Just six years earlier, in Washington, D.C., he had lobbied the U.S. government to become the first major power to dignify dozens of the Independent State's purchase contracts.[6] At one point, Williams even offered to recruit black laborers from New Orleans to the Congo for work as porters.[7] Like his budding contemporary, W. E. B. Du Bois, he hoped to see an international enterprise eradicate what remained of the eastern slave trade in Central Africa. Williams therefore had reason to believe in the Independent State, whose leaders, at the very moment Williams wrote his letter to Harrison, chaired an international conference in Brussels pledging to "put an end to Negro slave trade by land as well as by sea, and to improve the moral and material conditions of existence of the native races."[8] Yet, once Williams actually traveled to the Congo interior to see matters for himself, his credulity gave way to suspicion. Those treaties which should have given the Independent State its legitimacy—treaties which the United States hastily sanctioned, allowing a fledgling polity to convince European investors of its bona fides—had been, according to sources on the ground, obtained through either duress or trickery. This was when the treaties had been obtained at all, and not fabricated outright.

Williams might never have learned these things had he heeded warnings from Belgium's Leopold II, "King-Sovereign of the Independent State," not to enter the Congo or speak with any residents.[9] Once Williams did go, the truth proved explosive enough to make him fear for his life.[10] As he told President Harrison, the Independent State had never appeared in some of the places where it claimed to have bought sovereignty through treaties. Many indigenous leaders did not even know the supposed government's name, with one official report, published in Brussels in 1889, estimating the latter employed only fifty-two civil servants in Africa.[11] Moreover, in several of those areas where the civil servants had arrived, their most visible activity so far had been to engage in confiscations. Their regime asserted far-reaching claims to the soil, animals, and minerals—enough for one British informant to warn that the regime would soon, if unmolested, try to seize the entire country's supply.[12] Soon the new Independent State went so far as to enforce a law permitting seizures of any "non-state" boats sailing the Congo.[13]

Though Williams's reporting caused an uproar in the international press, it had little impact in Washington, and its author succumbed to a lung infection on his return voyage from Africa.[14] True, his charges of "crimes against humanity" would later resurface as part of an international humanitarian campaign against the Independent State featuring Sir Arthur Conan Doyle and Mark Twain.[15] But by then the U.S. State Department had long been aware of what Williams had uncovered; embarrassed diplomats simply resolved to conceal it.[16] One reason why was that, in late 1884, around half a year after the U.S. Senate first extended its approval for the Congo treaties, agents of the State Department moved to sway European powerbrokers, in an international conference convening in Berlin, to lend their imprimaturs to the Independent State of the Congo.[17] So forceful and efficacious was this support that, for a time, European diplomats referred to the Independent State as "the United States of the Congo."[18]

Shortly after Williams's death, the authorities of the Independent State moved deeper into the territory that was nominally theirs to govern.[19] Along the way they uprooted entire villages, took hostages, followed East African slavers into conscripting forced labor, and governed largely by virtue of a number of unpublished, and at times conflicting, decrees.[20] The Independent State set up courts of justice as far east as Leopoldville (Kinshasa), beyond which only martial law was held valid.[21] And courts were certainly needed, not least because the foreign traders endowed by the state with absolute control over villages included an ex-American who periodically dressed like the devil, raped villagers' daughters, and summarily executed his victims.[22] Alas, nary an official in the few judicial venues that existed spoke African languages. Perhaps worse still, there were three proper jails in the entire country, and the supposed "interpreters" offered by courts to accused defendants were, by the admission of the state's own judges, often cheats with nothing but poor French to conceal their venality.[23]

Over the next several years the Independent State did not officially condone slavery—arguably a measure of progress, even if so-called Arab slave raiding remained endemic in eastern, Swahili-speaking sections of the Congo Basin.[24] Nevertheless, many European missionaries came to fear that the unfortunates living along the Congo—where population estimates ran as high as forty-nine million, though the first census was not undertaken until the 1910s—were on their way to annihilation through cruelty.[25] Millions would verifiably perish between 1890 and 1908, when a disgraced and dying Leopold II sold off control over the Independent State, in yet another treaty, to Belgium. In the interim the bartering of human lives continued de facto, with countless laborers losing limbs to the hatchet men of the Force Publique, the Independent State's version of a police force.[26]

As reports of atrocities slowly leaked to the West—a German government official noted as early as 1887 that the Independent State treated African workers in an "inhumanly raw" way—it was logical to ask how the world had endorsed the Independent State in the first place.[27] Historians continue to search for answers to this day, with many writers, notably Adam Hochschild, seeking to disentangle a web of social, moral, political, and economic interests about which the scholarly community has struggled to achieve consensus.[28] Using pieces of such literature as the starting point for a new set of arguments and insights, this book examines the global confusion over sovereignty wrought by the Independent State of the Congo and a host of related political forms. The book shows how a particular type of treaty was a sine qua non for some pivotal developments in nineteenth- and early twentieth-century imperialism. To understand this treaty and its relationship with a fundamental concept in our world—sovereignty—we have to situate the Congo within a larger, global setting. We have to include Washington, D.C., London, Berlin, numerous other points in Africa, and, somewhat counterintuitively, Southeast Asia. Doing so will help to clarify how these treaties came to be, and why so many of them came to look the same way at the same time around 1884, arguably the decisive year in the partition of Africa and, most infamously, the time of the Berlin Conference.

In the 1880s a race was on among Europeans, spanning virtually the entire African continent from Tunisia in the North to the Orange River in the South.[29] Some of its nicknames are familiar: the "Steeplechase" in France, the "Scramble" in England.[30] What is less known is that this was a race, not necessarily to conquer or take land by force—most of that came later, starting in the 1890s—but to claim treaties, or paper deeds, which nominally sold to Europeans the titles to govern various territories.[31] The competition was so prolific as to cause a noticeable surge in the world's treaty production: as much as a 100 percent increase, according to one metric.[32] For instance, in addition to the hundreds of pacts made by Leopold's men in the Congo area, British businessmen in East Africa produced 389 treaties that allegedly showed indigenous leaders signing over sovereignty.[33] This effort slightly outpaced that along the Niger River, where the total amounted to 237.[34] Meanwhile the Germans, French, and Portuguese also produced cartloads of such documents in East, West, and Southwest Africa respectively.[35] To the extent that this torrent of treaties appears in histories of the period, it generally does so in isolation: as a part of the origins of colonialism in a particular place—Cameroon, say.[36] Often, the pertinent treaties are held to be merely a prelude to the establishment of serious European colonization. Or they are seen as a deceitful, abusive sign of colonialism that was used, typically in the 1890s and 1900s, to justify the exploitation of indigenous lands and labor.[37]

There is much merit to the interpretation of the treaties as "lawfare," even if it tends to overlook the diversity of treaties involved. Documents purporting to sign over sovereignty in African territories sometimes went untranslated in African languages.[38] On paper, they often stated that pieces of cloth or copper wire were to suffice as cash equivalents to rights of sovereignty.[39] Given all that, it is tempting to say that the treaties were simply a cover for theft from indigenous peoples.[40] Indeed, some Europeans involved in making the treaties later repudiated their own handiwork. Friedrich Fabri, a missionary who assisted German imperialists in Southwest Africa, talked of "paper agreements whose sense and meaning, whose consequence necessarily remained hidden."[41] In the case of East Africa, a young Frederick Lugard confided similar doubts to his diary, in part, he said, because many pacts' particulars could not be translated into indigenous languages.[42] Lugard oversaw and enforced dozens of such arrangements in his career before he decided, from the comfortable seat of his post at the League of Nations in Geneva, to deny their legitimacy in public.[43]

We know today that treaties signed in the African Scramble not only helped to redraw the map, but also often determined to what degree indigenous populations controlled the continent's mineral wealth.[44] Those consequences continue to manifest themselves in court disputes.[45] Crucially, though, despite the general air of opprobrium that envelops the treaties, they are still considered valid by customary international law.[46] But—what is a treaty? What did the concept mean in the nineteenth century? This was a time, as Edward Keene has argued, that witnessed an explosion in treaty making, with the number of interstate agreements growing nearly sevenfold relative to the previous century.[47] Owing in part to the proliferation of European diplomatic academies and legal codifications, these new agreements were proving increasingly significant in world affairs on the eve of the African Scramble. Yet one must note that not all such agreements took the title of "treaty," because Europeans negotiating with polities in Africa and Arabia—a practice increasingly common starting in the 1810s, with the onset of Britain's antislaving initiative—never quite agreed what a treaty was, who could make it, or how it differed from some other common forms: pacts or contracts, for instance.[48] Without firm demarcations, European officials often designated pacts and contracts as treaties for practical purposes.[49] Thus, although this book uses the word "treaty" broadly and loosely in order to refer to interstate agreements generally, as European diplomats did in their own documents, readers need to keep in mind that around 1884, problems of treaty definition and nomenclature were very much at issue, both within and without Africa.

The treaty race, carried out in Africa in the 1880s and 1890s, was itself far from uniform, for the treaties signing over titles to govern parts of Africa claimed to do very different things.[50] Some were drunken farces; some were sober products of negotiation. Some were vague; some were quite literal. Some were leases; some were sales. Some held the formal title of "treaty" and had the appearance of a compact between equals; some, not titled at all, merely amounted to protection contracts resembling the arrangements a mafia foists on shop owners.[51] But throughout all this tumult in early colonial Africa there was one curious, abiding fact: Hundreds of the treaties purported to transfer control of entire countries to one man, or to a company, rather than to a preexisting European state.

A "private" treaty signing over sovereignty, not to a European government, but to Europeans: That was what had appeared, by 1890, to have made the Independent State of the Congo possible. But such treaties were not restricted to the case of the Independent State. On the contrary, they appeared widely throughout Sub-Saharan Africa during the late nineteenth century, and especially in areas that fell under German, Belgian, and British control circa 1884. Moreover, the treaties in question came about as conscious imitations of arrangements made far away from Africa, on the Southeast Asian island of Borneo. How a template began on Borneo, then made its way to Europe and to Africa, is an unexplored subject with major implications. It adds new chapters to the story of the African Scramble, changing both when and where the story begins and ends. It alters how we understand the role of treaties in the partition of Africa. It also changes our understanding of sovereignty itself. Accordingly, this book spotlights the subject as an overlooked precondition for three major developments: the surprise entry of Germany into the formal race for overseas colonies; the creation of Leopold II's empire in Central Africa, that is, the Independent State of the Congo; and the improbable revival of the chartered-company system of colonial government by Germany, Belgium, Britain, Portugal, and Italy.

There is a distinct, albeit forgotten, history embedded within the European partition of Africa from 1882 to the 1890s. This particular history has affected modern Namibia, the Democratic Republic of the Congo, Togo, Cameroon, Tanzania, Uganda, Nigeria, and Malawi directly; indirectly, it has touched Kenya, Zimbabwe, Zambia, Botswana, and Mozambique, with residual effects in Asian locales like Brunei and Malaysia. Its essence was not fraudulent treaty making by Europeans—that kind of duplicity occurred intermittently in European interactions with non-European communities from at least the late fifteenth century. No, this forgotten history consisted of a moment when treaty-making adventurers and cynical statesmen manipulated a particular loophole in international law to their own ends. The loophole theoretically allowed private individuals or companies—as distinct from preexisting states—to claim first that they bought sovereignty through treaties, and thereafter, with some luck, to found an empire accepted by the international community as enjoying equality and reciprocity with its other members: states. On paper, the powers accrued by such private actors were priceless. They included the authority to claim eminent domain over all land and mineral wealth within a given territory. They also included such traditional state prerogatives as rights to tax, police, mint money, make war, control courts, and dispose over the life and death of inhabitants. Endless fortune, endless power: It was all within reach.

The loophole in question was controversial at the time and, at least in a sense, short-lived, owing in part to its eventual concealment and denial by an embarrassed European legal community. Today, historians generally do not acknowledge the loophole, let alone its impact, choosing instead to depict entities like the Independent State of the Congo solely as "private empires" or "fiefdoms" whose operations sometimes behooved, but rarely concerned, European leaders.[52] Here revision is necessary. For one, the concept of a "private empire" can easily be applied to a global business—say, De Beers—and does not capture what distinguished a De Beers from the Independent State of the Congo. More important, the term "private empire," if deployed without context, obscures that from the 1880s to the 1890s, Western governments extended diplomatic recognition to several independent, for-profit governing entities in Southeast

Asia and Africa, including two in Borneo; one in the Congo; and others in Southwest Africa (Namibia), Tanzania, and Nigeria. Although allegations of ethical lapses rightly surrounded these embryonic empires and their treaties, European leaders overwhelmingly brushed the doubts aside for a decade, elevating the would-be powers to a legal status and breadth unknown before or since.

A more fitting epithet to apply to these unique political forms is "rogue empires." "Rogue," of course, is a tricky term. To many, the term suggests illegality. Yet, from the perspective of people living under imperial control, even as far back as Julius Caesar's Gallic Wars, there has likely never been such a thing as a non-rogue or legitimate empire. Moreover, the designation of a "rogue" empire risks implying that other empires founded by traditional European authorities—say, in Algeria—were legitimate. A key point of this book is that the Independent State of the Congo and its ilk were not illegal; rather, their claims to govern were advanced by ethically flexible men who, for a moment, successfully exploited European legal opinion and attitudes toward governance. Nonetheless, the term "rogue" helps to recapture a sense of fraudulence that surrounded particular empire-builders in the nineteenth century. The term also speaks to the unpredictable character of their ventures, which shared DNA with traditional empires in a place like Africa, but could also look and feel elusive. These "rogue" empires were qualitatively different, not because they proved illegitimate for colonial peoples, but because of the way in which they challenged Europe's laws while only briefly winning approval from Western legal institutions, as well as from traditional seats of imperial power.

"Empire" is a problematic concept in its own right. Even in the twenty-first century, it is difficult to agree where old "empires" ended and "states" began; accordingly, the two concepts often appear interchangeable in this book. Again, such blurring of definitional lines paradoxically speaks to key points. When evaluating claims to statehood and empire made by rogue actors in Africa into the 1890s, traditional European states had to examine their own claims to rule, some parts of which rested on treaties and principles no less dubious than those of their interlocutors. Figuring out how much "statehood" to attribute to a rogue empire in Africa meant revisiting the desired legitimacy, not just of a distant French or British colony, but also of potentially imperial governing foundations closer to home: say, the treaty that transferred authority over Alaska from Russia to the United States; or the transfer of federal powers in a newly unified Germany. Without the rogues, therefore, one might miss a crucial aspect of perception about how European powers proper got so hands-on with African colonization in the 1880s.

More than a dozen different explanations exist for why the African Scramble occurred.[53] Every historian seeks to solve a riddle: Why did Africa, where Europeans had contented themselves with mostly informal control prior to the 1880s, and that at only a handful of coastal spots, undergo a near-complete partition by the end of the century? According to what is perhaps the most famous answer, (1) Britain's transition from informal to formal empire never really happened; (2) the rash of British imperial expansion in Africa during the later nineteenth century mostly emerged as a response to instability in Egypt and South Africa; (3) the decisive cause for this expansion was strategic, not economic, involving as it did a wish to maintain access to India via certain points on the African continent; and (4) this British expansion set off a kind of territorial arms race among European powers that became known as the Scramble.[54]

A fresh answer lies, not just in Europe, or even in Africa itself, but in Southeast Asia. The flood of private treaties and states that dominated the African 1880s did not happen because of international lawyers. On the contrary, the flood happened in spite of them, because of a series of variably clever copycats employing a single, powerful precedent.[55] One could easily call the latter behavior legal posturing, thus borrowing a term from Lauren Benton and Daniel Hulsebosch.[56] One could likewise, to borrow from C. A. Bayly, define it as a kind of imperial ricochet from Southeast Asia to Africa.[57]

No diplomatic, political, or legal study has addressed this phenomenon at length, notwithstanding that it, too, featured heavily in the equation of African partition. Of course, readers might well expect economic theorists of imperialism to have studied the matter exhaustively. By all rights economic theorists should have had the most to say when it came to any Anglo-European people or companies claiming to pay for sovereignty in foreign lands. But consider the case of J. A. Hobson, who, along with Vladimir Lenin, dominated early twentieth-century discussions about imperialism. Hobson, whose work continues to stimulate Marxist historians, noted the presence of privately governed empires in Africa in his landmark book, *Imperialism: A Study.* Yet, Hobson made no comment on their origin, their status in law, or the curiosity that was their existence. Why his interest in the phenomenon proved so cursory is a mystery: It may have owed to the fact that, during the 1880s (the heyday of the rogue empires), he actually championed overseas colonization via what he called "commercial advances."[58] The rogue empires had mostly vanished by the time of Hobson's work as a newspaper correspondent in the Second Anglo-Boer War—arguably the decisive phase in his development of a thesis about the prostration of European foreign policy to finance. At any rate, Hobson's scant examination of privately governed empires, coupled with the now widely accepted inapplicability of his theory of imperialism to the Scramble, is another cause for renewed scrutiny.

This book aims to reexamine the African Scramble by recovering some contemporary debates and confusion about what a state was, and about whether sovereignty existed as a commodity. Perhaps the most important aspect of these exchanges was to assess the way legalistic or quasi-legalistic manipulations of the sovereignty principle in one part of the globe (Southeast Asia) were closely studied and adapted for use in another continent. This was a process in which private entrepreneurs, established European governments, and international lawyers interacted in a complicated dance that existing theories of imperialism—widely insistent on particular case studies—have failed to capture.[59] Obviously the process proved devastating to many Africans; they were often victims of a treaty fraud, if to varying extents.[60] But, in order to better understand why, one must make certain inquiries, not just about results, but about the way in which Europeans carried out their work. Where and when did the idea of "private" buying of sovereignty through treaties germinate? How did European states support this idea in the late nineteenth-century partition of Africa, only to deny it later on? Finally, what effect did this curious idea have, not just on certain African or Asian populations, but on Western institutions and the Western international legal corpus?

1

The Man Who Bought a Country

THE MORNING OF SEPTEMBER 24, 1841, James Brooke woke up a stranger in a strange land. By the end of the day, he had been crowned a king.

Born in India, Brooke set foot on the island of Borneo for the first time in September 1839.[1] Back in England, Brooke's ancestral home, Borneo was terra incognita.[2] Despite scant information owing to a ban on missionary travel through the late 1830s—imposed by Dutch colonial officials who had gradually taken over the island's southern half since the seventeenth century—one commentator joked that less was known of Borneo than "of the North pole or of the headwaters of the Nile."[3] Nonetheless, this place had been attracting attention from international traders for more than a half-century.[4] Britain's empire was cementing a crucial period of expansion in Asia, and Borneo lay in the middle of a thriving maritime network between China, India, and Australia.[5] Borneo's location gave it great value, especially in view of the contemporaneous expansion of trade with China via the First Opium War. Many British ships started in India, passed through the Straits of Malacca, and then rounded the western and northern shore of Borneo before arriving in the South China Sea and moving on to Canton. Whoever controlled the Borneo coast could assist this China trade—say, by providing wood and supplies with which to refuel ship crews. They could also throttle it.

James Brooke admired the British colonization of Singapore, begun twenty years earlier by Stamford Raffles, and he wanted to extend what he saw as a superior civilization, as well as free trade, to areas even farther afield.[6] Brooke grew interested in some large parcels of jungle in the northwestern section of Borneo, collectively known as Sarawak. This seemed a dangerous place, a hunting ground for pirates and the orangutan. The brush was so thick as to allow easy ambushes, and, among the most populous indigenous people, the Iban, marriage was conditional upon young men taking a head.[7] Any European visitor would have to take this mystique into account, if tropical disease, leeches, or a crocodile did not overtake him first.

Sarawak was one of many polities then comprising the northern half of Borneo, which remained largely free of the sway Dutch colonists had established over the island's southern half.[8] At the time of Brooke's arrival, the northern polities existed as dependencies under the rule of Omar Ali Saifuddin II, the sultan of Brunei. The sultan was the latest in a line of warriors who, several centuries earlier, had begun to Islamize a Brunei-based, Malay-speaking empire of Sumatran extraction. Primarily confined to the coast at first, the Islamized Bruneian power gradually became a paramount authority in Borneo's interior, from whose subordinate kingdoms it exacted tribute.[9] Its sultans commanded respect as far abroad as Manila and even earned the attention of Qing official Wei Yuan, who analyzed them in his landmark *Illustrated Treatise on the Maritime Kingdoms.*[10] But by Brooke's time Brunei's imperial system teetered on the brink of dissolution, riven by civil wars, increasingly unable to defend against raiders based to the east, in the archipelago of Sulu, and struggling to adapt to European penetration of trade—much like Johor and Aceh, two neighboring Malay empires and competitors for regional supremacy. An uprising in Sarawak was the latest problem facing Brunei. Its cause was Mahkota, the sultan's cousin and Dutch-educated provincial governor, who coerced local residents into mining antimony in an attempt to cash in on a booming export trade to Singapore.[11] Mahkota's tax regime proved so exacting as to make enemies out of Sarawak's Ibans, as well as the Bidayuh, the area's second-most numerous indigenous people.[12] Most important, it also alienated the three leading *datus,* or aristocratic chiefs, whom Brunei had earlier placed in charge of administration, and with whom Mahkota and the sultan shared an ethnic heritage.[13]

By the late 1830s, Mahkota grew overwhelmed with his efforts to put down the revolt. Concerned about lost revenue, his cousin, the sultan, looked for outside help. One idea was to sell governing rights over Sarawak to the sultan of Sambas, a relative of Mahkota in southern

Borneo with a vested interest in antimony mining and a formidable private army.[14] The prevailing alternative, however, was to seek aid from a series of European adventurers who, at that time, cruised the ports of Southeast Asia looking to use their guns to make a fortune. James Brooke was such a man. A veteran of the Bengal army of the East India Company (EIC), he had retired from active duty after an injury in the First Anglo-Burmese War, then inherited a small fortune from his father. Eventually a wandering Brooke outfitted a yacht, the *Royalist,* and sailed to Kuching, the administrative center of Sarawak, with a crew of a dozen or so men, aiming to deliver a desultory message from the governor of Singapore to the sultan's uncle and designated heir, Muda Hassim, but also interested in prospecting for minerals.

The plan to seek minerals stemmed in part from reports made by a missionary, George Lay, but also from a general atmosphere of permissiveness, including pleas from the navigator George Windsor Earl for Britons to extend their influence in Southeast Asia.[15] Lay did not yet know the word "Sarawak" literally meant "antimony" in the sultan's official language, Malay. But he nonetheless wrote favorably of Brunei's antimony ore, as well as its coal deposits—certain to catch the eye of the British navy's steamship captains—and the likelihood that Brunei could soon entice its northern provinces, including Sarawak, to join a kind of confederacy. Brooke's arrival in Sarawak led to the desired meeting with Muda Hassim, who was then visiting in order to assist Governor Mahkota. Hassim hoped Brooke, his yacht outfitted with heavy guns, could bring Western firepower to bear on Brunei's enemies. "Could" was the operative word. Mere money did not sufficiently tempt Brooke, and besides, Brunei was, like its Dutch neighbors to the south, suffering from a major recession.[16] However, after multiple interviews and the ouster of Mahkota, Hassim allegedly proposed a more palatable trade: Brooke would help crush the insurgents in exchange for the rights and title of a *rajah* (Malay for "king") in the province of Sarawak. This offer, Brooke later recalled, included the country's trade and government rights, provided Brooke made annual tribute payments to the sultan.[17]

If taken at face value, the offer was not quite so novel as it may appear today. When one looks into the Malay tradition that gave rise to the Brunei Empire, one encounters numerous cases of bartered political control and, at least among aristocrats, a lack of differentiation between trade and governance. The *Sejarah Melayu,* a series of sixteenth-century annals whose most reliable iteration was published in English in 1821, tell how Malay rulers, whether local or imperial, consistently put a price on governmental powers, without ethical scruples. One such case took place around 1700, when Brunei sold control over the Kimanis River to Sulu; another saw Brunei acquire control over five districts, including Sarawak, from the sultan of Johor.[18] Sovereignty, the annals say, is thus a cash register.[19] Add to this that the Sultanate of Brunei had begun, several centuries before 1839, with what the anthropologist Marshall Sahlins has called a series of stranger-kings.[20] Even outside Brunei, the hundreds of Dayak peoples comprising the indigenous population of Borneo—among them the Ibans and Bidayuh—had a long history of such dynasties. Some of them had even come about through transactions made in part by non-Dayaks and non-Malays: men like Sharif Abd-al Rahman, who in the 1770s acquired the Sultanate of Pontianak in an area that later, by the 1800s, fell under Dutch control.[21]

Brooke, of course, was European. Thus it would not be unreasonable to assume that at least *this* aspect of his deal was something new in 1840. But here, too, the reality looks otherwise, for he was merely the latest in a series of Europeans in receipt of a virtual kingdom in Southeast Asia.[22] From the early eighteenth century on, certain English traders working for the East India Company around the Malay Peninsula had made similar arrangements, though sometimes without a formal transfer of title. In 1713, for instance, Joseph Collet reported that, thanks to his negotiations with the indigenous rulers on Sumatra, he had become a king, with the inhabitants of Bengkulu obeying his commands as if they came from a sovereign ruler.[23] In 1812 Raffles's colleague Alexander Hare went one step further, convincing a ruler in southern Borneo, the sultan of Banjarmasin, to give him a title to govern 1,400 square miles at Moluko.[24] Banjarmasin was uninviting: English colonists had already failed there in 1707.[25] But a crucial precedent was that Hare acted on his own initiative.[26] True, he used his license to cultivate a large harem of women. True, his efforts at pepper cultivation failed, despite the importation of some 3,200 workers from Java, and he surrendered his country after a few years, leaving behind only a few copper coins he had minted as a new currency.[27] But Hare's story became known to British and Dutch traders in the area, many of whom went on to engage with Bruneian officials. The sultan and his uncle, the familiar Hassim, were two such figures.

When Hassim offered control of Sarawak to James Brooke, the latter was only thirty-eight years old. Brooke's diary, accordingly, revealed plenty of self-doubt about governing.[28] As regarded battle, though, he owned six heavy guns, which might allow him to do the improbable in a society whose firepower did not extend beyond darts. It took little time to end the revolt; not long after accepting Hassim's offer, Brooke hired a diverse team of mercenaries, blew up the main opposition base, and initiated a rapprochement with the local Malay elites. Following a sojourn to Singapore, where he received encouragement from British officials, Brooke returned to the island of Borneo in 1841 intending to take formal control of Sarawak and its population: 45,000 souls, according to one contemporary estimate, with perhaps 1,500 of these living in Kuching.[29]

Such an ascent became the stuff of colonial fiction; Joseph Conrad used it, one of his childhood fixations, as material for the novels *Lord Jim* and *The Rescue;* less cerebrally, the popular Italian writer Emilio Salgari cast Brooke in his serialized adventure stories.[30] In 1841, however, questions abounded about whether Brunei would honor the agreement Muda Hassim made. Not long after Brooke returned from Singapore, Hassim—who did not enjoy a reputation for honesty—denied any arrangement to transfer Sarawak's government. That same day, Brooke's interpreter died after eating rice laced with arsenic, probably at the behest of the sidelined Mahkota.[31] Eventually, after another trip to Singapore and more encouragement, Brooke warned of retaliation. He headed back to Sarawak onboard the *Royalist,* its guns loaded, for what he hoped would be the final round of negotiations. On September 24, 1841, at around ten o'clock in the evening, a cowed Hassim declared Brooke "Rajah and governor of Sarawak, amidst the roar of cannon and a general display of flags and banners on the shore and the vessels on the river." For his bona fides Brooke even got Hassim to write out a formal deed according to which he, "with a clear conscience and integrity," transferred to Brooke power over the country of Sarawak, along with all governmental revenues.[32]

The only copy of this document to have survived is in English translation. In it, Hassim speaks of the "transfer of the Government" to Brooke. He acknowledges that Brooke is to "be the sole owner" of government revenues, even guaranteeing that "no person is to meddle or interfere with [his] government on any pretense, whether of politics or trade." But there were caveats. For example, Hassim calls for Brooke to ensure respect for the rights of indigenous peoples—"to preserve their laws, and not to meddle with their religion."[33] Brooke's control is also said to derive from annual cash payments to the sultan and various other officials, thus seemingly remaining contingent on Brunei's oversight.[34]

Sarawak's Malay elites, who had earlier rejected Mahkota, did not easily accept Brooke's ascendancy, either. To be sure, the sultan of Brunei, Saifuddin II, signed a document supporting Hassim's decision on August 1, 1842—again at ten o'clock in the evening, and again with the only extant copy being an English translation. This time, though, the document emerged across from the bow of a Royal Navy ship, ostensibly in town to ensure the release of two private British vessels captured by the sultan. A harried Saifuddin confirmed that Brooke would make regular payments in exchange for control over Sarawak, with the provisos that payments would increase if Sarawak's trade flourished, and that "James Brooke Esquire covenants and undertakes to observe the orders, custom, laws and regulations of His Highness the Sultan."[35] But the sultan's decree would be challenged in Sarawak; that had been the whole message behind the rebellion. He was also, by Brooke's reckoning, highly unreliable. He had made lots of false assurances in the past, and his health was quite poor. Besides, Malay elites tended to believe Brooke's lease on control was akin to Mahkota's old governorship—and thus revocable at the pleasure of the sultan.[36] The sultan could remove Brooke, if he so chose—as easily as the sultan removed Hassim from his position as designated heir to the throne from 1842 through the fall of 1844.

A gap began to emerge between this qualified interpretation and the one espoused by Brooke, who harbored ambitions of full independence from Brunei. In the period from 1843 to 1846, the gap widened to a chasm when Brooke made multiple visits to the sultan with the purpose of reinstalling Hassim as the heir and repeatedly confirming Sarawak's independence, each time in a more elaborate way.[37] Out of sympathy for Brooke's putative antipiracy initiative and keen to support informal British domination in north Borneo, members of the overgrown British navy typically escorted Brooke on these visits, only to find the sultan's advisors building up forts along the river out of concern for invasion. In one instance, Admiral Thomas John Cochrane dispatched eight warships from Singapore to Brunei simultaneously.[38]

Throughout this cycle, British vessels turned their guns directly on the sultan's palace, where negotiators discussed a series of treaties. The palace was located to the northeast of Sarawak in Brunei Town (in Malay, Bandar Brunei), a city of perhaps twenty-five thousand surrounded by hills and situated fifteen miles down the Brunei River, which ran from the egress of the South China Sea at the northern end of Borneo down into the interior. Though Brunei Town contained pockets of settled land, virtually every one of its buildings sat on stilts, with the houses seeming to float on water. Antonio Pigafetta, the first European chronicler to visit, reportedly called this place the "Venice of the East," but being himself from Venice, he must have known that servants there did not wear clothes made out of gold and silk, whereas here they did.[39] Pigafetta arrived in 1521, when the sultan of Brunei sat at the head of a prosperous maritime empire, and when Brunei Town served as the region's Islamic trading hub with a population as high as 375,000.[40] One sack by Spain and three centuries later, fortune had taken such a toll that the famous naturalist Alfred Russel Wallace mocked Brunei Town as a "Venice of Hovels."[41] Yes, local authorities still ensured that a market opened daily, allowing countryside growers to sell small produce, usually by way of canoe. But European competition crowded out a once-lucrative trade with China, and what little industry remained operated in filth, without any infrastructure, and, perhaps worse still, without any defense against semi-regular raids that ravaged the coast and surrounding countryside in a quest for forced labor.[42] Brunei Town, like the Brunei Empire around it, seemed stuck in a process of decay. Houses, which Brooke's official biographer described as "built on the slenderest of piles—mere palms," typically rotted within a few years. Population totals dropped yearly. And then there was the water, which harbored effluvia offensive to noses and capable of turning "the gold and silver of uniforms to the color of dirt."[43] Even the palace at which British negotiators met the sultan fit neatly into a narrative of decline. Although the palace's prodigious facade attested to its past greatness, and although servants rushed to offer visitors tea and cigars, the atmosphere inside was dingy. One admiral complained that the furniture consisted almost entirely of mats and rickety wooden chairs.[44]

Brooke regularly pressured the sultan, whose advisors at one point allegedly hired assassins to kill Brooke, Muda Hassim, and a host of their entourage.[45] But the true threat came from the British navy. In 1845 and 1846, its admirals presented evidence—provided by Brooke, now doubling as Britain's consul general to Brunei—that members of the sultan's council were aiding and abetting slave raiders out of northeastern Borneo, in return for a share of the spoils. Trade in Singapore, Brooke alleged, had experienced setbacks because of this system. The sultan should make amends, and when he did so, he should make them with Brooke, recently named Britain's lead negotiator.[46]

With gunboats at his doorstep, the sultan acknowledged the charges and promptly made three main concessions.[47] First, he ceded to Britain his sovereignty over the island of Labuan, a strategically important, if thinly populated, site off Brunei Town's coast where the Royal Geographical Society had once hoped, and the Royal Navy in 1844 had demanded, to turn a safe harbor supposedly loaded with coal into a refueling station.[48] Second, he agreed not to make any more transfers of provinces under his sway without prior approval from Britain.[49] Third, he recognized James Brooke as the independent sovereign of Sarawak.[50] From this point on, Brooke was allowed to discontinue the tribute of roughly 2,500 Spanish dollars he had been making every year.[51] In theory, Brooke also could try criminal and civil cases under whatever law system he liked, without Brunei's oversight. He could levy his own taxation and customs, he could fly his own flag, and he could even pass his rulership on to "whomever of his family that may be left wishing to govern the country of Sarawak . . . in the event of [his] demise."[52] Given all this, and given that Brooke no longer needed to worry about Brunei's interference in the religious or personal affairs of his subjects, talk of his arrangement as "feudal" ended—at least for several years, until Brooke moved to expand Sarawak's borders by leasing yet more territories from the sultan.[53]

The Western world rushed to celebrate Brooke.[54] President Zachary Taylor sent the "Sovereign Prince of Sarawak" a formal letter proposing the establishment of diplomatic relations and a treaty of commerce.[55] The United States acknowledged "His Highness" Brooke as an absolute, independent ruler.[56] In Britain, Queen Victoria made "Sir" James a Knight of the Order of Bath; and the Royal Geographical Society awarded him its gold medal.[57] Alfred Russel Wallace attached Brooke's name to a magnificent butterfly specimen discovered on Borneo, *Trogonoptera brookiana* (Rajah Brooke's Birdwing).[58] James Brooke was thus becoming a household name, with Alice Kipling—soon to give birth to a writer named Rudyard—said to have idolized him.[59] Donations for his cause followed, principally from one of Britain's wealthiest women, Baroness Angela Burdett-Coutts. The baroness, sometimes thought to have fallen in love with Brooke, began to pay Sarawak's bills more or less as an act of philanthropy.[60] Her largesse helped the new ruler to repulse raiders in northwest Borneo, to encourage forestry projects (especially the cultivation of sago for export to Singapore), and to curtail, though not abolish, debt bondage and the taking of captives for labor.[61] Reforms in turn attracted greater settlement from abroad, especially Chinese migrants displaced by civil war in Dutch Borneo. Within a decade the population of Kuching alone quintupled, accelerating the city's development into a major entrepôt.[62] Exports increased tenfold.[63]

On balance Brooke developed into a competent colonial administrator.[64] Backed by a team of imported European civil servants, many of whom functioned as regional supervisors known as "residents," he set up a court of justice at his palace, a modest house with little to recommend it but wooden floors and walls.[65] His main achievement was to effectively merge distinct polities of Sarawak into a federal system, amnestying and salarying the *datus* who had opposed Mahkota—and who were eager to exercise power disproportionate to their one-third share of the population—while endowing regional Dayak authorities with more autonomy than Brunei had granted.[66] At the local level this kind of indirect rule allowed latitude for discrete ethnic and religious communities to govern themselves, often as it related to intra- or intertribal disputes.[67] Brooke's residents reserved the right to intervene but mostly focused on the solicitation of foreign investment, the building of infrastructure, and the repression of major criminal activity and dissidence.[68] Early on, such an approach—championed through the successful publication of a number of flattering, and frankly orientalist, biographies—helped Brooke to establish a cult of personality within Britain's middle and upper classes.[69] A steady supply of Chinese immigrant capital and labor also greatly assisted the process, as was common at most spokes of Southeast Asia's trading networks.[70] Hence, *The Economist* could not help but heap praise on Brooke.[71] Even William Gladstone, allergic to colonial panegyrics, made an exception for the "White

Rajah," whom he deemed "as gentle-hearted as he was brave and good."[72] After all, James was a fellow free-trader who almost entirely eliminated customs and tolls from his domain.

Influenced by numerous endorsements, the public initially came to believe that the rajah was a liberal agent of civilization working to overcome a disloyal staff of Mahkota holdovers in Sarawak's bureaucracy. In a further romantic twist, audiences read how Brooke was winning the consent of a Dayak majority by reinstating several ancient customs that predated the more recent rule from the sultans in Brunei.[73] To what extent such claims held remains debatable, as does the efficacy of Dayak participation in Brooke's government. But John Walker is right to argue that Brooke's power, personified in a yellow umbrella he wielded at public gatherings, owed to remarkable prowess.[74] His mystique was so potent that many Ibans asked him to spit in their cooked rice, hopeful that the addition would improve their health.[75] At least one Dayak dignitary abjured resistance because he believed Brooke held supernatural powers.[76]

Throughout the 1840s the British government proper mostly overlooked Brooke's rule as an anomaly, though technically they might have objected by citing the 1824 Treaty of London, which stipulated that "no territorial acquisitions could be made in the Eastern seas henceforth either on behalf of Great Britain or the Netherlands, except by the authorized officers of either Government."[77] For his part, Brooke did not strongly assert Sarawak's independence before the British public, preferring instead to solicit direct British colonization, or to say that he ruled with British interests at heart and coveted protection.[78] The Royal Navy helped to nurture such sentiment through the 1840s. But this modus vivendi would change irrevocably in 1851, when the Scottish Member of Parliament (MP) Joseph Hume—reinforcing arguments made by his better-known colleague Richard Cobden—aired a list of grievances against Sarawak's leader, whom he accused of "bad motives, ambitious designs, violence, tyranny, falsehood, injustice, and petty larceny."[79]

Hume laughed when colleagues referred to Brooke as "His Excellency."[80] Somewhat more fairly, he reminded these politicians—many of whose constituents still celebrated Brooke as a folk hero—that Brooke had extorted his title to rule.[81] While this fact alone did not invalidate agreements in international law at the time, Hume thought it must impinge upon the government's position. Given his immoral foundation, Brooke ought to appear in British eyes as nothing more than a "filibuster," and in fact Hong Kong and London newspapers, along with Dutch officials jealous of his incursion into Brunei, came to label him as such.[82] This charge carried cultural weight both good and bad: By 1850 the term "filibuster" was used to describe men like Josiah Harlan, an American army veteran who, in 1840, variously connived and fought his way into becoming the king of a province in Northwestern Afghanistan. (Several decades later, Rudyard Kipling would draw inspiration from both Harlan and Brooke when writing his short story, *The Man Who Would Be King.*[83])

Hume recalled the battle of Beting Maru in 1849, when Ibans loyal to Brooke, along with some moonlighting ships in the Royal Navy, mounted a nighttime assault in which they surprised and killed some 1,500 people living on the Saribas and Skrang rivers. Local residents had long shunned Brunei's Malay tax collectors; more recently, they had warred with the Ibans in Sarawak, fighting in favor of a less hierarchical and more mobile society that Brooke deemed piratical.[84] Now pamphlets from the Aborigines' Protection Society described a gruesome fate. Gladstone—once an admirer—urged parliament to look into a "large, easy, and unsparing slaughter" led by Brooke, who supposedly pursued victims "without resistance, or after resistance had ceased."[85] "I cannot conceive," Gladstone exclaimed, "a more shameful misdeed."[86] A formal inquiry in Singapore—conducted nearly a decade after the fact, from 1854 to 1855, as a gift to Hume and other British Radicals in exchange for support of Lord Aberdeen's cabinet—eventually confirmed some horror stories.[87] "Various shocking murders and dreadful atrocities in the way of head-taking and head-roasting," wrote the royal commission, "were committed by the native [Iban] forces under the said James Brooke, without any restraint or punishment thereof."[88]

Though such findings damaged Brooke's reputation, the commission's inquiry yielded few tangible results.[89] At the time, the main concern was whether to define those killed in the incident as pirates.[90] If one did so—as was easy, given the exceedingly vague definition maintained by British law through 1850—then the conduct of Brooke, his forces, and their associates in the Royal Navy, far from violating any British legislation, actually fell under the umbrella of its antipiracy provisions.[91] From 1825 until after the time of Brooke's alleged massacre, parliament even pledged to pay soldiers and freelancers alike a bounty for any pirate body: or, in a term perhaps more familiar to many Dayaks, "head-money."[92] In 1849 alone, the government at Singapore had disbursed £20,700 for this purpose to diverse parties.[93] Failing that, however, the commission would still have had to reckon with precedents. More or less contemporaneously with Brooke's initiative, British warships had annihilated a host of forts maintained by "pirate" units along the Saribas and Skrang.[94]

Faced with such glaring contradictions, it looked incongruous for the British government to condemn Royal Navy officers involved in the incident, let alone to apply its writ in Sarawak. If Brooke really owned all the rights he claimed, then that should suffice to keep Britain from interfering with his affairs one way or the other, however capacious their jurisdiction in matters of piracy had otherwise grown.[95] Brooke, in other words, could do whatever he pleased in his Sarawak, where he was the absolute lawgiver. At the same time, however, Britain seemed incapable of escaping from some form of involvement in Brooke's affairs. He was still a British subject, and the queen had even appointed him governor of Labuan—at least until the commission's inquiry recommended his removal from British posts.[96] A final wrinkle concerned Brooke's private property rights. Because Britain had pledged to uphold its subjects' property when they traveled abroad, an inventive mind could even argue—as Brooke did, on occasion—that Britain had a duty to protect Brooke's rights from foreign threats.[97] Precisely this had been the tenor of Foreign Secretary Palmerston's controversial *civis romanus sum* principle, adopted before the House of Commons in 1850.[98] "A British subject, in whatever land he may be," said Palmerston, "shall feel confident that the watchful eye and strong arm of England will protect him against injustice and wrong."[99] As if to punctuate the argument, the latest treaty with Brunei confirming Brooke's rule over Sarawak had been signed under British oversight, with an effective British guarantee—and a vague commitment to fight piracy.

Although Brooke resigned from his consular and gubernatorial posts amid all this complication, the Singapore commission returned an indecisive verdict. Its two members left open the question of a nonstate empire, with one deriding the idea as outlawry and another willing to admit it as a legitimate possibility.[100] Thereafter, however, developments in Sarawak added a renewed sense of urgency to the debate, with many in a Chinese cabal beginning to doubt Brooke's future support from the Royal Navy. In 1857—obviously the early days of the Second Opium War, but, as importantly, the first year of the India Rebellion—a sizeable contingent of Chinese launched an armed assault, murdering several Europeans and torching Brooke's home with the assistance of some Malay elites.[101] As Brooke secured loans and Sikh mercenaries to reestablish his control in the capital city, which experienced days of bloody reprisals from Dayaks loyal to the rajah, he continued to think about what would become of his rule when he died. His health suffered a dramatic downturn, Sarawak's extractive industries stagnated, and his reliance on Baroness Coutts to pay state bills—estimated at £55,000 to this point—could not last forever.[102] In fact, the proximate cause for the explosive violence in 1857 had been an attempt to replenish Brooke's coffers: His award of monopoly mineral rights to a new European consortium led to a struggle for trade supremacy with gold miners in Bau, a town two dozen miles upriver from Kuching, and a gathering place for aggrieved Chinese and Malay mining investors.[103]

Brooke had sired no legitimate heirs and questioned whether his potential successors could match his supernatural mystique, which had long been pivotal for rulers in Malay societies.[104] Furthermore, a succession dispute was brewing among three contenders: Coutts, the philanthropist to whom he had pledged his state as collateral for a debt; Brooke Brooke, his nephew; and Charles Brooke, another nephew.[105] Instead of consistently supporting a successor from this pool, James Brooke revisited the notion that he might place his government in the hands of a major European power.[106] The latter could likely offer Sarawak's burgeoning population—on track to reach 240,000 by the 1870s—more enduring stability.[107] It could also preserve Brooke's legacy from encroachment by Dutch officials, whom he not incorrectly believed likely to annex Sarawak as soon as he died.[108] In turn, British commerce would benefit, not only by winning tighter control of a strategic maritime route, but also by securing a key point through which to connect telegraph lines from India to China. Brooke's longstanding preference was to offer Britain first refusal. Now he introduced a scheme whereby Britain would become the owner of a Sarawak public debt, contingent upon a British license to intervene in the country in an emergency.[109] In November 1858 a delegation of MPs and businessmen visited London from Liverpool, Manchester, and Glasgow to press this idea on to Prime

Minister Derby, even carrying a deed—apparently forged—that showed Brunei endorsing Brooke's plan to transfer his rights immediately to Britain.[110] Derby rejected the idea, partly because he feared complications from the impact of a British fiscal regime on Sarawak's residents, who exercised considerable discretion in setting their rates of taxation. So Brooke considered selling his rights to "France or Russia, or Brunei again"—"anything . . . rather than the Dutch."[111]

Brooke had cleared this path legally by 1853 at the latest, when a new sultan, Abdul Momin, not only confirmed the grant of Sarawak made by his predecessor, but also declared that Brooke could "transmit the district of Sarawak and its territories in whatever way he may please, either to his heir or to any other person."[112] The opinion of Britain, however, remained another, and more important, matter. For years the Foreign Office had proceeded from the premise that Brooke governed Sarawak de facto, "going by the name of Rajah," to quote Queen Victoria.[113] But that left thorny legal issues unaddressed. Could a ruler, for one, simply alienate or sell his legal powers by means of a contract? Derby expressed misgivings. Also, in the meantime, what was to be Brooke's official status in Britain, where he remained a citizen?

In the background of this debate lay a controversial, and somewhat confused, doctrine. Since roughly 1773, the House of Commons had maintained that any English person acquiring sovereignty outside England necessarily did so on behalf of the Crown, not for himself.[114] As early as 1846, only some experts recalled that resolution, and, even among those ranks, most had to rely on secondhand summaries.[115] By the 1850s, however, lawyers at the Foreign Office, scrambling for answers on Brooke's case and having already produced several conflicting reports, turned more intently to their archives to consider the origin of this jurisprudence: England's East India Company.[116]

IN 1600, TWO HUNDRED merchants combined to form the EIC, one of the then-novel corporations that could outlive their founders, engage in lawsuits, and limit shareholder liability.[117] The company's early days saw it send ships east, around the Cape of Good Hope and as far as the Malay Peninsula, to establish trading posts. The hope was that English merchants might share in the profits of the Dutch in the Spice Islands, or duplicate the success of the Portuguese *Estado da Índia* at such ports as Goa.[118] Despite false starts, which saw the abandonment of a number of forts along the Indian subcontinent, English traders eventually established a network of control over key positions at Madras and Surat, as well as more remote spots in what is today's Indonesia. Thanks in part to the EIC's oft-renewed charter from the Crown, which guaranteed a monopoly on all trade east of the Cape of Good Hope, as well as relative immunity from parliamentary oversight, this network proved so lucrative over the next two centuries that its members often returned to Britain with astounding wealth at their disposal.[119]

For varying durations, the EIC and other corporations held charters formally permitting them to exercise a wide range of governmental functions around the world. One thinks immediately of famous cases—at Virginia, Massachusetts, and Hudson's Bay, for example.[120] But there were also-rans such as the Royal African Company, too, along with numerous imitators abroad: from the Netherlands (1602, 1621), Denmark (1612), France (1664), Brandenburg (1682), Scotland (1695), and Sweden (1731), among others.[121] Charters for English organizations sometimes featured verbatim recycling of text from the EIC's founding document—a sort of preview of nineteenth-century behavior.[122] The North American charters, in particular, encouraged talk of autonomy from England—the uncertainty surrounding which provided a necessary, if not sufficient, condition for the revolution of the thirteen colonies in the 1770s.[123] But, from its birth, the EIC remained a singular phenomenon, rightly earning a reputation as "an extraordinary and anomalous empire, which has no parallel in the history of the world."[124]

Though the EIC's inaugural charter from Queen Elizabeth I proved relatively modest in scope and lasted only fifteen years, that particular charter's multiple seventeenth-century iterations expanded to include the acknowledgement of what many historians later called "quasi-sovereign powers."[125] These included rights to make treaties; to maintain armies; to mint money; to administer civil and criminal justice over English subjects within the EIC's domain; and, eventually, to maintain a system of judges and courts for such purposes.[126] A number of nineteenth-century historians, among them John Robert Seeley, later contended that the EIC did not come to take on such rights until the mid-eighteenth century, and only then by a sort of accident.[127] That depiction—encouraged in part by Warren Hastings, the first British governor of Bengal—does not withstand scrutiny.[128] Without question, EIC management in the seventeenth century generally loathed the idea of acquiring territory by conquest, even going so far as to criticize Portuguese rivals for their resort to violence.[129] But it would be a mistake to assume this aversion meant reluctance to rule. The company independently bought formal titles from Indian rulers who granted them permission to trade and to govern a selection of sites on the periphery of the embattled Mughal Empire.[130] This practice sometimes rendered the English Crown's charters and their attendant grants of rights more reactive than prescriptive—especially before the 1690s, when the Glorious Revolution and a rise in parliamentary power prompted a successful campaign for regulating the EIC.

Recent research has shown how lawsuits raised the issue of EIC autonomy at the Court of King's Bench through the early 1680s. Partly in view of such evidence, historians are right to argue that for most of the seventeenth century the EIC asserted itself as a state: by denying its own subjects appeals to other courts, issuing passports, policing against piracy, and even bringing its own lawsuits in London, when necessary, to guard its prerogatives from possible interference from the English government proper.[131] Such assertions took place both legally and practically, thanks to an influential lobby at home.[132] There were also instances of more direct muscle flexing, as when, after a dowry from Charles II's Portuguese bride briefly made Bombay a Crown possession, the EIC, from its perch in nearby Surat, refused to cooperate by citing its status as a body free from royal control. In the meantime the EIC looked increasingly stable from the late seventeenth century on, despite being forced to undergo parliamentary inquiries after 1688, to widen the availability of its stock, to make repeated tax concessions and loans to London, and to fend off rival companies and so-called interlopers seeking to challenge its monopoly privileges. As the Mughals, Portuguese, and Marathas pursued a series of destructive wars across the rest of the subcontinent, areas coming under the control of EIC, including the former Crown holdings at Bombay, frequently provided a safe, profitable refuge for trade in commodities: silk- and cotton-textiles, and, increasingly, saltpeter and indigo.[133] Nonetheless, the company largely remained confined to a few coastal enclaves, its presence contingent upon a mixture of physical might and licenses issued by a complex of indigenous rulers operating to various extents of self-interest.[134] Only in 1765, on the strength of Robert Clive's famous victory at Plassey eight years earlier, did the EIC finally acquire a formal title to control an expansive territory. This was the Kingdom of Bengal, along with Behar and Orissa (today's Bihar and Odisha, respectively).

Around eight years after this turn to expansive control, whose legal basis lay in a *firman* (royal decree) from the subdued Mughal emperor, Alam II, the House of Commons passed a hurried resolution in which it submitted that the EIC's acquisitions overseas, however significant they might grow, did "of right belong to" Great Britain.[135] This doctrine, though it came only after a considerable parliamentary inquiry, was not entirely new: It was a more public, and more encompassing confirmation of an opinion produced by Britain's solicitor general and attorney general in 1757.[136] That opinion had also been tacit in the regulations imposed on the EIC by parliament in the 1690s, and earlier still in a decision by the Court of King's Bench.[137] But the doctrine nonetheless marked a departure from the status quo ante, which had seen the Crown take vague stances on the EIC's jurisdiction and ability to act independently. Coinciding with an overall British reorientation toward imperial paternalism as a result of the Seven Years' War, the doctrine meant an ad hoc rule seemed to have become akin to law, despite lingering uncertainty about how far the ambit of the British parliament could possibly run in India.[138]

After receiving its most comprehensive *firman* yet, which had come in exchange for an agreement to pay annual tribute to the Mughal emperor and his local governor *(nawab)*, the EIC, still operating more or less autonomously from Britain in practice, began to perform the most simple business of government in Bengal: revenue and customs collection, also known as the *dewany*. To what extent this transition affected the everyday lives of the population remains controversial.[139] Within a decade, the company unquestionably found itself doing more in Bengal than revenue collection, just as it had done in enclaves such as Bombay since the 1670s.[140] Clive wondered whether the company's extended sovereignty might prove incompatible with its mercantile objectives.[141] Yet, in a continuation of its earlier behavior, the EIC proceeded to try civil and criminal cases for all English subjects, as well as European nationals and Indians generally.[142] The EIC took over much of the civil service in Bengal, and then unilaterally launched new wars with its own army.[143] It minted money, at first retaining the Mughal emperor's seal, but eventually discarding it.[144] Most important, the EIC also signed treaties with Indian rulers to buy control over ever-larger expanses of territory.[145]

Contracts produced in 1768 with the *nawabs* of the Deccan and Carnatic saw the EIC start to replicate the same formula obtaining in Bengal.[146]

In public, though the Crown still claimed to let the company do all these things on behalf of its home country, neither party had declared unequivocally that the Crown held sovereignty in Indian territories.[147] This was one reason why no one working in the British Foreign Office—or in parliament—could agree on where the EIC's rights ended and Britain's began.[148] Rather than publish this disagreement broadly, officials generally hedged, much as they would do with James Brooke several decades later. When making settlement treaties with France in 1783 and 1787, for example, British negotiators faced major difficulties, owing not only to the EIC's unclear status at home, but also to its exercise of de facto control in Indian polities where it disavowed de jure control.[149] By one extreme logic, if the company was practically, though not formally, the sovereign in a given polity, then one could argue that Britain, the EIC's overseer, was—at least in the system of overlapping and mixed sovereignty then prevailing under the Mughals—nominally subservient to the Mughal emperor.[150]

This definitional problem never met with neat resolution in parliament, which preferred to focus on investigations, as well as bills of legislation to curb the company's allegedly corrupt administration: most famously Lord North's Regulating Act in 1773 and the East India Company Act in 1784.[151] Of course, detractors argued that the EIC was ruining India. One such critic was William Bolts, a disgruntled former employee and adventurer who would make a large fortune by shipping opium from India to Southeast Asia. Bolts, like Edmund Burke, urged Britons to reform the EIC for the good of their own society. But he also spotlighted how a lack of clarity about sovereignty, when forcefully acquired in practice by the company but not definitively avowed by Britain, could weigh down the Indian population's juridical and trade affairs.[152]

Efforts to reform the EIC arguably reached their apex in the infamous trial of the former governor-general of Bengal, Warren Hastings.[153] Burke helmed the prosecution, accusing Hastings of overseeing the looting of India and disproportionately favoring Scots in civil-service patronage.[154] In a sense, Burke, who had a broad base of support or acquiescence from leading MPs, acknowledged a high degree of company autonomy but insisted that it must remain faithful to a particular definition of empire: "the aggregate of many states under one common head."[155] As important, though, was that neither Burke nor the lawyers at the Foreign Office ended the company's reign: The EIC's continued independence in practical matters remained at issue well into the nineteenth century.[156] Parliament continued to take steps toward oversight, including an explicit declaration that the Crown held "undoubted sovereignty" over EIC territories.[157] But these same gestures also led to further confusion, for parliament could not even define what its declared Indian territories were. In the interim, the EIC continued to perform many state functions, including employing Thomas Brooke—James Brooke's father—as a judge of a high court in the system it had set up to administer justice in places like Varanasi.[158] As regarded British courts, the EIC stayed immune from British jurisdiction after 1813, except in matters related to its commercial activities.[159] Likewise, the company's British employees were still said to have lost their domicile and acquired one in India because the company was "in a great degree . . . a separate and independent government, foreign to the Government of this country."[160]

By the time of the Singapore inquiry into James Brooke's affairs, the EIC remained in business; the commission appointed to examine Brooke's case was even staffed by EIC employees.[161] This composition attested that the company retained great influence throughout Asia, despite mounting debts incurred from wars and the loss of its trading monopolies, first for India and then, in 1833, for China.[162] In Britain, the company's lobbying, including banquets at the celebrated London Tavern, helped to keep it in the good graces of the middle class and many members in the Commons, even as Brooke generally fell out of favor with both.[163] Brooke, who also dined at the London Tavern, knew well how a more regulated version of the EIC still took responsibility for ruling over much of the colonial map in East Asia.[164] From 1784 to 1854 the company had actually expanded its portfolio by buying sovereign rights to a host of smaller Indian territories, thus enlarging its administration to the point that it concerned roughly one hundred and fifty million subjects, or around the populations of France, Austria, Prussia, and Spain combined.[165] The company had even acquired grants to extend its writ beyond the subcontinent and into Southeast Asia. The more famous case was Singapore, where a company agent, Stamford Raffles, would become known to posterity as the man who had bought and asserted control more or less by himself, albeit on behalf of the EIC. Brooke was an admirer of Raffles's written works, and, even if he hated the company by adulthood, he idolized the man.

In 1857, the year when Brooke's rule grew most tenuous, the issue of the EIC's status resurfaced with great fanfare when a group of its sepoys (soldiers) sparked a series of bloody uprisings among diverse forces resentful of British disruptions to their religious, social, and trade networks. Some historians place blame for this "Great Rebellion," once known as "the Mutiny," on the policy of Governor-General Lord Dalhousie, who angered certain Indian princes by insisting on formal expansion of British control through a notorious "doctrine of lapse."[166] Others have shown how land reforms kept much of rural India in upheaval through 1857.[167] Nearly every nineteenth-century observer, however, above all faulted the EIC as an institution.[168] The moment, one commentator wrote, had "arrived for it to be utterly condemned and cast aside as the relic of a past age and an exploded policy."[169] Whatever the validity of such claims, they followed in the wake of British parliamentary acts in 1855 and 1856 that, for the first time, allowed a host of corporations to limit their liability to company assets, rather than individual shareholders, when it came to the payment of debts.[170] This overlooked debate meant that just before India erupted, the role and public utility of corporations came under renewed debate in Britain, with the EIC figuring as one of many talking points. Nor was the audience confined to the British Isles. In Russia, Grand Duke Konstantin Nikolayevich cited the events in India as cause for a review of all remaining privately run governments—especially as it applied to his country's empire in Russian America.[171]

By New Year's 1857, the British parliament, in accordance with Queen Victoria's request, had prepared a bill to take over all governmental functions in the EIC's Indian domain.[172] Prior to this moment, the Crown had asserted its ability to theoretically subsume the company's rights and responsibilities, but it had settled for pressuring the EIC's boards for reform. Several months into 1858, Britain succeeded in transferring to the Crown a formal title of the EIC's sovereign functions. It is often said that Britain stripped the company of these rights; in reality, it bought them by executing a trade of "great difficulty" with a "company-state."[173] In a sense, this formula inverted that which England had earlier applied at Bombay, whose title it transferred to the company in the 1670s. This time, money would flow to the company via a more complex arrangement. All EIC debts, within India and without, would be paid by, and charged to, the future public debt of India. So, too, would a steady dividend for shareholders.[174] In exchange, the Crown would receive the company's rights and a declaration that the Crown now held full legal authority.

On the one hand, the Crown reaped the benefit of better public relations while embracing a nascent European consensus against nonstate sources of violence: A multilateral declaration signed in Paris in 1856, for example, had banned privateering and restored exclusive control of the seas, at least legally, to traditional maritime powers.[175] On the other hand, the EIC secured another couple of decades of dividends to please its shareholders, whose ranks at times included a certain Joseph Hume, MP—the sometime antagonist of Sir James Brooke. "The doom of the East India Company," wrote Karl Marx in 1858, thus amounted to little more than a cash transaction. Whereas the company "commenced by buying sovereignty" in the seventeenth and eighteenth centuries, it "ended by selling it." It was not legal niceties that brought England the rights it alleged to have had all along, but the "hammer of the auctioneer."[176]

It was entirely appropriate to wonder what was to become of Sarawak and Borneo, with Britain taking over the East India Company's interests. In the short term Brooke, whose case was much less topical, continued his quest to transfer Sarawak to a European power. Several suitors expressed interest in paying off the public debts of Sarawak in order to acquire the title to Brooke's territory. What they wanted first, however, was a definitive sense of Britain's attitude. If consistency with the EIC case had been paramount, Britain would be hard pressed to deny that Brooke could sell his title. After all, one key to the agreement between the EIC and the British government was that the Crown had legitimated all transactions for sovereign rights the company had made, so that the new colonial government in India, that is, the Raj, legally had a title by which to govern the affairs of the Indian and East Asian territories transferred by the company. In the end, despite Brooke's protestations that he hated the EIC, its case should have lingered in everyone's mind when Brooke made appeals to British officials.[177]

Brooke's status abroad had always been tied to that of the EIC. Like them, he sometimes asserted that he saw no conflict in the act of governing and profiting as a businessman simultaneously—a view illustrated by his abortive attempts to monopolize antimony mining in Sarawak.[178] At one point he even sought to follow the EIC by founding a corporation in London that could purchase his governing rights, thus ensuring Sarawak the protection that flying the British flag afforded a business when it came to foreign affairs.[179] Still, when Brooke argued "his tenure" in Sarawak "was as good as it possibly could be," based as it was on "as good a title as the Company's," he was inadvertently grouping himself with a body that at this point clearly fell under British oversight.[180] For foreign audiences, this link implied that, whatever Britain might say about Brooke's day-to-day autonomy, Britain ultimately intended to keep Sarawak under the influence of the British Empire. His title was thus imperfect, even damaged.[181]

Britain did not tell foreign governments what it planned to do about Sarawak; rather, it essentially dared Brooke to sell his rights to those governments in the absence of British guarantees. His most viable option was probably France, where his offer of sale reached the desks of the Foreign and Marine ministries, as well as the incipient Colonial Ministry.[182] True, French officials' temporary free-trade orientation discouraged direct responsibilities overseas. But France surely did have a habit of acquiring Far Eastern colonies.[183] Between 1853 and 1864, it annexed New Caledonia and the Loyalty Islands; Cochinchina; and, at least in practice, Cambodia.[184] In 1862, Napoleon III also approved and signed the so-called Lambert Charter, by which the queen of Madagascar transferred sweeping powers over part of her kingdom, including mineral and currency rights, to the businessman Joseph Lambert. One could certainly classify several such sites as akin to Borneo—along with veritable neighbors like Basilan, an island in the nearby Sulu Archipelago that France annexed in 1845.[185] Kuching and Saigon, in French hands from 1859, occupied two commanding points for Indian routes to China. Hence at least some French periodicals conducted inquiries on Brooke's *"petit royaume."*[186]

One could further argue that France already had in place the kind of support system Brooke desired. A vague protectorate over "civilizing" or religious missions, claimed by Paris since a concordat with Rome in 1801, might conceivably substitute the Brookes for clericals as a low-cost alternative for colonial expansion in Borneo.[187] It was perhaps for this reason that the more serious his negotiations grew, the more Brooke's case won attention from the British government. Whitehall, repeatedly, had declined to buy rights in Sarawak from Brooke; for a brief moment Palmerston offered a protectorate, but only on the unpalatable condition that Brooke retain responsibility for his state debts.[188] British diplomats, still digesting their formal takeover of three-fifths of the Indian subcontinent, did not want to commit their government to further direct rule on the far side of the world.[189] However, there were additional alternatives—notably in the other two-fifths of India.[190]

During and after the tumult of 1857, the rulers of many Indian polities known as princely states came to occupy a quasi-sovereign position in relation to the emerging British Raj. Exactly what the relationship constituted was never settled: British colonial officials often treated the princely states as fully sovereign, asking for mere tokens of recognition for British paramountcy; Britain ambassadors also maintained foreign relations with, rather than for, the states concerned.[191] In other instances, though, British lawyers dismissed talk of princely sovereignty as "niceties of speech," to quote the contemporary legal theorist John Westlake.[192] Amid this intricate backdrop of possibility, and as a low-cost alternative sporadically proposed by Brooke, Britain moved to recognize Sarawak's independence via backchannels, in the expectation that it would cement Brooke's bond to his mother country.[193] A first step in this process had come when vessels of the British fleet, taking their cue from the verbal approval of Palmerston, rendered Brooke a royal salute. British ships entered Sarawak and treated its flag—"a cross, half red, half black, on a yellow field"—as that of a full and equal member in the international community of nations.[194] A second, arguably more significant step consisted of an acknowledgement from London that within Sarawak's borders, Brooke's courts would adjudicate all cases, including those of British nationals, under the unique set of laws he had compiled, rather than under the English common law in which Queen Victoria's travelers in the Far East typically took refuge.[195]

The Economist consistently endorsed these steps, lauding Brooke's "liberal commercial policy."[196] Several other prominent figures, including the bishop of Oxford, recommended a formal declaration of independence as the best way to prop up the finances of Sarawak, which might offer British merchants a chance to circumvent a tariff system then being run by the Dutch in their East Indian colonies.[197] As for Britain, the act of formal recognition remained, to quote former U.S. president Andrew Jackson, "at all times, an act of great delicacy and responsibility."[198]

Recognition held a particularly dangerous potential as Britain entered the 1860s, with regime changes in Spain and Greece on the horizon.

To understand why, it is first necessary to understand the act itself. Tasked with explaining British recognition of former Spanish colonies in Central and South America, which came about after bloody revolutions in the 1810s and 1820s, George Canning once offered the following definition, which one contemporary author accepted as the standard in the 1860s:

> If the colonies say to another State, "We are independent," and that other State replies, "I allow that you are so," that is recognition. . . . That other State simply acknowledges the fact, or rather its opinion of the fact; but she confers nothing, unless, under particular circumstances she may be considered as conferring a favor.[199]

Recognition, in Brooke's case, amounted to more than a favor. With it, he would possess a legal mechanism to ensure that foreign states respected "the acts of (his) legislative, administrative, and judicial organs," including tariffs or trade monopolies. Recognition would afford Sarawak diplomatic standing to pursue disputes as a plaintiff in foreign courts.[200] This would help to "improve its credit . . . not only in the City (London) but also in Borneo."[201] Likewise, a recognized government in Sarawak, as distinct from an unrecognized one, would see consuls repeatedly appointed to its territory by foreign states, including Britain.[202] Those consuls would in turn give Brooke an invaluable means with which to facilitate business between his territory and markets abroad.[203] Such, at any rate, had been the findings of other recently recognized countries in receipt of consular appointments: Belgium, France post-1848, and the Bolívarian states in Latin America.[204] Partly out of this same awareness, the Confederate States of America spent the early 1860s trying in vain to lobby Britain and France to receive their own consuls.[205]

For Britain, which had never arrived at protocols for the EIC's consular appointments, a major risk lay in instantiating firm criteria to evaluate such requests. A misstep could backfire, especially in Southeast Asia, where British recognition of shaky rulers in the Johor Sultanate underwrote the legality of colonial settlement in Singapore and the Malayan peninsula.[206] Expecting other states to follow their lead, British officials also considered morality when evaluating Brooke's request for de jure recognition of his de facto independence. Many politicians viewed Brooke's deeds buying sovereignty from Brunei with incredulity; Derby scoffed that Brooke had "entered into a treaty or arrangement, or whatever they pleased to call it, into the terms of which he need not inquire too closely."[207] But a closer look at Sarawak would show how Brooke, whatever his evils, probably had an ethical record superior to that achieved by the EIC.[208] More than one commentator argued that he enforced the rule of law and allowed equal protection under it for all his subjects.[209] Even Brooke's residual doubters admitted that he differed from most colonialists in his sincere regard for the welfare and customs of his official subjects. It did not suffice to say that he had become a small-scale EIC. Arguably, he had become something better.

In 1863, Britain finally recognized Sir James Brooke as the independent, sovereign ruler of his territory by appointing a consul to Sarawak.[210] From this point on, Sarawak started to figure among lists of foreign nations for purposes of trade and shipping.[211] In short order, Brooke also earned the right to appear at the court of Queen Victoria as a head of state.[212] These gestures, even if superfluous to most residents in Borneo—an understandable impression, given that the consulate at Sarawak opened its doors only intermittently—symbolized the kind of credence Brooke and his supporters had coveted for years.[213] "You will see," he wrote excitedly to a friend in London, "that England recognizes us at last."[214] Of course doubts lingered about the eighteenth-century doctrine, according to which, it will be recalled, any sovereign rights owned by English citizens automatically vested in the Crown. That said, legal experts in the government hereafter determined to sidestep these concerns by emphasizing that Brooke technically leased his rights from the sultan of Brunei, albeit sometimes without payment.

One of the perks of recognition was attested in the small-denomination bronze coins that Sarawak began issuing that year, in what constituted an inaugural attempt at controlling its own currency.[215] But Brooke still lacked sufficient means to run his government long-term, and, with his forces weakened post-1857, raiders were reviving their operations to the detriment of export trades.[216] All that left the prospect of a sale attractive to him, whatever difficulties Britain anticipated in his trying to find a buyer. Unwilling to strike a deal with Leopold, Brooke was also unlikely to secure one with France: Napoleon III's disastrous attempt to install an Austrian Archduke as emperor of Mexico was yet unfolding, and expensive French expeditions into China and Syria remained fresh in the public consciousness. Nonetheless, Brooke made plans for a return to Sarawak, a publicity campaign to repudiate all ties to Britain, and the start of another round of negotiations.[217] "Sarawak," the thinking went, remained "a great temptation to France, America, or the Netherlands."[218] This fear proved only somewhat accurate—by the early 1860s the Dutch, if they ever were a palatable option to Brooke, had their hands full with the Banjarmasin War in southern Borneo and had formally ruled out the possibility.[219] In the decade following 1857, Brooke could do little else than struggle to fund his state budget through additional donations. An audit of his personal finances showed he had made hardly any money during his reign, and Coutts now resolved to withdraw her financial support.[220] On one occasion, as the rajah began to book passage from Marseilles to Singapore, he had to ask for a loan of £500 just to make the trip. In 1866, as Coutts granted some money for such purposes—one of her final contributions—an increasingly infirm Brooke returned to Sarawak and chose to install his nephew Charles as successor. Already Charles had effectively ruled Sarawak in his uncle's absence. Bolstered by strong support from the "Sea Dayaks," among whom he had lived for several years, and keen to increase rice cultivation so as to reduce reliance on food imports, Charles promptly set his sights on continued territorial expansion.[221] He scraped together some funds to approach the sultan for a lease of additional territories closer to Brunei—certainly the prosperous and chaotic Baram River area, but perhaps also a slice of the eastern side of Borneo.[222] The main part of the second prospective territory comprised another one of the sultan's nominal dependencies, Sabah, which occupied the extreme northeastern coast.

Shortly thereafter the Brookes were surprised to find their push for Baram frustrated and their hopes for Sabah dashed. Sabah, it seemed, was no longer on the market, having been leased to an American group. As the rulers of Sarawak were about to discover, the latter men wanted to open up an entirely new chapter in the history of Borneo.

IN 1864, not long after resigning his commission in the U.S. Navy on account of illness, Charles Lee Moses won his appointment as consul to Brunei, the first-ever U.S. diplomatic post on the island of Borneo.[223] Moses's job description was far from grand: Unlike fellow consuls with more lucrative postings, such as Hong Kong, he was to receive no salary, with his sole responsibility consisting in the furtherance of U.S. trade in Southeast Asia.[224] Nonetheless, letters from the likes of Senator Charles Sumner and Abraham Lincoln's secretary, John Hay, attested high hopes for Moses's tenure.[225] As a retired captain, he had expertise in navigation of foreign waters—a crucial need for any modern navy, and one that prompted his relative, Judah Benjamin, to recruit him unsuccessfully for the cause of the Confederacy.[226] While in Brunei, Moses could also deliver competent reports on ship activity in the South China Sea, where the Spanish, British, and Dutch competed with Americans for access to the all-important China trade.[227]

From the moment Moses set sail for Brunei, he appeared psychologically unstable. This behavior was hardly aberrant: His flirtation with fame had started in 1861, when the *New York Times* reported his being shot in the head in a Parisian duel—his second severe concussion in recent years.[228] Not long after the commercial steamer carrying him rounded the Cape of Good Hope in 1865, Moses started bragging about his supposed commission from the president of the United States to negotiate with the sultan of Brunei for the cession of a strip of territory. In Singapore, enough people heard of this allegedly secret design that journalists reported it. He shared his news again over a stop in Jakarta, this time in a grandiloquent interview with Dutch officials. Then, after a brief layover in Hong Kong, he changed his tune, replacing bravado with extraordinary deference. He apparently did not have any financial resources left by the time he met with the British governor on Labuan. Far from it, he acknowledged his own destitution to the governor just days before he was set to announce himself as American consul to the sultan of Brunei. Moses explained that he had accumulated debts for living expenses during his eleven-month steamer voyage from America—a plight that looked worse because he traveled with his wife and three infants. The British governor expressed surprise, like his colleagues in Hong Kong, to find an American delegate would not be "attended with a little more show of pomp and state."[229] Still, whether out of pity or tact, the governor felt obliged to pay the debts of Moses's family, and the latter finally arrived in Brunei on July 12, 1865. They had neither money, nor food, nor accommodations.[230]

On the day of his arrival, Moses called at the palace of the roughly seventy-three-year-old sultan, Abdul Momin, at whose expense he soon found himself accepting sacks of rice and a freshly built attap palm hut, in accordance with local custom for receiving ambassadors.[231] One month later, Moses urged the sultan to turn Sabah—the least-profitable, least-loyal province in Brunei's empire—into an American colony.[232] The fate of this suggestion augured a great deal. The American proposed to lease governing rights over Sabah—on his own account, but with the implication that this would be done on behalf of the United States.[233] Even without direct U.S. involvement, his offer still held certain attractions. The most obvious was that, in exchange for the Sabah rights, the American consul would provide the sultan with some much-needed hard money in a climate of heavy currency volatility in Brunei. But there was also the less noticeable benefit that Moses would pay off one of the sultan's cabinet members, the Pengiran Temenggong, whom the sultan had appointed governor of Sabah and whose approval was going to be needed to put the seal of state on any deals Brunei made. These cash infusions could flow into the empire's treasury more or less gratis, for while Sabah hardly brought in any revenues aside from a few customs taxes on river transport, it cost nothing to police, defend, and maintain insofar as no one living there had really accepted Brunei's authority since the 1820s.[234] An additional possibility was that an American naval presence on Borneo might offer Brunei a counterweight to encroachment by Britain, whose navy had long ago encamped at nearby Labuan. Finally, as before with James Brooke, the residence of Westerners could serve to deter raids against merchant ships sailing along the Borneo coast, and thus help to revive Brunei's stagnant maritime trade.[235]

Momin agreed to Moses's proposal, for a term of ten years at roughly 9,500 Spanish dollars per annum.[236] Both men were convinced as to the benefits of their arrangement—it was a partnership, not subjugation. But the sultan soon began to doubt Moses's character, not least because Moses missed his first payment.[237] In reality, the U.S. State Department had merely deputized Moses to support American trade; it had no plans, official or otherwise, to approve him in the establishment of an American colony in Sabah, and his consular handbook specifically forbade him to seek more powers than Washington granted.[238] Whatever rights Moses acquired were his own affair. To make matters worse, Moses, who never bothered to learn Malay, was said by the sultan's informants to be "a disagreeable scamp"; reports around town quickly identified him as a serial abuser of servants, an inveterate cheat, and an unfaithful debtor.[239] But the man also remained the agent of the United States, which held a verifiable interest in Borneo from 1842, when Admiral Charles Wilkes visited with his storied exploring expedition.[240] That had set the stage for a second visit by the USS *Constitution* to Brunei in 1845, around the time when Brooke and an earlier sultan were negotiating for control of Sarawak; hence the bilateral treaty signed in 1850, its finalization in 1854, and, around 1860, a decision by Washington to found a consulate in Brunei Town.[241] It was also feasible—according to official statements made by the United States in the Oregon controversy of the 1840s—that American citizens could unilaterally take possession of foreign territory without express authorization from the United States, only to secure approval of this acquisition retroactively.[242] And so in 1865 it may well have appeared reasonable, even advisable, for Abdul Momin to suffer Moses on behalf of the government back in Washington.[243]

Little is known about Moses's motivation.[244] He may have wanted to build himself an empire out of *libido dominandi.* Or he may have wanted to parlay his newly acquired territory—theoretically the first American overseas colony—into fame back home. Then again, Moses may simply have wanted to sell his rights to the U.S. government at a premium, taking a handsome finder's fee for himself in the process.[245] A French consul had tried something similar with a port in today's Djibouti from 1856 to 1862, but Moses's tenure did not last long enough for anyone to test the analogy. A little over a month after arranging his lease with the sultan he went to Hong Kong. In November, he returned to Brunei intending to transfer his lease to the American Trading Company of Borneo, a firm headquartered in Hong Kong and managed by one Colonel Joseph Torrey.

Torrey sailed to Brunei in his own ship, along with several dozen Chinese laborers.[246] An evidently intrigued sultan promptly facilitated the transfer by conferring on Torrey control of an additional island, as well as the title once given to James Brooke: *rajah.*[247] This was still an *American* trading company, one must note, and Torrey presented himself as a colonel born in the United States. Moreover, Moses moved to place the company's activities under the official auspices of the American consulate, whose perception by locals, as was customary in Southeast Asia, meshed imperceptibly with that of an embassy.[248] At Torrey's urging, the sultan even agreed to sign a second, more extensive document enumerating the powers transferred by the lease.[249]

The American Trading Company now owned, this document said, "the rights of making laws and coining money" in Sabah. But that was just the beginning, for the sultan also acknowledged that the company held full title to all property that existed within the province of Sabah, whether "mineral, vegetable, or animal." Interpreted strictly, this meant that private property had ceased to exist in Sabah. The company could dispose over every single thing in its territory, simultaneously levying taxes and customs duties without oversight from a third party. And, just in case anyone might object to a future company policy, the sultan's enumeration of lease powers also declared that the company held "power of life and death over the inhabitants"—mostly a mix of Dusun peoples.[250] Every man, woman, and child among the perhaps two hundred thousand residents in Sabah would figure as the company's subjects.[251] The company could police them. The company could resolve their disputes. The company could even, if it wished, conscript them in order to "create and command a military or naval force."

Management of this bounty fell to Torrey; a U.S. government investigation claimed he had "staked all he was worth on the enterprise."[252] A charitable associate once called him "a businessman of varied experience": newspaper editor, shipping agent, legal reporter.[253] This was a relatively accurate description, to the extent that Torrey, originally hailing from Roxbury, Massachusetts, had worked odd jobs in Australia before moving on to Hong Kong as a sometime agent for an influential American trading firm, Russell & Company.[254] He even wrote some poetry for friends—though it apparently amounted to a series of puns.[255] But the thirty-seven-year-old Torrey, while regarded by colleagues as "a man of splendid education," also carried a checkered reputation. He was, complained some of those same colleagues, an "author of much mischief" and a "pirate" who had worn out his welcome in virtually every major East Asian city before arriving in Hong Kong.[256] John Mosby, the future U.S. consul at Hong Kong, recalled Torrey as "a low, disreputable adventurer—a man of utter profligate and abandoned character."[257] Such accusations of skullduggery looked quite credible in view of "Colonel" Torrey's introduction to the sultan. Despite claims to the contrary, the American had no identifiable connection with the U.S. Army; the closest he came to service seems to have been some time spent in the

Ancient and Honorable Artillery Company of Boston, a ceremonial honor guard for the governor of Massachusetts.[258]

It is not enough to suppose that Torrey hoped his new title would help support his family, which included a teenaged wife and four children. One has to bear in mind that Torrey—known for impulsive behavior and speculations—thought he was buying ownership of an entire country for the next ten years, in return for a mere 9,500 Spanish dollars annually, plus some smaller payments to Moses.[259] Certainly this prospect held great appeal to someone who had the advantage of pairing legal knowledge with ethical flexibility.[260] The trouble was that Torrey lacked the means to make it work. His American Trading Company had no viable business, having been formed abruptly for the purpose of taking over Moses's lease.[261] The company's initial capitalization amounted to roughly 10,000 Spanish dollars—more or less the cost of hiring workers and buying supplies for a colony. Most of this capital, in turn, came from a Hong Kong opium syndicate, Wo Hang, for whom Torrey's employer acted as an agent.[262] Such a private funding pool was unlikely to expand adequately, even if one British official theorized that Borneo would see an influx of Chinese in decades to come.[263] On the contrary, Torrey's funding appears to have come with a specific agenda attached. Wo Hang's leadership may have envisioned poppy fields in Sabah or the use of Sabah as a path to circumvent, and possibly even challenge, the monopoly on opium held by James Brooke's government in nearby Sarawak.[264] Most likely, they were eager to capitalize on the then-rising competitiveness of domestically produced Chinese opium. A privately managed empire in North Borneo could help to establish a new outlet for that product, and to afford Wo Hang easier access to Australia and Northwest America, where they were expanding their drug- and human-trafficking operations.[265]

Once the American Trading Company paid some preliminary expenses, its cash reserves dwindled. Torrey may have hastened this process through embezzlement; in any event, not enough money was on hand to pay the most important bill: the sultan's.[266] Torrey temporarily put that concern aside and focused on attracting new investors, only to meet with skepticism.[267] "No sane European," a contemporary British agricultural expert remarked, "would invest capital in land under the present Brunei Government."[268] Potential investors wanted Torrey to win some international recognition of Sabah's independence before they committed to the project.[269] Alas, getting recognition was going to prove difficult without further funding. Torrey was in the midst of drawn-out litigation with delinquent customers from his regular job; he needed a loan just to travel to Sabah, let alone establish his authority there.[270] As for the other employees in the American Trading Company, they needed food, medicine, clothing, and, not least, weapons in their efforts to set up operations and survey in the middle of a strategically located jungle.[271] Reportedly, these supplies would cost an additional 10,000 Spanish dollars, with agents stopping in Singapore to buy up boatloads of rice, four Dahlgren nine-pound cannons, and myriad selections from the Smith & Wesson catalogue.[272]

Compounding such difficulties was the general business climate in Hong Kong, whose financial houses were watching a credit crunch turn into an outright panic.[273] Despite these odds, at some point in December 1865 Torrey convinced one of his Chinese investors to disburse additional funds. This done, Torrey outfitted an expedition and sailed with around twelve Americans and fifty-eight coolie laborers to build settlements in Sabah.[274] Torrey's prospective colony would start in the interior along a river known as Kimanis, about eighty-three miles from Brunei Town.[275] Thick vegetation mixed with marsh there. Tropical diseases flourished. And there was always the menace of raiders trawling the coast in fast *proa* (sailboats) and looking to capture potential slave laborers.[276] Nonetheless, the coolies set to work planting crops, the Westerners prospected, and Torrey's "viceroy," a New Yorker named Wheelwright, predicted a major gold or diamond strike.[277] Initial reports were positive, especially about the soil.[278] In the meantime, Torrey headed to Singapore and began to look for new investors to turn his company's parlous finances around. His first step was to write letters to U.S. Secretary of State William Seward touting his new development, "Ellena," which he had apparently named after his newborn daughter.

"I now have the honor," Torrey wrote Seward, "to inform you that I have since the date of my last communication visited a portion of the territory granted to the Company I represent and taken formal possession of it under the Sultan's leases." Torrey told Seward he could write at great lengths about the land's excellent vegetation, its soil rich beyond calculation, its Dusun inhabitants friendly to Westerners.[279] So he did, even suggesting that the United States might make use of this territory as a solution to the unemployment of freed slaves in the wake of the

American Civil War. A more surprising point in Torrey's writing came when he requested that Seward declare official U.S. protection of the American Trading Company's rights in Sabah. For Torrey, "protection" meant the United States would periodically send a gunboat by Ellena to intimidate the local Dusun people and any pirates in the vicinity. The United States would also make an official announcement that the company, by virtue of its rights, now reigned as the legitimate government in Sabah. This announcement amounted to diplomatic recognition—the same kind of acknowledgement that James Brooke had striven after for decades.[280]

Though such a course offered obvious benefits to the American Trading Company, what the United States stood to gain from it was less clear. U.S. history was, of course, intimately tied up with the question of recognition; arguably the entire point of the Declaration of Independence in 1776 had been to situate the fledgling colonies as distinct and equal members in an international system.[281] Simply laying claim to equal membership—adopting the "regal stile," to quote one contemporary critic—was a way for American rebels to "rise in estimation and in rank." To many Britons, the claim even presaged an unfair conversion of the rebels' status as a pirate into that of an independent prince.[282] But the United States, aside from advancing its own argument in 1776, never agreed where to draw the line for others thereafter. Liberia and Haiti had to wait decades for their recognition, which finally came in July 1862.[283] Now Torrey was testing this fraught relationship anew.

Apparently making use of some familiarity with mercantile law and American treaties in the Far East, Torrey went on to argue that the United States already had no choice but to offer protection.[284] As he saw it, the rights to govern Sabah now figured among the assets of his American-owned company. That fact meant quite a bit, for in 1850 the American government had signed a treaty with Brunei pledging to uphold the integrity, not only of its citizens trading in Brunei, but also of their private property. While in normal cases such protection might amount to no more than making sure personal effects, shares, or real estate were not unlawfully seized, Torrey argued the rule still held in the case of the Sabah lease—his private property. Thus "our colony," he reasoned, "is [already] under the protection of the Government of the United States, in the same manner as private property of citizens is presumed to be everywhere." "All we require," he continued, "is an acknowledgement of our rights. . . . An intimation of this kind and no foreign nation will dare to infringe upon our privileges."[285]

No acknowledgement had come by the time Seward contemplated the developments in Sabah in early 1866. In the meantime, Torrey had to deal with Moses, his erstwhile partner, behaving even more erratically than had been his wont so far. Sometime around New Year's 1866, Moses accused the sultan and Torrey of conspiring against him "in pursuit of the fleeting dollar."[286] Writing to Seward, Moses complained that the American Trading Company had not yet paid the sultan, and that the company was also in arrears on its "back royalties" to Moses for the transfer of the lease. As a result, Moses demanded the sultan void the lease and arrange a new deal; the consul had "another company in readiness to relieve the present occupants" and "reestablish the confidence and good feeling hitherto existing."[287] For his part, Moses seemed to have little good feeling left, for, not long after writing Seward, he outfitted a crew of German mercenaries in Hong Kong for the purpose of mounting a raid on the Ellena colony.[288] Should the crew succeed in restoring possession of Ellena to the American consulate to Brunei, Moses agreed to pay them in spoils. To facilitate the effort in advance, he even arrested one of his creditors on the streets of Brunei Town, in the somewhat mistaken belief that his job as consul gave him such authority.[289]

Moses had certainly grown into an embarrassment by this point, even when compared with the oft-abysmal record of unsalaried consuls in the nineteenth century.[290] Torrey's assurances that he "had cast Mr. Moses aside as dust by the roadside" did little to placate Brunei.[291] Arguably the more potent threat to the American operation lay elsewhere, however, in a foreign power that dared to infringe on their privileges. This bête noire was Sarawak, where, for years, the Brookes had been attempting, unsuccessfully, to add Sabah to their growing swath of land in the northern section of the island. Accordingly, not long after news leaked about Torrey's efforts to establish his own rajahship in Sabah, Sarawak mounted a diplomatic campaign against the new lease. First, Charles Brooke harangued the British—who had just finished recognizing Brooke's independence—about the illegitimacy of Torrey's rights. Second, Sarawak encouraged Sabah indigenes to rise up in revolt over having had their political allegiance sold to Westerners.

James Brooke still figured as a hero in the Western world and a mythical figure in Southeast Asia. But it would be inaccurate to say he amounted to Torrey's rival, for he was also Torrey's role model, and, in a way, his best hope for success.[292] Yet, on hearing of the court intrigues between Moses and Torrey, James and his nephew Charles grew furious.[293] Legitimacy, for them, now consisted less in a paper contract with incompetent Americans than in the will of the people.[294] Charles quickly turned this position into a public debate, insisting to the press in Hong Kong that the sultan of Brunei had no moral authority to commoditize the right to govern the residents of Sabah. Papers in Singapore also expressed their own brand of skepticism—regarding the Americans' business skills. "We hope," joked the *Straits Times*, "the Sultan of Brunei will not find his ten thousand a year rather ephemeral in its nature and uncertain in its payment."[295]

James Brooke eventually got in touch with his old patron, Baroness Coutts, who promptly spoke with Prime Minister Palmerston and his soon-to-be successor, John Russell.[296] Around this time, Sarawak dispatched a spy to the area around Torrey's settlement to filter local intelligence.[297] In a further twist, Britain's ambassador to the United States called on Secretary of State Seward to pose questions about Sabah. Did the United States intend to protect Torrey's rights by annexing the territory? Or did the United States intend to support Torrey as Britain most recently supported the Brookes—that is, by recognizing that their rights made them an independent sovereign?[298] In either case, Britain mooted invoking the treaty it had pressured the sultan into signing long ago, in the 1840s. According to that document, the sultan of Brunei did not even have the ability to make additional transfers of his territory without prior British approval.[299] That probably would not block the Americans retroactively, unless Britain wanted war: What it would do was to delay the Brookes' scheme to buy Baram, another vulnerable part of Brunei.

On October 22, 1867, as Britain protested, Torrey arrived in Washington, D.C. hoping to unlock new sources of funding. The Hong Kong opium dealers bankrolling the American Trading Company had backed out the previous year; in the interim, Torrey had fallen deep into debt.[300] Making matters worse were the machinations of Moses, Torrey's one-time partner. At some point in 1867 Moses, while still serving as the American consul to Brunei, apparently slipped into madness. First he claimed to liberate several dozen Chinese "slaves" who had escaped from Torrey's colony to Brunei Town—a story the confused Chinese immediately denied under oath to the local British consul.[301] Moses's next move came around 3:00 A.M. one day in March, when the U.S. consulate—the same attap palm hut the sultan had given him—caught fire.[302] Moses explained the blaze as the byproduct of a raid by fifteen armed assassins whom Torrey and the sultan had hired to "get my head taken."[303] However, a formal investigation conducted by the U.S. Navy concluded otherwise.[304] Multiple observers, including President Andrew Johnson, placed the blame on Moses's shoulders, theorizing that the U.S. consul had burned the consulate down in the hope that Uncle Sam's navy would then turn their guns on the sultan, as John Bull's had done for Brooke decades before, and as the USS *Wyoming*, with Seward's blessing, had recently done after a Japanese *daimyo*'s attacks at the Shimonoseki Straits.[305] Whether Moses set the fire was to some extent beside the question. The man's "extraordinary hallucinations," as Seward saw it, tainted Torrey's every activity by association.[306]

Torrey struggled to recover from this bad publicity and heavy financial losses.[307] Back in Washington, he talked about Moses's "evident and undeniable insanity," which was "the only excuse that can possibly be advanced for his actions."[308] In the end, though, Seward associated Torrey's scheme with Moses, who struck polite society as a naval washout, if at all.[309] The secretary repeatedly told the British ambassador that the American government had no colonial agenda in Borneo.[310] At his recommendation, President Johnson presented to Congress a dossier with cause to remove Moses from his position; before long the president was shutting down what remained of the consulate in Brunei Town, partly because the sultan's staff were requesting settlement of Moses's debts before reaccrediting a new consul.[311] Likewise, Seward not only ordered a minion to write a letter refusing Torrey a meeting, he even declined to acknowledge his receipt of Torrey's letters, referring them instead to the Examiner of Claims, a sort of legal advisor in the State Department.[312]

Something frightened the U.S. government about being seen to negotiate with Torrey.[313] Torrey was not the only contemporary imitator of Sir James Brooke, but part of a broad trend. This trend represented a problem for the international system of statesmen, including Seward, who had still not figured out how to deal with the Brooke model of empire on more than a case-by-case basis. In the years between Brooke's ascent and through Torrey's public-relations campaign in 1867, a romanticized version of the Brooke story had gone global, reaching readers as far away as Morocco.[314] Reporting from Natal on Theophilus Shepstone, a major figure in Britain's South African expansion and then the commissioner for Zulu Affairs, an Anglican bishop wrote, "I never saw or heard of anything more surprising than the mastery he has gained over them, except . . . in the case of Sir James Brooke."[315] Back in Europe, a university lecturer compared Brooke's aura to that surrounding the missionary explorer David Livingstone, "assigning preeminence, however, to the late Sir James."[316]

From the 1840s on, imitators of Brooke flocked to East Kalimantan, in the eastern portion of Borneo, where a Scot and Englishman each unsuccessfully tried to set up their own kingdoms.[317] In the House of Commons, Radical MP William Molesworth warned of a future in which would-be Brookes founded "some half-dozen other Bornean principalities."[318] But the mimicry did not remain isolated to this island, or even to Southeast Asia. For proof, consider the trajectory of Orélie-Antoine de Tounens, an aristocratic French attorney who became the "King of Araucanía."[319] Tounens traveled to Patagonia to trade, only to find, or so it was said in 1860, that certain chiefs wanted to make him their king in an effort to get Europe to recognize their independence from the Chilean government.[320] Chile did not formally claim the territory in question, but authorities in Santiago promptly captured "Orélie-Antoine I" and placed him in an insane asylum. Napoleon III lodged a protest with the Chilean embassy, perhaps aware that the matter overlapped with some other concerns.[321] The emperor was, at that very moment, still engaged in negotiations with Sir James Brooke to take over Sarawak.[322] He was also eager to find American allies for his intervention in Mexico.

Rogues pursuing sovereignty, it seemed, had gained approval in France—and surely some notoriety, too, if Tounens's appearance in Jules Verne's work, *In Search of the Castaways,* is any indication.[323] What opinion the U.S. government held was less clear, precisely as it bore most heavily on the fate of Joseph Torrey. As mentioned, the United States extended its recognition for Sarawak in 1850, acknowledging that the kingdom belonged entirely to Brooke. On the other hand, many figures close to the U.S. government, including former secretaries of state, remained skeptical about Brooke's autonomy from Britain, and the United States mostly declined to provide recognition for several such figures elsewhere in the world, fearing slippage.[324] For example, the United States maintained—excepting a notable and aborted recognition of William Walker as ruler of Nicaragua—an official distance from a dozen or so adventurers who dispensed with the formalities of contracts and based their claims in Latin America on force of arms: filibusters such as Narciso López in Cuba.[325] Unhappily for Torrey, American newspapers sometimes thought of these brigands, too, as peers to Brooke, spurred in part by the claims of Brooke's Dutch antagonists and in part by reports from London. More than one American felt that it was "as near an approach . . . as can be imagined."[326] And the *New York Herald* wrote that "filibuster Walker and filibuster Brooke are gentlemen much alike."[327]

It is perhaps more accurate to say that the filibusters, Brooke, and Torrey more closely resembled genetically linked, but phenotypically different, descendants from a common ancestor: the East India Company.[328] American filibusters sometimes defended their enterprise by arguing, more or less as Brooke did, that they only followed the path of the "king of filibusters," the EIC, in India.[329] They did so in very different ways and with different goals, however. Most adventurers in Latin America relied on arms in a quest to perpetuate slavery, whereas Brooke, rather like the EIC, relied on a mixture of force, treaties, and genuine consent from portions of indigenous populations.[330] Moreover, filibusters and Brooke did not really come onto the international scene at the same time—even if both faced public, severe setbacks around the time that the EIC met with its winding down, with only Brooke emerging with legal sanction for his activities.[331] In fact, though the term "filibustering" entered the lexicon only around 1850, the practice among Americans stretched back to at least the late 1700s, and it could be found across the globe among many different ethnicities: French, Italian, even Japanese.[332]

Still, it is crucial to acknowledge the common ancestry of the EIC, and to understand how, in the Western zeitgeist of the 1850s and early 1860s, the filibusters' paths intertwined with the fame of Brooke and other adventurers in Borneo in the years preceding Torrey's own gambit.[333] One example was the case of Walter Murray Gibson, a Southerner who tried violently to carve out his own colony in the lower half of Borneo, over Dutch opposition, before becoming prime minister of the Kingdom of Hawaii.[334] Another, less apparent point of intersection was an analogy bandied about in newspapers: "private sovereignty" in Borneo, however acquired, might be said to place its owners in a relationship to their home countries like that between the states comprising the American union and the federal government in Washington, D.C.[335]

The United States repeatedly, if inconsistently, prosecuted filibusters for violating a law that prohibited the raising of armies in America for the purpose of overthrowing foreign governments in peacetime. This was the so-called Neutrality Act, passed by Congress in 1794 and renewed, with alterations, on multiple occasions thereafter.[336] The act, though, in no way proscribed the *lease* of a government such as Torrey made in the 1860s; nor did it prohibit the peaceable transfer of ruling powers in exchange for an equivalent value of goods or services.[337] This loophole also existed in Europe: Britain, notably, only forbade subjects' acquisitions of territory when made by conquest, occupancy, election, or descent.[338] So Torrey seemed to fit neatly within the contours of American and international law. For all his faults—and there were many—he did not browbeat anyone with guns. Nor did he challenge an established European colonial power, as Gibson had done with the Dutch. On the contrary, Torrey only wanted to become king in a foreign land through a business transaction, by buying governing rights from a sultan, as he put it, "on the principle on which the Honorable East India Company . . . founded" many of its Asian enclaves.[339] The law of nations had apparently approved that course in the case of Brooke, as Torrey pointed out to Seward more than once.[340] And so Torrey, the *New York Times* reported, felt justifiably "bent on following the example of the celebrated Englishman."[341]

Legal intricacies aside, the U.S. Congress—then in the middle of debating another revision of the Neutrality Act in the wake of Fenian raids into Canada—refused to countenance Torrey, and in the end he simply tried to raise operating funds absent any government assistance.[342] Without recourse to officials in Washington, D.C., he turned creative in asserting his government's independence. He knew the money markets on the U.S. East Coast did not wish to participate in an overseas venture without some sign of approval from American officials, if not outright recognition. So he took advantage of the U.S. federal system and cultivated approval from an individual American state: New York. Rather than continue to base his operations out of Hong Kong, Torrey nominally relocated them to the Empire State, incorporating there in accordance with state law.[343] Thus did his government begin to take on a more American guise.[344]

Torrey followed up by issuing more than two thousand prospectuses to potential investors.[345] Each one made clear that the new corporation's assets were nothing less than the rights to govern Sabah. And what a place it was, if perhaps only in Torrey's imagination. There was so much gold there, Torrey fibbed, as "only equaled by the Australian and California mines."[346] There were also, he claimed in another lie, somewhere between one and two million inhabitants eager to go to work, with "several chiefs" having taken "the oath of allegiance to the Yankee Rajah," and "no distinction of race or color being recognized."[347] Rather than focus on lack of approval from the State Department, each prospectus suggested that the Borneo company's basis in New York placed its operations under the protective umbrella of a well-known home state. To punctuate this argument, Torrey publicized a visit to Sabah currently being undertaken by the retired president of the New York Chamber of Commerce.[348]

The prospectus for the "American Trading Company of Borneo" reached out beyond Manhattan to the money markets in San Francisco, Hartford, Milwaukee, and Cleveland.[349] It is fair to say it achieved some measure of success; in 1868, Britain's ambassador to the Netherlands reported that Torrey was "an enterprising citizen" whose status as a ruler on Borneo was equal to those of James Brooke, the sultan of Brunei, and the king of the Netherlands.[350] Financially, however, the prospectus fell flat, perhaps because its improbable aim was to sell shares of a nonexistent, already insolvent state in exchange for US$500,000. Whatever the reasons for this failure, Torrey continued his efforts. For one, he added a royal motto at the top of his letters, *"Dextris deoque confidens"* ("Trust to God and to its right arm"), which he appeared to have borrowed from his childhood home in Massachusetts.[351] Torrey also recruited George Francis Train, railroad tycoon, founder of the infamous Crédit Mobilier of America, and admirer of James Brooke.[352] Train had known Torrey earlier in life, when the two were in business in the Far East; now Train did Torrey a turn by promoting him.[353] In a final effort to overcome skeptics, Torrey cultivated a loftier physical presence than perhaps was his due. Throughout his trips around the United States to drum up business, the "Rajah" of Sabah traveled in the company of a royal entourage, replete with an entirely invented costume and an aide-de-camp.[354]

Eventually "His Highness" claimed to visit General Ulysses S. Grant, soon to become president of the United States, though there was no corroboration for this story.[355] In San Francisco, one newspaper reported the arrival in town of "the famous American Rajah of Borneo."[356] Another writer was even more hyperbolic, reporting that "the governor of Borneo is said to be an American, named Torrey."[357] Finally, Torrey placed a "royal" seal on his letterhead—two concentric circles embedded with a red star—and appointed a consul from Sabah to the United States, in another attempt to replicate some of the trappings that would have come with diplomatic recognition.[358]

Alas, by this time Torrey's settlement at Ellena had collapsed.[359] The tea and coffee crops planted by his agents had all failed. Likewise the attempts to strike gold. Worse still, officials of Brunei—as well as local traders along the Kimanis River—were trying to track Torrey down to make good on outstanding bills left behind by his employees, many of whom were reputed to live in debauchery.[360] Nor was there hope of starting over, for the dozens of coolie laborers hired to work had long since departed, their wages also unpaid.[361] Beyond a patch of terraced earth, plowed for projects that never took hold, the sole vestige of Torrey's colony consisted in a tombstone for his friend and business partner, a fellow New Englander who had contracted a fatal illness during an expedition into the jungle.[362]

The entire Sabah scheme appeared destined for obscurity by the early 1870s. The United States closed its consulate in Brunei in 1868, not long after an extensive *Atlantic Monthly* article on Borneo mentioned nary a word about American interests.[363] Moses, unemployed and severely depressed in Bangkok, eventually vanished on a voyage to San Francisco.[364] As for Torrey, he declared bankruptcy in July 1869, shelved his royal ambitions, and began to pay off his bills by managing a sugar refinery in Hong Kong.[365] Soon, however, he would rebound by meeting a man who shared his vision for Sabah. Within a decade, this pair would spearhead a change that transformed the political map of Southeast Asia. Then, in what surely represented one of the century's most improbable turns, they would launch an idea powerful enough to help enable the infamous Scramble for Africa.

2

The Emergence of an Idea

Gustav von Overbeck met Joseph Torrey in Hong Kong in 1870, when Torrey came asking for a personal loan and listed among his assets a ten-year lease on sovereignty in Sabah.[1] Overbeck hatched a plan to partner with the American and assist him in renewing his rights before they expired at the end of 1875.[2] Torrey was a kindred spirit, albeit a bankrupt one who had "lost about all he was worth," according to the American consul at Singapore. Torrey was now "living in reduced circumstances" and "struggling to get along . . . in connection with his unfortunate enterprises in Borneo."[3] Still lacking significant political connections, he had gotten no closer to Hong Kong's elite than giving a lecture at City Hall on poetry.[4] Overbeck, by contrast, lived in a posh neighborhood on Pedder's Hill, helping to direct the Chamber of Commerce, networking with the managers of the Hongkong and Shanghai Banking Corporation (HSBC), and maneuvering in Western diplomatic circles.[5] He even carried a knighthood from the Habsburg Emperor Franz Joseph, and he had served as the accredited Austrian consul in Hong Kong since 1867, before which time he also enjoyed stints as consul for Prussia and Mexico respectively.[6]

It was conceivable that Overbeck could secure international recognition for Torrey's rights; he was no ordinary speculator.[7] Born to an esteemed pharmacist in the tiny German principality of Lippe, Gustavus, as he was originally called, chased gold strikes at age twenty, fled from military service, and trekked to California. One whaling tour in the Arctic and a stint in Honolulu later, he went to work for Dent & Co., one of Hong Kong's major trading firms.[8] By age forty he had made a fortune selling insurance to rich Chinese fleeing the Taiping Rebellion, to the extent that Germany's ambassador to Japan described him as "swimming in gold."[9] He partied in Paris; he wore pearl-encrusted necktie-rings and smoked cigars from a golden case; and he was not afraid to flout social convention, sometimes showing up to dinner in his pajamas.[10] Early in 1870, the year when Overbeck met Torrey, he married Romaine Goddard, the beautiful daughter of an assistant secretary in the U.S. Department of the Interior and the stepdaughter of Rear Admiral John Dahlgren, lately of the Union navy. Goddard's family had major connections in D.C.; President Grant and Chief Justice Chase each attended her marriage ceremony.[11] In ensuing years, the newlyweds took up a sort of triple residence in Washington, Hong Kong, and London, socializing with people who would later take their own interest in Torrey's lease for Sabah.[12] These were figures such as Lord Redesdale, then secretary to Her Majesty's Office of Works.

The biggest obstacle facing the new partners was insufficient capital. Torrey continued to advertise himself as "a high Asiatic dignitary, a monarch whose sway was unbounded over millions of people"; still, he needed a loan to make ends meet.[13] As for Overbeck, he was making money shipping silk but had recently seen his fortune decline to the point of having to auction off furniture.[14] One can adduce plenty of reasons: the collapse of the Hong Kong real estate market and attendant demise of Dent & Co.; stabling for a fleet of expensive racehorses; maintenance of a home that was part villa, part château; an armed home robbery of cash and diamonds; extensive international travel, which included trips with an entourage of eight to such destinations as Bad Ischl in Austria; and, perhaps most acutely, the failure of a Siamese sugar refinery in whose future he had invested heavily.[15] In the event, by the early 1870s Overbeck, whose annual income had reached 80,000 Spanish dollars in the 1860s, could not even muster a quarter of that sum to put into Torrey's venture, which technically still existed under the title of the American Trading Company of Borneo, with Torrey as the only living partner.[16]

Hence the German moved to raise additional cash in London, meeting with Redesdale, as well as the Austrian ambassador to England, Count Montgelas. Overbeck put up £2,000, the others £1,000 each. All resolved to buy out Torrey once the American helped Overbeck renegotiate the lease with the sultan of Brunei.[17] The men hoped to publicize and resell Torrey's sovereign rights to some Western state: either the

Austro-Hungarian Empire, the United States, Germany, or even Italy, which was then beginning a tentative foray into colonialism at East Africa's Assab Bay, on the coast of what Italians eventually called Eritrea.[18] Western trade with Southeast Asia was primed to grow rapidly on the strength of the recent inauguration of regular, trans-Pacific steamship service to Hong Kong.[19] Overbeck, described by Lord Redesdale as ever "trembling with excitement," appeared to be a man "with prophetic powers." He told Redesdale, "You will get anything you wish."[20]

The first nibble came from the Italian government, which, newly unified on the strength of another *filibustero*, Garibaldi, had extended its official diplomatic recognition to Sarawak and won Brooke's admiration.[21] Italy had freshly qualified as a sovereign, independent state, and they were interested in building a penal colony somewhere in the vicinity of New Guinea.[22] In 1867 Baroness Angela Burdett-Coutts, via intermediaries, approached Prime Minister Urbano Rattazzi with an offer: An Italian company, not Rome, would pay Brooke four million dollars for the rights to govern Sarawak.[23] Deeming the price too steep, Rattazzi refused; some of his countrymen, though, shifted their attention toward Sabah, with one naval captain rumored to covet "an informal Rajahship, without British consent, as a private enterprise," in view of the trend developing among Brooke's imitators.[24] After a preliminary scouting trip by this same naval captain, the Italian Foreign Ministry dispatched negotiators to Brunei to acquire sovereign rights to the island of Banggi, located just off the coast from the former Ellena colony.[25] Even before setting out from Hong Kong, the Italian sailors heard about Torrey when he approached them at the city docks and expressed a desire to offload his rights over Sabah, the original title to which lay under lock and key in the local American consulate.[26] The Italians fumed.[27] Torrey, they claimed, was purely the "titular governor" of Sabah; his rights had not been used since 1866.[28] Over the next two years "His Excellency" Torrey would nonetheless lodge protests with the Italian consulate in Hong Kong, ordering the Italians not to undertake "occupation of any territory" without his "leave or license."[29]

Faced with such a threat, Overbeck could try to call in favors with Washington, D.C.[30] The U.S. Navy had begun snooping around Sabah in the late 1860s, when a Rear Admiral Bell stopped in Hong Kong to visit Torrey and discuss the possibility of taking over his lease.[31] Bell dismissed that idea, proceeding to rescue shipwrecked Americans at Formosa, of which far better placed U.S. officials urged a purchase from China. Still, and perhaps for this reason, reports continued to credit the United States with a strong interest in the entire area.[32] Asian newspapers repeatedly spoke of U.S. negotiations with the American Trading Company of Borneo to lease ground for a naval station.[33] Whatever that claim's veracity, Italy supposedly agreed, after indirect pressure in the form of a U.S. warship shadowing Italian vessels off Borneo, not only to back away, but also to honor the Torrey contract with Brunei as if it were a treaty between two states.[34] Torrey's rights, to this extent, started to appear more legitimate in the West.[35]

Starting in 1873 Overbeck took leave of his duties in Hong Kong to prepare a series of presentations for the Austro-Hungarian government in Vienna.[36] An attendant publicity campaign had begun in Europe, with flattering newspaper articles touting Overbeck. Here was a "virtuous man dedicated to the interests of Austria"—a man who had earned status not only as "the richest and greatest promoter in South China," but also as the newly minted king of an island in the Far East, albeit through a temporary proxy.[37] Such hype continued at the Vienna World's Fair, where Overbeck set up an exhibition booth for Chinese porcelain, but with the added agenda of advertising Borneo under a sign bearing a stretched tiger pelt and his own name.[38] By 1874, he took his sales pitch away from the masses of the *Prater* to a smaller audience of what he called "intimate friends and men of state." Austria-Hungary, his voluminous proposal ran, should agree to pay 5,000,000 florins to acquire Sabah.[39] Control there would assist the empire in expanding its trade with British India, then on its way to becoming Austria-Hungary's largest trade partner overseas.[40]

Officers of the notoriously modest Austro-Hungarian Navy appeared interested.[41] The head of the fleet pronounced Sabah superior to any spot held by the Dutch or British in the same region. Count Gyula Andrássy, the foreign minister, perused a prospectus delivered by the Austrian Trade Ministry on Overbeck's behalf and even approved a plan to scrape together funds, perhaps because he was impressed that his subordinate, Montgelas, belonged to the project.[42] But everyone expected tough sledding in Vienna, because the prime minister recommended foregoing all colonial schemes in favor of a redoubled emphasis on the Balkans.[43] Besides, Britain, though by all accounts fatigued with colonies, was making inroads in the area near Sabah. Between 1873 and

1874, British "residents" assumed administrative duties in the sultanates of Selangor, Perak, and Seremban (Sungei-Ujong), thus expanding a Malayan peninsular portfolio that already included Singapore and parts of Penang, Pangkor, and Malacca.[44] As a result, the market in Southeast Asian territory looked especially robust by 1874, despite the advent of a worldwide economic depression, which, coincidentally, had begun with the Vienna stock exchange crash less than one year earlier.

In early 1875 Franz Joseph's navy dispatched one of its few corvettes, *Herzog Friedrich,* on a mission to circumnavigate the globe. The *Friedrich*'s trip began with a pass around the African Horn and across the Indian Ocean.[45] In May, an official government order charted a course for Torrey's Ellena.[46] The prospect of Austria's seizing the area by force was palpable in Brunei, but such talk dissipated when a group in canoers—perhaps Dayaks—decapitated two armed Austrian sailors and wounded several more.[47] Following up with British authorities in nearby Sarawak, the *Friedrich*'s captain, a man appropriately named Österreicher, learned that Torrey's company had disappeared from Sabah years ago, leaving unpaid bills behind in Brunei, Singapore, and Hong Kong.[48] This revelation mirrored statements made some years before, by two visiting vessels in the United States navy.[49] One of those ships, the USS *Wachusett,* complained when it found no evidence of Torrey's supposed regime.[50]

Whether because of this fiasco or because of more pressing concerns about a prospective Ottoman-Serb war, Austria-Hungary soon exited the bidding war.[51] With Italy and the United States also out of the picture, Torrey now found himself without any prospective clients. Worse still, observers in Europe could not help but note that his lone assets—the agreements he and Moses had signed in 1865—were still set to expire at the end of the 1875.[52] True, it was possible to argue that, depending on how one interpreted the lease with Brunei, expiration would not necessarily void the agreement: Moses had inserted a clause into the contract allowing him to renew the lease for a few more years without the sultan's approval—perhaps through 1878. But the sultan had not received a dollar from Torrey in years, and, during a meeting with Overbeck and Torrey in 1875, the sultan refused to countenance even a short-term extension of the lease, absent payment of arrears.[53] This was apparently the first sighting of Torrey in Brunei since the late 1860s, when the sultan's officials started soliciting information on Torrey's whereabouts from his associates in an effort to track him down as a delinquent debtor.[54]

Such issues did not abate by the beginning of 1876, when a smuggler named Cowie arrived in Hong Kong to discuss some developments in a place called Sulu.

IN THE SECOND HALF of the nineteenth century, as the Spanish struggled to hold onto what remained of their Pacific empire following the devastating Napoleonic Wars, they turned their sights on the Sultanate of Sulu.[55] This was a vaguely defined archipelago located roughly halfway between Borneo and the Philippine island of Mindanao. According to contemporary Western commentators, the archipelago comprised a wild kingdom where a population of around one hundred thousand Muslims, known as Tausug, functioned more or less without the rule of law.[56] Spanish rumor had it that Tausug cut out the tongues of enemy prisoners.[57] Stories also abounded about another group harbored by the Tausug, the Iranun, who had earned a reputation for raiding foreign shores and taking perhaps hundreds of thousands of prisoners, only to sell the latter into slavery in an economic climate thirsting for labor to make goods for sale to China.[58] Such slaves, opined one observer, were "not well treated, for their masters exercise the power of life and death over them, and sometimes kill them for trifling offenses."[59]

When the Spanish made their first attempt at annexing Sulu around 1850, it came as part of a campaign with two objectives: to break the back of raiders who had menaced the Philippines since at least the 1820s; and to counteract the influence of Britain, on whose behalf James Brooke had just negotiated a stillborn treaty with the Sultan of Sulu.[60] Through the next two decades, observers in Manila and Madrid saw little success.[61] Although repeated bombardments of Jolo, Sulu's capital, did disrupt the slave-taking that powered the Sulu economy, they failed to force Sultan Jamal'ul Alam into submission, and Spain changed course by implementing a full-scale blockade in 1870.[62] In theory, this effort would cut off supplies of weapons (mostly from British India), create a shortage of food (mostly from Spanish Manila), and hasten the unwinding of Sulu's key export business, which involved shipping pearls, edible sea cucumbers, and birds' nests (mostly to China).[63] Instead of strangling their enemy, however, Spain's elimination of licit trade to the island enticed a series of smugglers in and around Borneo to trade with Sulu. Worst of all for Spain, some of these smugglers, known as the Labuan Trading Company, started flying British and German flags along their routes.[64]

The Labuan Trading Company employed several dozen expatriates, one of whom, a Prussian by the name of Hermann Schück, followed Joseph Torrey in becoming a titular ruler on the far side of the world.[65] Schück's status as a German subject accorded him certain privileges overseas.[66] A Spanish naval squadron could not easily molest a ship known to carry Schück, so long as that ship cavalierly flew the flag of his home country.[67] This was true especially because Germany, whose merchants chafed most under the blockade, had been pushing London to force Spain into free trade.[68] That was good news for Schück, who ran contraband through the Spanish blockade to Jolo, where he usually arrived at dark with opium and rifles, then took payment in the form of slaves.[69] Spain may have carried an awesome reputation around Manila. Yet, as Schück soon told Jamal'ul Alam, Spain was nothing more than a second-rate power on the European continent when compared with Germany.

Sulu's sultan was a young man, without much experience in negotiation and at the head of a weakly centralized polity that more closely resembled an oligarchy than a monarchy.[70] In 1866, at the suggestion of German traders, he wrote to William I, the king of Prussia, to ask for assistance in the war against Spain. The sultan suggested that the North German Confederation take a slice of his territory on the northeastern coast of Borneo, in exchange for recognition of his authority and, not least, German naval protection of Sulu.[71] The latter kind of deal had become fairly common since the late 1700s, when Sulu began licensing Tausug aristocrats *(datus)* to create their own principalities in Borneo, in a sort of mutualistic relationship of profit.[72] William I liked the idea but deferred to Bismarck, his chancellor.[73] In 1872, as Spain intensified its blockade, Jamal'ul reiterated his as yet unanswered proposal—aware that his fellow sultan in Brunei had recently offered the same territory to a disbanded American group, with one of whose ex-members, Wheelwright, Sulu now traded for guns.[74] Of course, the last German attempt at formal colonization overseas—a fort on the West African coast known as *Groß-Friedrichsburg*—had ended in ignominy roughly a hundred and fifty years earlier.[75] At the same time, Prussian naval planners were known to be interested in establishing a base in Southeast Asia:

Beginning in 1860, they had tried to negotiate one in Siam, Japan, or China, and by 1872 this informal preference had become an initiative in Bismarck's chancellery.[76] Beyond naval strategy, Jamal'ul also told William that the Reich's foreign trade could benefit immeasurably from owning an additional fueling point on the way to China. He even suggested that German businessmen should take an interest in the vast timber resources to be found along the Kimanis River, which ran from the egress of northeastern Borneo toward Brunei.

The *Nymphe,* a German corvette that happened to be in the area carrying two hundred sailors, inspected the coast of Sabah in May 1873, not long before Overbeck's Austrians did the same.[77] Writing back to Bismarck, the *Nymphe*'s captain acknowledged commercial potential but cautioned against governing any part of Borneo, especially since Sabah was an area that was only intermittently under Sulu's control in the first place, and whose vicissitudes had quickly decimated an American colony.[78] Bismarck, notorious for his aversion to overseas entanglements, promptly dispatched the *Nymphe* to Jolo with an order declining the offer from Sulu. As it happened, however, the ship's captain arrived at Jolo in the company of a familiar translator: Schück. Schück—who had once worked in the consular service of Prussia—politely told the sultan that Germany did not incline to govern a colony so far away from Europe.[79] But then Schück deviated from the script, so to speak, by providing the sultan with a translation that asked the sultan to give territory to Schück's company, in order that Schück might govern it "for" Germany—apparently, as a Tausug *datu* might have.[80] By the end of this parley Jamal'ul signed a contract giving Schück what he wanted. On paper, Schück and his company now owned rights to govern a piece of land on the coast of northeastern Borneo by themselves, with the tacit understanding that they might do so on behalf of Bismarck's mighty nation.

Schück was an official translator. So it was true that, as with Moses and the United States some seven years earlier, he really did have a connection to the German government. Still, on balance this was an audacious man who simply wanted a *kampong,* or village, at which to safely restock his smuggling vessel, a fifty-three-foot steamship named the *Argyle.* He had no designs to build a state out of his rights, even after the Labuan Company sent several more of his countrymen to the new site, appropriately named "Kampong German."[81] On the edge of a jungle, the men took equal shares in building a sort of smuggler's paradise where nearly every resident carried a weapon and bore a name like Hofft, Olzen, or Sachsze.[82] In the meantime, everyone—including Sulu—earned major spoils for their troubles.[83] Thanks to their refuge on Borneo, the smugglers spent years more or less immune to stolen cargo and Spanish capture. Sulu's regime continued to benefit from such contraband as opium, integrating its economy and investing the profits into state-building at home while rivals, notably Brunei, suffered by comparison.[84]

Schück disappeared from recorded history at some point before 1875, by which time his company had come to claim a virtual monopoly on smuggled goods to Sulu for use in the ongoing war with Spain.[85] In the interim Schück's boss, a Scot named William Cowie, took over the duties of ruling Kampong German. Cowie showed up in Hong Kong sometime in 1876 and started to advertise his fiefdom, only to find himself accosted by the American manager of a local sugar refinery.[86] This man was Joseph Torrey, who demanded that Cowie pay 10 percent export duties on a cargo of pearls he had acquired in Sulu and was hoping to run through Sabah to Hong Kong, before moving on to mainland China.[87] To substantiate his demand, Torrey produced lease contracts signed not with the Sultan of Sulu, but with the Sultan of Brunei. Torrey claimed these contracts made him the ruler of a vast territory, in which Kampong German figured only as a small part.[88]

Cowie hardly needed to stomach Torrey's demands, so long as his interest was smuggling. But Cowie, like Torrey, had larger ambitions. Clearly Kampong German lay inside the boundaries of the American's territory, as construed by his lease contract with Brunei; but Brunei's own claim had been weak. The lease presupposed that Brunei actually disposed over the area at the moment to transfer. In reality, Cowie could confirm for Torrey—who had never really set foot in "his" territory, aside from a brief visit to its coast—that Brunei had exercised virtually no authority in northeastern Borneo since the eighteenth century. Sabah's residents could find Sulu's predominance attested by some two thousand wandering elephants originally sent from Jolo as a projection of power.[89] Besides, Cowie correctly noted that the Sultanate of Brunei had sold its claim to the territory to Sulu long ago, in exchange for military assistance during a protracted seventeenth-century civil war.[90] Sulu, in turn, had unsuccessfully offered Sabah to the British in 1763, over a century before granting a lease on Kampong German to Cowie's company.[91] To illustrate this control, Cowie had even stopped calling Kampong German by its European name. He now preferred to call it "Sandakan"—a Tausug word meaning "the place that was pawned."

These disclosures suggested that the Sultan of Brunei might have tried to swindle Torrey and Moses, even as the two Americans presumed to have done the same to him; any strong American foray into Sabah would have bolstered Brunei's tenuous claims there, without cost to the sultan.[92] Nonetheless, Cowie indicated that he would assist Torrey and Overbeck in acquiring a new lease—only this time from the Sultan of Sulu, and with a fee for his trouble. First, however, Overbeck needed to come up with yet more money in Europe. Appeals went out again to Teutonic elites, including an invitation-only reception at Vienna's Palais Windisch-Graetz.[93] When no donors came forward, Overbeck went to London and solicited the aid of a merchant named Alfred Dent.[94] The thirty-three-year-old Dent was the nephew and successor to Overbeck's former boss of twenty years, Lancelot Dent, whose machinations on behalf of the eponymous Dent & Co., a firm best known for trading opium, had helped to precipitate the First Opium War with China.[95] Dent & Co. fell on hard times in the wake of the Overend Gurney crisis in 1866.[96] With many of the firm's bank deposits lost and their cash reserves depleted by horse racing, the firm had no other choice than to sell its vaunted fleet of clipper ships, and eventually to declare bankruptcy.[97] Still, by the 1870s the Dents still disposed over far more capital than Overbeck, Torrey, and Cowie combined. Alfred Dent, now taking command of his inheritance for the first time, claimed he was working "like a Trojan" to reestablish the family business.[98] As important, he retained impeccable political connections. These extended to the British Foreign Office, the agency most responsible for determining Britain's overseas relations, as well as to the navy, one of whose rear admirals, Richard Charles Mayne, had married Alfred's sister Sabine.[99]

Overbeck, to whom Torrey had signed over power of attorney, emphasized how rare it was to have won control of prime territory in Southeast Asia "in a perfectly peaceful and legal way . . . in exchange for the payment of a certain sum of money."[100] Dent, for his part, identified strong financial incentives for his participation. For one, the prospect of putting Sabah's estimated 22,000 square miles of fertile land under new ownership would generate lots of interest among cash-rich coffee and tea planters in Ceylon, where the newly christened "Alfred Dent and Co." had a significant presence.[101] It was also plausible that if Western "law and order" could be established in Sabah, many "strong Chinese emigrant colonies" that had dispersed decades before might return to the Borneo coast, thus restoring "the moving and living element" of "an extensive trade" with China.[102]

Dent proceeded to tell Overbeck that he would participate in the scheme, on certain conditions. First, the group needed to secure another lease from the Sultan of Sulu, in order to render Torrey's title beyond reproach. Second, Dent would direct these upcoming negotiations, with Cowie as his proxy. Third, Overbeck would travel, not just to Jolo, but also to Brunei Town, where he would pay the Sultan of Brunei for a new, still more explicit lease of sovereign rights than had ever been granted to Torrey. Fourth, Dent would buy into the project and hold a slight majority of shares in a new company, to which Overbeck and Torrey would transfer their leases. Fifth, as soon as Overbeck finalized the deal in Brunei, he would help Dent jettison Torrey. Overbeck, by this time in jeopardy of bankruptcy, agreed. In early 1877 Dent transferred money into an account for the new corporation, the "Dent and Overbeck Company."[103]

Drawing from the company's coffers, now flush with an additional £6,000 of Dent's fortune, Overbeck traveled to Singapore with Cowie to outfit an expedition.[104] After purchasing guns and cannons, the pair joined a larger party for two journeys: one to Brunei, one to Sulu.[105] Torrey had already taken another boat to the palace in Brunei Town, Moses's original lease in hand, in the hope of negotiating for another deal. Keeping him company was the British governor of Labuan, William Hood Treacher, for whom Dent's involvement had served as a spur. Treacher's presence ensured that "the natives," as one witness remarked, were "under the impression, an impression as to which no attempt was apparently made to undeceive them, that the negotiations were in some way specially recognized by the British Government."[106]

The Sultan of Brunei decided to repeat the experiment, agreeing to a new lease at a greater annual rate.[107] Still persuaded of Torrey's connection to the U.S. government—a perception the American reinforced by anchoring at the site of the ruined consulate—the elderly sultan put aside his contempt for Torrey, fueled as it was by the latter's failure to pay anything or stay in touch during the last ten years.[108] After demanding a mere few thousand dollars up front, "to satisfy him for all there was due under the old lease," the sultan relented.[109] Overbeck agreed once he arrived to join Torrey at Brunei Town. Their pact sealed, the expedition then sailed up the Sabah coast, past the abandoned Ellena colony—more or less the most eastern point of any vestigial loyalty to Brunei—and on to Jolo, where they met with the Sultan of Sulu to negotiate for yet another lease.[110]

Arriving at Jolo in a ship named *America,* Overbeck implied that the United States, yet again, was thinking about committing itself to colonization in Southeast Asia.[111] This second round of negotiations lasted just a few days—"an astonishingly short time," according to an American diplomat keeping tabs from Singapore.[112] Sulu's sultan had already formed a business partnership with Cowie to split the 5,000 Spanish dollars Dent offered Sulu for control of Sabah. Add to this that the sultan liked the idea of a British- and American-supported refuge in the event of a Spanish invasion of Sulu, and the brisk pace of talks is unsurprising.[113] After a sendoff that featured horseracing, bullfighting, and a grand dinner with giant pearl-shell plates, the visiting party left behind a cash deposit and returned to Singapore to cable London with the good news.[114]

Now came Dent's turn. Writing to colleagues in London, he asked what it would take to secure for Sabah what Britain had given Brooke's Sarawak in the 1860s: diplomatic recognition. Unlike Brooke—and very much like the failed interloper Torrey—Dent's rudimentary government in Sabah had acquired the title of ruler before it could claim de facto control throughout its nominal territory, then in a condition of anarchy.[115] It was partly for this reason that, when word of the new leases reached London in April 1878, several members of parliament cautioned the cabinet against legitimizing whatever rights Dent claimed to own. Charles Dilke, a Liberal Party MP then viewed as a future prime minister, led the way. Dent's company, he charged, was nothing but a pack of fortune seekers looking for quick profits, worst among them Overbeck. Rumor had it that the German still preferred to sell his company's rights to a Central European government, and Overbeck's recurring presence at official meetings in Vienna was confirmed as late as the winter of 1877–1878.[116] Dilke therefore wondered aloud why Britain should do this opportunist the favor of recognizing those rights as valid.[117] Fellow members of parliament ought to consider whether Sarawak, still under the control of young Charles Brooke, might do better to take control of northeastern Borneo. The Brookes were somewhat constitutional and philanthropic rulers—a broad majority, including labor activist Edith Simcox, agreed on that.[118] Whatever Charles Brooke's reputation for being jealous of his European rivals, he did not want to become the ruler of hundreds of thousands of people just to make a profit off of selling their government.[119]

Further complicating matters was the growth of opposition abroad.[120] Mere months after Dent and Overbeck struck their bargain with Sulu, the Spanish navy finally overran Jolo. Immediately they coerced the sultan into publishing a statement in which he proclaimed that all he owned—including the territory he "leased" on Borneo—had actually been under Spanish sovereignty since time immemorial. Nor did Spain stop there. Midway into 1878, a flotilla of their ships dropped anchor off Sabah, menacing the provisional government that Dent had set up in Cowie's old haunt, Sandakan.[121] The Spanish could already see clearly that the new "emperor" at Sandakan had no clothes—or at least, only one transparent set. True, some of the Dent and Overbeck Company's buildings flew the Union Jack.[122] More often, though, they flew their "national flag," a banner with a miniature version of the Union Jack in its upper-left hand corner.[123] To put things further into perspective, one must consider that the supplies passed out by one of Dent and Overbeck's officers amounted to six rifles, a barrel of flour, and seventeen chickens. When asked to assess the provisional bureaucracy under this new regime, an insider worried that a staff of four men was to police three hundred miles of coastline.[124]

While this bureaucracy may have sufficed to collect customs revenue on the coast, it was hardly enough to repulse Spain. Hence, absent some kind of intervention from Britain, the experiment of the Dent and Overbeck Company looked likely to end poorly.[125] Spanish officers in the Philippines started sending Dent's officers what amounted to eviction notices; they even forewarned Brunei officials against cooperation.[126] Madrid, fully expecting Britain to refuse Dent its permission to continue his indirect claims, simply awaited confirmation from London before authorizing direct military action.[127]

As the Foreign Office turned to tackle the matter, it found itself addressing the same thorny issues it had addressed with James Brooke.

Questions flooded in from parliament: Was it legal, as at least one prominent politician asked, for the Dent and Overbeck Company to exercise sovereignty over a territory? A kind of amnesia had set in since the battle over Brooke's recognition. MPs now declared it (again) "free from objection" if the Sultan of Brunei wanted to lease his sovereign rights to "any recognized sovereign power," such as Britain.[128] No such indifference would greet the matter if the sultan intended to strike a deal with someone like Overbeck, whose expedition appeared "to have been somewhat of a filibustering nature."[129]

Spain, eager to sustain this negative proposition, had an easy series of precedents at their command: Spanish settlements in the Americas. The court at Madrid had insisted since the days of Hernán Cortés that European powers must hold sovereignty over any provinces acquired by *conquistadores* overseas.[130] Put differently, however much mineral wealth might flow into private coffers, any administrative rights exercised in newly settled areas would be held as privileges dependent on a given Crown's pleasure. In Spanish colonial history, there were occasional gestures toward subverting this rule, as when Gonzalo Pizarro, angered with the New Laws issued from Madrid, considered declaring himself an independent king of Peru by virtue of a marriage contract with an Incan princess.[131] In 1528, Charles I, in exchange for a loan, even authorized agents of the German Welser family to take control for themselves of what is now Venezuela.[132] Notwithstanding this last partial exception, though, Madrid held firm through the nineteenth century, never making the "mistake," as one opponent of the East India Company put it, "of perpetuating a gigantic monopoly, bartering its territorial rights for money to a company of merchants, [or] delegating to them the awful and almost incommunicable attributes of peace and war."[133]

Legal experts at the Foreign Office saw no reason to concede the point to the Spanish, however. In 1880 they told their boss, Lord Granville, that the proposition brought to the fore in Borneo was one to which no "valid exception could be taken in point of international law."[134] For the first time, Britain recalled Brooke's precedent to explain why "the Government of the territories in question" was not less legitimate by virtue of "being vested in a private Association."[135] Nor was that all. Some lawyers now argued that, if it was acceptable in international law for the Dent and Overbeck Company to acquire sovereign rights, then the company should be recognized as a state wherever it exercised those rights.

This logic seemed all the more significant in view of debates over Sabah's incipient justice system. Unlike Torrey—who never really attempted to dictate law to the locals, or to expand the visibility of his presence on the ground—Dent knew that if he could not make a respectable show of power, foreign governments would assume his want of sovereignty and withhold diplomatic recognition. Accordingly, he circulated copies of a letter from the Sultan of Brunei to "warn and advise all people on the coast to obey and respect [Dent's] . . . orders as our own."[136] Dent also instructed his men to instantiate a system of criminal and civil law, covering a host of matters including murder, robbery, and property disputes.[137] A cornerstone of this campaign was administering justice through courts, which the Dent and Overbeck Company set up in ramshackle markets at Sandakan and two other posts.[138] Humble as these facilities appeared, they helped to arrange a performance of the company's sovereignty, which had hitherto existed only on paper. The more the company performed and made declarations of its rule in public, the more likely it was to establish in the West a principle Bismarck had made famous that same year in negotiations concerning Russia: *beati possidentes*.[139] Put crudely, this principle meant that when it came to control of territory, possession was nine-tenths of the law.

To its credit, Sabah's fledgling court system did produce peaceable resolution of conflicts between some groups, many of whom came to appreciate the benefits of more or less objective arbitration by a third party.[140] These outcomes compared favorably to the kind of performances of sovereignty seen in Spain's overseas colonization, which, for a time, included the reading of *requerimiento* (pronouncements compelling indigenous peoples to accept submission or die).[141] On multiple occasions Dayaks at the coast even refused Spanish demands to replace Dent's flag.[142] Within a short span the company would go on to introduce the Indian Penal Code of 1860, along with Indian standards for judicial procedure, into its domain.[143] Still, as early as 1878, European nationals working as smugglers in Sabah began to challenge the court's authority when seeking to escape criminal charges.[144] For instance, one smuggler fled prosecution after assaulting a customs official, thanks in large part to encouragement from his boss, the disgruntled Cowie, Torrey and Overbeck's onetime partner.[145] Such moments obviously hurt the company's image. They also lent credence, not just to rivals in Spain, but to the Dutch, who consistently maintained that Dent's rights as leased by the sultans had "a strictly private and commercial character, free from all political function, and without the slightest political design."[146] Politicians in Amsterdam saw Borneo, and the East Indies generally, growing in economic importance; before long the area would contribute 10 percent of Dutch national income.[147] Although less aggressive than their counterparts in Madrid, therefore, the Dutch cabinet did speak out against the "invasion of our East by a foreign power."[148] Their officers in lower Borneo even staged a protest of their own by hoisting their national flag at a town located just inside the southern limit of Dent's territory.[149]

Local populations waged their own struggles. "The country is of the best," Overbeck once complained with evident prejudice, "but the people of the worst."[150] Having never employed more than two hundred policemen in its first seven years, Dent's company largely failed in enforcing its prohibitions on the trafficking of slaves—and sometimes did not bother trying.[151] It also met with resistance when attempting to collect taxes.[152] On one occasion this dynamic led devotees of Mahomet Asgali, a former Sulu governor in the region, to tear down the company's flag at Sandakan.[153] More troublingly, the company executed a leader in western Sabah who argued that "the country did not belong to the Company," but to the indigenous population.[154] Finally, while Dent's agents did provisionally convince many established leaders, located throughout Sabah, to let them try some of the cases involving locals, these gestures toward authority often floundered.

Such developments took place partly because the company's prestige, not unlike that of its Dutch rivals to the south, sometimes rested more on contractual "rights" than on any ability to wield overarching power. But other factors contributed, too, including an inability to stop attacks from indefatigable raiders moving between the coast of Sabah and the Sulu islands to the east.[155] Not long after these raiders murdered the crew of a schooner that had stalled off the coast, company magistrates attempted to make arrests.[156] Again, though, a lack of resources—planters complained that this vast country was "without a road or a wheeled vehicle"—hampered every effort.[157] A Royal Navy gunboat, HMS *Kestrel,* helped out occasionally, even destroying a nearby Iranun base.[158] But generally company employees had to sail over to Labuan, hire constables, and mount joint expeditions to arrest suspects wanted within Sabah.[159]

For a time, Dent's company could get around such problems by bluffing that British warships would visit an area imminently unless everyone complied with its directives.[160] But this pattern could not continue indefinitely, for tax collections were not running smoothly, and Dent was flirting with bankruptcy by trying to fund all the expenses of running a government. The financial strain grew so desperate that Dent and Overbeck sent an emissary to Brunei, tasking him with lowering the amount paid to the sultan for the lease on sovereign rights.[161] The company's two leaders even bickered over a sale of their shares.

For its part, Britain needed to choose between a few alternatives. First, Britain could recognize the Dent and Overbeck Company as an independent state, leave it alone, and abstain from exercising any voice in its affairs.[162] This course would embolden bureaucrats running the new justice system in Sabah to try all cases within the leased territory—whether they involved locals, visiting Englishmen, or any other foreign national. It would also free Britain from any responsibility. On the other hand, this course risked the wrath of Spain and local pirates, who would likely overrun the company and proceed to imperil British commerce. It also allowed for abuses by the company against indigenes. A second option was for Britain to annex the Sabah territory to keep it out of "foreign" hands. On some level this course made sense. Dent had little hope to fortify his territory long-term unless Britain offered to supplement his ragtag forces with a major military presence. That said, such a development could only occur in stages. Britain would not only have to buy out Dent and Overbeck, but also meet the very expenses of governance driving the pair bankrupt. This was a major worry, for Britain's success in keeping an empire in the nineteenth century generally depended in large part on making colonies pay for themselves.[163]

From such a viewpoint, there remained only one viable alternative: inaction. But Governor Treacher, the head of the nearby Crown colony of Labuan who had helped Overbeck and Torrey renegotiate with the sultan of Brunei, took some pressure off London by making his own move to endorse Sabah's independence. Treacher appointed an unpaid British consular agent to Sabah in 1878, thus providing an instance of recognition that Britain—after years of debate—had given James Brooke some fifteen years earlier.[164] Into this fray Overbeck soon brought an idea radical enough to solve more problems: to "form a British Company somewhat, though on a smaller scale, after the manner of the late East India Company."[165] The new company could sell stock to buy out the rights currently owned by the Dent and Overbeck Company, allowing both men to exit their positions with a modest profit. Then the new company could operate under a royal charter.

A charter would incorporate the company in Britain, but under specific conditions that benefited all participants. On the one hand, the company would gain British military protection for its "rights," as well as an implicit seal of approval from the British Empire. On the other hand, Britain would pay nothing up front to keep the territory out of foreign hands, while reserving a theoretical veto over the company's foreign policy. This veto was enough to make sure the company did not start or lose any wars the Crown deemed inexpedient. But the veto did not take the responsibility for day-to-day governance away from investors in the company. "The British Government," declared one minister proudly, would thus assume "no sovereign rights whatsoever in Borneo."[166] As an added benefit, while Britain would not pay to collect taxes, staff a civil service, or build roads, the company would be obligated by a charter to remain "British" in its character. No foreign nationals could take its helm.[167]

Thus, decades after the Indian upheaval of 1857, a new firm would inherit the status enjoyed by the old East India Company.[168] Overbeck and his associates cannot exactly be credited with originality here: Similar proposals to establish new chartered company governments had circulated unsuccessfully from at least the early 1870s in various quarters, their persistence owing in part to the rather tortuous decline of the Hudson's Bay Company.[169] Overbeck's, however, was the first such scheme to gestate in a fertile climate like that produced by Brooke on and for Borneo. While other projects asked to start fresh in the Pacific or Zanzibar, this one would take hold in a place blessed with a preexisting British license, where the footprints of the East India Company still lined the soil. Official British opposition could follow only with great logistical difficulty, and therein lay the brilliance.

Dent quickly launched a public relations campaign to win over reporters in Southeast Asia, some of whom had displayed an animus against the scheme. T. S. Dobree, a respected planter, produced a favorable report on the soil in Sabah.[170] Then, in a published interview given to the

Ceylon Observer, Dent repudiated "all idea of filibustering," assuring local notables, not entirely truthfully, that the company's "every step" had "been made known to, and approved of by, the authorities of the Foreign and Colonial Offices." Less inaccurately, Dent also touted that, in a manner "rather different to the inception of the Sarawak Rajaship . . . no contest or loss of life" took place during the preliminary establishment of the company's rule.[171]

London saw Dent's politicking to win a charter and confirmation of the company's "anomalous" statehood. Two influential international lawyers in Lombard Street, Stephenson and Harwood, helped him draft a formal application for incorporation, making several recommendations designed to iron out rough edges.[172] At the top of their list was the swift removal of any involvement by "foreign" parties, notably Overbeck and Torrey. The latter simply offended elite circles.[173] Overbeck posed a more philosophical obstacle. He owned only slightly fewer shares of the sovereign rights than did Dent, and he still hoped to sell the company's assets to the highest bidder—especially since he had just declared bankruptcy.[174] Dent, by contrast, hoped to get a charter for the purpose of actually running the government of Sabah at a profit, like a commercial trading venture. Overbeck, accordingly, still wanted to find the highest bidder for his rights, be that bidder's nationality German or Japanese.[175] In the summer of 1879 Overbeck convinced the Japanese ambassador in Berlin to approach Tokyo with a 1,000,000 Spanish dollar sale price, to be paid in three installments; the two even drew up a contract and secured the support of the Japanese foreign minister before the project faltered.[176] This was a sizeable retreat from earlier appraisals, which called for a price between two and three million.[177]

Dent promptly took his lawyers' advice, buying out Torrey for US$25,000, or 10,000 more than Torrey had asked of Overbeck a few years earlier.[178] Thus ended the American involvement in the original scheme to acquire a colony on Borneo. Dent in the interim turned to buying out the enigmatic Overbeck, whom he eventually persuaded to capitulate in exchange for a cash infusion Overbeck needed to settle with creditors.[179] With Overbeck, still known as "King of Borneo" in Germany, now consigned to a consulting role, Dent moved to enlist more than sixty members of the British elite as supporters.[180] These included former governors of Hong Kong and Singapore, as well as bankers in the City who resented the Brooke family's control over Sarawak and wanted to disrupt that state by building up a significant neighbor in Sabah.[181] Like Dent's lawyers, most of this group had strong connections to the China trade. Several of them were veterans of the Royal Navy's China Station; others were influential diplomats. To their ranks Dent added a final heavyweight in the form of Sir Rutherford Alcock, the president of the Royal Geographical Society.[182] The lobbying group wrote to the Foreign Office urging that "on no account commercially or politically should that portion of N E Coast of Borneo lately ceded to Messrs. Dent & Co. with its fine harbours and mineral production be allowed to fall into the hands of Spain or any other European nation."[183]

In the weeks after Dent submitted his first application in December 1878, the likelihood of its success grew steadily higher, thanks to the lobbyists' interventions. However, the outcome was far from fated, with British recognition of Dent's nascent state, as in so many other cases, remaining less a question of law than of politics. Britain had seen the concept of chartered company government fall out of favor in the nineteenth century.[184] Well before the country wound down the affairs of the disgraced East India Company, many saw the unpopularity of chartered companies as an inevitable result of social progress.[185] Adam Smith once remarked that "the government of an exclusive company of merchants" was "perhaps the worst of all governments for any country whatever."[186] A company of merchants, because responsible to shareholders, was widely assumed incapable of keeping commercial motives from predominating over the greater good. Smith, for example, had criticized the East India Company for avoiding payment for essential public services. His logic persisted in the 1820s, when a former governor of Sierra Leone, Thomas Thompson, doubted whether anyone could "be at the same time successful traders, and virtuous rulers."[187] That position only bolstered the resolve of the coming generation of liberals and free-traders, who associated company-governments with mercantilism, colonial quagmires, and monopolies that retarded economic development. Over the next decades skepticism greeted proposals for chartered companies. Sites mentioned but rejected included Central Africa, New Caledonia, and even an uninhabited Pacific archipelago known as the Auckland Islands.[188] And the Royal Geographical Society, for example, refused overtures that it reboot the system.[189] Finally, by 1869, even the board of the world's last charter company, the Hudson's Bay, had come to admit they must "abandon either their commerce or their sovereignty," provided the British government could arrange appropriate cash compensation.[190]

Well after the halcyon days of free trade had gone, chartered company governments still seemed passé. As part of the fallout from Dent's charter application, an editorial in the *Economist* roundly dismissed the proposal that Britain revive the institution of chartered company government. Yes, Dent's request for a charter appealed to history. But that hardly represented a virtue. Perhaps "the granting of charters to trading companies was a thing natural enough at the time when commerce even with the Mediterranean was so uncertain that the 'Levant Company' had to be formed to carry it on."[191] The 1880s were different, however, and the idea of Dent's company had already, according to reports, troubled many members in the House of Commons.[192]

Whatever gripes critics had about the granting of a charter paled in comparison to doubts surrounding the validity of the two leases. Dent and Overbeck convinced some officials that they had acquired the powers of government in Sabah, but an equally large contingent accused the pair of exaggerating their company's presence on the ground by representing hopes as facts.[193] The War Office, for example, marveled at the two men's "full sovereignty"; and Granville, the foreign secretary, pronounced it impossible to "confer any greater privileges than" what they claimed.[194] But because Dent and Overbeck kept the original lease documents guarded closely, transmitting only copies, and showing those copies to only a few people high up in the government, it seemed fair to wonder whether they had modified the content of the contracts in the English translation, so as to inflate their own personal claims to rule.[195] Few had seen the proof, outside the cabinet and some high-level diplomats; and that situation would remain so for decades.[196] "There were," complained one MP, "no Papers upon which to found an opinion."[197]

The rights supposedly transferred in the leases were, as *The Spectator* noted, greater than any European sovereign currently possessed.[198] That two ordinary citizens now claimed to own such rights by themselves greatly aroused the interest of the public and "almost took their breath away." It was hard to believe that "Mr. Alfred Dent," a man "of no political importance," had awoken "one morning to find himself" so powerful. One joke ran that Dent was so "oppressed by his own greatness" that he had, out of necessity, "resolved that others should share his honors and responsibilities" by means of a company incorporated in Britain.[199]

Yet a still greater philosophical question remained. One could argue that a state or empire was the organic result of the governance it provided to a large group of people—to the public. One could also insist that state and imperial territory was rather a kind of commodity—something to be passed back and forth between various parties in exchange for cash, as circumstances warranted. Which alternative prevailed was of more than an academic interest, for any charter granted by Britain would hinge on the presupposition that Dent's group was in fact an independent, autonomous governing body. Accordingly, some critics asked "what right" had a group of "semi-barbarous Sultans . . . to transfer not only all the lands over which they reigned, with all their resources and treasures, but the people who inhabit and possess those lands?[200] A hundred or so miles away from Sabah, Charles Brooke, ruler of Sarawak since James's death, joined the skeptics. Angered that rivals had kept him from annexing all of northern Borneo—his latest attempted seizure of territory had come along the Baram River, in the wake of another civil war over excessive Bruneian taxation—Charles cast doubt on the notion that the sultans of Sulu and Brunei could simply dispose of the inhabitants in Sabah, as if the latter should have no voice in the process.[201] One columnist loyal to Charles pointed out that Sabah was not "likely implicitly to submit to be handed over like flocks of sheep to new and strange masters." They would not "patiently and implicitly acquiesce in the bargain by which their Sultans, on receiving an annuity of £5,000 for themselves, have sold them to a set of foreign trading adventurers."[202]

Yet, as the Foreign Office considered Dent's request for a charter, Charles Brooke's challenge looked shaky.[203] This, notwithstanding that when the second "white Rajah" of Sarawak began to foment insurrection among Sabah's people, he had a strong moral argument behind him. As Charles would soon complain to the sultan of Brunei in a personal interview, "what the Brunei government had done was to sell the lives, rights, religion, as well as the land of a large population," and this practice was entirely contrary to the precepts of modern governance.[204] But, to impartial observers in London, Charles's quarrel also appeared petty.[205] He clearly resented Overbeck and Dent, both of whom had also received titles of "rajah" from the sultan of Brunei. Besides, the foreign secretary believed that Mr. Dent would administer his territory "precisely as Sarawak has been administered since its cession to the late

Rajah Brooke."[206] Brooke's family was less the exception than it was the prototype. Accordingly, should Charles further challenge the proceedings he risked undermining his own rule's foundation, insofar as it too originated with a perpetual lease on sovereignty in Sarawak.

In the event, Charles improved his standing with the Colonial Office but did not have enough friends in the Foreign Office to topple the schemes of Dent's upstart company. What he and other opponents of Dent could hope for, however, was help from William Gladstone, the legendary, and legendarily anticolonial, prime minister.[207] Gladstone took control of British foreign policy in April 1880, on the strength of his Liberal Party's election victory. Over the next two years, he would decide the fate of the Borneo idea.

When the newly formed Gladstone ministry turned its attention to Borneo, it found itself beset with so many foreign-policy issues that its ambassador to Russia mused about Britain being "in dispute, if not at war, with all the world."[208] Recent struggles with the Zulus and the Afghans had made it seem that Britain was succumbing to imperial overreach.[209] Coming campaigns in the Transvaal and the Sudan would further strain public finances, just as they tested the public's tolerance for bloodshed. Add to this a series of diplomatic challenges—the Ottoman Empire, Egypt, India, and, not least, Ireland—and it hardly came as a surprise that Gladstone initially expressed little interest in the schemes of a few adventurers in Borneo.[210]

Dent's proponents had already made significant inroads with the Disraeli cabinet.[211] Surely, they argued, "the Government that annexed the Transvaal and Cyprus would scarcely hesitate to grant a charter to a Trading Association to govern a slice of territory in Borneo acquired peacefully by purchase, and under circumstances eminently satisfactory to the natives."[212] But now that Gladstone's Liberal Party was in power, having run on a platform opposed to "imperialism"—an old word once employed to describe Roman dictators and Bonapartists, but now attached pejoratively to rival Disraelian conservatives—some speculated that pleas for Dent would result in "an instant and emphatic negative and repudiation."[213] Gladstone was not inclined to add pieces to an overflowing portfolio of overseas territories; rather, he believed, as the Duke of Wellington once said, that "the extension of our territory and influence has been greater than our means."[214] Buttressing this point were critiques of empire from Radical Liberals, who argued that India in particular was a moral and fiscal drain on the British public. Empire, in the view of this increasingly clamorous contingent, favored elites and contributed to class conflict at home by diverting the government from the cause of reform.[215]

Starting in the 1840s, Gladstone consistently opposed British territorial aggrandizement by aligning himself with economic arguments against colonies in places like West Africa, where more than one official saw Britain's handful of possessions as wasteful. He held this line through 1881, when he rejected two indigenous leaders' offers to take over the government of kingdoms in West Africa.[216] Gladstone reserved a special opprobrium for adventurers trying to acquire kingdoms for themselves. He protested when members of parliament, as well as the secretary of war, proposed a resolution approving freelance attempts to acquire sovereign rights in New Zealand. At issue, Gladstone announced, was whether "any body of private gentlemen were to be at liberty, first, to purchase and exercise the rights of sovereignty in a foreign country, and then to frame laws, at their pleasure, for the country so acquired." For him, "no subject demanded more circumspection."[217] His verdict fell no differently a little over two decades later, when he resisted James Brooke's attempts to sell Sarawak to Britain.

Events from 1881 to 1882 again forced Gladstone to take a stand on empire, private governance, and the sale of territory in Southeast Asia. Would it be acceptable, one MP asked the prime minister, for the Crown to sanction the proposed Borneo Company "to acquire and take by purchase" the powers of "life and death?"[218] As it happened, Gladstone turned to answer this question just seven years after a letter to *The Times* heralded the final demise of the East India Company.[219] The company had never really gone away; it was still a fresh issue in late 1881, when the High Court of Madras found itself forced to consider with what ramifications the East India Company "had been invested with powers usually called sovereign powers" through 1857.[220] Given the court's deliberations, Gladstone would find it difficult to assail the legality, or even the topicality, of such a scheme as Dent proposed. Meanwhile, officials around the prime minister, including the colonial and foreign secretaries, prompted him to think twice about the matter. Dent was running out of money. He needed some sort of decision from Britain, and he needed it soon.[221]

When the decision finally came, Gladstone treated the British public to a surprise. "I am not," he said to the House of Commons, "about to use the language of mistrust and condemnation as regards the Company . . . which has obtained these remarkable powers—powers involving the essence of sovereignty."[222] For Gladstone, who made his speech while standing in front of the future chairman of the North Borneo Company, the essential point was not what Britain might offer the company; rather, it was what the company would surrender to Britain.[223] Gladstone told members of parliament that the company already owned every imaginable right when it came to North Borneo. Hence, Britain had no authority to regulate the company unsolicited, and "it would be an act of confiscation if" Britain attempted to claim the company's rights without consent.[224] That said, the company, as currently configured, needed supervision. This fact held, not just for British capitalists who wanted recognition of Sabah for the benefit of their finances, but also for the conscience of British citizens, who should take an interest in ensuring fair rule for all populations.

There was no better method by which to tackle Dent's scheme, Gladstone concluded, than to circumscribe the powers of the company through the issuance of a charter. The prime minister believed that the very suspicions surrounding Dent's enterprise encouraged such a move. Gladstone did not necessarily disagree with the conventional wisdom that chartered company governments were frightful.[225] Nonetheless, he consented to issue a charter because it would place firm requirements on the company. For example, Britain would receive the prerogative to ensure that the company kept its directors British; that the company sold no territory or rights to foreign powers, except Britain; that the company protected indigenous customs; that the company ended slavery in its territory; and that the company surrendered control of foreign policy to Whitehall when it mattered. In return, Britain would merely agree to incorporate Dent's preexistent state as a business.[226]

"Incorporation" itself masked the transfer of some of Dent's rights to Britain, and seen strictly in these terms, the idea of a charter looked viable. True, Gladstone noted how the specter of the East India Company loomed large. But the two situations themselves now appeared "totally different."[227] The era of the East India Company was over, he said—part of an "old system" of mercantilism and trading monopolies dismantled by 1858. Under a "new system" first demonstrated in Borneo, Britain could use "our negative and restrictive powers," as confirmed in the charter, to shield an otherwise independent enterprise like Dent's "from the temptation to be led into unwise and aggressive action."[228] Men like Dent would not vanish; inevitably, they would continue to travel outside the empire and seek to acquire sovereign rights from foreign governments, often without authorization. This behavior was part of a long tradition that ran from Francis Drake's Pacific expedition through James Cook's trip to New Zealand, of which Britain had "disowned" an annexation in 1770.[229]

To pass a law prohibiting British subjects from traveling beyond the empire hardly represented a liberal proposition. On the contrary, Gladstone felt it meant "sitting by with folded arms" while such things went on anyway.[230] The tendency for adventurers to acquire ruling powers was strong, "perhaps irrepressible." So too was the tendency toward "man's inhumanity to man" on account of "greed of gold."[231] Hence it was best to recognize these twin tendencies, put contractual limits to them in a charter, and provide for monitoring by Britain, should abuses transpire.[232] As a Belgian observer put it: "The only question which the Government had to decide," in the end, "was, whether it should or should not leave [Dent's] company to act without hindrance, and entirely without control."[233] This view was consistent with Gladstone's stance on the regulation of joint-stock companies in Britain, which had seen the government, under a succession of acts since 1844, grant companies easier access to incorporation and its attendant privileges while simultaneously subjecting them to greater regulation.[234] It also represented an alternate route to something Gladstone once said he hoped could emerge from the British Empire: new states, run on British values but functionally independent, that amounted to "so many happy Englands."[235]

Finally, Gladstone's approach to Borneo dovetailed with larger attitudes toward India. In each case, Britons had already acquired an empire. Yet, unlike Disraeli's supporters, Gladstonian liberals felt moral obligations to peoples affected—a "civilizing mission," in effect. Forging a compromise with Dent could thus reinforce Gladstone's stance on another, far more significant policy in India, where Gladstone's leadership hardly meant retreat, but would rather spearhead efforts at moral "improvement" and undertake to increase the governmental role of educated elites from urban Indian populations.[236] An engagement with Borneo on similar terms could serve to differentiate the new liberal government from that of its predecessors, simultaneously glossing over the complex and oft-discordant attitudes held by many British liberals toward imperialism: The new leaders, whatever their disagreements, looked for creative solutions to an acknowledged problem that they could not solve quickly.[237]

Perhaps, too, Dent's nascent state in Borneo could come to rest comfortably on the spectrum of sovereignty which was crystallizing throughout imperial realms: the princely states of India, Basutoland (today's Lesotho), and the German Empire.[238] It is worth noting that, while the 1860s and 1870s are often regarded today as a great era of state-building and territorial consolidation—from Italian and German unification, to the American Civil War, to the Meiji Restoration—these two decades also saw renewed efforts to determine what sovereignty looked like in polities that defied easy identification as a "nation-state." In the princely states of India and the new German Empire, to cite just two cases, there was a continual re-thinking of jurisdiction and a constant process of negotiation in which degrees of state independence waxed or waned, in accordance with exigencies as interpreted by figures like Gladstone and Bismarck.[239] In any event, notions emerged that sovereignty consisted of divisible prerogatives passing back and forth between polities—the prerogatives to control educational curricula and tariffs, for example.

By the time Gladstone delivered his public defense of his arguments about Borneo, the Borneo charter stood as a fait accompli. In August 1881, the Crown officially approved Dent's application, thus clearing the way for Dent not only to lease more territory from Brunei, but also to issue one-cent and half-cent coins for his realm.[240] This currency bore the new state's Latin motto, *Pergo et Perago* ("I undertake a thing and go through with it"), suggesting great confidence and tradition.[241] HSBC even weighed a proposal to open a branch in Dent's territory.[242] For the other, less reputable players in the scheme, though, the outlook looked more muddled. By now Overbeck had been completely cut off from the Borneo Company; he was to live out the rest of his days in obscurity. Torrey, his former partner, had moved on to other confidence games: first, landing the paid jobs of U.S. vice consul and clerk of a consular court at Bangkok (he later resigned amid allegations of bribery and extortion); second, ingratiating himself with retired president Ulysses S. Grant; then, in what might have been his second-most improbable feat, claiming to win an appointment as an advisor to King Chulalongkorn of Siam.[243]

Back in Britain, the debate rolled on, as somewhat surprised critics began to doubt Gladstone's notion of a separation between Britain and the company; there were not two empires but one, and Britain was, so complaints ran, "filibustering by proxy."[244] "We have established a new East India Company in Northern Borneo," reported the *Pall Mall Gazette* with a measure of pride.[245] But the East India Company, it was recalled, had expanded its territorial portfolio almost continually in the two centuries preceding 1857, while placing Britain on the hook for Indian government in the event of its default. Now, when some officials looked at Sabah and Borneo, "there was a parallel and an analogy between the two cases which was very striking."[246] A small coastal enclave, an ex-governor of the Bombay presidency told a meeting of the Royal Colonial Institute, was "exactly the way in which the East India Company began its career."[247] Accordingly, when the public read new reports of the North Borneo Company's desire for further territorial aggrandizement—to be accomplished, in competition with Sarawak, through fresh leases from a shrinking Brunei—it was easy to wonder whether Britain was placing itself into *precisely* the same predicament as it had encountered with the East India Company. It could be disadvantageous if "the North Borneo Company" was "in most essential respects . . . as closely as possible a reproduction of the old East India Company."[248]

Dent's government might rule Sabah for a long time, as the EIC had ruled in India. It might even go on to capture the imagination of the British Empire's leading writers, including Kipling.[249] But no handbook existed should anything ever happen to incapacitate Dent's operation.[250] It was unclear who would fill the resulting power vacuum in an area "half as large as France," astride the vital trade route to China, and right in the middle of a region where Britain delivered 26 percent of its total exports.[251] The party filling the vacuum might be Sarawak, which won British permission to annex Baram as a quid pro quo for accepting the North Borneo charter.[252] For the time being, though, one could only suspect that the final liability for both projects lay with Britain, which

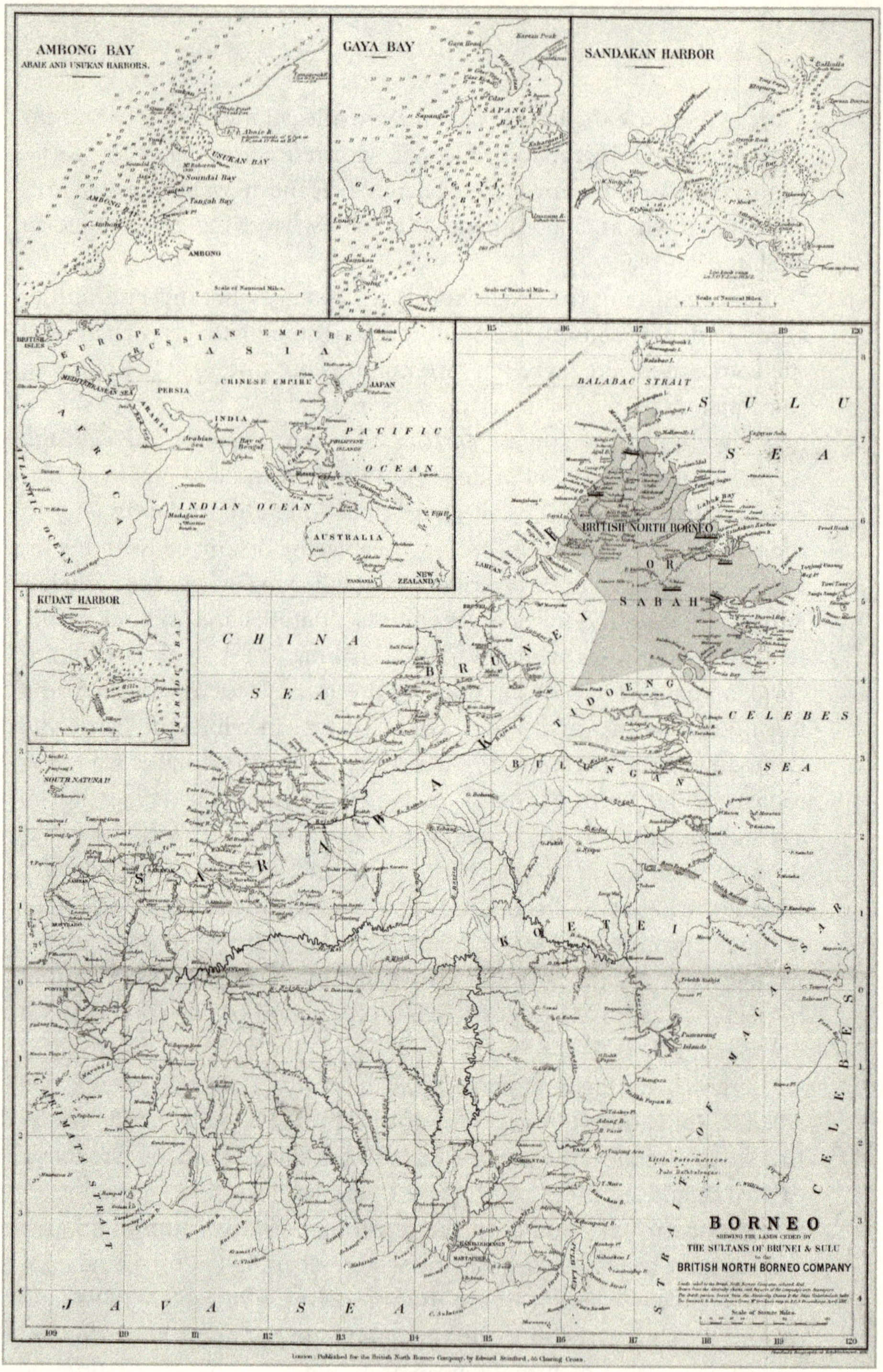

Map 1 Borneo, 1881. The territory claimed by Overbeck and Dent is shaded. Note Kimanis Bay, the base of the ill-fated American colony, near the western edge of Sabah. *Source:* Edward Stanford, *Borneo: Shewing the Lands Ceded by the Sultans of Brunei & Sulu to the British North Borneo Company* (London 1881). Courtesy of Library of Congress, Control Number 2007630401.

promptly sold Dent heavy weaponry in order that he might build an army.[253]

Irrespective of whether Gladstone's cabinet paid insufficient attention to the risks of Borneo—meetings at the time focused almost exclusively on passing Coercion and Land acts for Ireland—the affair's impact certainly surpassed expectations.[254] Far from being an aberration, Britain's approval of chartered company government represented the revival of an idea "which the abolition of the Honourable East India Company and of the Hudson's Bay Company was supposed to have destroyed."[255] The Parisian socialist publication *Le Devoir,* for its part, credited Britain with prudence for resurrecting an old approach to foreign policy.[256] Nor was the effect limited to opinion: As a jurist in Vienna remarked, the revival gave as much inspiration to politicians and economists as to geographers.[257] Most of the inspiration concentrated on Africa, where Britain had waged a short war against the Boers in the months preceding the issuance of Dent's charter and, as in princely India, again arrived at a treaty arrangement in which the empire would take just a sliver of sovereignty while otherwise recognizing the self-rule of a (Boer) state in the Transvaal.[258] Despite Britain's nominal defeat at the hands of the Boers, and in view of major diamond finds drawing the Cape Colony further into Southern Africa, the continent now seemed more likely to repay even unconventional colonization attempts. Hence, just months after the full Borneo charter appeared in print, Edward Hewett, a British consul in West Africa, proposed that a chartered company be formed to acquire sovereign rights over a hypothetical territory running from the Cameroon River to Benin; the company, Hewett said, might spare Britain "the assumption of the responsibility attaching to the government of a country."[259] Similar proposals emerged from a series of Manchester businessmen concerning Cape Juby in Morocco.[260]

Late in 1882, meanwhile, rumors began to circulate in London concerning George Goldie Taubman, a longtime admirer of the Brookes battling with English, French, German, and African rivals to dominate palm oil exports in the vicinity of the Niger River. Taubman had grown up, by his own recollection, when "Rajah Brooke's name was a household word"; he "was never likely to forget the effect that the legend of Rajah Brooke had on his youthful mind."[261] By the early 1880s, Taubman was reacquainting himself with Borneo through a mutual friend, Sir Rutherford Alcock.[262] Alcock had acted as a lobbyist for Dent and thereafter became the North Borneo Company's managing director in London. In 1882, partly at Alcock's instruction, Taubman grew "fully determined" to build "an African Sarawak."[263]

As of 1881 the palm oil trade, while still lucrative, lingered in a slump: Because petroleum could now lubricate industrial equipment as effectively, prices had fallen by roughly 33 percent since peaking in the 1850s.[264] Keen to reverse this decline, and also aware that hitherto discarded palm kernels were finding a market as ingredients for vegetable margarine, Taubman tried buying out his rivals.[265] By 1879 he amalgamated three of them into his own vehicle, the United African Company.[266] This scheme, however, still did not bring the monopoly he wanted: Wealthy indigenous merchants, including the famous King Jaja of Opobo, circumvented it by shipping palm oil directly to Europe.[267] With prices continuing their downward trend, Taubman set to work on securing a monopoly via a circuitous route. He would make his company the government in the heartland of palm oil.[268] The company would then, through skillful manipulation of laws, cut African coastal middlemen and European competitors off from their share of exports from, and imports to, the interior.[269] Profit margins would soar.

Taubman's first step was to form a new venture, the National African Company, whose charter allowed it to assume political and governmental duties in foreign states, and whose much higher capitalization (at least on paper) could support the transition.[270] He instructed employees along the Niger to sign treaties supposedly purchasing sovereign rights from a host of political figures.[271] Next, he commissioned a legal brief. Its subject was an application for a royal charter that would allow the National African Company, under Britain's aegis, to govern vast territories. With a charter confirming his rights, Taubman would have a kind of ultimate authority with which to contest any contracts or treaties concluded by his competitors, whether indigenous or European.[272] Simultaneously, he would have an international legal pretext with which to move into the interior and challenge indigenous middlemen's stranglehold on the supply of palm oil, the Niger's most precious commodity and still a sure source of profit when it came to European soap manufacturers like A. & F. Pears'. Subsequent historians have rightly noted Taubman's ambition to imitate the East India Company.[273] The more salient linkage, however, was to Borneo, as he later recalled in a board meeting.[274]

In the background to these negotiations loomed a European threat to British preeminence on the Niger. By late 1882 the French had missed their opportunity to dominate trade on two of Africa's great rivers, the Nile and Zambezi. British officials anticipated a French push against Taubman on the Niger—the principal fear being, as the president of the Royal Historical Society speculated, an "energetic and ambitious traveller" who, perhaps without authorization or even approval from Paris, landed the Third Republic in a diplomatic imbroglio from which she would "find it difficult to withdraw."[275] This last thought owed its genesis to the struggle for Africa's other great river, the Congo.

3

King Leopold's Borneo

IN 1861 LEOPOLD LOUIS PHILIPPE MARIE VICTOR, the Duke of Brabant, was heir apparent to the throne of Belgium, a country hardly able to defend its own borders.[1] Belgium had no armed forces of consequence, and its citizenry lived in fear of French invasion, with the sole consolation—or was it a curse?—that, in 1839, six European powers had signed an agreement to uphold its neutral status in continental wars.[2] Leopold hoped to improve Belgian financial and industrial health by acquiring control over territories outside Europe.[3] The problem he faced was that his fellow citizens saw colonies as unwise deviations from the then-prevailing doctrine of free trade—as commitments that invariably drained more wealth from the public treasury than they added.[4] Not so Leopold, who saw opportunity *only* in colonial systems.[5] The duke had spent his adolescence studying overseas ventures undertaken by his Dutch neighbors. He had concluded, albeit somewhat erroneously, that the Dutch still owed their disproportionately large financial clout to profits from Java, where crops and minerals abounded.[6] If Belgium wanted to become great, then the duke believed Belgium needed its own, similar empire of exploitation.[7]

How to achieve this goal was unclear.[8] Parliament in Brussels, the duke's secretary lamented, had practically "decided never to have colonies," thanks in large part to the free-trade orientation of the Liberal Party that had dominated politics since 1848.[9] That orientation strengthened in 1849, when a skirmish nearly forced the Belgian navy into war with Britain over control of West Africa's Nunez River.[10] Throughout the 1850s, the majority of liberal notables in parliament, despite essentially sharing legislative power with the duke's father, refused to countenance any overseas schemes put forward by the royalty and a budding colonial lobby, including a faltering venture in Guatemala. It was fair to assume that if Leopold's father had failed to realize such plans, then surely his son would, too. Leopold may have passed for a tireless worker when compared to his relatives. But insiders in Brussels held little faith in his ambitious projects, which some would later liken to Napoleon III's ill-fated adventure in Mexico.[11] At least one critic thought Leopold imbecilic.[12] Finally, there were moral concerns: Rumors about underage prostitutes, greed, and a lack of scruples so obvious as ultimately to prompt Cecil Rhodes—hardly a paragon of virtue—to liken visiting Leopold to meeting the devil.[13]

The duke, in any event, had no solution to his country's anticolonial stance by the beginning of the 1860s.[14] He seemed open to any overseas site. But the Orient held a special allure, thanks mainly to the increasingly rapid deterioration of the Qing Empire. Inspired by the Opium Wars, the duke began working to acquire territory in the vicinity of Beijing, Shanghai, or Canton.[15] But Leopold's most realistic, and most enduring, target turned out to be a kind of compromise between China and the Philippines: Borneo.[16] Leopold's relationship with the island began in February 1861, when he asked Belgium's ambassador in the Netherlands to compile a list of potential sites for colonies. Borneo stood out.[17] Its southern half, although potentially loaded with coal and gold, was proving a financial drain to the Dutch government. As for the island's northern half, it fell mainly under James Brooke, whose dire financial straits had recently induced him to make inquiries in Amsterdam. Brooke, it seemed, had been speaking to a group of financiers there about setting up a commercial company which, modeled on the old Dutch East India Company, would buy Brooke's governing rights and administer Sarawak for profit.

An intrigued Leopold soon took what was, for him, an unusual step: He bypassed his secretary and urged his ambassador to move forward.[18] By this time, Sarawak was a state with a population approaching two hundred thousand—small beer when compared to Belgium's four and a half million, but enough to form a significant colony. Brooke opened negotiations with Leopold, discussing a price of roughly £130,000.[19] Brooke did not necessarily mind if Leopold, in the fashion familiar to Dutch East India, wanted to send an expedition of six hundred mercenaries and two ships to Kuching, a city whose population was about eighteen thousand.[20] No, Brooke's primary reservation was that Leopold only intended to treat everyone in Sarawak as cheap labor, with "no notion of native rights" or indigenous land ownership, and a vision of foreign-owned plantations throughout the countryside.[21] Brooke, whatever his faults, wanted guarantees of respect for the religion, laws, and customs of his subjects, as well as a certain caution in economic development.[22] Besides, he did not know exactly who would be buying the rights to Sarawak.[23] The duke might be acting as an official agent for the Belgian government. Or he might be working for a new kind of East India Company, to be run out of Brussels.[24] Finally, the duke might somehow be negotiating on his own account, in a bid to fill James Brooke's role as an absolute monarch.[25]

Brooke's designated heir, Charles, temporarily ruling Sarawak while his uncle recuperated in Britain, wrote a letter to Brussels in which he explained that the indigenous people of Sarawak, with whom he advocated the gradual intermarriage of Europeans, would violently resist Leopold's rule.[26] James Brooke's own rejection of the duke soon followed; Brooke failed to show up in Brussels for a planned meeting, despite the duke's having funded the destitute Brooke's passage back from the Far East.[27] Sarawak thereafter appeared to be out of the question as a potential colonial site. The rest of the island of Borneo, though, was still in play, for the duke had become, in his own account, inspired by Brooke's example.[28]

Leopold admired how Brooke's story involved the building of an empire without the military muscle of a great power. "Filibusterism," announced one contemporary source close to Brussels, "is an aspect of this enterprise which should not be lost sight of."[29] At the same time, Leopold also liked the idea that one man had acquired absolute, uncontested powers of ownership over tens of thousands of human beings—quite a contrast to Belgium, where government bureaucracy moved slowly, and where parliament had circumscribed the king's powers in diplomacy.[30] Finally, and particularly in the 1870s, Leopold seized on a second, less clearly selfish, thread in the Brooke story: the possibility of turning one's personal colony into a social and economic safety valve for one's home country. Many experts believed tiny Belgium would always struggle to overcome internal strife between Catholics and Protestants, between aristocrats and bourgeoisie, between labor and capital. However, if Leopold could found a "Belgian" colony by himself, then there would be a new market for Belgian exports and labor.[31] There would be cheap raw materials for manufacturers. There would even be a mission to unite different religions, and an additional bureaucracy into which to insert young middle-class men, as well as Catholics largely excluded from state positions at various intervals prior to 1884.[32] This complex of factors—as much as, but not in exclusion of, plain avarice—likely induced Leopold to hope, in a somewhat confused way, to take credit for saving his country from its problems.[33]

Leopold had learned something else from Brooke: The idea of buying control of a country "out and out as a property" was not necessarily outrageous.[34] In December 1865, the duke ascended the throne and became Leopold II, King of the Belgians. After the new year, he started negotiations with the Dutch government to buy part of their colonial territory in the southern half of Borneo, just beyond the reach of Brooke and the Sultan of Brunei.[35] The Dutch expressed interest in a deal but backed out, embarrassed, when news of the discussions leaked to the public. Sensing distrust, Leopold II issued public denials; instead, the new king spoke only of his wish (again) to participate in a company with governing powers. Over the next several years he shifted his gaze to the Philippines, with two critical changes. First, Leopold now insisted on acquiring a state independent of Belgium: something he could control without Brussels's parliamentary oversight. Second, Leopold insisted on forming a company that could rule this independent state under the nominal "sovereignty of the King of the Belgians."[36] Skeptics challenged these notions, saying companies could not govern people. To this charge, though, Leopold preliminarily cited the precedent of Sarawak.[37] His reference was misleading and inexact; Brooke was not a company, but a man. Nonetheless, Leopold's comparison represented the first significant step in his lifelong utilization, and distortion, of the Borneo story.

Leopold never succeeded with the Dutch; in a later complaint to his secretary, he deemed them indisposed to sell.[38] At one point, he offered in vain to use some money he had made off shares in the Suez Canal to "lease" sovereignty over the Philippines from Spain. Despite budgetary crises, Madrid would not agree to part with the islands until over thirty years later, when the United States turned its guns on Manila. Temporarily, Leopold's frustration induced him to fixate on New Guinea, a cheaper destination. Then, in 1872, he was back in the market for pieces of territory in Northern Borneo. His new obsession was a miniature state on the other side of Brunei: Sabah.[39] As it turned out, the adventurers who had acquired sovereignty there had put into place something Leopold liked: a ten-year lease with options for unilateral renewal by the lessees, and no defined process of cancellation for the lessor.[40] They had also begun to cultivate terrain in the vicinity of the Dutch colonial system Leopold so admired, more or less next door to Java—the most profitable colony in the world, according to J. W. B. Money's then-recent international best seller, *How to Manage a Colony*.[41]

Leopold's negotiations with the Sabah group faltered; perhaps they were too disreputable even to him, or he to them.[42] In the interim, he took the advice of one of his ministers and reverted to Sarawak, where James Brooke and the successor he had originally chosen had long since passed from the scene.[43] Charles Brooke, a very different man, now stood as absolute ruler.[44] Late in 1875, the Belgian king asked his cousin, Queen Victoria, whether Britain would oppose him should he succeed in purchasing the governing rights from the latest Brooke. In April 1876 Victoria replied, professing ignorance on the subject but offering to inquire with the Foreign Office in London.[45] By July, after Leopold made a personal visit to Balmoral Castle, Victoria could communicate more freely.[46] To start, no one in the Colonial Office foresaw success for a potential Belgian colony in Sarawak; the place was a money pit. Moreover, the Colonial Office cautioned Leopold not to look at the Brooke family's rights as simple commodities. Legal inquiries were pending over what the rights meant, as well as over Sarawak's relationship with Britain, whose subjects the Brooke family remained.[47]

Leopold kept prying. Through the summer of 1876, he told Victoria he did not care about the demerits so far attributed to Borneo. At this juncture Britain's Foreign Office modified its stance from one of discouragement to active prohibition. The foreign secretary in London informed Leopold that Her Majesty's Government did not want any European interference with Sarawak or Sabah. Both places, it turned out, were now seen as vital to the British navy, so Britain would have first right of refusal on any sale. At one point the foreign secretary told Leopold flatly, "Do not go there."[48]

Meanwhile, under the influence of geographical societies in Brussels and Antwerp, Leopold's fixation on East Asia, though still alive, gave way to an intensified interest in Africa.[49] This shift in orientation owed overwhelmingly to developments in the weeks following November 7, 1875, when a British naval lieutenant named Verney Lovett Cameron stumbled into the Portuguese town of Catumbela, located in what is now the Angolan province of Benguela.[50] Crucially, however, Borneo never left Leopold's thoughts. It would stay with him well into 1882, when it helped to achieve his plan in Africa, as well as to fuel the general European rush for African territory.

CATUMBELA WAS A DINGY outpost in what was then one of Portugal's small colonies on the Southern Atlantic coast of Africa.[51] An emaciated Verney Lovett Cameron appeared to be near death when he arrived there after spending two years in the interior.[52] A local doctor diagnosed Cameron's illness as scurvy—which, along with doses of alcohol, drugs, and tropical fevers, had rendered the patient one of many explorers who went out of their minds in terrae incognitae.[53] In the event, however, Cameron was no ordinary traveler. His expedition, originally formed to "find" the mythical Dr. Livingstone, had just walked 1,200 miles of unmapped land across Equatorial Africa, leaving Cameron as supposedly the first European to survive the trek.[54] What is more, Cameron had in his possession several treaties that purportedly annexed the bulk of Central Africa to Great Britain.[55]

Cameron said he had spent the last year mapping territory and concluding these treaties with a host of local potentates who agreed to set their polities under the sovereignty of Britain, "in the name of Queen Victoria," in exchange for certain payments.[56] To Cameron's mind, the treaties were necessary because French traders were soon going to push into Central Africa, implement tariffs, and, in the process, deny British merchants an opportunity for free trade.[57] Cameron believed Britain could ill afford to lose out on the continent's coming economic boom.[58] He also believed local Africans would benefit from British rule—particularly since, as he saw it, advancements in religious and cultural civilization would follow.

The centerpiece in Cameron's campaign was to be the Congo River—the body of water that Joseph Conrad's famous narrator Marlow likened to "an immense snake uncoiled, with its head in the sea, its body at rest curving afar over a vast country, and its tail lost in the depths of the land."[59] So dense and inhospitable was the river that its name among Kikongo-speaking peoples, *nzere* (later transliterated by the Portuguese as *Zaire*), meant "the river that swallows all rivers." It was reasonable to ask what allure it might hold for a European government. To some veteran explorers the river's banks conjured thoughts of a graveyard.[60] Certainly the place often proved a harbor for tropical disease: African sleeping sickness, malaria, elephantiasis, schistosomiasis, and a host of hemorrhagic fevers which, in some cases, would later take the name of an obscure tributary named Ebola. The dimensions of the river itself were also staggering—up to 720 feet deep and as long as the distance from London to Moscow.[61] Likewise, the force of the Congo rapids was so great that when they discharged into the Atlantic, at the river's mouth, they created a pocket of freshwater at least forty miles into the ocean.[62]

Nor was the river the only thing for European explorers to fear. Rumor had it, albeit with exaggeration, that cannibalism was prevalent in certain among the Congo's eastern, Swahili-speaking reaches, and many indigenous groups were afraid of traveling to a few sectors along the river because they perceived such a threat.[63] At one of these places—a village known as Maniema—it was once said that history was nothing but blood, cannibalism, slaves, and ivory.[64] One could speculate that Cameron, like the contingent of other Europeans crossing Africa in the nineteenth century, did not believe these sensational stories of danger; at least for a few more decades, the majority of extant travel accounts and diaries would deal with the western portions of the river, where, to the comfort of many Europeans, a form of Christianity had long ago established itself.[65] But it may be more accurate to suppose that Cameron and his fellow explorers embraced the prospects that such sensational stories held for glory and attendant physical harms.[66]

Regardless, there were compelling commercial reasons to press on, for, to hear some observers describe it at the time, the Congo amounted to an El Dorado. The Congo, gushed one American somewhat inaccurately, "affords 4000 miles of navigable waterway, and on either side stretches a country of the most exuberant fertility." Planters might cultivate sugar, cotton, palm oil, and rubber in abundance here; sportsmen would find elephants, lions, buffalos, hippopotami, and crocodiles. Also waiting were millions of indigenous laborers with a supposedly endless demand for European goods.[67] The Congo, in short, induced Europeans to think about a "white line across the Dark Continent," even if the river sometimes proved so treacherous that neither man nor animal could cross it.[68]

Cameron, as it turned out, had done his mapping work with flawed instruments.[69] Further, the reports of fertile soil held only in certain spots; the Congo River had plenty of rainforests and grass, but also abutted brackish swamps and stretches of parched savanna.[70] Still, by May 1876 Lieutenant Verney Cameron was back in London, where he explained his recent journey to the Royal Geographical Society and made celebrity appearances.[71] Leopold II, an honorary fellow of the RGS, happened to be in town vacationing at Claridge's, a hotel beloved by Queen Victoria's entourage.[72] Leopold invited Cameron for a chat, with exactly what the two men discussed remaining the subject of conjecture.[73] What is clear, though, is that by February, a few months earlier, the Belgian king had familiarized himself with Cameron's reports, and the British cabinet had already rejected Cameron's treaties.[74]

The documents turned in by the explorer so far had remained hidden from the public, but members of the cabinet began discussing them internally in late 1875.[75] Sir Robert Morier, an influential diplomat, was said to support the adoption of Cameron's treaties.[76] Some of his colleagues even believed the documents constituted a fait accompli, since the Crown and parliament had declared, in the famous case of the East India Company, that any territorial acquisitions made by British subjects automatically vested sovereignty in the home state. At the same time, a number of officials, including the colonial secretary, doubted Cameron's bona fides.[77] Paper annexations by British subjects, they said, did not necessarily warrant British recognition. After all, there had been a similar case in the 1820s, when Britain disowned annexations attempted by a Royal Navy captain near Delagoa Bay, in what became Portuguese Mozambique.[78] Farther afield, there was also the more recent case of James Brooke.

Parallels with Brooke were intriguing, if not exact. As with Brooke, no one in the British government had authorized Cameron to acquire political control overseas. Quite unlike Brooke, however, Cameron made his deals in an illiterate society, and Cameron's treaties, far from being made in Malay-English duplicate, were English-only papers bearing marks of "x" for indigenous leaders' signatures.[79] A further complication was that Cameron's expedition had traveled under a *firman* (decree) of authorization from the Egyptian Khedive Isma'il Pasha, along with financing and porters from the Zanzibar Empire.[80] The British government thus thought it probable that Cameron's treaties might prove void even with British authorization ex post facto. Partly for this reason, it seemed to many that Cameron had just presented British diplomats with documents fit for a previous generation: for the days when pirates wandered the world in search of plunder.[81]

Of deeper concern was the way Cameron's treaties, if dignified by Whitehall, might impinge on European-African relations.[82] Since the advent of its antislaving policy in 1807, Britain had concluded a number of compacts with indigenous African rulers, often called "princes," allowing for cooperation in the interdiction of suspicious ships and persons.[83] Initially British negotiators had labeled these compacts "treaties" and acknowledged their African counterparties as equal members of the international community, if only on a formal basis.[84] As late as 1879, the American navy would do likewise.[85] By the 1870s, however, such respect was eroding on account of notions of "civilization" and "barbarousness," with many British, though not all, insisting that contracts signed with African leaders not take the title of "treaties," or even appear in official records, on account of African inferiority.[86] Because this dynamic was still in play by the time of Cameron's return, one can infer that the act of defining his documents as "treaties," to say nothing of accepting their contents, risked compromising residual aspects of Britain's policy in Africa. As significant, Cameron's willingness to commit his government to heavy financial involvement in the middle of Africa did not hold much appeal in 1875, especially in view of budget constraints then under discussion in parliament. Britain's most recent expansion project in Africa—undertaken in the 1860s and early 1870s, along the former "Dutch Gold Coast"—had already occasioned the Third Anglo-Ashanti War and proven a costly addition to the 279,000 square miles of African land previously under formal British control.[87]

When the cabinet sided with skeptics in the Colonial Office, declining the proposed Congo annexation, Cameron appeared to give the issue of his treaties up, unaware that the British navy had begun to retrace his steps and sign new treaties "with the chiefs of the River Congo," albeit on different terms: the prohibition of human sacrifice; cooperation against piracy; antislavery; assistance for British trading vessels; and free access for missionaries.[88] In the interim, though, Cameron had, as mentioned, already made a profound impression on Leopold.[89] In July 1876, two months after meeting the explorer, Leopold wrote Queen Victoria to talk about Borneo. At the same time, he pivoted to note how impressed he was by the British explorer who had traversed Africa. Cameron's treaties with Central African leaders, Leopold knew, had been made in the name of Queen Victoria. But neither Victoria nor anyone else in Britain agreed on what that meant, even if she thought Cameron a "wonderfully enterprising young officer" who was "nice looking and very modest."[90] Nor did anyone know what was to become of those rights that Cameron's treaties theoretically transferred away from indigenous control to Britain. A critic could argue that Cameron, as the owner of certain property (treaties), possessed whatever part of that property Britain did not want to take. Upon finding Britain unwilling, Cameron could simply have kept the rights and formed his own empire. Cameron himself left this possibility open, eventually proposing a kind of East India Company that would manage governing rights in the Congo and Zambezi river areas.[91] The time, however, was not yet ripe for such a revival; by 1877, British officials particularly seemed to fear complications that might result if, as in earlier eras, private individuals or companies had the legal authority to wage wars.[92]

Leopold launched another phase in his initiative in June 1876, just as he made his last unsuccessful inquiries about Sarawak.[93] Leopold now called a conference of the world's geographers to Brussels for the ostensible purpose of discussing aid to Central Africa. The conference founded the International African Association (AIA), a society with the goal of wiping out the slave trade along the Congo. This concern had little to do with the Atlantic slave trade, which had a long history in the Congo dating back at least to the sixteenth century, when Portuguese explorers, enticed partly by glowing reports from the familiar traveler Antonio Pigafetta, started selling arms to Bakongo rulers in the western interior—the grandest of whom, the Mani Kongo, had a long tradition of enslaving foreign captives before he ever consented to ship bodies across the ocean to the New World.[94] On the contrary: Leopold knew that by 1876 Britain had crushed the Atlantic slave trade, to the point that apologists for Lisbon could tout—albeit prematurely and somewhat as free riders—that there was "no longer a single slave in any Portuguese colonies."[95] True, the demise of the Atlantic trade, soon hastened by Cuban and Brazilian prohibitions, did not mean the concomitant eradication of interior slavery in the Western Congo: Through 1876—the year of formal abolition in Portuguese Angola—a British consul at

Luanda reported that nearly every European factory on the Congo still bought slaves from indigenous traders, if not always in name.[96] Nonetheless, Portuguese officials at least passed legislation acknowledging the gap and began to craft a plan to improve the condition of bonded laborers under their nominal colonial jurisdiction.[97] Moreover, the abiding international concern at the time lay with the mostly Swahili-speaking east, spanning at least from Portuguese Mozambique to the Zanzibari mainland.[98] There Europeans encountered the internal East African trade.

Preying on what seemed a limitless supply of East and Central Africans, the nature of this trade was not always clear cut: Some scholars have argued that the bondage it entailed often existed on a sort of continuum with kinship that rendered the categories of slavery and antislavery problematic.[99] That said, the internal East African trade was as complex and replete with horrors as its Atlantic counterpart, with raiders regularly torching villages, especially in the area near Lake Tanganyika, partly on the strength of muskets imported by European traders.[100] The British government consistently pledged itself to work against this phenomenon; the Portuguese and the Zanzibari sultan were seen as abetting it; and Belgium's liberal cabinet would support antislavery work as a matter of course, however dubious its nomenclature.[101] There was a global dimension, too: Between 1820 and 1880, slavers exported some two million souls across the Indian Ocean to South Asia.[102] Growing awareness of such statistics eventually prompted the world's major antislavery organizations, the British and Foreign Anti-Slavery Society and the Aborigines' Protection Society, to undertake a fragile international cooperation with Catholic missionary groups operating out of Belgium and other traditionally less active locations on the European continent.[103]

In view of this conjuncture, Leopold could not possibly ask for a better veil behind which to conceal a Central African business project.[104] Taking care to portray himself as a disinterested philanthropist, the King of the Belgians invited notables from around Europe to fund national committees of the AIA and eradicate a trade that annually took an estimated one hundred thousand Congolese from their homes only to ship them, via grueling marches, to plantations in Zanzibar and other coastal locales.[105] Influenced in part by pamphlets tailored for mass consumption, the Prince of Wales and the German emperor William I each announced his support for the agenda.[106] So, too, did famous scientists: men like French zoologist Armand de Quatrefages and the Spanish cartographer Francisco Coello.[107] Finally, at least two other philanthropists, both familiar with Borneo, heeded the call to action. There was Baroness Burdett-Coutts, Brooke's longtime benefactor.[108] And there was Sir Rutherford Alcock, arguably the greatest lobbyist for the consortium now active in Sabah, Borneo's second fledgling rogue empire.[109] Contributions from these notables were expected to generate a climate of small donations from among the people at large; one of Leopold's lobbyists even delivered a rose-colored projection in which "150,000 persons of all classes" pledged $80,000 in the first year alone.[110] Donations came from abroad thanks to committees set up in Switzerland, Germany, Hungary, and the Netherlands, among other countries.[111] In the end, they amounted to little, and the Belgian public also greeted the campaign tepidly.[112]

By early 1879 the AIA was moribund, if not dead.[113] Despite claiming devotees as far afield as Budapest, it had met only once since its inception and quickly abandoned its national committees.[114] In November 1878 Leopold quietly replaced the Belgian committee with a body that shared the same address and office space: the *Comité d'études du Haut-Congo*.[115] For the first time, he began to speak privately of "procuring an African possession" in the Congo.[116] The new *Comité* seemed noble enough on the surface, even if its covert conceptualization as a limited liability company seemed at odds with its philanthropic trappings.[117] In its bylaws, it claimed a capitalization of one million francs and vaguely purported to continue the work begun by the Brussels Conference in 1876 and in the single meeting of the AIA in June 1877. Focusing publicly on the exploration of the Congo—but, in a subtle shift, no longer determined to end the slave trade—the *Comité* would "erect stations," then "establish steam-communication wherever available and safe" between those stations.[118] To this end, the *Comité* would scrupulously obtain land for its stations and roads, acquiring it as private property from indigenous rulers. "By lease or purchase," a spokesman said, "ground enough was to be secured adjoining the stations so as to enable them in time to become self-supporting if the dispositions of the natives should favor such a project." Finally, the *Comité* would buy land for road routes to connect the stations, as well as "land on each side of the route adopted for the traffic."[119]

It goes too far to accept, as nearly all historians do, that the *Comité* dispensed with any pretense to internationalism.[120] At least initially, its finances looked more international than those of its predecessor. Though the majority of the *Comité*'s funding stemmed from the Low Countries, there was now an important, and surprisingly overlooked, component elsewhere. Magnificent investments in the enterprise came from Baroness Burdett-Coutts, who renewed her interest in Leopold's projects via a series of letters, as well as the banker Maurice von Hirsch—later to realize tremendous profits in Congolese railroad development.[121] Nor was the *Comité* itself the fixed, rigid product many have claimed it to be. Rather, this was still very much a malleable vehicle through which Leopold attempted to inch closer to a kind of international recognition as a monopolistic trading concern or a governmental organization. One attempt to boost such prospects came with the establishment of the "Stafford House Upper Congo Exploration Committee" as an English branch of the *Comité*.[122]

In the event, the *Comité* now stood as an embryonic empire that, at least in part, owed its gestation to Henry Morton Stanley.[123] Stanley, then best known as the man who "found" Livingstone, had recently improved upon Cameron's trek by taking an even more dangerous route across Central Africa—starting from Zanzibar in the East, then moving west to Lake Victoria, and finally arriving, more than five thousand miles of hitherto-unmapped territory later, in the Portuguese-influenced town of Boma.[124] By the time Stanley reached the Atlantic coast in 1877, he had traversed the entire Congo River from its source to its mouth at the ocean, passing over dozens of unnavigable waterfalls—and, rumor had it, many innocent corpses he had mowed down along the way.[125] Because conditions killed more than half the members of his expedition, he was one of the few Europeans alive who could claim he knew the Congo thoroughly.[126]

After several months of courtship, Stanley agreed to meet Leopold's representatives on a series of occasions in 1878, suggesting—evidently for the first time—that the AIA give way to a kind of commercial company.[127] By early 1879 the *Comité* emerged to fill this role, thanks in part to capital from the Dutch African Company, a firm interested in Congo trade. One of the *Comité*'s first actions, not surprisingly, was to hire the man who had partly conceived it: Stanley. In theory Stanley accepted the assignment to lead an expedition into the Central African interior, but what Leopold really wanted him to do with his knowledge started to become clear in July 1879, when Stanley stopped in Gibraltar to meet with Maximilien Strauch. Strauch, a colonel in the Belgian army, nominally ran the *Comité* but in reality served as Leopold's proxy. He presented Stanley with a letter outlining a mission remarkably different from that set out in the *Comité*'s charter. Whereas the bylaws had spoken only of acquiring land as private property, at the pleasure of Africans, Strauch told Stanley at Gibraltar that he wanted him to acquire political control along the Congo.[128] The *Comité* supposedly intended to help the indigenes found a "Confederation of Free Negro Republics."[129]

Strauch—probably inspired by John Latrobe, president of the AIA's American chapter and head of the American Colonization Society—told Stanley that the Congo republics would eventually join together to form a new state resembling Liberia, which Latrobe's American Colonization Society had helped to set up in West Africa in the early nineteenth century.[130] Like Liberia, Strauch's confederation would be an independent body of districts populated by ex-slaves.[131] Crucially, however, its supreme authority would not reside with indigenes or Americanized Africans. Instead, each "independent republic" would fall under the absolute political sway of a president, who would live in Europe and "hold his powers by grant of the King," Leopold II.[132] Strauch did not yet say whom he had in mind for president. Clearly, though, there had been yet another shift from the bylaws: from disinterestedness on the part of Leopold to ruling ambitions. The difference was not lost on Stanley, who suspected Leopold's ambition to colonize the Congo for himself.[133] Colonization in turn might pay dividends, for, at the time, ivory traded along the river represented one sixth of all the supply passing through London."[134] Prices for ivory, unlike those for nearly every other commodity, were rising consistently in the tough economy of the 1870s.[135] They also came with margins high enough to withstand the costs of river transport, freight to Europe, and tariffs in major ports.[136] Thus, whichever organization dominated trade in the Congo stood to make a fortune.[137]

Less than one month later, the king went even further in a confidential letter delivered to Stanley, now making his way down the West African coast toward the Congo mouth. "The king, as an individual," Leopold wrote via Strauch, wanted to acquire full control over any lands

Stanley might buy along the Congo. Stanley needed to maneuver Central African opinion for this purpose. First, he "had to buy lands or get them transferred to him" through a contract drawn up on paper and signed by an authority. Then he had to "attract natives to the lands" by whatever means necessary. Finally, Stanley had to "declare the independence of these agglomerations, provided the *Comité* approves." In other words, the proposal floated by Strauch a few weeks earlier, in which free "negro republics" would emerge, did not encompass Leopold's true intentions. The latter's goal for the Congo was not so much to create the second Liberia as it was to replicate "Sarawak on Borneo," which was "ruled by a white family, the Brookes, who have never had the support of any other government and who carry on very well."[138]

With the advantage of hindsight and a global perspective, it might seem plausible that Leopold hoped to advertise himself as a version of the "stranger-king," a charismatic outsider selected by warring factions to bring unity to a polity.[139] There was some reason to believe this was feasible: not just the recent experience of Brooke, a stranger-king par excellence, but also the rituals and lore of cultures indigenous to Central Africa.[140] The great Kongo Empire, which had spread its control across three hundred thousand square kilometers beginning in the late thirteenth century, soared under the leadership of Wene, an African stranger-king; over generations it celebrated the trope of a heroic immigrant seizing sovereignty in each one of its coronations, which lasted at least into the 1850s.[141] To the east of the Kongo polity, one could find similar, if less clearly apposite, motifs. The Luba Empire allegedly derived from Kalala Ilunga, a nomadic hunter who overthrew an established tyrant.[142] Finally, the Lunda Empire celebrated Tshibinda Ilunga, a Luba prince who, having emigrated, deposed a Lunda tyrant and then became emperor in his new, adopted land.[143]

Such lineages notwithstanding, Brooke's Southeast Asia of course differed fundamentally from Leopold's Central Africa. First, Leopold did not actually want to reside in, or even visit, his projected colonial empire, so any speculation about his stranger-king aspirations must remain quite tempered, even if he did periodically employ symbolism designed to evoke the Kongo Empire. Second, nineteenth-century Southeast Asian rulers had a tradition of bartered sovereignty into which nonindigenous peoples, including Westerners, could fit more or less neatly. Central Africa did not. It is unclear whether this discrepancy was lost on Stanley as he prepared to land at Boma, the seat of Portuguese influence on the coast. But Stanley had not yet seen his new employer's colonial vision in full—and never would—partly because he identified Leopold as a relatively benign source of money which he could use to achieve his own vague goals for Central Africa.[144]

Almost immediately after the *Comité* hired and dispatched Stanley to the Congo, it too ceased to exist.[145] In November 1879, around six months after the bankruptcy of its only other significant backer, the Dutch African Company, the *Comité* saw its members agree to accept buyouts from Leopold. The king was now operating with an infusion of cash from Léon Lambert, an agent of Gustave de Rothschild in Paris.[146] Relieved that "we are no longer exposed to see our purposes delayed by the necessity of obtaining the consent of a great number of persons"—that is, any other persons—Leopold promptly dissolved the *Comité* and, surreptitiously, replaced it with new bodies that (again) operated under the same coordinates, with the same telegraphic and postal addresses.[147] Most famous among these names was the International Association of the Congo.[148] Less known was the generation of such also-rans such as the International Association of the Upper Congo, the International Expedition of the Upper Congo, the International Expedition for the Study of the Upper Congo, and the International Committee for Studies of the Upper Congo.[149] The sheer volume of these avatars soon proved overwhelming. Even one of Leopold's lobbyists had to ask how he was supposed to explain the confusion.[150]

Unaware of each detail, Stanley went on to conduct his expedition in the name of at least eight organizations, some defunct.[151] In September 1879, he took his steamship and motley crew east from the Atlantic coast, traveling upriver until he met with impassable waterfalls. At this point, Stanley left his boat behind, moving onto land and to a place called Vivi. This was an insalubrious hill that, while known to Europeans for breeding malaria, was located just far enough in the interior not to arouse the jealousy of Portuguese traders. On arrival, Stanley sent out word that he wanted to meet with "the five chiefs of Vivi," whom he identified as the sovereigns of a very large surrounding area. The designated chiefs had some familiarity with Stanley; one of them had even become friendly with him on his previous trip down the Congo, and they could all converse in a regional Kikongo dialect, as well as in Swahili.[152] More to the point, Stanley now offered to bring prosperity, building roads where there was wilderness and thus putting local villages into contact with a larger trade community.

Residents at Vivi had made a number of exchanges with European traders already; this was why the five chiefs negotiated in third-hand military coats and cotton linens. Stanley's journal also attested a second mode of contact: alcohol. Remarking that the respective leaders arrived "sober and cleanly"—a fact called into question by his admission elsewhere that "each of the chiefs begged for, and received, a bottle of gin"—Stanley alluded to the way in which a host of Europeans had been selling liquor at the edges of the Congo interior in recent years, often with serious social consequences.[153] One could certainly read Stanley's protestation of sobriety as sensitivity to allegations of impropriety. But one could also read it as a reflection on him and his retinue: on *their* battle to remain clear-headed in spite of being intoxicated with a variety of substances and conditions.[154] Whatever the case, it was in such a hazy atmosphere that the negotiators assembled at Vivi to consider Stanley's proposal.

Stanley's account of what followed does not fully withstand scrutiny; another, less famous series of letters from an eyewitness visibly contradicts it.[155] Nonetheless, extant sources confirm that, in September 1879, the Vivi chiefs eventually agreed to lease Stanley and his men a modest parcel of land in the vicinity. According to a document advertised as a true copy of a written contract, Stanley agreed to make a down payment of £32 in cloth and deliver monthly fees of £2 in cloth. In exchange, the defunct *Comité* that Stanley claimed to represent received not only the land, but also an exclusive economic license. The latter included "the right to make roads wherever it is necessary," as well as some supervisory powers: first, that "all men that pass by those roads must be allowed to pass without interruption"; and second, that no Europeans other than those friendly to Stanley be allowed to build near, or make use of, those same roads.[156]

Simply to take this political contract at face value is too generous to Stanley, who threatened the chiefs at Vivi "about destroying the place, in case they allowed any white man to build [there]" or refused to sign the contract.[157] At the same time, it is not entirely proper to treat this kind of transaction as farcical simply because it was attested via a written contract. Written contracts were not common in the Congo Basin, but they did have precedents, especially in the Western Congo.[158] The indigenous kings who ran Boma, for example, had been registering land deeds, sales, and transfers for some time.[159] Moreover, disinterested visitors—including lieutenants in the U.S. Navy—confirmed in interviews in 1879 that several of the area's leaders understood treaty contracts they had signed with the British in 1876.[160] Another murky issue is that the preferred form of deal making in Central Africa was the ritual exchange of blood.[161] Yet, while Stanley and his contemporaries would have freely attested this fact, they were also aware that one Central African polity would not necessarily recognize another polity's blood brotherhood, to say nothing of the European community's preference for the printed word.[162] So the expedition members simply participated in both written and ritual performances, often acquiring so many cuts on their arm as to render it glaring reality.[163]

Nor is it proper to dismiss the contracts because they did not involve conventional Western currency. Europeans like Stanley kept cloth, beads, and wire on hand precisely because they understood how these items functioned as a form of currency in the Congo Basin, having been used as such since before the seventeenth century; well before European arrival, "money" in Kikongo derived from words either for cloth mats or seashells, which existed in numerous denominations as units of account, and whose skillful manipulation helped some polities dominate others via a sort of regional reserve currency system.[164] By the 1870s, the items still carried enough legitimacy that indigenous traders, in times of famine, attempted to use them to buy food from Europeans; farther to the east, meanwhile, cloth evidently served as payment for slaves.[165] More broadly, the European use of such items could have very real effects on the money supply and inflation.[166] That European traders made a habit of clipping brass rods in circulation and pocketing the difference only reinforces this point: Rods, cloth, and the like were very real currencies whose rises and slumps could cut both ways. A few years later, as the *Comité* considered selling some of its Congo claims to France, its negotiators requested compensation for sums already paid to "native chiefs."[167]

How to pay in contracts was thus a matter of great insecurity exacerbating an already hazy atmosphere for African-European contracts in the Congo.[168] At least one important town proved willing to accept only gin as payment in trade for market activity.[169] Two regional ports insisted on colored beads or cloth.[170] So Stanley needed to prepare multiple forms of commodities for use as currency in advance of his travel.[171] On one day he might succeed in buying thirty pounds of ivory for an empty vegetable can; on another day, he might be unable to buy vegetables for thirty pounds of ivory.[172] By 1881 the discrepancy popped up in relation to an examination of the Vivi rights: "Do you know," complained one of Stanley's fellow expedition members, "that we do not pay as much for Vivi, including original presents, as I am now paying for the small piece of ground purchased at Boma by Mr. Gillis? Such is a fact, however."[173]

Stanley did not specify how strictly he intended to interpret the rights he had purchased at Vivi, but, in any event, he had acquired for the *Comité* its first paper claims, including a license to effectively control Vivi's "roads" and—as important—the toll on goods that traversed them.[174] Around a year later Stanley left Vivi in charge of an American superintendent, having built a few wooden homes and constructed fifty miles of road westward, around the waterfalls and back to his abandoned steamship on the Congo. Throughout 1881, his expedition moved forward with orders to found a handful of additional stations farther east, most based, at least in theory, on contracts signed with chiefs, subchiefs, kings, or other figures of political authority.[175] At each new station—sometimes no more than a slapdash barrack—Stanley acquired papers assigning his expedition small economic privileges and landholdings.[176] In exchange, he gave either gifts or guarantees of aid and protection. He also started to raise unique flags on the instructions of Leopold, who believed this was a significant step.[177]

Early on it was reported, and is generally still accepted, that these flags included a golden star to represent the richness of civilization, amid a dark blue background that stood for barbarity. "Out of darkness cometh light," a suggested motto developed around the same time, appears to confirm the interpretation.[178] It does not suffice, however, for the flags' design was almost certainly an attempt to evoke the nearly identical flag adopted by the indigenous, and voluntarily Christianized, Kongo Empire.[179] Notwithstanding that civil wars and major economic changes had started robbing the Mani Kongo of his significance as a middleman in Congo trade in the seventeenth century, the king still nominally ruled over swathes of the territory Leopold now hoped to claim.[180] A symbolic continuity could thus lend Stanley's operation additional prestige during negotiations with polities formerly or tenuously falling within Kongo territory. In the process, Leopold's fantasies of control might appear like serendipity, not imposition.[181]

Just how feasible this proposition was is borne out in the work of anthropologist Jan Vansina. In his path-breaking book, *Oral Tradition as History,* Vansina posits a gap in cultural memory among Central Africa's illiterate peoples. According to his model, one can infer that by 1880, there would have been much talk about the origin stories and heroes of Kongo rule dating back several centuries; however, there would have been less knowledge about life just before and after 1800, when the Kongo Empire had begun to disintegrate.[182] People in the Western Congo Basin thus would have remembered Kongo power, not through written means or documented chronology, but through an abridged tradition that made no mention of the circumstances of the ancient empire's decline. This situation only improved the odds that Leopold's inroads would initially meet with positive associations.[183]

Europe was a different matter. It had long been the custom of Europeans doing business along the Congo to fly their home state's flag over their factories. But unlike Canton (Guangzhou) in China—a spot famous for its array of foreign flags over warehouses—the factories on the Congo were typically little more than ramshackle houses or vacated barracks (barracoons) left over from the Atlantic slave trade.[184] As such, they were vulnerable to incursions by rival traders, and, in some cases, hostile indigenes.[185] Some enterprising souls might try to mitigate such threats by forming an enclosure out of coal sheds or broken-down wagons.[186] A flag could go still further, the thinking being, recalled one law professor, that "the flag of the nation from which the trader" hailed offered him "protection if he should be wronged by a native chief or by a trader of another European nation."[187] British nationals, for instance, could claim protection on the basis of the Union Jack, hoisted at some seventeen posts by the late 1870s.[188] Now, however, Stanley's expedition was putting a curious twist on the practice by raising its own "national" flags.[189] Accompanying the innovation was considerable growth in the number of people who might be affected: Though the number of European factories did not amount to much more than a hundred, the population of residents inside them multiplied several times, with as many as 1,300 men, women, and children living under their roofs in one city alone.[190]

Portuguese in contact with the affected areas asked what it meant to fly the flag of something other than a country.[191] Inquiries were made as to whether Stanley's men were "authorized by the International

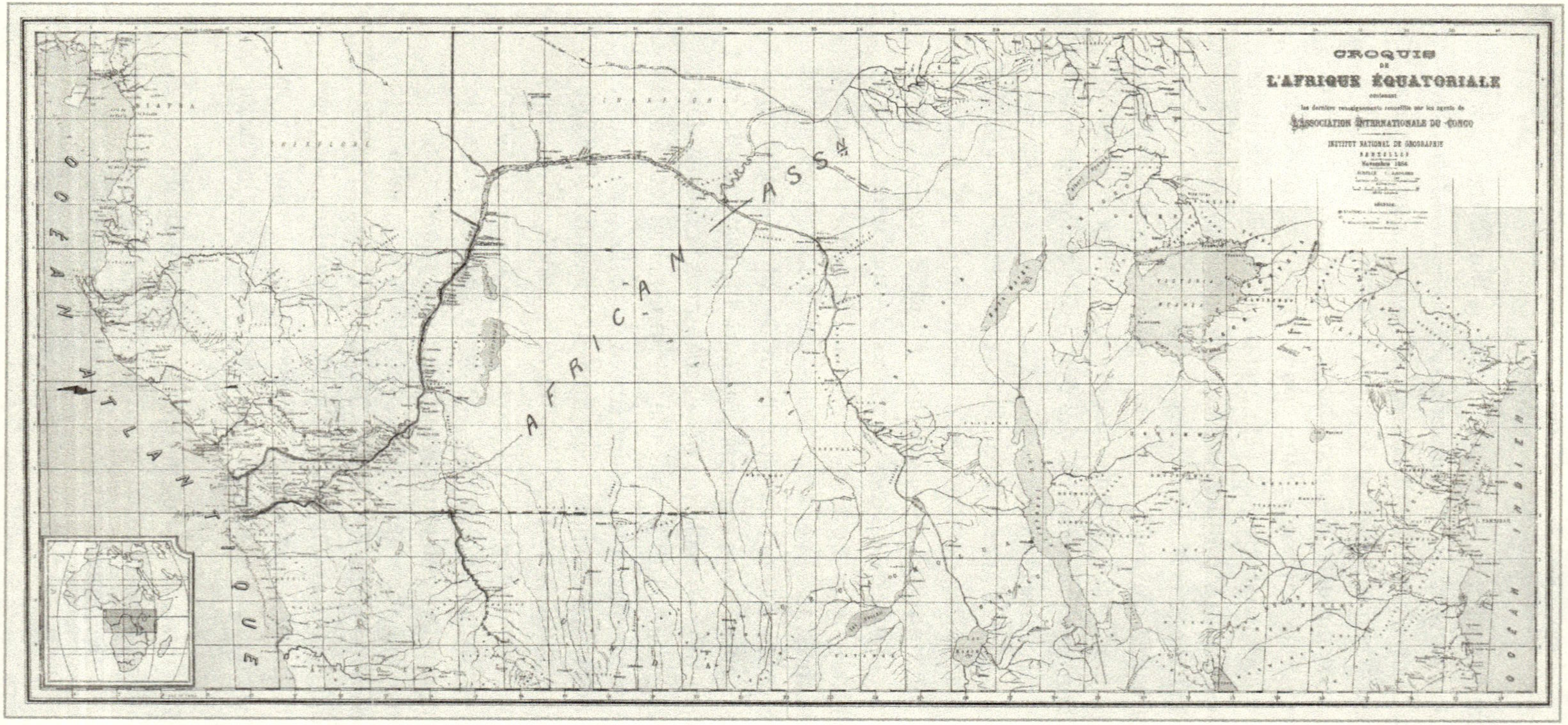

Map 2 Penetration of Congo River and Basin, November 1884. A copy of this map, made using data of the "International Congo Association," found its way into the possession of American diplomats lobbied by Leopold II. The association's putative territory lies to the right of the darkened line—a glaringly blank space. Note the areas marked "French" and "Portuguese," to the top and bottom, respectively, of the darkened lines nearest the Atlantic Ocean. *Source:* Institut National de Geographie, *Croquis de l'Afrique Équatoriale* (Brussels 1884). Courtesy of Library of Congress, Control Number 2006627675.

Association" to make "treaties and compacts of a political nature."[192] Leopold's organs quickly issued a reply, which was technically true inasmuch as it denied that such treaties had been signed by the "International African Association"—a long-defunct body.[193] Alas, it turned out that the flag of the International African Association was also that of the *Comité*, the International Association of the Congo, and all of its other avatars.[194] Things of a political nature were afoot, but under a smokescreen.[195] Already, Leopold had pushed to complicate this picture further by having the Belgian cabinet found an official consulate at one of his Congo stations—perhaps in an effort to afford his settlements the kind of legitimation Brooke sought for Sarawak.[196] Belgium's prime minister refused, but Leopold eventually made a similar request to the president of the United States, offering to pay the hypothetical American consul's salary himself.[197]

In the meantime Stanley's and Leopold's visions of the stations had begun to diverge. A very sick Stanley nearly died as he oversaw the construction of public works in summer 1881. At this time he sent letters to Leopold attesting that the contracts signed so far had placed the *Comité* only in the position of a tenant who, though not necessarily living under indigenous control, was also not empowered to treat indigenes as conquered peoples.[198] An additional volley came in the language that Stanley used when instructing his subordinates to found new stations. Whereas Leopold spoke of arranging "the cession of a territory"—unquestionably an action of states or empires—Stanley employed the term "concession" and placed his possible acquisitions of rights on the same plane as those usually accorded to European missionaries and trading companies. In one case, the discrepancy manifested itself in overlapping communications from the two sources, with one lieutenant receiving conflicting directives to secure a "cession" and "concession" along the Kwilu River.[199]

Leopold did not brook dissension easily. Writing from his palace at Laeken, he urged all expedition members to shed their concerns and move quickly to produce documents attesting the acquisition of full political rights across the Congo Basin. Leopold could not decide what he wanted to call these rights: he oscillated between the words "suzerainty" and "sovereignty."[200] The upshot, though, was that being a tenant on indigenous land was not a sufficiently convincing claim "to enforce respect, toward intruders, to the rights which the chiefs . . . have granted us."[201] At a minimum, Stanley ought to develop a claim for turning indigenous populations into *his* tenants, in line with the plan for a "confederation" discussed in 1879. He could throw up a few token buildings at each station, fly the flag of the association, attract a sizeable group of dignitaries to sign a form to "associate with the aim of civilization," and then move downriver and farther to the east.[202]

Into 1882, Leopold continued to press such schemes on Stanley in the belief that the *Comité* was falling behind other rivals.[203] His anxiety owed nothing to the construction of actual stations—that was proceeding apace, even if it amounted mostly to modest wooden houses. Rather, Leopold feared that European rivals might grab superior titles to the same territory he coveted. Stanley's contracts looked somewhat like regular land purchase contracts being signed by British missionaries, some of whom were shadowing the *Comité*'s route and building their own stations.[204] These missionaries, or indigenous leaders, could easily start flying the Union Jack, and then claim the protection of the British Empire.[205] Alternatively, they could simply flout the *Comité*'s lack of jurisdiction over Europeans, as happened with a Dutch trading company whose flag Stanley later tried to remove forcibly.[206] Stanley had not been specific enough in establishing the *Comité*'s right to exist vis-à-vis, and over, other European enterprises that might make their way into the Congo; he could, again according to the British, only do so by establishing "sovereignty."[207] Contributing to this explosive mixture were physical threats from rival Europeans, including a few from the Portuguese settlements at the mouth of the Congo on the Atlantic.

Portuguese economic interests, mostly forgotten until 1879, had once again become important enough that Lisbon was making claims to hold sovereignty over almost all of Equatorial Africa.[208] "Portugal had never bothered herself about the Congo Country," joked an American, "until someone one else became interested in it."[209] That was not exactly true—Portugal repeatedly attempted to inject its own minted coins into the local currency system, and it somewhat rationally planned to increase its African involvement from at least 1860.[210] That year, amid a major renewal of the ivory and gold dust trades in the Central African interior, Portuguese colonial officials in Luanda worked to install Pedro V on the Kongo Empire's throne, with the result that the new ruler pledged vassalage to Lisbon.[211] By 1881, colonial officials in the metropole also sensed that "civilizational" rhetoric was an untapped resource with which to drum up public support for their expansionist projects abroad.[212] Portugal was therefore going to make a concerted effort to convert its longstanding titular claims to the Congo—which a British foreign minister had once called "barren sovereignty"—into something more concrete.[213]

Arguably the greatest obstacle facing diplomats in Lisbon—as well as domestic geographical societies seeking to defend them—was that they could make only flimsy arguments about governing most of Central Africa, relying as they did on accounts of the planting of a few large stone crosses *(padrões)* along the coast, some by the explorer Diogo Cão, starting in the late fifteenth century.[214] These accounts had yet to be backed up through armed force: The last attempt to move a Portuguese army squad into the Congo interior, in 1857, had ended, somewhat pathetically, with the squad's expulsion by a British antislaving patrol on the river.[215] But the calculus in Lisbon was changing, and before long Portugal would weigh not just reprisals against Leopold's men in the Congo, but also diplomatic retaliation against his kingdom in Belgium.[216]

Through early 1882 the contracts signed by Leopold's *Comité* did not clearly look better than Portugal's claims, when one compared the two.[217] At best the *Comité* documents were assurances of vague trading privileges related to roads or construction.[218] At worst they were contracts with an air of duress likely to arouse protest when revealed to the public. By 1882 missionaries were reporting that several recent treaty negotiations had taken place in the presence of African mercenaries foreign to the area, whom one commentator likened to a terror.[219] A leading newspaper in Lisbon, *l'Economista,* later relied on such accounts to argue that if Portugal's rights, "founded on priority of discovery," were "of no value," then "those of the International Association, which, so to say, arrived yesterday at the Congo and which only by threats and by subtlety obtained them and imposed them on the natives," were "truly ridiculous."[220] In the event, though, not every Portuguese trader called the association's treaties "pseudo-contracts."[221] Some even shifted their tactics to imitation, signing contracts for land purchases and rights in areas adjacent to the holdings of their upstart rivals.[222]

Amid this fight both Leopold and the Portuguese also had to contend with another entrant into the arena: France.

FRANCE'S INVOLVEMENT in the Congo began with one man, Pierre de Brazza. Brazza, an Italian-born count and a sublieutenant in the French navy, led an expedition from French-controlled Gabon down to the Congo Basin in 1880. Officially, Brazza worked on behalf of the undead French committee of the AIA, which had hired and funded him in late 1879.[223] Brazza's trip had a dual loyalty, however, as his finances attested.[224] In part his duty was to Leopold, who added parcels of his own money to Brazza's payments from the AIA; the greater obligation was to the French government, which, with the strong support of then minister of education Jules Ferry, had contributed additional, even more substantial funding for the purpose of opening up a viable trade route between Gabon and Central Africa.[225] The latter gesture spoke to an anxiety, shared among many members of the French committee, that Leopold's *Comité* would either deviate from the AIA's humanitarian goals, or cut off the growth of French trade from Gabon to the Congo, or both.[226] Some of the members heard rumors about the monopolistic terms of Stanley's recent agreement at Vivi.[227] Brazza also had inside knowledge as to the *Comité*'s intentions, for Leopold had tried to hire him directly in 1878, shortly after he returned from a three-year mission navigating the Ogooué River—a path that led him more or less from the Gabon coast to the Congo, possibly offering a more effective route to the riches of Malebo Pool and the upper basin than Stanley's.[228]

Moving into the interior with about a dozen Senegalese soldiers on loan from French colonial authorities in Gabon, Brazza deviated from his modest charge to found two stations.[229] This was not altogether surprising: In a meeting with French AIA members he had proposed occupying an immense territory with the stations as mere launching points for the projection of power.[230] But soon there was more to the story. In late 1881 Brazza left Africa behind, his debts heavy, with the exact details of his trip a mystery even to many Europeans along the Congo.[231] He now returned to Europe with treaties, just as Verney Cameron had returned in 1876. As Brazza explained it, a king in the Congo had signed over his governing rights to France.[232] The man in question, Iloo, was a *"makoko"* (a paramount authority in the Tio kingdom) who had inked his first contract with Brazza on September 10, 1880.[233] That much was certain; the problem was figuring out what the contracts actually meant.[234] The most important of them, complained the American ambassador to Paris, was "drawn up in such language" that it was "not easy to understand exactly its meaning."[235]

That Iloo had simply transferred all political authority over his kingdom was a debatable interpretation of events, to say the least. The full text of the key treaty remained closely guarded until well over a year later; as late as June 1882, high-ranking officials in the French Ministry of Foreign Affairs had not had the opportunity to peruse it, and the minister of the navy said he could not produce the original.[236] Around the same time, in Brussels, a member of Leopold's *Comité* qualified Belgian accounts of its provenance by adding a sardonic phrase: "so it is said."[237] When a substantial number of Europeans finally did obtain a full copy, they saw a somewhat less clear story than had been advertised. To begin, the main treaty said that Iloo was agreeing to accept a "cession of territory" made to Brazza, "the representative of the French government," by one of Iloo's vassals, Ngampei, the territory in question being a patch of land along the river "for the establishment of a French station."[238] So far, so good: But did Ngampei's "cession of territory" also alter the political situation of Iloo's realm generally? It was unclear who would govern the territories in question post-treaty—both the "French station" given up by Ngampei, which was located some ninety-three miles away from where Iloo sat with Brazza, and Iloo's kingdom itself.

It is probable that Iloo, photographs of whom show a thin, wizened man, negotiated with Brazza in hope of valuable assistance: the extension of his kingdom's vast agricultural trading network to the Gabonese coast; an alliance to fend off internal challengers; and, finally, some protection against even less pacific exogenous threats, such as Stanley's expedition.[239] Such behavior was not unique: Starting in the 1860s, ruling elites among the Kongo population of northern Angola also tried to direct their heightened encounter with (Portuguese) Europeans in order to prevail in a climate of economic disruption and dynastic struggle.[240] Still, it remains unclear what Iloo was willing to give up to Brazza. The text of Iloo's main treaty with Brazza began with a confirmation of Ngampei's cession, the result of around two weeks' negotiation. But then, in its next lines, the treaty included a clause in which Iloo agreed to surrender his "hereditary rights of supremacy" over all "his territory." The treaty thus started by talking about some land on the bank of Malebo Pool, at the periphery of Iloo's control, ninety-three miles away, only to end by concerning Iloo's entire area of control.

As one analyzed the whole document, the point about peripheries broached another question: whether Iloo was really, as Brazza said he was, the latest head of a dynasty dating to the fifteenth century.[241] Subsequent research has answered in the affirmative, however tenuously.[242] Provided this condition was met, most European lawyers would have agreed Iloo had the right to sell France control over a vast portion of African territory, some of which overlapped with the northern portion of Leopold II's desired African empire. But Iloo's role as leader was actually placed in doubt by a second treaty, which Brazza produced about a month after the first, on October 3, 1880. In this document, signed by a proxy of Iloo and four of Iloo's vassals, Brazza confirmed that he was, "in the name of France," going to "take possession" of certain territory "by virtue of the rights which had been conferred on him on the 10th of September 1880 by" Iloo, "the King Makoko."[243] The territory in question had comprised Iloo's whole kingdom. Paradoxically, however, the "supreme authority" of Iloo now appeared to cover less than that kingdom. The four vassals signing Brazza's second treaty evidently did not accept that Iloo, their "supreme" leader, could serve as an adequate proxy for their own voice.[244] They, too, had to sign off, whether by Brazza's admission, their own, or that of Iloo—who sent his own representative to the signing ceremony to confirm its legitimacy.

Because the second treaty called into question the thoroughness of the first, it may seem proper to agree with one missionary working in the Congo at the time of Brazza's expedition, who complained that Iloo was nothing more than a village elder "of the kind you meet every few kilometers in Africa."[245] But the status of Iloo was merely one of several disputes that exemplify a recurring problem in Europe's encounter with Africa: what to make of the precolonial African political landscape.[246] European treaty negotiators, who ordinarily dealt with kings or emirs in other, non-Christian parts of the world, frequently misread the powers of such men as Iloo in Sub-Saharan Africa.[247] An optimistic explanation is that Europeans simply did not comprehend the immense variety obtaining in the status of political systems across Africa; and, no doubt, there are numerous instances in which employees and contemporaries of Leopold appear to have taken indigenous kinghood seriously.[248] A more common explanation is that the misreading of indigenous powers was deliberate, with the result, to quote Sir Richard Burton, that "every fellow with one black coat becomes a . . . prince, and if he has two he styles himself a 'king.'"[249]

Whatever one's perspective, one must concede that immense variegation played a role in generating confusion for Europeans—and even in motivating certain indigenous political figures to try to use outsiders like Brazza for their own ends.[250] Sometimes titular African rulers held something approaching ultimate authority, in a polity fairly called a state; as often, they did not. Rulers in Yorubaland, for example, typically had well-demarcated boundaries and defined their control within a static territory.[251] Islamic authorities in Morocco, by contrast, interpreted their writ as extending wherever their subjects happened to be.[252] In this sense, the Congo region through 1880 figures as a microcosm: Like precolonial Africa generally, it can perhaps be described as a hodgepodge that periodically included everything from strongly centralized monarchies, to feudalism, to stateless agglomerations of families.[253] Iloo's polity existed on this spectrum but was perhaps shifting in the direction of feudalism at the time of Brazza's arrival. At Boma, meanwhile—a major port near the mouth of the Congo—several kings shared authority.[254] There lay a key difference: Like many other African figures of the time, not just in the Congo but also in other areas farther afield, Iloo might understandably balk at arrangements whereby he shared political power with numerous other sources: religious leaders, generals, and the like. Outside assistance, though risky, promised a path to consolidate his otherwise diffuse power and raise him to the same level as that of other political figures in Boma and elsewhere. From this perspective—as a world away in Brunei—a deal with the right European could appear much more as a mutually beneficial partnership than as the kind of one-way transaction most would later assume.

European legal considerations on the nature of African territoriality had not yet achieved any consensus, however, leading to heavy debate by the time of Brazza's initial return to Europe.[255] Brazza's documents, despite the fanfare that would soon surround them, looked overhyped and padded to astute observers.[256] To further clinch that point, one has only to consider that Brazza brought back two different versions of his initial treaty with Iloo. In the first version—never published, but far less neat—Brazza declared that Iloo had "supremacy" *("suprématie")* over his kingdom.[257] In the second version—published widely in 1882 and many times since—Brazza declared that Iloo had "sovereignty (*"souveraineté"*), even as he mentioned that Iloo was transferring vague "rights of supremacy" to France.[258] If the first version was authentic, then France was not dealing with a king, at least according to European standards. On the other hand, if the second version was authentic, then France, in only receiving "right of supremacy" from the "sovereign," was still acquiring less than ultimate control.

Discrepancies of this kind were by no means unfamiliar to French imperialism in West Africa. Between 1882 and 1883, a number of French treaties employed the terms *"suzeraineté,"* "cession of territory," and *"souveraineté"* indiscriminately; some even met with an upgrade to *"souveraineté"* retroactively.[259] Still, Brazza's work quickly won broad acclaim from the French public, among whose geographers and journalists the makings of a small "colonial party" had been in place for several years.[260] Popular writings such as Paul Leroy-Beaulieu's *De la colonisation chez les peuples modernes*—reissued in 1882—certainly encouraged activity in the Congo, even with the lingering shock of Paul Flatters's doomed Trans-Saharan Railway expedition in February 1881.[261] In a turn consistent with the notion of an imperial "civilizing mission," fantasies soon emerged of turning the Congo into a Brazil-sized area where only French would be spoken.[262] Brazza, compared with the generals making headlines for bloodshed in Tunisia, Madagascar, and Indo-China—or a decade earlier, in the suppression of Cheikh Mokrani's Algerian uprising—appeared to have ushered in a viable opportunity for inexpensive French expansion.

In official circles, however, Brazza struggled to surmount a high degree of skepticism. To begin, France never publicly authorized him to conclude a treaty of annexation. That begged the question of exactly what France *had* asked Brazza to do. As it turned out, Brazza reached a tacit agreement with part of the French cabinet, albeit not the parliament, in advance of his journey: He was to raise the Tricolour where possible, preferably over stations he had founded.[263] This permission did not necessarily entail authorization to make binding pacts, however. The navy, Brazza's erstwhile employer, had been apprised of Brazza's intentions from the start but confided various misgivings about annexing territory through June 1882, after the French parliament had already declined an initial opportunity to ratify the Brazza treaties.[264] Like

Brière de l'Isle, the colonial governor who had recently forced expansion into the Senegalese interior without authorization from Paris, Brazza found it more difficult to ask permission than to beg forgiveness for his roguish move—which he did in a report of August 1882.[265] That report made clear that forgiveness would require multiple stages, for, according to Brazza, his expedition had already formally placed the *makoko*'s territories into French administration, if not that of the French government proper. Indeed, multiple ceremonies had taken place in which indigenous leaders, having been informed of Brazza's treaty terms, explained the new regime to their subjects.[266] More Tricolours were flying with each passing month, and in the meantime, with or without Paris's consent, Brazza's agents were attempting what Verney Cameron never had: governance.

Both because the credentials of Brazza were in doubt and because the navy was reluctant to take on additional expenses, ratification did not occur until November 1882.[267] Even then, it did not succeed because the treaty won esteem in the Chamber and Senate.[268] Transcriptions of parliamentary debates show overwhelming indifference, with many deputies not caring to ascertain the dimensions of Iloo's territory—the part of Central Africa that France was supposedly annexing by virtue of the treaties.[269] Was the kingdom's largest side nine miles long, or ninety? Did it include the left bank of a spot on the Congo River, as well as the right?[270] Was Iloo a "sovereign," or was he a "suzerain," as President Jules Grévy called him?[271] No block of politicians bothered to demand answers. And while it is not entirely accurate to say that parliament approved a wildly popular colonial venture for fear of losing the French public—lobbying by French manufacturers and chambers of commerce, jarred by a Bourse crash in January, also played a role—it is certain that there would have been no ratification without press agitation and colonial mania seizing the French public.[272] (Partly the latter phenomenon had to do with Egypt, where, in September, Britain had destroyed Urabi's army at Tell El Kebir absent any French input.)

As the French committee of the AIA presented its possessions to France in a ceremonial exchange, there was a final element to consider.[273] In the background of Brazza's maneuvering, observers had to concede that his treaties, because signed by an African authority under questionable circumstances, resembled certain "protection" treaties on which the French based their control of other coastal territories in West

Africa. Some of these dated back to the early 1840s.[274] Some were more recent, such as that concluded along the border with Liberia in 1868 by a naval lieutenant.[275] Some, like "a pact of friendship" in the Bafing region (today's Ivory Coast), were just coming up for review in parliament.[276] Judging Brazza's documents too harshly might besmirch the integrity of these others, and few in Paris really wanted that.[277] This issue, after all, would only resurface in the coming years as France—its colonial policy under the influence, if not the letter, of Charles de Freycinet's plan for public works—saw its bases for control in Senegambia expand still further in preparation for railway construction in West Africa.[278] Arguably the ramifications could extend still further—and not just to Britain, which had made thirteen treaties with Congolese dignitaries by 1884, some in an attempt to combat French treaties.[279] As at least one contemporary noted, the pacts signed by Brazza with Native Africans looked much like those signed by the United States with Native Americans.[280]

Back in Brussels, the machinations of Brazza left Leopold facing a dilemma in the months leading up to November 1882.[281] On the one hand, the King of the Belgians could abandon his political ambitions in the Congo, choosing instead to focus on commercial possibilities and trade.[282] This path might spare him further haggling with French ministers over the meaning of treaties. On the other hand, it would probably leave France as the unquestioned master of the Congo interior, with Portugal remaining as a substantial power on the coast. Neither France nor Portugal, in such a scenario, would be obligated to respect any preexisting commercial contracts Stanley had signed with indigenous authorities. On the contrary, both empires would likely proceed to void these contracts, since the latter claimed to vest in the *Comité* the control over export and import tolls that indigenous authorities had previously levied.[283] If this fear materialized, it was unclear where Leopold would stand financially, absent such an advantage as his contracts afforded. The outlook was poor, for British traders could already rely on more experience in the Congo than could any Belgian or member of Stanley's expedition. Finally, French traders would likely receive preferential treatment from the new colonial authorities, whatever their legitimacy in law.[284] Brazza had been pushing the creation of a large French company with a state-guaranteed monopoly on Congo trade since 1881.[285]

The stage was set for a diplomatic fight with France over control of the Congo River area.[286] As of early 1882, the physical threat remained meager: With Brazza back in Europe, the entire French "army" in the area consisted of a skeleton crew with poor communications.[287] So Leopold could make do for a while with rudimentary security measures, such as replacing his ships' flags with the Stars and Stripes whenever danger loomed.[288] This situation would not last, however, for by the end of 1882, France looked to augment its forces after finally ratifying the *makoko* treaties and even agreeing to fund a further expedition by Brazza.[289] An initial countermeasure was to supplicate France; so far its cabinet had given vague assurances for Leopold's project, but the king now tried to pin Paris down on specific recognition of its rights.[290] In the meantime, complaints flooded into Britain, where Leopold lamented to Queen Victoria that France wanted Tunis, the Niger, the Congo, and Tonkin all to herself.[291]

Leopold made another unsuccessful attempt to hire Brazza away.[292] Then he turned to discredit Brazza, with Stanley spreading word among travelers that Brazza was a charlatan, and with Henry Sanford, the king's man in America, telling the U.S. secretary of state that "the so called treaty of Mr. de Brazza was a flimsy and specious pretext . . . with an ignorant chief." Sanford, a sometime spymaster, claimed to have heard compromising details about Brazza's treaties from "one who had seen them."[293] This talk was consistent with Brazza's reputation in Britain; as early as 1875, *The Times* reported that he carried an electric battery under his coat sleeve in order to shock indigenous people whose hands he shook to make them think he was superhuman.[294] Elsewhere, several critics partial to Leopold dismissed Brazza as a poseur riding on Stanley's coattails. Whereas the latter understood Africa, the former was, or so the argument went, variously a publicity hound and a confidence artist. He would prey upon poor potentates; he would stage scenes of amity with Africans; he would even pass out small French flags to give visitors to the Congo the impression of widespread support for France.[295]

But perhaps the best chance to mitigate the French threat was to acquire treaties awarding political rights superior to the kind claimed by Brazza, and then to get these treaties recognized by other European powers eager to balance against French predominance.[296] Signing a treaty of commerce was the preferred form of recognition, but making so much happen at once posed a considerable challenge.[297] The deals

Stanley had secured so far concerned only vague landholdings and economic privileges. Leopold was, moreover, just a citizen acting without the sanction of the Belgian prime minister and his government.[298] Happily for Leopold, events in London soon afforded a weapon: the debut of the Borneo principle onto the international stage.

MOST HISTORIANS RECORD that Leopold discovered the idea of Borneo in March 1882.[299] It is more accurate, however, to call this moment a rediscovery. On the mornings of March 14 and 18, as Leopold began to read his sanitized copy of *The Times*—he feared the germs—he came across articles recapping debates in the House of Commons. According to these pieces, the House had just considered a royal charter for Alfred Dent's North Borneo Company.[300] Leopold had never forgotten this case, though he did remember it with some distortion; he had mentioned it earlier in the month when casting about for a way to justify his rogue empire-building in the Congo.[301] Just around eight years earlier, Leopold had come close to a deal with Overbeck, backing out not long after Britain urged him to do so. Now, as Leopold continued to read over his newspaper, he saw that Dent intended to fold the rights into a new company-state—something Leopold had conceived of for the Congo as recently as 1880, albeit with the Hudson's Bay Company in mind and with himself as projected president and lead shareholder.[302]

That was where matters grew especially intriguing. *The Times* outlined how the status of Dent's company had won approval from Prime Minister William Gladstone, who argued that Britain would charter Dent's new company in exchange for the company's consent to certain provisions, including—in a flourish evocative of Leopold's own—the abolition of slavery in its territory. Gladstone announced that the company itself was a state, its title "already perfect previously to the grant of the charter," full, and sufficient to be recognized by all states under international law. The company did not need Britain's approval. And the legitimacy of Dent's title was enough to override ethical or international legal protests.

For the second time in his life, Leopold developed an obsession with Borneo. The first time Leopold had hoped to help himself to a chunk of Asia; this time, he hoped to help himself to a chunk of Africa. Nine days after reading the article in *The Times*, Leopold dictated a letter to Strauch in which he laid out a new plan for the Congo. "In consideration of a certain annual charge," his letter began, "the sultans ceded to Mr. Dent, a private individual, the property of a vast tract of territory: larger than the half of France, with all the privileges of sovereignty, such as the rights of life and death, to coin money, raise an army, organize a public force etc. etc." Noting that "the importance of these declarations will not escape you," Leopold proceeded to argue that if Stanley could sign such declarations on behalf of the *Comité*, then "nobody would ever contest the rights and authority" of the *Comité* in the Congo area. A "decisive precedent" now existed to help the *Comité* establish itself—despite its status as a body with no official "commission from a government"—as a power capable of making treaties and acquiring kingdoms by contract.[303]

Leopold believed in this precedent for several reasons. First, the Westerners in Borneo had not bought their rights per se; they had leased them indefinitely. This slight difference could prove crucial to propaganda about Africa, where, according to one well-placed Belgian source, indigenous communities generally recognized *sales* of rights as invalid, but not perpetual leases for annual or monthly payments.[304] Second, and not least, Britain, the preeminent factor in Africa, had gone on record saying it was quite sure about the legitimacy of freelance empires in Borneo.[305] At the fore of that position stood Julian Pauncefote, a major figure in the British Foreign Office. To this point Pauncefote had refused Leopold's attempt to win recognition as a legal power in the Congo, on the grounds that his *Comité* lacked complete and uncontested "sovereignty" there; during one meeting, Pauncefote even rejected an arrangement by which hundreds of Central African polities would contribute troops to a military confederation under loose supervision by the *Comité*.[306] By contrast, Pauncefote had steadfastly supported the Borneo Company from its inception through its recent negotiations with the British cabinet, so he acknowledged that Leopold's plan could work if he secured similar control, "for all administrative purposes," over the Congo population.[307]

Paris, Washington, and Berlin were also on the hook, having begun to recognize the new order in Sabah in certain diplomatic and legal affairs.[308] Even the Dutch were crafting plans to accredit consuls to the North Borneo Company.[309] In other words, unless these great powers wanted to contradict themselves mere months into the Borneo experiment, they could not possibly refuse to recognize an organization with identical credentials to govern in Africa.[310] And so Leopold's treaties, if fashioned after Borneo, could "prove" the *Comité*'s ownership of governmental powers in the Congo and become "quite sufficient to authorize and justify the recognition" needed for entry into the international system of states.[311] An astonished servant to Leopold soon expressed amazement at this proof "of states founded by private persons without any official mission."[312]

Leopold now felt "the success of the enterprise" in Africa depended on exploiting the developments in Borneo—on casting Stanley's outfit in the mold of Sir James Brooke and the other Borneo adventurers.[313] "It is," remarked one of Leopold's cabinet members, "the same process."[314] Accordingly, Leopold insisted it was necessary for his agents to start producing treaties different from the kinds they had concluded so far. Stanley's first batch of treaties had spoken only of renting land or territory, and he had complained as recently as June 1881 that he was finding it difficult to extract even these concessions.[315] Leopold had shaken this status quo in January 1882 by instructing his agents to procure signed contracts in which indigenous leaders transferred to the *Comité* "the largest possible concessions of earth for the culture and foundation of stations."[316] Now that was not enough: The new treaties ought to mimic, as closely as possible, what appeared to be in the Borneo treaty then under debate in Britain. In theory, this would mean putting words in the treaties to the effect that the visitors were leasing in perpetuity sovereign rights over a vast territory, not just a parcel of land, and that these rights amounted to absolute power without "restrained" prerogatives such as existed in Europe.[317]

Leopold's new documents would thus not just equal Brazza's treaties, but surpass them. Yet this trick was easier said than done. One could say that, by early 1882, Leopold had to rely on secondary sources: reports such as those issued by one of his charitable causes, the *Société belge de géographie*.[318] He did not have a copy of the original Borneo documents. A translation evidently did not surface in France or Austria until at least late 1885, and in Britain the originals remained closely guarded, with mere paraphrases being provided to parliament.[319] So Leopold did not know the magic formula by which these documents had won over Whitehall, and he was already making mistakes when speaking about Borneo to his lieutenants. To refresh his memory, the king soon requested that his secretary retrieve his files on the island of Borneo from the royal archives, no doubt hoping to find a transcription of the treaty given to him in the negotiations with the Borneo businessmen many years before.[320] In the event, he continued to recommend that Stanley "take the concessions granted to Mr. Dent as a type for the treaties which you are to conclude in the name of the *Comité* with the principal chiefs of the Congo."[321]

Leopold was unfazed by subsequent reports in *The Times* that the Borneo treaties had not "been accepted and in practice submitted to" by the population of Sabah, and that the Borneo Company lacked "an adequate force at their command to admit of their actually exercising the sovereign powers of government and administration."[322] At this point the king only cared about marketing his claims to fellow Europeans, not about eliciting authentic or enduring African approval. Personally he never cared much for written contracts, preferring verbal agreements.[323] He also knew that "it would seem that these natives are not very desirous to see strangers establishing themselves amongst them and that they are not very disposed to grant them the territorial concessions which are indispensable to us for the realization of our kind intentions." But unless this opposition was overcome, "our establishments will not enjoy true security and we will not be able to secure pecuniary means for giving the enterprise the intended development."[324] Here, however, the issue of Stanley's compliance would resurface. Stanley certainly thought it realistic to duplicate aspects of the Borneo story in Africa, since the Congo was "a sanatorium compared to Borneo."[325] Stanley also had no compunction about trumping the French and Portuguese. That said, he expressed reservations to Leopold about the notion that paper treaties could grant a European jurisdiction over Africans.[326] Stanley, for all his faults, insisted that the *Comité* could not simply buy the rights to an empire.[327] Moreover, any pretensions to govern, he protested, were impractical, given that he estimated the Congo's population at between 49,000,000 and 80,000,000, and Leopold's ranks at less than 1,000 men, with no common culture or language to speak of.[328]

Leopold sought to reassure Stanley: "You know that we don't pursue conquests on account of Belgium in Africa; we have already told you this; we repeat it once more . . . let the chiefs accept our guardianship, delegate us their authority as the sultans of Borneo did, and, on our part, we will take care that they may not be reduced to a state of servitude."[329] Yet, in the summer of 1882, the king started to circumvent the man nominally in charge of all indigenous negotiations in the Congo. This circumvention—a tactic familiar to Leopold, who generally disowned uncooperative members of his inner circle—was made easier when Stanley, still severely weakened by illness, returned to Europe for a sojourn. By September, with ratification of Brazza's treaties by France a month away, Leopold distributed his Borneo plan to various other expedition leaders he was funding in the Congo area.[330] "The treaties must be as brief as possible," he said around this time, "and in a few articles must grant us everything."[331] There was some room for negotiation: An indigenous leader could choose a "political treaty," in which he accepted monthly payments for control of "strangers of all color" and stranger-native relations; alternatively, he could opt for an even shorter "territorial cession" and transfer "his rights of property and sovereignty on all the territories submitted to his authority."[332] Nothing less than "very extensive" spans of earth was in view, and territories ought now to be "connected one to the other so as to form later one entire lot."[333]

Leopold directed Strauch to enclose one or more treaty templates in letters to agents.[334] "The question" of treaties, he added, "is currently the thing that occupies us the most."[335] Thus were a host of other men tasked with the mission Stanley refused. These fresh recruits, many of whom set out to do their work without experience in indigenous affairs of the Congo, represented a fraction of the roughly 128 Europeans working for the *Comité*.[336] Many were veterans of the Belgian army; others were German, British, Austro-Hungarian, Swedish, or even American free agents imported to the Congo.[337] All relied on hundreds of mercenaries and laborers imported from regions of varying proximity: Cabindas from the Congo mouth; Hausa from the Niger Basin; Kru from Liberia; Zanzibaris from East Africa; and, most distantly, Chinese "coolies."

Some of the new agreements came shortly after these instructions, from September to November 1882. At Bolobo, a figure named Ebaka accepted *Comité* money in the hope of increasing his power over rival Bobangi traders, as well as reaffirming his dominance over religious authorities; in exchange, Ebaka signed a treaty giving the *Comité* the right to forbid Europeans from entering the area without its authorization.[338] Farther down the river, Lutete, known by Europeans as a "powerful chief" of the Ngombe, agreed to let the *Comité* provide aid and assistance to those people who "recognized" its authority.[339] In other areas, even these formulations ceased to look bold: A treaty signed near Manyanga claimed to witness two geographically disparate dignitaries "recognizing" the authority of the agents of the *Comité,* though within vague parameters.[340]

Thus 1882—and especially March 1882—was as a crucial turning point for the Congo.[341] Only by using Borneo as its model could Leopold's group start to assert itself in Europe as a unified state with supreme power over Congolese territory, as well as the Africans and Europeans residing within it. Through early 1882, the *Comité* had maintained visions of acquiring economic monopoly rights or, at most, supervisory rights over existing African polities: A "confederation of Free Negro Republics," to recall Strauch's phrase.[342] From March 1882 on, the *Comité* was dreaming bigger.[343] It was seeking, improbably, to be recognized as no less than an independent authority that had swallowed "Negro Republics": as a body that possessed, so it said, "independent territories with prerogatives that allow it to govern, to introduce the beginning of organization, and to raise a public force in order to maintain order and respect people and properties."[344]

A key component of this approach was to flex muscles: Instructions went out to increase the number of loaded guns at stations and to put on a show of crushing indigenous resistance, perhaps the largest case of which happened at Manyanga, less than two weeks after the signing of a treaty there in October.[345] Over the next two years, Leopold commissioned the installation of cannons and other heavy weaponry outside of key towns.[346] A less bloody, but more controversial, tactic was to sign contracts leasing *Comité* land to other Europeans not affiliated with the *Comité* or its avatars.[347] One such deal saw Baptist missionaries looking to protect themselves—and forestall Catholic rivals—negotiate for a seven-year tenure on a two-and-a-half-acre plot of land around Malebo Pool. The caveat was that they engage in no commercial trade and recognize the *Comité*'s political and military supremacy.[348] While a power with a tenant's rights, or even the supervisor of an African confederation, could not arrange such terms, an independent state or empire could, and if missionaries spread that impression around Europe, all the better for Leopold.[349]

At any rate, the flying of flags and the stationing of a few guards would not suffice to substantiate the *Comité*'s claims to have gotten independent polities to "close their countries for us," as a subordinate of Stanley put it.[350] Nor would a second plan—weighed for a brief time—to send indigenous leaders loyal to the association as delegates to the United States.[351] Only a Borneo-inspired treaty, cleaned up for presentation and stripped of its social messiness, would clinch the point. As the waxing ambition of the treaties made them more difficult to obtain, the *Comité* also tolerated forgery and deception on a new level, both of which in turn exposed the operation to heavier criticism. Leopold's men, often going behind Stanley's back, claimed to have concluded a few handfuls of purchases of sovereignty by early 1883, with many coming in January of that same year.[352] In reality, these purchases consisted of contracts that still read very differently, in the form of several fundamentally different templates. Some merely spoke of trading privileges; others purported to deliver the *Comité* full governing powers and looked, in the confidential assessment of Belgian prime minister Walthère Frère-Orban, like the handiwork of a slave trader.[353] But the *Comité* advertised them all in the same way, whether to Europe, to the Belgian cabinet, or—by early 1884—to the very same Congolese political leaders who supposedly agreed to them.

This new generation of treaties, unlike its predecessor, saw multiple indigenous Congolese authorities denounce the *Comité*. The depiction of treaties they had "signed" months before, once revealed, was said to bear little resemblance to what had been agreed.[354] In one case, a Dutch trader visiting the town of Palaballa obtained a copy of the treaty allegedly signing the area away, then translated the copy aloud for the indigenous inhabitants.[355] "The chiefs," he recorded, "were much surprised at the conditions, and declared that they never understood the full meaning of the treaty imposed upon them, that they had no wish to sell their lands on those terms, that they were given to understand that the expedition intended to establish a factory."[356] In April and May 1884 the several kings of Boma encountered a similar circumstance. Alexandre Delcommune, a veteran factory owner there and sometime agent for the *Comité*, claimed to have signed treaties with them in which sovereignty was exchanged for merchandise.[357] The kings felt otherwise, fearing an influx of new laws in disharmony with their own, and they joined Dutch and English traders at Boma in making a formal complaint to the Portuguese governor-general of Angola.[358] "Steps should be taken," the complaint demanded, to address the fraud of the "truly laughable" claims made out of proportion to the modest documents signed.[359] Around a year earlier, an agent of the *Comité* protested that his superiors were making him a "liar" and a "thief" not only by asking him to invent some signatures, but by asking him to misrepresent a treaty orally as a mere land sale, despite the more robust claims advanced within its twenty-five lines of French text.[360] When Lutete, the leader of the Ngombe, at one point tried to assert his supremacy in matters of trade in the understanding he had only signed away certain land rights, he was imprisoned.[361]

Stanley had once written, in 1879, that he was exhausted from the four hours he spent haggling with chiefs at Vivi over a contract for land use. Stanley had known the Vivi leadership beforehand, and he apparently counted several of them as his friends, despite making threats to their livelihood. It was therefore fair to ask how Leopold's other negotiators farther to the east were now entering negotiations with the expectation that they could arrange "the transfer of sovereign rights to the Association" in a matter of a few hours.[362] Portuguese officials noted that eight treaties ceding sovereignty had supposedly been signed in different locations on the same date in April.[363] Of course, there was some truth to the idea that Leopold's negotiators tried to succeed by making palatable bargains; on one occasion, Strauch authorized an underling to spend "25,000 to 40,000 francs in merchandise" to secure political control over a wide area disputed by the French.[364] Certainly, such employees could still offer desirable commodities in high quantities, with one negotiator dispatched to the left bank of the Kwilu River being told to "take a couple bales made up of military coats, caps, shawls, large knives, some boxes of gin, looking glasses, etc. with you to purchase the concession."[365] The problem was that Leopold's negotiators paid for one set of rights—usually land, sometimes economic privileges—only to claim to have bought a much grander set thereafter, generally by means of a heavily altered copy of whatever original agreement had been made. In scale this practice may not have been unique: From the 1840s on, Algeria, for example, would witness extensive land transfers through outright confiscation and deception.[366] But the Congo saw differences in kind: The object was not just exaggerated claims to landholdings, but to absolute political control over people, that most valuable of resources.

The treaties, from late 1882 on, came in many different templates, perhaps the most common of which was one in which agents proposed to pay for "suzerainty." One Belgian spokesman boasted that Leopold obtained "more than five hundred treaties of suzerainty."[367] But even if genuinely transferred on payment, "suzerainty" was at the time a "general, vague, intangible claim" that could mean anything from the absolute political control and ownership of an area, to a merely titular presence with no practical effect: "sovereignty with the bottom knocked out," as one British observer put it when describing the Pretoria Convention, which Britain signed with the Transvaal Republic to end the First Anglo-Boer War.[368] In 1880, as Brazza closed deals with the *makoko*, he wrote in his journal that Iloo's influence was declining, reducing him from the position of absolute sovereign to that of suzerain.[369] Accordingly, if other Congolese potentates had agreed to sell "suzerainty" to the *Comité*—and that was the exchange many "treaties" purported to make after Leopold's Borneo epiphany—then they had sold something the dimensions of which might prove nonexistent or infinite.[370] Compounding it all, many of the treaties existed in duplicate translation—with one version in English using the word "suzerainty," and the other using the French word *"souveraineté"* (sovereignty)."[371]

It is difficult to reconstruct what suzerainty meant to Europeans in the early 1880s. Clearly it functioned as an equivalent to "sovereignty" for several translators who transcribed agreements; one whistleblower said its transfer, interpreted so broadly, "would simply have enslaved the whole" population.[372] Yet, in parts of Africa, the Ottoman Empire, and South Asia, the word "suzerainty" meant nothing beyond the ceremonial acknowledgement of friendly protectors or neighboring parties.[373] All this confusion suggested, to quote one British official, that the diplomatic community had "no means of judging . . . who or what the Association may become."[374] Still, such confusion was not accidental.[375] The Belgians' translations look especially misleading when measured against the conflict heating up between the Boers and the British after their Pretoria Convention in 1881, in plain view of many free agents Leopold was using to sign treaties in the Congo. No less a figure than Lord Derby confessed before the House of Lords in 1884, when asked about a treaty acknowledging British "suzerainty" over the Transvaal in 1881, that it was impossible to agree what the word meant.[376] British doubts allowed a high degree of flexibility for Leopold II—who not only made a habit of contortions in his complex web of self-promotion around Europe, but who was also still trying to decide exactly what form his ideal project in the Congo would take.[377] The doubts also made an impression on Stanley, who was complicit in perpetuating the suzerainty problem. While Stanley refused to employ the word in treaties circa 1881, by 1883 he counseled some indigenous leaders that it was better to sell suzerainty than to sell ownership of their land.[378] Hence, Stanley's eventual preference for the transfer of vague political rights—rather than merely tenancy—might easily be adduced as evidence that Stanley resolved to take more, not less, from African signatories.

Diaries written by some of Leopold's agents indicate that the "suzerainty" treaties they signed with Africans were negotiated mainly as an obligation.[379] For example, entries from 1883 show that "suzerainty" was seen as comprising armed protection, which Leopold's men covenanted to grant to indigenous leaders in exchange for the use of land for stations.[380] "Suzerainty" as ceded to the foreign agents would not give Leopold's association any control over the land itself; it would merely give it the title and duties of a protector. In secret, Edmond Hanssens, who worked in the Congo with Stanley on behalf of the association, admitted that this "protection" carried no further legal effect than obligating his men to wield guns against possible threats to a nearby chief; hence he still referred to Africans as the owners of the land. Likewise, a colleague of Hanssens—Liévin van de Velde—allegedly signed a treaty with several kings to buy control of territories near Palaballa, only to negotiate separately for the right to "trade freely" with those kings' still existing "states."[381] To further complicate this farce, Stanley later felt impelled to sign a second treaty with these kings in order to "explain the meaning and the spirit of the term" "suzerainty" in van de Velde's treaty—even though that term never appeared in the earlier document, which instead spoke of "sovereign rights."[382] At any rate, van de Velde's and Stanley's reckonings both suggest that, even in their differing views, the first treaty had still left indigenous chiefs with independent juridical authority sufficient to conclude treaties for the land in question.

A final problem with all the treaties now being signed by Leopold's men was that no impartial observer could verify their contents, however vague or illegitimately obtained. Early on, a treaty was conceptualized as a weapon to ward off threats from whites on the ground: "I have our contract with the Vivi chiefs safe . . . and am ready . . . for any one else who wishes to establish at Vivi."[383] But by mid-1883, Leopold was unwilling or unable to produce any of the original documents giving the *Comité* suzerainty, imparting to allegations about their clauses the taint of "rumor."[384] A French naval captain, having managed to intercept copies of three agreements on their way to Brussels, immediately forwarded his finds to Paris.[385] Generally, though, such moments proved few, and interlocutors in Europe, including the Belgian prime minister, had to settle for "very incomplete dossiers," with the originals supposedly under lock and key in Brussels.[386] This, too, was an echo of proceedings in Borneo, with the difference that Leopold developed a reputation for manipulating documents, and in many cases should be suspected of having committed outright forgery. For instance, consider a treaty supposedly signed by Augustus Sparhawk at Vivi, June 13, 1880. In early 1884 Leopold's representatives handed a copy of this document over to the U.S. Senate. Yet, Sparhawk's generally unedited, exhaustive personal diary makes no mention of such a treaty on June 13, 1880 or any of the surrounding dates, recording instead that other than "packing goods" and battling fever, he had "nothing particular to note" at this time.[387]

Trusting Leopold's "copies" was always problematic, even if one was able to look past the often questionable content on paper. Confidentially, a superintendent of the Vivi station even admitted to endorsing some copies as "true" without having had any witnesses present at the signing.[388] Portugal quickly distributed dossiers mocking the treaty copies Leopold had produced, and Jules Ferry, in Paris, expressed his own qualms.[389] It came as no surprise that, when Leopold approached the German chancellor Bismarck in 1883 to seek help against France, Bismarck dismissed his claims to political control in the Congo as a "swindle."[390] Skepticism abounded in Britain, too, where some Tories compared Leopold's expedition with Caribbean pirates from the seventeenth century.[391] Acute incidences of criticism even came from sources close to Brussels. Leopold's secretary and lawyer eventually confessed that Leopold was "very ignorant" when it came to "the science of international law," as well as "matters of geography." Leopold apparently had trouble keeping track of the differences between the pieces of his Congo network, when left "without instruction."[392]

All this and more found broad public confirmation in early 1883, when Eduard Pechuël-Loesche, a German geographer selected to fill in for Stanley while the latter was in Europe, grew disgruntled after not receiving supplies and nearly being killed by martial locals—people over whom Leopold's negotiators assured European officials they had peacefully purchased control in October 1882.[393] Pechuël-Loesche returned to Germany, where he promptly published several confidential documents from the comfort of a professor's chair in Jena.[394] Exposés appeared in, among other places, the magazine *Die Gartenlaube*, Germany's largest periodical by circulation.[395] Pechuël-Loesche showed readers orders from Leopold to conceal the true contents of the contracts indigenous chiefs were signing with the *Comité*. "The king knows," wrote Leopold's secretary, "that the natives in their current condition are not capable of comprehending his plan." For good measure, Pechuël-Loesche also published a damning letter outlining Leopold's attempt to market treaties in Borneo as being equivalent to those in the Congo—even though the legal and political circumstances in these two places were fundamentally different.[396]

Needless to say, such leaks did not please Leopold. The king soon impelled Stanley to return to the Congo and set to work anew.[397] By April 1883, shortly after France sent Brazza back to Africa with better funding, tremendous weaponry, and a new appointment as "commissar," Stanley began to dispense with his scruples, fashioning a treaty to buy "fullest powers" of jurisdiction over "non-domestic" matters at Kinshasa, for example.[398] Leopold, for his part, began a new stage in his international publicity campaign, intending to legitimize his enterprise in the European public eye by using the Borneo proceedings from early 1882 as his precedent. In July 1883, Leopold rolled out the first phase in this plan when he hired an eminent British bureaucrat as the "administrator" of the territory where the *Comité* had supposedly made treaties to govern.[399] The man chosen by Leopold was Major-General Sir Frederic Goldsmid, a veteran of the defunct East India Company who also had ties to Sir James Brooke and Borneo.[400] Leopold commissioned Goldsmid to travel to the Congo and personally inspect the villages signed over to Leopold's *Comité* by treaties.

In theory, Goldsmid was to verify that the treaties had been negotiated in the same reliable manner for which the EIC had been known, thus fostering good will in Europe.[401] Instead, his work bordered on farce.[402] Goldsmid, a sixty-five-year-old who rode a mule everywhere because his doctors discouraged walking, contracted a fever almost immediately on arriving in the Congo in September, forcing him to lay prostrate well into October.[403] By November, having traveled about one hundred kilometers into the *Comité*'s supposed territory and suffered a "complete breakdown of his health," Goldsmid felt compelled to return home and deputized his personal aide to make his inspections.[404] It is doubtful that even the aide visited all the areas in question, though he did demote one agent for depraved conduct at Boma.[405] Nonetheless, Leopold later published statements professing that Goldsmid *personally* made each visit—including to places much farther down the Congo River than Goldsmid ever saw.[406]

This was only the initial stage of Leopold's misinformation campaign.[407] Early in 1884, the Belgian king claimed that some of Goldsmid's British aides had concluded several dozen additional treaties in the Congo Basin.[408] Once again, many of these new treaties purported to be purchases of "suzerainty" by the *Comité,* while some spoke of "sovereignty."[409] Goldsmid, asked by British skeptics to address why agents working for a philanthropic organization were on a quest to sign dozens of such treaties handing over what looked like governing rights, now wrote to *The Times* with curious explanations for what was "perhaps the most interesting point" of his time in the Congo.[410] Yes, Goldsmid said, the *Comité* was acquiring governing rights by purchasing them from indigenous rulers. But these rights, he argued, had "only been acquired for the express purpose of never being enforced."[411] The *Comité* had no designs of its own, he protested in letters screened by Leopold; it was merely working against threats to freedom of trade.[412] Portugal and France were the villains.

Small wonder that more than a few critics continued to lambaste Leopold's group—which, in the wake of Goldsmid's departure, had added yet another name to its litany: the International Association of the Congo. "Mixing the International Association of the Congo with the African International Association and with the Expedition for the Study of the Upper Congo," complained one Portuguese journal, was causing "an inexplicable confusion" in the halls of European governments.[413] Alas, although Leopold edited many already dubious treaties prior to their publication, even the printed treaties contained numerous errors: for instance, the open use of the *Comité* as a buyer of sovereign rights, long after the *Comité* had ceased to exist. Then there was the embarrassment of stories told by employees that did not match with Leopold's account of events.[414] Grant Elliott, the head of one expedition, reported "the desertion of [his] interpreter a few days' journey from Issangila," leaving him with no other option than to pantomime in his subsequent negotiations with village authorities—some of whom, Leopold boasted to the United States and other nations, signed treaties with him.[415] Edward Delmar Morgan, the aide who supposedly verified a majority of some three hundred treaties signed during Goldsmid's tenure, provided another such example. Speaking to the Royal Anthropological Institute in London, Morgan confessed that at the very treaty signings he was supposed to be authenticating, he was told by a Belgian military officer "to remain a passive though interested spectator, the talking being" supposedly "all done by the Belgian officer" in an African language of which Morgan admitted not to understand one word.[416] Full awareness of this "palaver," as the Belgian officer called conferences with indigenes, was something Morgan, the supposed umpire, verifiably lacked. All Morgan knew for sure was that the Belgian officer left a flag from the "International Association" as a gift—just as Brazza had passed around French flags in Iloo's village three years earlier. It turned out that the flags of the International Association of Africa, the *Comité*, and countless other organizations were the same, and that Leopold's men only heightened the confusion by occasionally planting a Belgian flag, then denying that they had put it there.[417]

In Europe, Leopold continued to combine professions of philanthropy with less public promotions of a vast speculation.[418] True, Leopold's charitable claims were made more plausible by his frequent use of the name "International Association of the Congo," which harkened back to the International African Association convened at Brussels in 1876. "I will pierce the darkness of barbarism," he told an applauding Belgian senate.[419] Reached for comment around Christmas 1882, the Italian foreign minister even appeared to buy into the idea.[420] But could any amount of dissimulation help Leopold protect his trading concessions against threats from Portugal?[421] Or France? Or Britain? The Belgian army officers in Leopold's employ could torch helpless villages along the Congo, but they could neither ward off a man-of-war sent by Lisbon, nor attract other major investors, in the absence of their recognition by the West as a sovereign state.[422] Add to this that Leopold had laid out a reported eight million francs of his own money to keep operations running, with outlays and revenues often so embarrassingly mismatched as to remain unpublished for years to come.[423] The thinking around the royal palace at Laeken was that something needed to change in the Congo: Perhaps Leopold might fire half the European employees there, or, at minimum, reduce expenses by a two-thirds margin.[424]

Winning the open support of the Belgian government proper was, at this point, highly unlikely; that said, through at least November 1883, Leopold spent much time begging a reluctant Prime Minister Frère-Orban to placate his rivals.[425] Sometimes this approach worked, as when Auguste Couvreur, vice president of the Belgian house of representatives, made incognito visits to the French Foreign Ministry offering to broker a deal whereby Leopold would split his claims with France. Success, though, proved fleeting, with Jules Ferry in particular unwilling to sign any treaty with what he still dismissed as a private body.[426] Instead, in 1884 Leopold tried to improve his lot through yet another targeted publicity campaign, which involved the mobilization of the Borneo idea in scholarly, press, and diplomatic forums across the Western world.[427] An early success in this direction came when various chambers of commerce—notably those of London and New York, the one-time flirtation of Joseph Torrey—publicly endorsed the Congo venture.[428] Another coup came in President Chester Arthur's congressional address, in which Leopold's association, likened to a company with a chief executive officer, won much praise.[429] This push coincided with efforts by an even more commanding European leader seeking to capitalize on the Borneo precedent. That man, Bismarck, would almost single-handedly convince Europe to recognize Leopold's "Compagnie," as he called it, as the ruler of a "new" Congo state.

4

Bismarck's Borneo

As GERMANY'S CHANCELLOR, Otto von Bismarck never seemed to like the idea of overseas colonies.[1] In 1870 the French empress, Eugénie, eager to end her country's war with Prussia and its allies, was said to have proposed giving the new German Empire two billion francs and Cochinchina, a region comprising the southern portion of today's Vietnam. Bismarck shrugged his shoulders at the offer and insisted on Alsace-Lorraine.[2] Over the course of a decade Bismarck verifiably declined a host of other exotic proposals: Mozambique, Ecuador, Tunis, Curaçao, Formosa, and Morocco.[3] In 1878 he even overturned a semiofficial annexation of the Pacific island chain of New Britain (ironically later named the Bismarck Archipelago), where the German consul to Samoa and the commander of a visiting warship, *Ariadne,* had conspired to hoist the German flag.[4]

Nearly every refusal prompted questions about why the leader of Germany did not want colonies. It was possible to argue, as an assortment of predominantly moderate liberal intellectuals did from the 1840s on, that acquiring control over territories overseas might further Germany's ascendancy as a world trader by legally inscribing its sway over exports, transport, and raw materials in certain foreign markets.[5] No one could deny that the German share of worldwide trade and migration grew immensely from roughly mid-century; those trends had prompted Article 4 of the new Imperial German Constitution in 1871, which gave the imperial parliament the power to regulate possible "colonization of, and emigration to, lands outside Germany."[6] But public finance was another matter.[7] By the end of the 1870s Germany was suffering from a series of recessions later known as the Long Depression.[8]

As a result, cash proved a salient issue in the Reichstag, which was busy with empire-building "at home."[9] The parliament in Berlin, endowed with veto rights over budgets submitted by Bismarck, broadly refused to approve spending money for projects overseas.[10] This reluctance owed something to the peculiar federal structure of the German Empire, which, as distinct from its member states, could levy only indirect taxes.[11] Since most of that tax revenue was already tied up in military and social spending, even after the inauguration of higher tariffs by Bismarck in 1879, the hypothetical expense of running colonies looked certain to cripple the federal government with even larger budget deficits than those it was running. The government already had to rely on annual subsidies from member states, who promptly passed the costs along to their constituents in the forms of higher direct taxes on land or property.[12]

From this angle German "colonial policy," as one deputy scoffed, resembled "a luxury."[13] Such reluctance—typified by Ludwig Bamberger, leader of the Left-Liberals and one of the key opponents of all government-sponsored colonial activity—could further justify itself by reference to other European powers. Throughout much of the era Britain was supposed to have abandoned the notion of acquiring more colonies. Prior to 1877 even the majority of French officials—despite committing to expand their colonial presence in areas such as Senegal—still generally held little regard for the value of overseas territory.[14] If Alsace and Lorraine were two children lost by France in 1870, then colonies overseas, as the nationalist founder of the League of Patriots Paul Déroulède put it, were merely a bunch of house servants by comparison.[15]

As late as 1882, Italian diplomats discussing Brazza's fame lauded Germany for staying out of the emergent colonial race and focusing on informal commercial development abroad.[16] But this was not to say no one expected otherwise. As the 1870s drew to a close, and as Britain and France snapped up new colonial holdings in a kind of burst, a growing variety of agitators urged the government in Berlin to overlook any financial misgivings.[17] Overseas colonies might divert the flood of emigration from Germany into another "German"-controlled space, rather than to places like the United States.[18] They might also provide room to relocate some of Germany's burgeoning population—set to grow by three million between 1875 and 1885.[19] Domestic missionary and geographical societies, too, had cause to champion colonial expansion. Nonetheless, caution prevailed at the *Wilhelmstraße* through April 1880, when Bismarck supported a bill that would form a company to rescue some borderline-insolvent Hamburg merchants doing business on the far side of the world, in Samoa.[20] After Social Democrats and Left-Liberals in parliament combined to strike down this "Samoa Bill" by a slim margin, Bismarck opined that his homeland would never agree to administer colonies.[21] Bismarck's opponents, whom he likened to accountants, looked certain to vex any colonial efforts indefinitely, particularly with the parties loyal to the government losing seats in an election held in 1881.[22]

But Bismarck qualified his pessimism over the next two years, claiming that German businessmen, not their government, needed to take the lead in funding colonial development.[23] In June 1882, in a rather revealing conversation with Bismarck's top lieutenant, Friedrich von Holstein, Italian prime minister Francesco Crispi heard that Germany "had no need to colonize, *or rather, the time has not yet come* for establishing colonies."[24] Whether Bismarck had really begun to covet a colony as such was questionable.[25] But whatever one's opinion on the *why* of Bismarck's change in colonial outlook, the *how* of it all certainly had to do with developments abroad, in London. This particular contingency not only enabled him to undertake his mission; it also represented a kind of intellectual structure without which no such mission would have emerged in the first place.

In November 1881, the British government announced its chartering of the North Borneo Company. German newspapers quickly produced articles about Overbeck and Dent's adventures.[26] Not every detail was accurate, but a basic outline became available to members of the Reichstag around the same time.[27] Initially Overbeck had offered to sell his rights to Germany, among other powers. In 1880 he even encouraged rumors that the troubled Samoa bill and his own scheme were intertwined.[28] By late 1881, though, he had changed the equation by forming a British-backed governing company, whose genesis Bismarck followed in dispatches written by his underlings in Southeast Asia.[29] The German chancellor was, British sources noted, "becoming suspiciously interested in Borneo."[30]

Advisors close to Bismarck noted that the company Overbeck founded intended to run a "British" colony by itself, with the British government proper providing only minimal diplomatic support.[31] Whether such a model could work to facilitate German colonialism, too, had become a popular question by this time—not just in the works of economists like Wilhelm Hübbe-Schleiden, but also among grassroots advocates urging a purchase of Sabah as well as the Brooke holdings in Sarawak.[32] The makings of a strong reply popped up in Bismarck's office in November 1882, in the form of two long-winded letters from Adolf Lüderitz, a Bremen-based merchant. After an unsuccessful stint in Mexico, Lüderitz had bought a tobacco farm near the Niger Delta in Western Africa only to see the British annex this land to their Lagos colony and introduce what was, to him, an unfavorable tariff policy. Now Lüderitz told Bismarck he wanted to be free from any British interference. One path to that goal lay along the Southwest African coast. Britain did not claim sovereignty there, but it did seem likely to annex it at some point in the near future. Before that happened, Lüderitz wanted to pay indigenous authorities in the vicinity of the coast for a deed to a large portion of land.[33] Afterward, with this deed in hand as his private property, Lüderitz hoped to claim "the protection of the German flag" and turn his land into a German colony.[34]

What "protection" meant was unclear.[35] Like all Europeans, German citizens were typically entitled to guarantees for the safety of their private property when doing business abroad, though the extent of this service had been contested since at least 1849, when the National Assembly at Frankfurt meditated a vague law to protect emigrants.[36] Test cases usually appeared in places already on the diplomatic map—China, the Ottoman Empire, even Morocco.[37] The problem was that no one knew exactly how Germany would protect Lüderitz's rights if he intended to operate in an area more remote from the international state system.[38] This was an uncertainty felt by governments other than Germany's, but it looked all the more salient in Berlin after the recent founding of a lobby, the German Colonial Society, whose roughly eight thousand members called for their politicians to protect German business overseas.[39] Early in 1883, Bismarck asked for further details about Lüderitz's plan in relation to his request.[40] His timing was apropos, for it fell amid the backdrop of Bremen, Lüderitz's home base, negotiating to end its longstanding holdout from the German Customs Union.[41]

Lüderitz—in the first of what would be many lies—told his powerful interlocutor that the land he coveted was a fertile gateway to the African plains, where visitors could expect to see elephants, trees, and grass.[42]

Bismarck found himself intrigued, even though Germany's closest existing export market lay far to the north, in the Congo River Basin.[43] German imports from West Central Africa were steadily growing, with one firm, C. Woermann, having built several palm oil factories in the vicinity since 1868. German exports to the area were likewise increasing, especially liquor and rifles, with tonnage multiplying by a factor of ten between 1868 and 1883.[44] It was thus not outrageous to hope that southwest Africa either offered similar potential, or contained an undiscovered, felicitous path to the preexisting markets for Germans.[45] Nor was it unrealistic to think that support for German merchants in such a colonial sphere would appease some of the protectionist impulses that had been in the ascendant in Germany since at least 1879, when Bismarck famously shifted his policy away from free trade.[46]

In reality the southwest African coast seemed one of the least hospitable places on Earth to Europeans who visited.[47] The few settlers living there resided next to the rough waves of the Southern Atlantic, with inadequate vegetation and minimal access to drinking water. In order to survive, residents needed to rely on boats from the British-controlled Cape Colony to bring them regular shipments of fresh water and food. This delivery hardly posed a small task, when one considered where supply ships had to land. The German Navy later reported that the local coast, known as the "Skeleton," displayed numerous wrecks and visible bones—at least, once the morning fog cleared.[48] Here was a stretch of terrain so jagged that one nearby people, the San, called it the "land God made in anger." To make matters worse, the "Skeleton" had horrid weather. Daytime temperatures routinely reached 95 degrees Fahrenheit during the dry season, before turning bitter cold at night.[49] As for the air, it was, recalled one prospector, "a sort of semi-solid mixture of whirling sand, that cut and stung, and choked and blinded, and permeated every orifice and crevice, and generally made life utterly unbearable."[50]

Lüderitz knew that a setting like this would do little to win support from the public.[51] So Lüderitz told yet more lies, writing to Bismarck about troves of minerals he knew lay buried along the southwest African coast—even though neither he, nor any professional engineer, had yet been there. He avoided mentioning that according to the accounts of Portuguese sailors who had seen the coast, its cliffs posed a threat to every landing. Silence on this subject was appropriate, because as intimidating as the coast was for Europeans, it looked quaint when compared to the desert that adjoined it: an infertile, Mars-like terrain known as the Namib.

The Namib comprised the land north, south, and east of Lüderitz's projected colony. It was a place where hurricane-force winds swept over an endless series of sand dunes, which often ran as high as church towers and sometimes covered up cliffs hidden amid a forlorn expanse of orange-brown soil. Lüderitz claimed that his waterfront settlement, once launched, would attract German settlers seeking agrarian opportunity. But rain hardly ever fell, making agricultural plans seem like fantasies; besides, the shifting sands made tracking animals exceedingly difficult. Finally, whenever the dunes cleared enough to allow a glimpse of the soil beneath, the earth appeared so full of iron as to make the planting of crops appear an absurd exercise.[52]

Fortunately for Lüderitz, agriculture was not the only reason Bismarck might consider providing him help. There were other forces at work on the German chancellor, starting with some questions about foreign policy.[53] Would the establishment of a German colony in Africa lead France and Britain into more direct competition over an African partition, simultaneously distracting them from European affairs and perhaps even paving the way for an improbable Franco-German entente?[54] Alternatively, would a German foray into colonialism make Britain, Germany's likely colonial rival and an icon of the kind of parliamentary government Bismarck feared, deeply unpopular with a majority of the German electorate?[55] Further wrinkles existed domestically. It was not lost on Bismarck that the presumptive long-term threat to his power in Germany, the crown prince, had attached himself, by affect and marriage, to the British royal family. Nor could Bismarck overlook the frailty of reigning Emperor William, soon to enter a phase of acute illness and frequently holidaying on doctors' orders.[56]

Much could change should the crown prince accede to the throne in the midst of a heated Anglo-German conflict over colonies. While his wife, Crown Princess Victoria, privately believed England should determine the rules and race for Africa, German liberals mostly wanted German colonies, whether at England's expense or not.[57] Still, even as the future Frederick III turned out to embrace the national zest for colonies, Bismarck calculated that an Anglo-German rivalry might cost the prospective king some liberal allies in any battle over noncolonial domestic policy.[58] By then, mistrust toward England's colonial predominance and toward the crown princess—who happened to be Queen Victoria's eldest daughter—might have easily mixed with protectionist impulses to distract much of the electorate from agitation for social and political reform.[59] German subjects would focus on whether Britain was jealous of Germany or had helped bring cholera to the continent through poor management of its colonies—not on German structural inequalities that the government in Berlin abided, such as high unemployment.[60] And the crown prince would find it hard to remain on good terms with Britain and its prime minister, Gladstone.

Which factor predominated in Bismarck's mind is impossible to identify, but it is appropriate to build in a few caveats. First, while Bismarck did wish to drive a wedge between France and Britain via Africa, the French were hardly unaware of that notion when arranging their own plans, and Bismarck knew it.[61] Second, one must not overlook how domestic business and religious lobbies also figured quite heavily in Bismarck's deliberations.[62] A string of Hanseatic merchants had become involved in African trade from the late 1840s on.[63] By 1884 they had built sixty-seven factories on the western coast, and Hamburg alone accounted for roughly a third of all foreign trade in West Africa, with two-fifths of global German liquor exports also headed to this region.[64] That meant something, because 1882 and 1883 saw major slumps in an otherwise burgeoning economy. Meanwhile, starting in the 1840s, members of the Rhenish Missionary Association had traveled from Germany to the Namib Desert, hoping to convert local residents to Protestantism.[65] One such figure, Friedrich Fabri, eventually came to spend much of the 1870s unsuccessfully lobbying Bismarck to annex the desert and turn it into Germany's first overseas colony.[66]

Around 1882, Fabri mobilized yet again by assembling some other associates into a campaign to gain favor with Bismarck. Thanks to the German Colonial Society, the new pressure group founded by some of Germany's wealthiest industrialists, Fabri's effort came to the fore around the same time as Lüderitz's.[67] The society intended to push for bold colonial activity during the upcoming parliamentary elections, set to take place late in 1884.[68] The support of this lobby, combined with the favor of numerous Hanseatic states committed to overseas trade, would not just help Bismarck maintain his popularity; it would likely increase it, according to the British ambassador to Germany.[69] In turn, that fortified standing might win the deputies loyal to Bismarck's cause tens of thousands of votes, thus easing the path for all legislation championed by the chancellor. But the magical formula would work only if Bismarck succeeded in getting Germany some kind of overseas colonial claim exotic enough to excite the public.[70]

For several reasons, including the lobbyists, Bismarck began to involve himself with Lüderitz in March 1883.[71] Did Britain, Bismarck asked—or the semiautonomous Cape Colony whose foreign affairs it controlled—have any designs to annex the southwest African coast? And what was their current relationship to the area? For the next several months, as Bismarck awaited answers, he began to look more carefully into whom and what he was dealing with.[72] So far Lüderitz had talked only of plans to buy southwest African land from indigenous authorities. Eventually, he would claim to have bought his own kingdom, complete with sovereign rights and powers over life and death.

ADOLF LÜDERITZ was a wonderful character, if a loathsome person.[73] Photographs from 1882 show a mustachioed man of forty-eight years, wearing a white pith helmet and wire-rimmed glasses over heavy, drooping eyes.[74] By all accounts he talked quickly and often, impressing reporters with his "extraordinary energy" and claiming to have kept a youthful appearance by spending so much time in a tropical climate.[75] It was once said—by Lüderitz—that the only thing faster than his mouth was his pen.[76] Although he disposed over only a modest, inherited fortune, he was prone to megalomania and fancied himself the German Rhodes.[77] He also crowed that, with a small army behind him, he could "make it too hot for the Portuguese" in Mozambique.[78]

When Lüderitz first wrote to Bismarck in late 1882, he was running a factory in West Africa just outside Lagos, near the Niger River.[79] Officially, Lüderitz's firm dealt in growing tobacco for export to Europe, but that proposition had started to look dubious with Germany weighing a government monopoly on tobacco production.[80] For the time being, Lüderitz's real business profits derived from selling liquor and ammunition to warring peoples in the African interior.[81] While in his hometown of Bremen, in the months prior to contacting Bismarck, Lüderitz conferred with a twenty-year-old veteran of South African trading, Heinrich Vogelsang.[82] Lüderitz discussed a tip about a large stretch of desert much farther down the West African coast than his then choice of base near Lagos.[83] The desert was, he came to believe, perfectly beyond Britain's colonial sphere: Located just to the northwest of the British-run Cape Colony, it also lay neatly to the east of Walfisch Bay (today's Walvis Bay), a port the British had annexed in 1878 but only staffed with three people.[84] Lüderitz was interested enough to dispatch Vogelsang to Cape Town in January 1883 for further research on possible landing sites. At that point the latter spoke with Theophilus Hahn, a German missionary periodically working in the Namib Desert.[85] Hahn convinced Vogelsang to focus his efforts on a port called Angra Pequeña, located only about four to five days' sailing distance from Cape Town.[86]

Angra Pequeña, whose name was Portuguese for "little bay," started appearing on European maps shortly after 1488, when Bartolomeu Dias sailed along the southwest African coast on his way to the Cape.[87] Legends have it that Dias called the place "Angra dos Ilhoes," or the "bay of islands," as well as "Angra de São Cristóvão" after one of his ships, but early cartographers evidently preferred something else and made a substitution.[88] Either way, the beauty of late-nineteenth-century Angra Pequeña—as Hahn told Vogelsang—was that it had virtually no European or African settlers.[89] True, Dias had installed a monumental white marble cross *(padrão)* nearby in 1488, officially claiming the territory for King John II of Portugal. But, by the time of a visit by an American Confederate naval raider in 1863, the cross had decomposed as a result of wind and surf.[90] Consequently, a handful of German missionaries traveling from Angra Pequeña to the Namib Desert did not even notice the remaining cross fragments on their visit in late 1882, when the local population consisted of three British fishermen scraping penguin excrement off rocks.[91] The absence of any markings signaled that the area largely lay beyond even the prying of fellow Europeans.

Why there was such fuss about the lack of settlement in this place requires some explanation. Angra Pequeña sat at the end of the Namib Desert, where a sporadic civil war had been underway for three decades between two ethnic groups, the Nama and the Herero. Both groups wanted guns and ammunition to win their skirmishes, a new round of which had begun since 1880, after a Nama cattle-raiding expedition along a disputed border gave way to evening massacres in which Herero reprisals killed hundreds of sleeping Nama.[92] Here Lüderitz saw opportunity. From Angra Pequeña, he could mount expeditions to visit the Nama and sell them weapons, in exchange for mining rights in the desert they owned. The rights were likely to prove valuable, since the desert lay next to the kimberlite pipe in South Africa where, just a decade earlier, the great diamond rush had hit Kimberley and ushered in a new era of interest in southern Africa's mineral wealth.[93]

Looking at Angra Pequeña on a rudimentary map, Lüderitz grew increasingly convinced that no European power could levy import or export taxes on goods transported in the Namib.[94] The Cape Colony did not yet control the area, by Britain's admission, and indigenous authorities in the desert appeared quite willing to live alongside Europeans at the coast peacefully, according to missionary accounts.[95] These claims were more or less true, but they were also made by Germans who had scouted the area before Lüderitz—including Hahn, Friedrich Fabri, and agents of the Düsseldorf industrialist F. A. Hasenclever.[96] Fabri, in particular, had lobbied Bismarck as recently as 1880 to have Germany annex the territory, put an end to the legal vacuum, and pump money into mining ventures outside Angra Pequeña.[97] Lüderitz thus had rivals, even as late as 1884.[98]

None quite shared his ambition, however. As he saw it, if diamonds and copper really did lay buried in this desert, then he stood a good chance of exporting them out through Angra Pequeña at no cost, and making a fortune with which to start still more investments in southwest Africa.[99] Lüderitz just needed a little help from Bismarck first. So he wrote to the German chancellor, hoping to strike up a correspondence that would lead to protection for the rights he hoped to acquire. Next, he resolved to outfit an expedition to the Namib, to be led by Vogelsang.[100] One method to raise money for such a trip would have been to find investors in Germany. Alas, despite his inflated notions of self, Lüderitz barely knew anyone outside his hometown.[101] The few people who had heard of him in the German capital, Berlin, thought him a scoundrel, and skepticism abounded when he first hinted that he intended to turn Angra Pequeña into a "German" colony.[102] It was possible for Lüderitz to solicit the special interest groups lobbying for German colonies; they disposed over considerable funds. But Lüderitz was wary of these same groups, viewing them as potential threats. Not surprisingly, therefore, he used his personal savings. At the Cape, Vogelsang was to wait for the arrival of another ship sailing from Germany, which Lüderitz was clandestinely outfitting with stacks of gunpowder and rifles, along with a small crew.[103]

Shortly before Vogelsang's planned departure date, the missionary Hahn reported that ownership of Angra Pequeña and most of the Namib itself lay with a single figure named Josef Frederiks II, and that Frederiks was amenable to a sale.[104] It was not uncommon for Frederiks to levy transit fees on foreign visitors, and some Cape agents had bought mining permits in his territory in the 1870s, albeit with little success.[105] After several delays the ship ordered by Lüderitz at last arrived, full of contraband weapons whose export to southwest Africa was banned by the Cape authorities. Vogelsang and the crew, with the aid of some forged documents, sailed for Angra Pequeña on April 4, 1883. On April 9 they anchored in the bay of Angra Pequeña, not far from the wreck of a Portuguese treasure ship that sank with loads of gold aboard in the sixteenth century.[106] Once on shore, they encountered a few British fishermen. This unassuming pair spoke only English, but Vogelsang, the German, had English speakers among his crew, so the men welcomed Vogelsang and eventually put him in touch with an indigenous messenger.[107] Vogelsang dispatched the messenger with the duty of delivering a note to a German missionary living in the interior. That missionary was to set up a meeting for Vogelsang at the town of Bethanie, the home to roughly nine hundred members of a Nama clan.[108]

Bethanie was located about 124 miles away from Angra Pequeña, just past the edge of the desert.[109] As its name attested, missionaries passing through the Namib in 1814 had originally founded Bethanie as a station.[110] By the early 1880s, many of these missionaries had been scared off by the civil war's most recent outbreak, leaving Bethanie best known as the place where Josef Frederiks II, supposed "king" of the Namib, lived and presided.[111] Vogelsang was so eager to reach this place that he split his group into two factions shortly after coming onshore and dispatching his messenger. One faction remained at the coast to erect prefabricated houses made in Germany.[112] The other faction, including Vogelsang, set off into the desert with the goal of finding Frederiks.[113] Shortly into the journey, the group led by Vogelsang again stood on the precipice of disaster, their canteens having run out and their journey sputtering due to near-fatal falls in the shifting sand dunes. Fortunately, they soon ran into a welcoming committee sent by Frederiks to escort them.[114] The committee led the group for two more days to Bethanie, where the groundwork had been prepared for a meeting in a modest wooden house built by German missionaries.[115]

Frederiks was a reputed inebriate who wore the clothes of a European and spoke in sentences littered with Dutch words; his most common appellation, in the Dutch fashion, was "Captain."[116] As these facts attested, Frederiks and many of the leading figures at Bethanie were not simply Nama, but rather Orlams: a set of relative newcomers to the Nama group who had arrived in commando units after fleeing from the Cape Colony to avoid conscription, enslavement, and loss of livestock in the early nineteenth century.[117] Before escaping oppression at the Cape, the original Orlams settling at Bethanie had learned Dutch and marksmanship.[118] As it turned out, though, the Orlams had gotten still more from their former Cape masters, for those who encountered them at Bethanie noted "a considerable infiltration of white blood," as well as a religious and military culture that looked quite familiar to a European like Vogelsang.[119] Since the first settlement at Bethanie under Frederiks's father, Josef Frederiks I, the Orlams had effectively become an outpost of the Dutch Reformed Church. They were literate and had some written records, unlike many other Sub-Saharan peoples. They also implemented what one might call a system of private property, complete with contracts, deeds, and archived documents.[120] By 1883, these innovations and the ongoing civil war had produced seismic shifts beyond Bethanie and throughout the Nama territory.[121] Trade with the Cape expanded dramatically, with elephant ivory, ostrich feathers, and especially cattle being exported in return for ever-larger quantities of guns, horses, coffee, sugar, and brandy.[122] Social changes took hold, too: greater militarization and use of Western technology such as rifles and ox wagons; a move away from pastoralism and toward increased reliance on credit from Cape traders; more permissiveness for the work of Christian missionaries; and the spread of a hierarchical tribal structure in which Orlams with connections to the Cape came to dominate the old Nama as a kind of colonizing authority.[123] It is not a stretch to say that by the time of Vogelsang's arrival, with the Orlams having effectively remade Nama life to their own specifications, Bethanie had become one of the most Europeanized places in Sub-Saharan Africa. To illustrate this point, the French Foreign Ministry referred to Frederiks as the area's "legitimate sovereign."[124]

German was not a language Frederiks could speak, so he could not converse directly with Vogelsang. It took little time, however, for the latter, with the aid of a translator, to declare in Dutch that he wanted to buy Angra Pequeña and all the land within five miles of it, in every direction. To sell this land was hardly an outlandish idea. Frederiks acknowledged that his ancestor had bought the land in question from Tsaomab, an indigenous Nama chief of the "Red Folk," roughly a hundred years earlier.[125] More recently, starting in 1870, Frederiks's predecessor had made other sales: first, a large plot of land to a group of mixed-race exiles from the Cape (Basters); and second, a series of licenses allowing Europeans to conduct everything from game-hunting to mining in Nama-Orlam territory.[126] The territory was spread out enough that Frederiks never even went to Angra Pequeña, which was, so ran Cape intelligence reports, "a long way from everywhere" and not remotely close to Bethanie, the center of his power.[127]

Frederiks had both means and motive. The guns Vogelsang proffered could help the Nama in their war against the Herero; and the money Vogelsang promised to include could prove a godsend in the area around Bethanie, where tireless workers were starving on account of a downturn in the cattle-based economy.[128] Frederiks and approximately forty elders at Bethanie eventually assembled in a sort of parliament to consider Vogelsang's offer. As the men debated by making what struck Vogelsang as incessant "click" sounds, Frederiks told the translator he would need a few hours for some more contemplation.[129] Vogelsang agreed, leaving his hosts with some presents: a shiny European rifle, horse saddles, blankets, and lead-soldier toys.[130] Vogelsang closed by telling the assembly—still at war with the Herero people to the north—that his home country, Germany, was a great military power. Germany, Vogelsang implied, might be able to offer assistance, but only if Frederiks let him acquire Angra Pequeña "on behalf" of Germany.

On May 1, 1883, Josef Frederiks signed a "sales contract" with the "Company F. A. E. Lüderitz of Bremen in Germany."[131] The beneficiary of this contract was Lüderitz, to whom Frederiks sold Angra Pequeña and all the land within a five-mile radius in exchange for two hundred loaded rifles and gold valued at £100. Lüderitz, a German subject, now had the deed to a big parcel of land in a strange place. But within twelve days, as Vogelsang began flying the Imperial German flag off the coast, another question had emerged. This was whether Lüderitz had acquired not only land, but also political rights.

No one in Germany saw the details of the contract with Frederiks in the months following the sale, but on August 8, 1883, after some preliminary meetings with Heinrich von Kusserow, a then-unremarkable foreign ministry official, Lüderitz arrived at the *Wilhelmstraße* and asserted that he had bought something more than land off Frederiks: specifically, the rights to tax; to control customs; to adjudicate disputes; to keep a military; and to dispose over all land and water.[132] To the amazement of many seasoned diplomats, Lüderitz now claimed the status of a king and began to style himself as such, arguing that his sovereign rights endowed him with fabulous wealth and control that trumped whatever land or permits rival traders might claim around Angra Pequeña.[133] In a second twist, Lüderitz also announced that Vogelsang was serving as his viceroy, even taking measures to erect customs frontiers and ceremonially levy duties.[134] He was rechristening Angra Pequeña as "Lüderitzland."[135] And soon he would introduce a tax on water use at select locations.[136]

Of course, Lüderitz was lying when he told the officials in Berlin about his "rights." The contract with Frederiks made no reference to political control of any kind, and Lüderitz had bought only a title to land, albeit a large parcel. However grandiose his manner, Lüderitz was still a man who did not even have enough muscle to ward off thieves from his cotton stores outside Lagos.[137] Nonetheless, Vogelsang wrote back to Lüderitz from his new "capital city," a set of buildings on the coast modestly named Fort Vogelsang, to confirm that he was attempting to govern the five-square mile territory as Lüderitz had requested.[138] In the meantime Lüderitz began yet another campaign of deception. In July, he planted newspaper reports at Cape Town that "the Germans"—implying the German government—"had bought and occupied Angra Pequeña and some miles of inland territory."[139] British traders prospecting for copper in the Namib quickly went into a panic, fearing confiscation of their rights by the new German regime. The traders considered settling with Lüderitz, who, according to the Nama, was some sort of agent working on behalf of Germany. But then the dust started to settle, and the traders saw that Lüderitz was acting alone, without the official backing of Germany. The traders took reprisals, even sneaking into Fort Vogelsang at night to hoist the British flag above some buildings.[140]

Before long the British Foreign Office became involved and decided to look more closely into the matter of whether Lüderitz or the German state proper had bought rights. Although Whitehall had not yet begun seriously to weigh the option of seizing Lüderitzland, it had to take into account the Cape Colony's concerns about the possibility of a connection between Lüderitz and various Boer parties hundreds of miles to the east of Lüderitz's claims.[141] Commissioners in the Transvaal speculated that the ammunition already imported to Lüderitzland could sustain such a combination.[142] In 1883 and 1884 the world also learned about the founding of Stellaland, which lay in the mineral-rich territory of Bechuanaland, or just to the north of the Cape Colony, to the far east of Angra Pequeña, and to the west of the independent Boer republic in the Transvaal.[143] At first glance, Stellaland was just another instance of filibustering: Some Boer mercenaries had provided local leaders in Bechuanaland with services in a civil war; in exchange, the leaders had "granted" the mercenaries land and rights with which to found their own republic. But there was more to this picture than met the eye.[144] Authorities at the Cape had reason to believe that those running Stellaland intended to link up with the Transvaal.[145] Rumor also had it that Lüderitz and the Germans were intent on forging close ties with the Boer states, and thence with Stellaland.[146] Lüderitz had already met with Bismarck to discuss the possible founding of a German colony in Boer country, just to the north of the Cape Colony.[147] At least one German consul hoped to secure Boer financing for such an operation.[148]

Whitehall was only a little paranoid to fear that "unless steps were taken at once, the whole of Bechuanaland might be permanently lost," especially because "German territory on the west might readily be extended to join with that of the Boers" in the Transvaal.[149] Bechuanaland was thought to contain vital deposits of diamonds and gold—commodities that were pivotal to the financial well-being of the Cape and, in the case of gold, to the British Empire's preeminence in international finance. In any event, by the end of the summer of 1883 officials in the British Foreign Office moved to act on complaints about Lüderitz's machinations at Angra Pequeña.[150] Evidence enclosed within these complaints suggested that, in 1863, "King" Frederiks's predecessor had sold British traders mining permits along the coast near Angra Pequeña—in territory that currently overlapped partially with "Lüderitzland."[151] All this had happened well before anyone in Frederiks's orbit ever met a German.[152] But it had also happened under another Orlam regime, and it was an open question whether regime change in the interim meant an end to earlier contracts. Lüderitz, for his part, quickly got Frederiks—whom he called by his first name, Josef—to deny the legitimacy of contracts issued under the aegis of his predecessor.[153] Lüderitz also tried a second approach, dismissing British traders' claims on the grounds that as the new ruler of the territory, he could revoke old grants "at any time."[154]

Britain's first intervention against Lüderitz was to challenge the German merchant's claim that Frederiks had sold him political rights. In a complaint lodged with the German ambassador, the Foreign Ministry said Lüderitz was only a common man, and as such ineligible to possess sovereign rights. Second, they said that even if Lüderitz did own sovereign rights, he could not override the preexisting contracts of British traders.[155] To follow up on the counterarguments made against Lüderitz, the British navy authorized one of its corvettes to sail for the coast near Angra Pequeña and await further instructions.[156] German newspapers immediately picked up the escalation.[157]

Britain was raising the stakes, with its most trenchant charge being the illegitimacy of Lüderitz's own contract with Frederiks, which was not as he had advertised. Some Europeans did believe that rifles and a wad of cash were all it took for Lüderitz to buy a chunk of Frederiks's kingdom; the rifles, it turned out, were sold at a cut rate amid a war, as well as a severe shortage of weapons thanks to the Cape embargo.[158] Investigations would also reveal that Frederiks's Nama translator understood written Dutch—the language in which the treaty had been signed. That said, the Nama translator likely did not speak enough German or Dutch to converse with Vogelsang and the Germans on particulars, and so had to rely on translations made by a German missionary loyal to Vogelsang.[159] This second translator, according to reports, also speculated in mining ventures when he was not writing dissertations on the Nama language.[160]

Though the British knew that Lüderitz's contract with Frederiks was weak, they could do little about it legally. They could talk at length about how Lüderitz was a man of ill repute who simply wanted to use Angra Pequeña as a smuggling foothold or a giant mining site.[161] But this talk would be in vain unless the British could convince Bismarck to refrain from supporting Lüderitz. The chancellor had so far conceded nothing, summoning Lüderitz to Berlin to review the matter in person on several occasions—with a telling acceleration from early 1883, when Bismarck began to demand reparations for German merchants expropriated during the British annexation of Fiji.[162] In his interviews Lüderitz behaved as usual, mixing lies with braggadocio, pleas for protection, and demands for Bismarck to fight the British. He was not, one advisor complained pithily, low maintenance.[163] Bismarck soon turned to discuss Lüderitz with the British ambassador, who hinted that Britain would view a German annexation of Angra Pequeña as a violation of Britain's regional supremacy in southern Africa. The ambassador reminded Bismarck that many British subjects had already signed contracts buying land from the Nama with the hope of finding diamonds in the desert. In a further twist, these merchants were urging that Britain's Cape Colony annex the Namib and Angra Pequeña.

Germany, the ambassador explained, need not worry about any such annexation by the Cape or Britain. The Cape government sat on the brink of insolvency, and most of its citizens knew nothing about Angra Pequeña.[164] But Britain was not going to recognize Lüderitz's rights, either. That balance placed Bismarck in an unenviable spot, and the stakes grew still higher on August 25, 1883, when Lüderitz told Bismarck he had expanded his polity with a second purchase contract.[165] According to this second document, again forged from negotiations with Frederiks, the Nama king was to receive an additional £500 in gold, as well as sixty of the rifles that had lately become popular among Boers fighting the British.[166] In exchange for this return, Frederiks agreed to transfer to Lüderitz a parcel of land far larger than he had earlier given up along Angra Pequeña: one that amounted to almost the entire Namib Desert. Starting with the Atlantic coast at 26 degrees latitude south, this additional zone stretched down 200 miles to the Orange River, and inward at all points to the extent of 91 miles, comprising an overall area of around 10,400 square miles.[167]

Leicester Smyth, governor of the Cape Colony, challenged Lüderitz to defend his new contract; in particular, he asked why Frederiks had agreed to a second sale, consisting as it did of a giant area roughly the size of Massachusetts.[168] No doubt Frederiks wanted more guns from Lüderitz, and more cash with which to pay off the Boer traders supplying his Nama in their war against the Herero. But these justifications did not suffice, for Frederiks was giving up most of the land worth defending against his enemies. One of Lüderitz's own agents soon suspected that Frederiks had never had any idea how large a parcel he was giving up.[169] The explanation for the discrepancy lay in trickery by Lüderitz's negotiator, Vogelsang. On instructions from Lüderitz,

Vogelsang negotiated with Frederiks to buy land measured in "miles."[170] To illustrate this proposal, Lüderitz eventually took out a compass and a map, on which he proceeded to sketch the sale area in pencil for Frederiks.[171] However, in another step that followed Lüderitz's instructions, Vogelsang deliberately had Frederiks sign a contract mentioning the more expansive geographical (German) miles, rather than the modest, nautical miles that Vogelsang had drawn, and to which Frederiks had been accustomed on account of his ancestors' experiences at the Cape.[172] This discrepancy caused Frederiks to sign over somewhere between four and five times as much territory as he expected; according to one estimate, it cost him more than half of his entire realm.[173] It also placed a reliable water supply—the only one in the vicinity—under the control of Lüderitz, rather than Frederiks.[174]

Displaying no scruples about his treatment of Frederiks, Lüderitz proceeded to regale Bismarck and the German public about his coup in September 1883.[175] In law, the best way to establish Lüderitz's supremacy—"my sovereignty," as he eventually put it—was to get it recognized by Western states such as Britain.[176] To that end, only two paths seemed possible for Bismarck, who never quite bothered to spell Angra Pequeña's name correctly.[177] First, and least likely, Lüderitz could take real control of Angra Pequeña and its surroundings, establishing his rule through force and successfully acting as a government long enough for world powers to take notice.[178] Second, Germany could annex the area he had bought. This latter path meant doing the very thing Bismarck loathed—committing to a colony whose governance Bismarck could never convince his recalcitrant opponents in parliament to fund.[179] In yet another complication, any attempt by Lüderitz to rule alone might prove illegitimate, according to opinions Bismarck had just commissioned from the lawyers at the German Foreign Ministry. These lawyers argued that sovereign rights could never rest with a German subject—even if such a man purchased his rights from a foreign ruler. Instead, Germany had essentially annexed Lüderitzland via Lüderitz, becoming a colonial power in a manner embodying John Robert Seeley's famous phrase, published that same year about the British Empire: "a fit of absence of mind."[180]

For Bismarck, the status quo was precisely the thing to avoid. Colonies, as the future Social Democrat Max Quarck correctly put it, were becoming "the lioness among the questions of the day."[181] Many in the procolonial lobby wanted—if not expected—Bismarck to travel down the path of direct, immediate annexation.[182] Moderate liberals generally felt similarly. Bismarck gauged their appetite in a clandestine press campaign in 1883, all of which confirmed a latent enthusiasm for colonies.[183] It was thus probable that a sizeable contingent would not forgive Bismarck should Britain annex Angra Pequeña before Germany.[184] To sum up, Bismarck could not afford to annex Lüderitzland; nor could he afford to let Lüderitzland go.[185] British officials could empathize, having had to appease pro- and anti-imperial lobbies around the Borneo question circa 1881.[186]

That the German chancellor needed his own solution was being made quite clear in other parts of West Africa. These included the harbor of Little Popo (Aného), one of a number of locations at which Hamburg firms were cashing in on the trade in palm oil.[187] Owing to an explosion in European popular demand for cleaning products, vegetable oils—and especially those extracted from the fruit of a palm tree indigenous to West Africa, *Elaeis guineensis*—had become a precious commodity with which to mix animal fats and produce soap.[188] So vital to this process was palm oil that the Hamburg firms were continually competing with French and British traders in a quest to monopolize access to the middlemen who supplied it.[189] The Germans, having experienced setbacks in their deals with indigenous middlemen beginning in late 1883—a sting felt all the more given a worldwide slump in prices—were seeking a more regular presence of German warships to protect their interests and give them an edge in trade negotiations.[190] In February 1884, the German cruiser *Sophie* visited Little Popo, took hostages, and forced concessions to local German traders. Then, in March 1884, indigenous chiefs allegedly sent Kaiser Wilhelm I a letter seeking German "protection" against incursions by the British, rumored to be meditating annexation of the area in order to secure themselves a monopoly on the palm oil supply.[191] Lüderitz, when seen in this context, represented one piece of a larger puzzle.

In April 1884, when Bismarck found his solution for the colonial dilemma, it all hinged on a provocative proposal: Lüderitz, or any German, could very well buy and run an empire by himself. The British Foreign Office opined that "the exercise of sovereign rights by private individuals would be anomalous."[192] But they made no prohibition against it. On the contrary: British officials had supported such a scheme in northern Borneo in 1881 and 1882. German officials were rediscovering this history thanks to a correspondence undertaken with Spain on navigation around Sabah in February 1884.[193]

From the moment the most famous author of the Borneo scheme—Overbeck, a German—started putting the finishing touches on a company that would run its own state, the German colonial lobby had also begun to catch what one columnist called "Borneo Fever."[194] Flattering portrayals appeared in magazines and newspapers, with some writers musing about the possibility of a "New Berlin and New Breslau on the island of Borneo," while others touted the agricultural prospects.[195] Karl von Scherzer, a noted explorer and Austrian consul in Leipzig, suggested Germany purchase the Borneo Company's territory.[196] So, too, did the head of the German Imperial Navy, Albrecht von Stosch. Finally, Berlin's ambassador in Washington D.C. vouched for Overbeck.[197]

By late 1881 all that was past. As was made clear in a leaked report to the *Kölnische Zeitung* in August 1881—two months before Bismarck suffered a major election setback, lacking support from the colonial lobby—Germany declined Overbeck's repeated sale offers, the first of which had come in 1875.[198] In the main, though, the Borneo company's effect on domestic colonial lobbyists was to be one of inspiration: The dream that Germans, having missed out on Borneo once, might replicate it in a new, African land.[199] This circumstance held through 1883, when lobbyists published several articles on the subject. Wilhelm Hübbe-Schleiden openly encouraged the German government to issue a charter to a governing company formed by Germans doing business in Africa. According to this plan, individual Germans might lawfully pay indigenous authorities for territorial rights, and in so doing bring the German nation their colonies without parliamentary support or oversight.[200] Ernst von der Brüggen, another propagandist, followed by arguing that the colonization of an overseas territory through a German company would represent a triumph of immense national benefit.[201]

Neither recommendation was lost at the German Foreign Ministry. Hübbe-Schleiden discussed the idea in early 1884 with Heinrich von Kusserow, the diplomat in charge of reviewing the many colonial proposals that had been pouring in since the 1870s.[202] Prior to this Kusserow was a man whom colleagues in the civil service dismissed as a bungler. His repeated requests for a better posting had been denied, despite his averaging fourteen-hour workdays.[203] He had also botched the translation of a key Anglo-French treaty in early 1883.[204] Still, in April 1884, having just finalized a renewal of the League of the Three Emperors and needing a primer on colonial issues, Bismarck looked to Kusserow.[205] The latter held views very similar to those of his brother-in-law, the influential banker Adolph von Hansemann.[206] In the late 1870s Hansemann had tried to convince Bismarck to buy up the Borneo rights. A few years after this effort failed, Kusserow announced "a personal conviction" in favor of Hansemann's proposal, which was then being revived thanks to repeated sales pitches by "King" Overbeck.[207] (Overbeck, often via the German embassy in China, had made himself known to Bismarck.[208] When he was not busy trying to woo the Austrians instead, that is.[209])

Kusserow and Hansemann never lost the scent of the Borneo story or its intrigues, which came to involve multiple agencies of German bureaucracy. The diplomatic service played its part, including Viktor von Bojanowski, an eventual coworker on the case of Lüderitzland.[210] So did the navy, aware that Overbeck's territory contained two harbors large enough to house the entire imperial fleet—and that the one colonial venture Bismarck had successfully implemented so far had been the acquisition of a naval coaling station in Samoa.[211] In April 1879, Kusserow dined with a Japanese diplomat who encouraged his superiors to enter into sales talks with Overbeck.[212] Through May 1880, Hansemann attended presentations with financiers in Berlin regarding German colonization in Borneo.[213] One year later, the Prussian Economic Council recommended setting aside ten million marks per annum for the purchase of overseas colonies.[214] Finally, in 1882, Hansemann compiled a dossier on the subject for review by colonial propagandists.[215] Kusserow, already a supporter of the Borneo project, was briefed again in February 1884, when the Spanish asked Germany for support in the South China Sea against the pretensions of the British on North Borneo, in exchange for a naval base on the West African island of Fernando Po.[216] Count Montgelas, Overbeck's sometime business partner and the new secretary of the British North Borneo Company, lobbied for support in Hamburg.[217] March 1884 brought further review when a German navy corvette wrecked off northeastern Borneo and undertook furtive repairs onshore.[218]

With the idea thus at the ready, all that remained was the right governmental opening. By 1883 Kusserow was becoming close personal friends with Adolf Lüderitz. It was only after meeting with Kusserow early in 1883 that Lüderitz decided, mysteriously, to misrepresent his land purchase over Angra Pequeña as a purchase of a title to territorial sovereignty. Such a misrepresentation ensured that just as Borneo was fading as a formal colonial destination for Germany, it was making a comeback in Africa. In April 1884, Kusserow took the idea of replicating "the Borneo model" to Bismarck.[219] Kusserow argued that its initial reviews were encouraging—especially when one considered how it was winning praise from domestic lobbyists.[220] Kusserow suggested to Bismarck that Lüderitz should form a similar company to buy the rights the latter had (according to misrepresentation) acquired around Angra Pequeña. The new company would inherit the duty of governing "Lüderitzland."

This particular conjuncture was maturing in the background of the shifting stance of Otto von Bismarck toward colonial affairs. Risk on the part of private businessmen, a focus on coastal sites, and a limited official German role comprised the elements that had convinced Bismarck to support the Samoa bill in 1880. But whereas Samoa had only involved a rescue package for merchants who held land rights, the rescue for Lüderitz would entail sovereign rights themselves.[221] Hence the chancellor came to believe in Kusserow's presentation, or at least claimed to do so: "Without your initiative," one of Bismarck's aides soon wrote Kusserow, "the boss will not be able to execute his current colonial agenda."[222] Now Bismarck accepted that Germany could, "according to an analogy" with Borneo, also give Lüderitz's company a royal charter.[223] The charter put the force of German law behind Lüderitz: That is, it "sanctioned the transfer of the territory in question to him." At the same time, a charter avoided German annexation while ensuring that Lüderitz's rights would be "protected," not only from legal challenges by any British merchants hovering around Angra Pequeña, but "from the possibility of annexation" by the British government.

Nor was this the end of the long list of benefits Bismarck would see. The ostensible merit of a royal charter was that it would incur for the German government "no more significant duties and costs" than would be involved in protecting a German citizen's property when abroad; for instance, through the establishment of consulates in the country.[224] Germany would not even be obligated to protect the territory in question in the event of a war.[225] There was a hidden political benefit, too. Opposition groups in the Reichstag would find it difficult not to fund "protection," amounting as it did (in theory) to what would be provided in any significant foreign city for a German entrepreneur.[226] If opposition groups declined or attenuated their support, they would appear insufficiently patriotic to the many voters who were, thanks to a press frenzy, enthusiastic about the colonial idea at the best possible time for Bismarck: election season and, still more immediately, the moment for parliamentary debates on the renewal of the antisocialist laws.[227]

Bismarck seemed to get everything he wanted under Kusserow's scenario; it even fulfilled some conditions he had long ago proposed for a hypothetical "ideal colony" when the subject came up in negotiations over the Franco-Prussian armistice.[228] Thanks to Kusserow's ingenuity, Bismarck would figure as the hero in a popular movement that could, through clever marketing, look like a "German spring." The lobbyists who once derided his caution would now hail him as their "pilot . . . steering with an iron hand."[229] Opposition groups in the Reichstag, by contrast, must either fall into line or pay the price, at best looking like reluctant followers, and at worst appearing to be an insufficiently patriotic "Loki" determined to subvert the Norse gods of German nationalism.[230] The day-to-day logistics of colonial government were a secondary concern. Bismarck intended to leave the details of governing to Kusserow, whom he proceeded to rely on so heavily that some plans for "colonial matters" emanated from Kusserow's hand without Bismarck's inspection—even instructions for raising the German flag overseas.[231] Bismarck hoped vaguely that Lüderitz would govern an "independent" Lüderitzland where Lüderitz, not the Reich, occupied the position of a sovereign state in international and domestic law. "Lüderitz I, Duke of Angra Pequeña," would need to become the recognized master of southwest Africa.[232] This technicality in turn might lessen trouble for Germany when it came to colonial rivals from France or Britain. But there was also no denying that Lüderitz's colony was "German," for Lüderitz was a German citizen, and Lüderitz's charter suggested that he governed by virtue of Bismarck's permission.[233] That was the key.

"We do not want to install colonies artificially," Bismarck soon said. "When they emerge, however, we will try to protect them."[234] The chancellor took the unusual step of inviting Lüderitz back to Berlin on April 19, 1884. Lüderitz was told to take a few days to produce a small memorandum detailing the plan for his own government—effectively a personalized constitution.[235] The Bremen merchant promptly complied, outlining a state that would do virtually everything a normal state did, albeit while reporting to an Imperial German consul stationed at Angra Pequeña—who, at Lüderitz's suggestion, turned out to be none other than his deputy, Heinrich Vogelsang.[236] On April 24, Bismarck announced to the British that Lüderitz's "acquisitions" were henceforth "entitled to German protection." By this time, however, Bismarck had diverted some of his attention away from Lüderitz and toward a group of more important German businessmen active overseas.

Just days before he gave Lüderitz his guarantee, Bismarck read over another memorandum proposing a new course for colonial questions generally.[237] In a highly significant escalation, the memorandum suggested that Germany not stop with assisting Lüderitz, but also help several German firms acquire the rights to govern diverse portions of Africa and the Pacific. All this activity would have been impossible as recently as 1880. Now, though, the memorandum Bismarck was reading claimed to know a way to get Germany an overseas empire at virtually no cost. The difference was summed up in a few words: Borneo and chartered company governments.

The particular companies envisioned in the memorandum did not yet exist, but, in a sense, they already had much stronger foundations than anything Lüderitz could muster in the Namib. It started with Kusserow's relative, Hansemann. In March 1883, for instance, Hansemann asked associates in Antwerp whether the Borneo idea might rescue certain factories he was building in the South Pacific, on the island of New Guinea.[238] New Guinea looked enticing from a business standpoint; politically, however, it was in a state of anarchy, with the British even overruling an Australian annexation attempt in 1883. Hansemann did not want to worry about running his business overseas in the absence of European-style laws. By the end of 1883, however, Bismarck had yet to sign off on an official colonization plan in the area. Investor confidence in the Far East had recently been undermined by the Marquis de Rays, a Frenchman put on trial in November 1883 for lies to Italians about easy riches in his fictitious kingdom on New Guinea.[239]

In April 1884, with Hansemann sensing an opportunity to capitalize on Lüderitz's success, Kusserow stepped in to offer Borneo as the solution to New Guinea, where Bismarck could "protect" Hansemann's governing company in the form of a formal charter and occasional military visits by men-of-war.[240] While Hansemann rechartered his own company to take on state functions in New Guinea—a process he would initiate in May 1884—Bismarck consented to test the charter system in other areas of Africa.[241] The German chancellor's decision resonated most forcefully in the case of Douala, a coastal site in Western Africa that sits in today's state of Cameroon.

Douala was the home to several palm oil factories owned by thirty-seven-year-old Adolph Woermann, then arguably the best-known of Hamburg's so-called merchant princes.[242] One cannot say definitively whether Woermann really made more money through importing palm oil to Germany or, as rumor had it, by exporting alcoholic beverages to Africa.[243] What is certain is that Woermann had designs on dominating trade routes to West Africa, and that his regional interests, like those of Hamburg schnapps manufacturers generally, had become synonymous with those of Germany in certain circles.[244] In 1884 Woermann became president of the Hamburg Chamber of Commerce and a delegate to the Reichstag, having already won a board seat at a string of elite firms: Hansemann's Disconto-Gesellschaft, Alfred Nobel's Dynamit AG, and, most relevantly, the HAPAG line.[245] Around the time of Lüderitz's travails in March 1883, Woermann wrote a memorandum asking Bismarck to turn the areas around Douala into an official German colony.[246] Bismarck refused at first, for familiar reasons. But then along came the notion of a colony modeled on Borneo.[247]

Woermann, Kusserow concluded, might arrange to buy a title to govern the area housing his seven factories.[248] He had only to copy Lüderitz, who, at Kusserow's prodding, had copied the adventurers in Borneo. Woermann's iteration was to begin with the people of the Douala area: the Duala.[249] He would instruct his lieutenants to negotiate there with two paramount, and sometimes warring, princes—or "kings," as the Germans and English then preferred to call them.[250] One of these men was an Anglophile spendthrift known as Bell (a corruption of Ndumbé Lobé); the other, a rich ex-slave named Akwa.[251] In the event, a company organized by Woermann would sign contracts with the "*États princiers*" granting the company "sovereign rights" over the Douala coast and the surrounding area.[252] Several months later it was said that Woermann would make these contracts on behalf of "His Majesty, the Emperor of Germany." In fact, however, the contracts were to deal exclusively with Woermann's company, with the tie to Germany only in the background as a possibility.[253] The company, Bismarck assured the emperor, operated as a "third party."[254]

Bell and Akwa had strong reasons to deal with any European outsiders who agreed to designate them as monarchs. For decades the Duala people, seen by Europeans as ideal middlemen for interior trade, had been witnessing great upheaval.[255] Thanks in part to Britain's successful naval campaign against the slave trade, Douala, like much of West Africa's coastal population, was undergoing a transition from a slave-based economy to one dependent on the export of palm oil and, to a smaller extent, ivory.[256] This economic transformation did not directly harm Bell and Akwa. They still collected "comey," or trade tax, on all local export transactions.[257] Likewise, they still controlled trade occurring up the Wouri, Dibamba, and Mungo rivers into the interior, thanks to the extension of credit in the form of goods from Europeans.[258] However, the shift away from slavery, beginning in the 1840s and occurring in tandem with missionary work by Europeans, had been gradually undermining social and political structures favorable to the rulers.[259] Former or potential slaves not only became wage laborers; they often sought to circumvent payment of comey by trading directly with whites at the coast. These efforts caused multiple civil wars.[260]

Disinclined to accept the loss of comey, Bell and Akwa looked for the help of Europeans to shore up their power.[261] At first they tried inviting Britain to rule in the late 1870s and early 1880s; Britain, after all, had begun convening a "court of equity" in the area periodically to resolve intertribal disputes. Notwithstanding one consul's suggestion that Queen Victoria place "the country under a chartered company of merchants . . . analogous, I suppose, to the North Borneo Company," the British cabinet rejected all such proposals, offering no concrete help to defend Bell or Akwa's interests.[262] Thereafter, the Germans assumed that the two local rulers would probably volunteer to sign a contract with traders of other nationalities.[263] In such a contract, Bell and Akwa would accept gifts, i.e. retention of comey, as well as protection against their enemies, in exchange for giving up their territories on paper. Woermann, treaties in hand, could thereafter run his own state, with politicians in Berlin calling it a "German" colony. As for the two local rulers, they had their own motives. The German colonial regime would witness the elevation of their own status on the international scene to that of "kings," thus bolstering their shaky claims to economic superiority vis-à-vis their

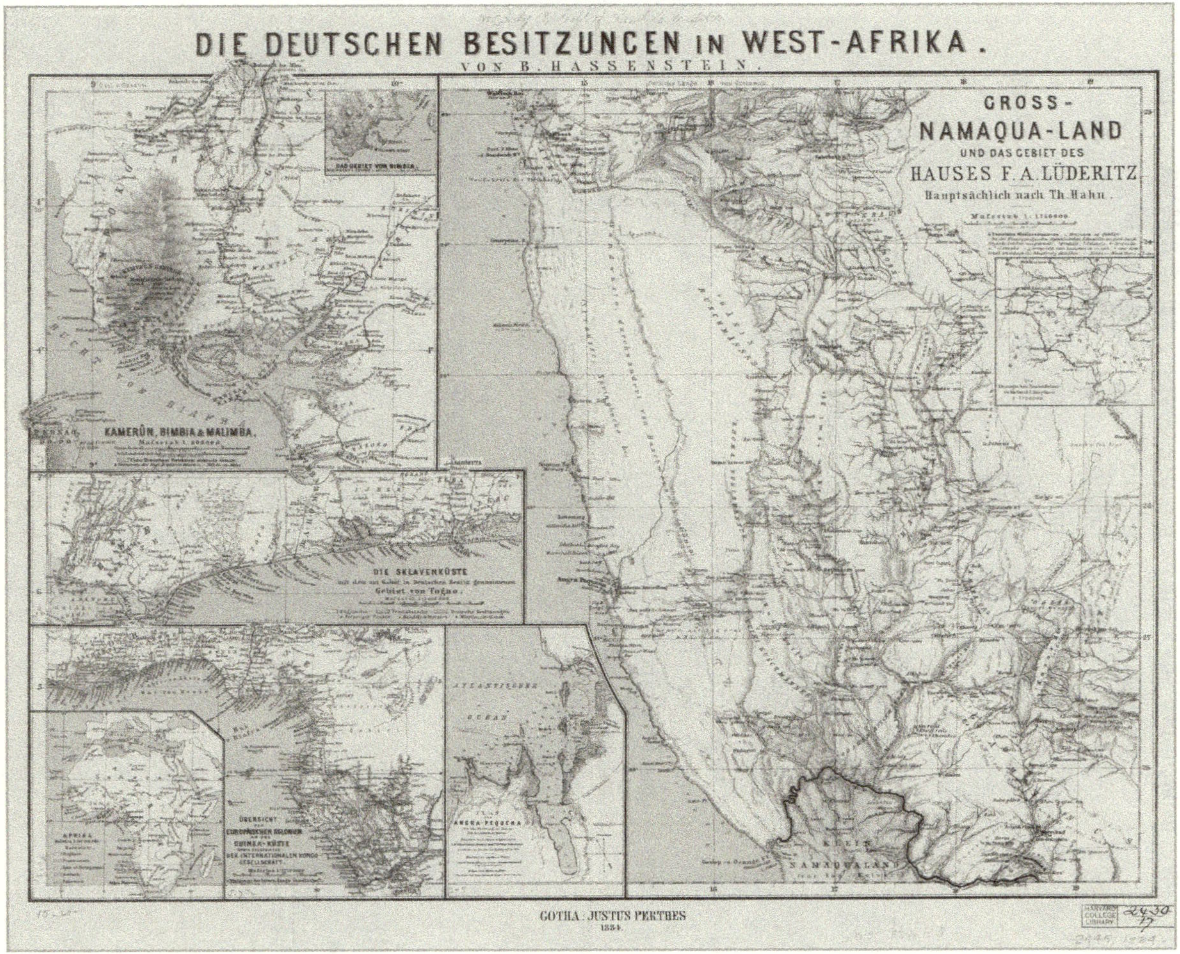

Map 3 German "possessions" in West Africa, late 1884. At right, a map with the territory of Lüderitz, as sketched by the missionary Theophilus Hahn, one of Lüderitz's early associates. Top left corner: The Bight of Biafra, home to Woermann's aspirations in the vicinity of the Cameroon River. Bottom middle: Plan of Angra Pequeña harbor, Lüderitz's operational base. *Source:* Bruno Hassenstein, *Die deutschen Besitzungen in West-Africa* (Gotha 1884). Courtesy of Harvard Map Collection.

own subjects, coastal rivals, and laborers at the interior. Royal credentials could form their own kind of economic security in a time of heightened risk.

The price of a deal with Bell and Akwa was not entirely attractive to Woermann; he later complained that it lost him a great deal of money. Even if he estimated that the cost of paying them off for parcels of land would amount to "almost nothing," buying a claim to sovereignty was expensive, especially since he had to guarantee Bell and Akwa that the Germans would let them retain their comey, as well as a large measure of jurisdiction over indigenous institutions and customs.[264] This at least was a plausible deal to which Bell and Akwa lent credence at the moment of signing, though the Germans over time made no effort to keep their word.[265] When the particulars appeared on paper, they consisted of the following:

1. Natives to be allowed to continue to buy women.
2. There are to be no taxes imposed.
3. There are to be no duties on trade.
4. The Germans are not to go to native markets.
5. "Comey" to be paid as heretofore.
6. Heavy penalty to be inflicted on Germans in case they rape native women.
7. Germans to have nothing to do with the farms of natives, i.e. the land in the occupation of the natives [is] to continue to belong to them.[266]

On April 28, the same day he announced his protection for Lüderitz, Bismarck and Kusserow called together a series of men who would run the proposed German empires. Meeting in Berlin, Woermann joined Lüderitz and various other Hanseatic trade princes ostensibly to discuss how best to protect their interests abroad.[267] It quickly became apparent that the real "theme" of this meeting, as Bismarck put it, was to develop a concrete plan for creating privately managed empires on the putative model of Borneo.[268] Over breakfast, Bismarck suggested that certain German traders active along the West African coast do their utmost over the next few months to pay indigenous authorities for titles to sovereign rights.[269] Thereafter, these traders might transfer all of their newly acquired rights to the German state, which would in turn "lease" most of the rights back to the traders in exchange for nominal concessions. The leased rights would include, among others, the right to set customs duties, to police, and to try legal cases. Bismarck went on to propose a scenario in which "the governing would fall to the beneficiaries of the colony," as if the task were an opportunity for profit.[270] Another attendee was less sanguine, observing, "The businessman will have to administer the colonies."[271]

A split of rights might please both parties.[272] Bismarck hoped Germany would keep only the right to control foreign relations, with "clerks from the trading houses, not German generals," handling all the other duties and functions of government. The traders, however, did not so much want to commence governing as they wanted extra assurance that Germany would provide muscle to protect their businesses from foreign powers—an uncertain prospect, given the proposal by Bismarck to establish German consulates in each of the new colonies.[273] Any foreign power—say, Britain—could challenge the fledgling empires, perhaps even convincing rival political figures in the area to sign treaties alleging annexation by non-Germans. Hence, Lüderitz insisted that an official German emissary travel to each of the areas in question to sign a redundant treaty of "protection."[274] In these supplemental treaties, loyal indigenous leaders would have to pledge to Germany, on the threat of reprisal, never to alienate any of their territory again. By this time, of course, the leaders would already have sold parts of their territory to German traders, and those earlier sales would remain valid.

Lüderitz's and Bismarck's new proposal for Africa had some parallels with what had happened in Borneo, mainly that here, as in Brunei, some indigenous rulers would prove eager to partner with Europeans in order to bolster their existing claims to economic and political supremacy. One crucial difference was that on Borneo, a group of adventurers had periodically produced treaties without sanction from their home state, or even any impetus from the same. In the event, however, Lüderitz and Bismarck's proposal looked enough like Borneo to satisfy everyone involved on the German end. The proposed companies would initially acquire their rights by paying for them, just as Lüderitz had. But Germany, too, would acquire certain rights in exchange for signing treaties of "protection." Subsequently, the companies would operate under the token "protection" of the German emperor, which would issue them a charter approving their rights to collect taxes, to police, and so on.

Redundant titles, all—but more than enough to keep foreign powers off the backs of Germany and Germans alike. In this manner, Bismarck would get to avoid the responsibilities he most loathed, with "the necessary government officials being hired and paid" by the ruling companies "themselves."[275]

Over the next few weeks discussions in Berlin shifted to the subject of Gustav Nachtigal, a famous explorer prepped by Kusserow to carry out the job of traveling to West Africa to lay groundwork for several empires. In May 1884 Nachtigal received a telegraph from Woermann with Bismarck's plan.[276] Nachtigal was to rendezvous with a German warship in Gibraltar before sailing on a two-month journey around northern Africa and down the entire Atlantic coast of the continent.[277] At the onset of this journey Nachtigal would conduct an inspection of German merchant welfare in Little Popo (Aného), a settlement of the Ewe people in what is today's Togo. However, at several other spots—Cameroon, Angra Pequeña, and Koba, Kabitai, and Sumbayland, the latter three being kingdoms along the West African coast located near the Dubréka River (in today's Guinea)—Nachtigal was to meet with local authorities, making sure not just that German traders were being given fair treatment, but also that these same traders had signed deals for sovereign rights over territory.[278] Thereafter, Nachtigal would sign separate "protection" treaties with each indigenous polity, directly on behalf of Germany.[279] The journey would end in Angra Pequeña, where Nachtigal hoped to sign a supplemental treaty with Josef Frederiks. In this treaty, Frederiks would formally grant Germany the right of "protection"—whatever that meant—just as Lüderitz himself granted Germany the same right over the territory he supposedly controlled.

Bismarck's overall plans for Africa remained shrouded well past July 2, 1884, when Nachtigal arrived at Little Popo after a disappointing visit to the Dubréka, where he found that local rulers had already signed treaties pledging themselves to the French.[280] Back in Europe, German newspapers already had plenty to talk about in the form of Bismarck's announcement of "protection" for Lüderitz. As a popular atlas quickly moved to color in Lüderitzland as a German possession, most observers took Bismarck's declaration as a sign that Germany had acquired its first colony, Angra Pequeña, albeit by a circuitous and limited path.[281] Others, notably the *Berliner Tageblatt,* even identified Borneo as the inspiration.[282] Crucially, however, most initial reports bought into the idea of private German states. No less than Munich's daily paper, otherwise quite skeptical of Prussian-led diplomacy, informed its readers that Lüderitzland would amount "not to a state German colony," but to an independent polity whose "sovereign owner," Lüderitz, had secured protection of his sovereign rights from Germany.[283] Here Bismarck's colonial vision seemed the opposite of utopian; it seemed more practical than that of Britain, France, or other powers.[284]

Of course, not everyone delighted in the prospect of protecting a stretch of desert in Africa. The British, who did not understand what Bismarck had meant when he said he was going to "protect" Lüderitz's rights, continued to consider letting the Cape Colony annex Angra Pequeña. In France, a confused Ferry read reports that German imitations of Lüderitz would soon follow in New Guinea and the Transvaal.[285] Meanwhile, several commentators wondered whether "protection" would constitute the first stage in a process of outright colonization similar to what the French had carried out in Algeria and Tunisia. In this event, Bismarck would no doubt face domestic roadblocks. The Reichstag wielded veto rights over every Imperial budget, and thus would have the prerogative to refuse any additions made for "colonial" purposes. It was not out of the realm of possibility that the Reichstag would refuse Bismarck permission to provide subsidies to Lüderitz or Woermann, both of whom seemed to have enough financing for the time being.[286]

Bismarck's next step was to meet with the British about Angra Pequeña in early June, around the time Wilhelm I was breaking ground on the new Reichstag building in Berlin. Britain still struggled to define its own opinion on Lüderitzland, partly because its involvement in Egypt was consuming the lion's share of its time.[287] Such indeterminacy had become an even greater problem by the summer of 1884, when Britain needed German support on the issue of Egyptian debts. Britain wanted to keep Bismarck happy. Because this wish coincided with a demand to resolve the Angra Pequeña question, the British view—as Bismarck correctly predicted—would be that "the support Germany could provide Britain and eventually will provide Britain" was "worth more" than disputes over places like "Little Popo."[288] That left Britain in a difficult spot. The British foreign secretary found it arduous to identify where Angra Pequeña was located, much less to decipher the meaning of Bismarck's "protection" declaration. But he also knew for a fact that Bismarck loathed the thought of overseas colonies. Thus, he told Bismarck proudly that in order to relieve him of any sort of colonial burden, the Cape Colony would annex Angra Pequeña. Lüderitzland was to become a thing of the past, and Bismarck would have no need to resort to "royal charters" for German citizens doing business abroad—a possibility he had mentioned to the British starting June 9.[289]

Bismarck likely would have taken this offer in 1883. Instead, the German chancellor announced that he wanted to follow Britain's behavior broadly in regard to Borneo, the seal of whose fate was still fresh with the wax of the charter signed in 1882. Germany, Bismarck said, was not going to ask any help from Britain; unless one counted it as help for Britain to leave Angra Pequeña and other ventures of German subjects alone. Instead, Germany was going to offer a sliver of "protection" for Lüderitz, and perhaps others, with Lüderitz promptly taking over all the duties of governance in and around Angra Pequeña. Should Britain doubt the legality of such moves, Bismarck wanted to tell them in advance that

> these are questions which may interest professors of international law as curiosities, but they appear to me to be without value. I do not know why we would split hairs in definitions over declarations of sovereignty, over a hosting of a flag or implementation of a protectorate or award of a Royal Charter. You have declared that this area does not belong to you, therefore I think it is a question of mere curiosity if you ask about the sovereignty: it can be all the same to you, what another power does in a country not belonging to you.[290]

Confused as the British were, some observers could see past Bismarck's façade, right through to his cynicism. In the last few years the British foreign secretary—the same man Bismarck was negotiating with—had allowed adventurers to take control of most of North Borneo because he wanted to save his government money while still reaping trade benefits and acclaim. Thus the British government were "like thieves caught in the act," unable to refuse Germany their permission "to proceed in Angra Pequeña as we have in North Borneo."[291] On June 16, 1884, in a final gesture of humiliation, an impudent Bismarck asked the British what kind of flag flew in North Borneo, only to find that the foreign secretary had to leave the room for several minutes before returning with an agnostic reply.[292]

Bismarck had overwhelmed Britain. "We are on a good path with Angra," wrote his son Herbert on June 18, and three days later the British cabinet decided not to contest the German "protectorate" in Lüderitzland, meaning, mused Charles Dilke, that Bismarck would get everything he wanted.[293]

Achieving similar success in Germany involved a different tactic, however. In an effort to maximize electoral gains, Bismarck delayed the announcement of his comprehensive plan for a series of German colonies until October 13, or about two weeks before the German elections.[294] To considerable fanfare, a newly christened, heavily armed squadron of German warships departed for the West African coast around that time, along with some three thousand personnel.[295] Meanwhile, the chancellor began to paint his opponents as anticolonialists. On June 23 Bismarck arranged to testify at a parliamentary budget committee hearing—the first he had attended in thirteen years.[296] Though this testimony ostensibly concerned steamship subsidies vetoed (again) by Bismarck's opponents, some of whom refused to stand when he was announced, he used his surprise appearance as an opportunity to contrast such recalcitrance with his successful support for Angra Pequeña.[297] His next move was to make a speech to the German parliament on the day his victory over Britain was announced in German newspapers, with his broader ambitions still concealed.[298] On June 26, the chancellor opened his remarks in the Reichstag with a reminder that he dreaded the thought of taking on colonies similar to those the French had been developing in Africa.[299] Colonization attempts, he declared, were a problem when they were "artificial": when they tried to start a harbor from scratch; or to create trade where there was really no money; or to spread moral values. As a result, Bismarck still did not like the idea of colonies per se. Nor did he want to start Germany down the road of "French-style" annexations.[300] That said, he told the audience of hundreds in parliament that he could no longer deny claims for protection coming from German businessmen overseas. If a German businessman in an area outside another European nation's control was operating without some sort of European law—be it direct colonial administration by a European power, or even consular jurisdiction as exercised by Europeans in places such as China—then Bismarck was henceforth going to make sure that businessman got the support he needed.[301] Like the British prime minister, Palmerston, in 1850, Bismarck invoked the idea of *civis romanus sum* to argue that a citizen's rights, wherever they might be in the world, and even if they included sovereignty, must be protected by the citizen's home state.[302]

Fortunately, Bismarck told the audience, this protection did not need to involve sending in garrisons—or any significant expense. On the contrary, the British experience, which Bismarck touted first by reference to the East India Company, and then by reference to an almost mythical company just founded in Borneo, proved that companies could do the job of governing territory by themselves. "I hope that we will come," he went on to say, "to a system like that which England has made so great in East India. There it is *the businessman alone* who rules and governs."[303] Germany would begin such an experiment in southwest Africa. There it would acquire some of Lüderitz's governing rights—the ones he did not really want to exercise anyway. Then, Germany would "loan" those rights to a company formed by Lüderitz, keeping for itself the "option" of protection powers in the event of overwhelming attacks on the company.[304] Germany might also keep an option to buy the company's rights first, should the rights ever go up for sale.[305]

The chancellor did not intend to inspire further unauthorized attempts at colonization abroad, such as Friedrich Nietzsche's sister was about to undertake disastrously in Paraguay.[306] Nonetheless, results with public opinion proved quite positive, even with southwest Africa as the only focal point yet revealed.[307] Unsurprisingly, the German Colonial Union *(Deutscher Kolonialverein)* expressed its approval for "the Borneo Company model" in a national meeting held on September 21, 1884.[308] More broadly, a foreign correspondent in Berlin reported: "The press here, without exception, lauds the colonial policy."[309] In the Reichstag, the chartered-company idea also seemed like a panacea to some: to Conservatives who always supported Bismarck and liked tariffs, and to National Liberals who strongly advocated the acquisition of colonies overseas and who were then embarking on a rapprochement with Bismarck after years of rancor. The chartered-company legacy even made a distinct impression on Eugen Richter, a staunch Left-Liberal who in principle opposed colonialism: Perhaps Woermann and Lüderitz, he speculated for a time, could emerge as the next James Brooke.[310]

Only a few deputies initially found the idea misguided.[311] They eventually demanded reports about what was actually going in Borneo, Bismarck's supposed model state.[312] One would ask whether Germany might have to pay to buy out a German company's "sovereign rights" overseas in a case of bankruptcy. But it was not until several months after Bismarck's coup—and comfortably after Bismarck had cost Left-Liberals a chunk of their popularity—that a significant domestic contingent really began to suspect that any company that Bismarck might ask to run a state was going to ditch or bungle its duties as a governor. By then, the German flag was already flying over Lüderitzland (it had been there since August 1884), complete with a pole declaring that Germany would do whatever it took to protect "the territory belonging to Mr. A. Lüderitz."[313] Affording such protection would prove much easier for Bismarck if he could win a broad consensus from Western powers to keep their navies and subjects away from German overseas territories. Happily for him, he was set to convene an international conference in Berlin with the goal of helping Leopold II convert most of Central Africa into another privately run empire.

5

The Berlin Conference

THE BORNEO SCHEME began with small-time rogues. It reached its apogee at the Berlin Conference of 1884 and 1885, when Bismarck teamed with Leopold to lend the scheme broad international approval. By the 1890s it would inspire yet more private empires, the combined extent of which included modern-day Tanzania, Kenya, Uganda, Nigeria, Zambia, Zimbabwe, Malawi, and Mozambique, as well as a chunk of Somalia.

MIDWAY THROUGH 1883 European statesmen were inundated with petitions on behalf of Leopold II's International African Association (AIA).[1] The AIA claimed to exist "in the interests of the civilized world and of the natives of Africa," and to carry out its work on the Congo in accordance with international law, by virtue of treaties.[2] But what did those treaties, if valid, make the AIA? France's prime minister, Jules Ferry, consistently expressed consternation on the subject.[3] Was the AIA, he asked, a state? Was it a company? Was it a company-state? Was it acquiring political privileges for its home country—wherever that might be?[4] Or was the AIA merely a group of "filibusters," as its lead agent, Henry Morton Stanley, confessed to a friend in a seeming moment of desperation?[5] The last charge circulated in Britain, where even opponents of Portugal spoke of the AIA as "a filibustering expedition, because one can call it by no other name."[6]

As Ferry's bemusement suggested, the European community was seeking answers. First, there was Portugal's colonial regime based in Luanda, which had recently begun pushing from its coastal enclaves to the Congo interior, where few Portuguese had ventured in hundreds of years despite Lisbon's longstanding pretensions to govern there.[7] Lisbon did not authorize a concerted inward move until roughly the same time as the AIA showed up; one observer joked that groundbreaking on a railway in Portuguese territory was the only such work done prior to 1884.[8] Once Portugal emerged from its torpor, however, its agents began running into camps sparsely staffed by Stanley and other AIA employees.[9] In short order they blustered about war, and Portugal even dispatched warships to the egress of the Congo in an attempt to frighten off boats supplying Stanley.[10] Yes, Lisbon's state finances lay in a parlous condition. But government ministers in Lisbon still hoped to leverage control over Central African trade into a more prominent role in intra-European markets.[11] As a result, they challenged the legitimacy of each treaty Leopold's men produced in Africa, protesting heavily whenever Leopold's men appealed to foreign governments for recognition.[12]

This was disturbing news for the King of the Belgians, who believed it would only take about "five hundred men with maxim guns" to overpower all the Zanzibari mercenaries he had hired to back Stanley.[13] Stanley himself put the number even lower.[14] With war between some combination of Portugal, France, and Leopold a distinct possibility from early 1883, even the otherwise reserved the Belgian prime minister, Walthère Frère-Orban, consented to encourage his counterparts in Lisbon to temper their opposition to Leopold's "private" colonization company.[15] The company, he protested, was legitimate and not "a violation of international usage."[16]

Leopold and Stanley most feared French intervention.[17] France's interest in the affairs of the AIA waxed with the advent of Brazza's Congo treaties. In Paris, one of the many objections to Leopold's "purchases" of sovereignty was that they partially conflicted with a treaty Brazza's group was purporting to have made elsewhere, with separate authorities.[18] Once Paris moved decisively to back Brazza it, like Portugal, denied the legitimacy of Leopold's operation, lest Brazza find himself forced to retreat from his maximum territorial extent.[19] French ministers could count as an added advantage their ability to intercept some of the AIA's confidential telegrams to Belgium via Tenerife.[20]

The veracity of these challenges was not universally accepted. France and Portugal talked at length about illegitimate treaties; a naval captain loyal to Brazza derided the AIA's flag as a "piece of common cloth," and

Portuguese ally Pedro V, king of the shrinking Kongo polity, argued that many of Stanley's treaties could not have been valid without approval from the Kongo capital in São Salvador (today's M'banza-Kongo).[21] Yet, according to the U.S. secretary of state and some Belgian parliamentarians who had recently opined on the subject, the treaties signed by Stanley and Leopold's other men in the AIA looked no less legitimate than those signed elsewhere in Africa by Britain and France.[22] Some of the latter had emerged from areas quite near Leopold's claims, and as recently as August 8, 1883.[23] Portugal, for its part, had even begun signing contracts for land rights modeled after those of Stanley's men, in a spirit of imitation.[24] Moreover, Leopold's propagandists skillfully contrasted their "peaceful" model with the method made infamous by *conquistadores* in the sixteenth century.[25] Though this technique did not adequately differentiate the AIA from Brazza—a man celebrated in France for his relatively nonviolent achievements—it did appeal to Britons, proponents of whose own empire had used a similar argument to claim superiority in relation to Spanish rivals.[26] Campaigns based on Leopold's treaties, an anonymous "participant in the enterprise" assured British readers, were not campaigns of "bloodshed."[27] Eager to keep its image as clean as possible, the association even reprimanded one of its future governors general for showing off his firearms when concluding a treaty.[28]

This tactic was potent, as some British officials acknowledged confidentially.[29] Nonetheless, for France and Portugal, the best way to discredit Leopold remained to label his outfit a group of filibusters or pirates: actors who, because they operated outside the established rules of international law and outside the state system, could never acquire territory legitimately. Ferry, then French prime minister, led the charge, telling the German ambassador in early 1884 that Leopold's association "always will be only a private association." Portugal's foreign minister was more vociferous, bemoaning Leopold's "temerity," "violence," "fraud," and general contempt for the spirit of laws.[30] As Ferry explained it, Leopold's association consisted of mostly Belgian citizens, along with the Belgian king. But the association was officially neither Belgium nor the Belgian king; as a result, France could never recognize the association's armies as legitimate, let alone its flags or claims to sovereign rights.[31]

Ferry conceded that the AIA might try to implement its own laws in parts of the Congo, citing certain treaties it had signed to supposedly buy sovereign rights. Still, given the lack of any actual courts in the AIA's territory, Ferry doubted that it was capable of producing laws, and suggested its control was a fantasy. He vowed "eternally" to oppose the completion of Leopold's aims.[32] In the event that they were not merely piracy, he surmised that the aims represented a sort of opening for Britain to rule the Congo by proxy, perhaps by lending money to the heavily indebted Leopold.[33] Stanley talked of Britain's annexing the Congo. And Leopold's cousin, after all, was the queen. Finally, many of the men in Leopold's camp were veterans of Britain's military and industry. There was Sir Frederick Goldsmid, helping to legitimate Congo treaties;[34] Major General Charles "Chinese" Gordon, who signed on to take over Stanley's expedition just before setting out to meet his end in Khartoum[35]; Rear-Admiral Bouverie, trying to sign up his children for Stanley's outfit[36]; and, not least, William Mackinnon and Joseph Hutton, both of whom figured as shareholders in Leopold's defunct *Comité d'études du Haut-Congo* and both of whom lobbied British chambers of commerce to support the AIA.[37]

This was where a third European factor came into play: British policy in Central and West Africa. As the 1880s began, Britain was the dominant Sub-Saharan force; several regions, not least the Niger River, were growing increasingly British thanks to the maintenance of a "trust" system that had tended to make Africans dependent on European credit since the advent of Atlantic slave trading.[38] Even in long-established French colonies, goods from Britain sometimes totaled as much as 95 percent of imports.[39] Notwithstanding this tremendous economic influence, though, Britain did not want to govern the Congo. On the contrary, many in London—relying partly on a study conducted by a select committee of parliament in 1865, amid the backdrop of a major Jamaican uprising—recommended dispensing with Britain's existing West African colonies and abjuring any future treaties of annexation.[40] Britain had been turning down potential annexations in Africa since at least the 1830s, when indigenous polities in the Rio del Rey basin, in what is now Cameroon, allegedly offered to cede some of their territory.[41] And while the government did not unilaterally agree with the committee formed in 1865—its reaffirmation by the Colonial Office in 1882 led one

Foreign Office official to complain that its recommendations "were too vague for any practical purpose"—Britain entered the 1880s with a preference to warn off other European powers from the Congo while letting its traders reap the spoils of trade.[42] That way, Britain never had to bother with infrastructure or the concomitant taxes at home.[43] Considerations of racial composition also proved a factor.[44]

One could thus say that a kind of Monroe Doctrine remained in place for Central Africa.[45] So it stayed, at least, until Portugal, France, and the AIA intensified their squabble about taking full control over certain areas.[46] Now, if France actually established itself as the government in the Congo interior—as British and German papers forecasted—then Britain's days as the unmolested trading champion might reach an end, despite preliminary assurances of free trade during the brief tenure of French prime minister Charles Duclerc.[47] The French might even, it was conjectured, sell weapons to the Mahdist Sudanese or invade Egypt in case of war with Britain.[48] In the interim, the AIA set to work lobbying Britain, as well as Bismarck, "to guard and watch over the general interests of [itself] by confirming its status in the territories in which it has obtained sovereign rights."[49] So far the treaties this mysterious body was signing—as best foreign diplomats could tell from the smuggled copies they received—appeared to confer on the AIA all those privileges that Portugal claimed to own already.[50] Britain, therefore, faced three alternatives.[51] One, it could support Portugal; based on terms proffered by Lisbon starting from the time of the Brazza treaties' ratification, this support would win Britons an exemption from future Congo tariffs and taxes, as well as guarantees for Protestant missionaries.[52] Two, Britain could cut a similar deal with Leopold, who had begun begging Queen Victoria to send a warship or two to the mouth of the Congo to frighten off the Portuguese.[53] Three, and least palatably, Britain could concede control over the region to France.

Otto von Bismarck watched these developments at a remove, often reminding colleagues that Central African trade amounted to a paltry percentage of European business overseas.[54] Early on, his lieutenants said Germany did not care which country claimed sovereignty in the Congo.[55] As a man allegedly preoccupied with intra-European and Near Eastern questions, the chancellor also professed little interest in ending the East African slave trade. In 1876, when Leopold convened his famous conference in Brussels, Bismarck's only concern was that heightened European missionary work in Africa might favor the Catholics with whom Germany was then locked in a *Kulturkampf*.[56] A similar cool prevailed in 1877, when the German emperor tried to tout the antislavery cause.[57] By the 1880s, new reasons existed for caution. Bismarck did not want to offend France by backing the Belgian king too forcefully.[58] Nor could he overlook that France's meddling in the Congo, as well as Morocco, would almost certainly mean further French entanglements outside Europe—in other words, a distraction from the disgraceful loss of Alsace-Lorraine to Germany.[59]

Bismarck's attitude stayed the same through early 1884, although several German manufacturers vainly lobbied him to intervene on behalf of Leopold.[60] The lobbyists included Bismarck's personal banker, Gerson von Bleichröder, as well as the explorer Nachtigal, both of whom had begun to benefit, on the side, from Leopold's largesse.[61] Prior to this point Bismarck had buried all Congo correspondence on the desk of his resident African expert in the Foreign Ministry, Kusserow, whose civil service career had entailed extensive work on Belgium.[62] As late as March 26, the Italian ambassador in Berlin even spoke confidently about Bismarck's "uninterest."[63] (The chancellor apparently did not remember that more than a decade earlier, in the middle of a war with France, he had called on Portugal to assert its "sovereignty" by impounding French warships near the Congo.[64]) But then, Bismarck suddenly changed his mind around April 11, 1884, one day after Kusserow delivered a memorandum on the subject and three days after Kusserow recommended the Borneo plan for Germany.[65] By this time Kusserow—the African expert in receipt of virtually all Congo documents—had risen in the ranks to become the point man for Bismarck's now far-reaching colonial schemes.[66] As it happened, these schemes looked "analogous to those" Leopold was attempting to implement.[67] So it was that Kusserow came to see support of the International African Association as inextricably linked to German colonial projects.[68] On the Congo as in Southwest Africa, Bismarck would follow Kusserow's advice, not just when introducing a new system for colonial government, but also when considering how to process new overseas alignments.

On April 17, a week before Bismarck fully embarked on his new overseas policy for Germany, he sent feelers to Paris suggesting cooperation against the Anglo-Portuguese Treaty of February 1884, by which Britain would have recognized Portugal's complete control over the

Congo.[69] He found a receptive audience in Prime Minister Ferry, already making his own protests to Lisbon.[70] On April 18, Bismarck informed his ambassador to Portugal that Germany would fight the treaty.[71] Starting a week later, he pressured the Netherlands to join his initiative, with plans to reach out to others.[72] Finally, he told the French he intended to support Leopold's project, expressing a wish to embrace calls for an international conference on Congo affairs.[73] France was game for a conference that would force Britain into retreating from its Monroe Doctrine for Africa, part of which now rested on the Anglo-Portuguese Treaty; without Portugal, only the near-bankrupt AIA would stand in France's way. France also—in a move destined to revive British fears—asked for the conference to implement international rules concerning the Niger River.[74] Germany, for its part, joined France in concluding that Britain was vulnerable enough to make concessions in West Africa on account of its Egyptian occupation, not least because, on April 22, the British Foreign Office sent out a letter imploring other great powers to attend a conference that would help wind down Egyptian debts.[75] In the event, April 1884 marked the first time Bismarck showed any solicitude for the Congo, let alone Leopold, aside from cursory discussions with lobbyists.

As is the case with his colonial turn, explaining Bismarck's volte-face on the Congo is complicated. Some biographers ascribe the maneuver to Bismarck's then waxing resentment of British policy.[76] Others find it satisfactory to credit economic self-interest.[77] After all, according to Bismarck's official statements, Hamburg traders—in particular Adolph Woermann—stood to lose vast potential profits if anyone but Leopold took control of the Congo.[78] The Portuguese were notorious for installing prohibitive tariffs in their territory, and their penetration of the Congo from the coast inward would take place in villages where Hamburg firms hitherto dominated the liquor trade.[79] Germany could expect no favors for Woermann and other traders, with Portugal having already committed to protect Britain's traders.[80]

Bismarck himself entertained the theory that he supported Leopold's Congo project for economic reasons, declaring that he could not "consent," in "the interests of German commerce," that the Congo, "which is of such importance, and has hitherto been free land, should be subjected to the Portuguese colonial system."[81] Despite his preoccupation with anti-British maneuvering at the time, Bismarck also endorsed a related argument about France—the other likely victor in the event that Leopold's AIA failed. French protectionism seemed invariably to follow French rule—they would, complained Americans, "bolt and bar the door against" foreign traders.[82] Continuing with the economic interpretation, one must note that, in mid-1884, Leopold told Bismarck through Kusserow that he was prepared to offer German traders in the Congo complete freedom.[83] With Leopold at the helm, German trade would (or so he advertised) enjoy safe, tariff-free conditions.[84] The offer also appeared at a propitious time, for by 1884 Germany's global liquor exports had entered a sharp decline since peaking two years earlier.[85]

Still, economics appears to have been only one piece of a larger puzzle. As mentioned, Bismarck approached the French to support Leopold not in February 1884, when he first learned of the Anglo-Portuguese Treaty, or even in early April of the same year, when British officials privately wondered why he had not yet asked them for favors in the Congo.[86] Rather, Bismarck made his approach on April 17.[87] Why he did so *then* is a question historians have not adequately considered from the perspective of domestic politics.[88] In May 1883 Leopold lobbied Bismarck unsuccessfully to support the AIA's "stations"; the king carefully avoided any use of the word "state," making analogy only to the Red Cross.[89] A little under a year later, Leopold's requests had shifted to resemble the concept of a chartered company government that fused commercial interests with a political constitution.[90] Now the king adduced arguments that fit perfectly with Bismarck's own colonial schemes, which, like the idea to call for an international conference concerning the Congo, originated shortly after April 8, 1884. The new German empires that Bismarck was preparing to recognize would rest on treaties purporting to transfer sovereign rights to Hanseatic companies, one of which, as announced on April 24, was to fall under German protection, having already occupied Bismarck in meetings around April 17. Sometimes these companies would buy their "rights" directly from local governments; on other occasions, Germany would replicate that procedure and then lease out its property. In any event, the key to this whole scheme was the idea that sovereign rights were commodities accessible to every kind of buyer—Africans, European businessmen, European states—and that certain experiences in Borneo, and even an announcement on April 22 that the United States supported Leopold's association, freshly affirmed this notion.[91] Proof that Leopold's Congo scheme fit into the picture lies in a meeting Bismarck held with Courcel, the French ambassador to Germany, again on April 24. At that time, Bismarck declared that he was pondering "to what extent [the association] was comparable . . . to the English Society that had taken possession of a part of the island of Borneo, not in the name of England, but merely with the consent of the English government."[92] From this day on, Bismarck would insist on the validity of such a comparison by telling the French how he did not really see the Congo scheme as that of an "association": He saw it, somewhat at Kusserow's suggestion, as that of a *company,* and he discussed it in parallel with the "private property of M. Lüderitz" at Angra Pequeña, since christened Lüderitzland.[93]

By May, Bismarck was also preparing to deal with the German parliament, where some deputies tried to disclaim the feasibility of overseas empires.[94] Such opposition took several forms, including newspaper articles by Social Democrats and Left-Liberals.[95] How fortuitous, then, that just as Bismarck started cultivating the notion of privately run empires, Leopold's lobbyists presented Kusserow, Bismarck's idea man, with a host of documents showing that Leopold wanted to do the same thing, on a far larger scale, in the entire Congo Basin.[96] The supposed model in Borneo was thus being brought to Africa, at the same time, by at least two different forces: the Germans and the Belgian king, and with each new report on the Congo, the combination was having a marked effect on thinking in the German Foreign Ministry.[97] Bismarck, like Leopold, was interested in emulating Borneo and the great "East India Co.," its spiritual predecessor.[98] One could thus argue that Leopold, as much as any German, might enable Germany's colonial turn.

With the Borneo linkage, Germany's designs looked increasingly legitimate in international law, and Leopold's scheme was the latest proof.[99] Without Borneo, the putative German and Belgian kings in Africa were nothing more than pirates, as Stanley had feared and as some others—including parliamentary deputies—would imply.[100] Defending the colonial foray by Germany would thus necessarily mean defending the one in the Congo.[101] This equation applied equally at home and abroad. In Munich, Catholic politicians mistrustful of German colonies also labeled Leopold's claim to statehood in Africa "fantastical": Both, it was implied, rested on dubious purchases of sovereignty from "sale-minded negro kings."[102] It was apropos when a French naval officer began comparing Leopold's treaties to those made by Adolf Lüderitz with the "King of Bethanie," Josef Frederiks.[103] Lüderitzland, Woermann's kingdom in the Cameroons, and the other private empires must either "enter the family of nations in both hemispheres" alongside the Congo venture, or not at all.[104] As important, their success would hinge on a single champion—Bismarck—in the run-up to the German elections.

An array of European officials noted, from April 1884 on, how well the debate over Leopold's machinations in the Congo could factor into Bismarck's evolving plans for colonies; even after Angra Pequeña won international acceptance from July through September, the terms for Cameroon and Togo remained on the docket in Whitehall and the Quai d'Orsay.[105] Bismarck confirmed the Congo's role in this process to select members of the Reichstag.[106] He also hinted at it in a personal letter to Münster, Germany's ambassador to England.[107] In late April the United States extended diplomatic recognition for Leopold's operation partly on the strength of a recommendation by Gustav Nachtigal; the next day, Kusserow telegrammed the German ambassador in Washington to ask for details about what form this recognition would take.[108] Meanwhile, Bismarck's interest in the Congo question soon intensified to the point that it fascinated Friedrich Holstein, who was essentially second in command at the Foreign Ministry. Holstein correctly theorized that Bismarck planned to use the Congo fanfare to help him win the upcoming German elections, to be held on October 28. This was why Bismarck originally proposed that the international conference concerning the Congo start sometime during the first two weeks of October, just before election day, and that the conference take place in Berlin, where future rulers of the German colonies could easily make the trip from their Hanseatic hometowns.[109] The proposed duration—"they say this thing will last three weeks," an American invitee reported—coincided nicely with the election timetable.[110] The conference was to form the capstone in a colonial publicity campaign that included a Bismarck-approved visit by a Moroccan delegation to the Krupp Works at Essen in early September, and the inauguration of a German West Africa Squadron around October 1.[111]

Along with the German colonial schemes Bismarck would announce to the public on October 13, the conference could prove a thorn in the side of his parliamentary opponents, simultaneously discrediting their legal arguments about company governments and encouraging the nationalist and industrial lobbies on whose support Bismarck intended to rely that fall.[112] It was common knowledge that Left-Liberals and Social Democrats objected to Leopold's "experiment" in the Congo.[113] Thanks to the conference, however, Bismarck's scheme would appear not as unique to Germany, but rather as "international," so far as legal sanction was concerned.[114] Hence Bismarck's eventual remark, during a meeting on the Congo, that West Africa, "even if it may objectively be worthless," had become "more important for our politics than all of Egypt."[115] Bismarck's son Wilhelm saw a connection, too: He confided that his father hoped to make use of the Congo for internal political purposes, perhaps by adapting Stanley's speeches for use in German colonial propaganda.[116] So far as the elder Bismarck was concerned, Germany was going to advertise Leopold's Congo "association" as a "compagnie du Congo," or the equivalent to what Bismarck was setting up in German colonial areas.[117] By May 31 Germany had told Leopold it was ready to do what no other European power would go on to do until November: recognize Leopold's venture as an independent *state*.[118]

Holstein's suppositions, which he eventually confirmed by speaking with an enthusiastic Bismarck, did not quite go far enough. The Berlin Conference, as initially envisioned by the chancellor, would bring the added benefit of forcing French and European consent to a set of rules for future occupations of coastline—thus limiting the number of possible scenarios by which Westerners could challenge the fledgling private empires run by Germans.[119] Moreover, and unknown to all but a few, Bismarck considered purchasing the Congo rights from Leopold and inserting them directly into the fledgling collection of empires he was planning to place under loose German supervision. Just two weeks into May 1884, a leading Catholic newspaper in Berlin, *Germania,* reported that the colonial movement was so strong that it "gave full right" to the government to annex the "paradisiacal environs" along the Congo.[120] At the same time, shops in Germany began selling a board game, "The Game of the Congo," in which players could seize control of the river as one of four countries: France, England, Portugal, or Germany.[121] Precisely at this moment, Bismarck invited two colonial advisers to his country estate to discuss the idea at length.[122] His guests were Adolf Lüderitz, "Duke of Angra Pequeña," and Gerhard Rohlfs, a famous German explorer. Rohlfs delivered a personal message from Leopold in which the king said he "would see nothing with greater pleasure than for Germany to take over the entire Congo enterprise."

Bismarck, for his part, was still dubious about Leopold's motives. "We do not know who the International African Society and the other associations are," he told Rohlfs, adding that Leopold was "hiding" something from Europe by cloaking his designs on the Congo in the garb of philanthropy.[123] Still, the chancellor was intrigued by the idea that would later be called "Mittelafrika," not least because the Congo offered him a chance to move toward linking up two disparate "German" empires—the Cameroons and Togo—with Southwest Africa.[124] All these territories, when apart, represented middling opportunities for German business overseas.[125] But together—with Lüderitzland as "a sure road to the upper Congo" and its supposed riches—they might well combine to create a "German India in Africa."[126]

Fantasies of a German Congo had been circulating at least since 1875, when the Berlin-based Society for the Exploration of Equatorial Africa dispatched Eduard Pechuël-Loesche—later a disgruntled employee of Leopold's—to survey the area directly north of the river's mouth. That same year, the German Foreign Ministry received letters from members of their navy urging annexation, albeit without clear dimensions.[127] In 1878, British missionaries spoke of a fear that German lobbyists would not allow Britain to retain political influence over the Congo Basin.[128] By 1884, overseas colonialism and the Congo had grown so intertwined in the public consciousness as to make talk of annexation sound credible.[129]

Leopold II, as mentioned, had authorized Pechuël-Loesche to chart the Congo and conclude treaties.[130] Now, not only did this same German, fresh from the Congo, travel to southwest Africa with the assignment of making new treaties for his home country, but one of his countrymen and another Congo veteran, Max Buchner, was replicating the feat in the future German Cameroon.[131] Meanwhile, the German Society for the Exploration of Equatorial Africa—still outfitting expeditions to the Congo, and now a key organization in the emergence of the colonial movement—was doubling as the national chapter of Leopold's International African Association.[132] That meant the indirect placement of some major German names behind colonialism in the Congo, including Krupp.[133] It also spurred expansionist hopes, for Brazza's coup had begun from an identical foundation. By the end of May 1884, Adolph Woermann was discussing with Kusserow the prospect of Woermann's signing treaties to purchase territory "south from Gabon to the Congo," as Stanley's acquisition of territory through treaties had made a "special impression" on Bismarck.[134] German flags already flew over a number of settlements and factories.[135] Bearing in mind that the gamut of Nachtigal's African mission remained unknown through August—newspapers printed rumors concerning everything "south of the Congo"—it made sense for the public to think big.[136]

A takeover through purchase seemed realistic to Bismarck, who suggested that Kusserow draw up the necessary plans. Leopold was running out of money with which to fund Stanley's stations and he had not yet convinced a single power to recognize his AIA as a state.[137] It was logical to ask how long he might hold out. The Portuguese were pressurizing him with warships, creating chaos to the extent that the Italian navy soon dispatched cruisers of their own to the area, purportedly to safeguard their citizens' factories. Add to this that in February 1884, the British, Leopold's most likely savior and Bismarck's temporary enemy, were still technically aligned with the Portuguese. Perhaps, then, Leopold would be inclined to sell the AIA's rights to Bismarck after all. Lord Ampthill, British ambassador to Berlin, spoke of "a report which has reached me confidentially, from a fairly good private source, that the King of the Belgians . . . is willing to cede the protectorate of that Association to the German Emperor, and that Prince Bismarck is equally willing to take the offer into consideration."[138] (This "good private source" was likely Bleichröder, who later revived the idea of the sale.) Watching from afar, Italy's foreign minister noted the uniform support of Hanseatic merchants for a Congo independent of France and Portugal.[139] How far would Germany go to make it a reality?

The German Foreign Ministry pondered this possibility through the beginning of summer, to the point that even diplomats without a stake heard the rumors.[140] In July Bismarck circulated a memo proposing that Germany undertake "the creation of installations like those in East Asia" in the Congo—a clear reference to North Borneo.[141] In August Kusserow telegraphed instructions for a German cruiser to raise the German flag in territory claimed by Portugal near the Congo, only to change his mind and ask for the telegram's repression.[142] Bismarck evidently toyed with similar ideas as late as December 1884.[143] As discussion about "the formation of a Congo monarchy under a German Prince" percolated among aristocrats, and Bleichröder reinvigorated talks of a German protectorate in the Congo with Henry Sanford, French officials began to list "German territories on the Congo" alongside those of Lüderitz, Woermann, and their fellow countrymen.[144] Earlier, in May, Bismarck even made a bold suggestion that Rohlfs ask Leopold to offload the Congo rights to a German super-company that would combine all the other German companies he was forming in the colonial empire into a single behemoth: a larger take on the Borneo idea, which itself was being hailed by Bismarck as the new East India Company.[145] This was perhaps the most apposite proposal, which led Bismarck to authorize an expedition to the south Congo basin to create "factories" and "stations," perhaps on the model of Lüderitz's empire in Southwest Africa; he even added a subsidy of 120,000 marks in the kind of move Ferry had made to help Brazza.[146] With explorer Hermann Wissmann mounting a separate summer trek from Malanje (in what is now Angola) to Kananga, and with Paul Pogge's own German-led team still a fresh memory around the Kasai, it was not surprising that several British navy officers believed Germany intended a formal seizure of territory in the area.[147] A Belgian consul at Sierra Leone independently made the same prediction.[148]

Whatever the sincerity of Bismarck's vision, little evidence exists that Leopold ever decided to sell his claims. Yes, he told Bismarck otherwise through Rohlfs in May—the very time at which Bismarck was determining the fate of AIA pleas for recognition. But Leopold made a habit of lying when convenient, and this was just one link in his own delicately arranged chain of duplicity surrounding the Congo. As Leopold was talking with Bismarck about a possible sale in one breath, he was courting France in the next. Just as Bismarck expressed interest in buying Leopold's rights, the German chancellor learned that the United States was going to officially recognize the AIA as a state in embryo in the Congo, with the Americans likely dispatching a consul there and appropriating $50,000 for diplomatic operations.[149] This was good news for Bismarck; along with a sort of declaration of independence published by Sanford in Brussels, the recognition bolstered Bismarck's assertion that Lüderitzland was a completely "independent" state despite the German nationality of its owner.[150] But then Bismarck learned about the side deal Leopold was trying to arrange with France on April 23, well before Leopold had taken up negotiations with Bismarck in bad faith.[151] According to this still-fluid deal—not published in full until February 1885—France would "respect" the boundaries of Leopold's stations, in exchange for first right of refusal in the event that he decided to sell.[152]

How France negotiated this offer remains opaque; it appears that Leopold proposed the terms more or less in step with receipt of American recognition.[153] Why France accepted the terms allows for multiple explanations: Perhaps it was a conviction that Leopold would soon go bankrupt and sell out, or a preference for Leopold over the unknown "adventurers" and unsupervised "negro republics" that might emerge in his stead should he abandon his Congo venture, or simply a wish to freeze African problems as the Sino-French conflict over Tonkin heated up.[154] It is important to note, though, that France's offer to Leopold came with explicit limitations, including repeated disclaimers by Jules Ferry that he in no way recognized its pretensions as a state.[155]

The offer, as internal sources admitted, was primarily a stalling measure for France that allowed Brazza time to sign further treaties acquiring territory in disputed areas.[156] Rather than make any mention of the word "sovereignty," the French continued for some months to attach the adjective "private" to all descriptions of the association's rights.[157] Still, however modest the French ante, by making the deal Leopold temporarily crossed off one potential rival. For the time being, France was going to back off of Leopold, and so too were Portugal and Britain, for these two powers feared pushing Leopold into selling his rights and "giving them the French as neighbors" in Angola and West Africa respectively.[158] Bismarck, meanwhile, faced a unique predicament. Appearing as a potential buyer might annoy France precisely at a juncture when Bismarck was seeking Franco-German rapprochement. That said, he did not necessarily have to *buy* anything; he could lease, France could refuse to buy, or the AIA's charge could be taken over with a legalistic trick: the assumption of Leopold's duties by a German member of his royal line, the House of Saxe-Coburg and Gotha.[159] This was a marketplace, and several kinds of arrangement were possible that would not violate the letter of the French agreement; in this sense, as Leopold told Bleichröder, the right of preemption he had sold to France over the Congo was merely "a façade."[160] The idea of some kind of "protectorate" lingered in Berlin.

Leopold had received a kind of reprieve from France and Portugal while indirectly winning German support; his one major concession to Bismarck, of tariff freedom for German traders, had already been offered to at least three other powers by this time.[161] Germany, by contrast, appeared to have done Leopold's bidding gratis by making protests against the Anglo-Portuguese Treaty that proved a decisive factor in the latter's defeat; Bismarck even quashed an Italian attempt to broker a modified treaty.[162] By late June, with the treaty abandoned, Leopold was taking a noticeably firmer tone in discussions with Berlin, even insinuating he might renege on his earlier commitment to give Germans free-trade privileges in his territory.[163] Leopold approved the signing of a border treaty with Arab slavers in eastern Congo, the upshot of which was to secure a kind of Zanzibari recognition for the *Comité*'s sovereignty in a particular territory, whatever European rivals said.[164] From Brussels, the king also informed Bismarck that he had sent a "governor" out to the Congo and was looking to bulk up his presence there, in preparation for what would become "an independent state" under the "monarchical . . . rule of King Leopold II or of his natural or adopted successors, or of a member of this family designated by him or by them in case of impeachment of the head of the family."[165] A meeting among nearly all Leopold's agents at Vivi in South Africa had spent four days crafting rules for the guidance of station chiefs—effectively laying the groundwork for a state constitution.[166] Having already received public statements of support from Bismarck in the Reichstag on June 23—it was, noted one observer, considered certain that Germany would soon recognize the AIA as a sovereign power in the Congo—Leopold also went so far as to say he would merely listen to Germany on the limits of the territory he was envisioning, rather than obey.[167] Finally, Leopold wanted Germany to understand that this territory would come under his autonomous control indefinitely.[168]

Bismarck periodically grew angry with this negotiation. It seemed "inconceivable" that he "should wish to promote and establish the claims of the Association, knowing that there was every probability of the vast territories they allege themselves to have acquired becoming the property of the French Government," and get nothing in the bargain.[169] Hence, Bismarck not only kept Leopold in suspense about possibly withdrawing his informal support; he also had his associates go on the offensive when necessary.[170] Their efforts resulted in a redoubling of commitment to the German expedition to the Congo, no doubt aware that it would be perceived as a danger to Leopold, and watched as the members went on to claim German "annexations" around Nokki, a strategic point along the river.[171] At the same time, Bismarck proceeded to enlarge his demands. In what constituted a highly creative legal departure, he asked that Leopold pledge to give German traders perpetual freedom of trade and exemption from taxation in the Congo territory, even if this territory should one day pass to French control.[172] He also introduced a new wrinkle by requesting that Leopold fold his territorial disputes with the French and Portuguese into the upcoming conference, now scheduled to take place at the Palais Radziwill, his residence in Berlin.[173] Linking Leopold's own would-be state's international recognition to that of German colonies was something the King of the Belgians had earlier refused to do.[174]

Over the course of the next months, with his finances increasingly desperate, Leopold gradually acceded to Bismarck's demands.[175] As Leopold refined his lobbying to the German emperor and crown prince, Bismarck moved to recognize Leopold's association, not just as an authority in control of "stations"—or even as a state in early stages of creation, as the United States saw it—but as a full, independent, and internationally recognized existing state, albeit one that yet lacked a settled name.[176] Crucially, Leopold hoped this recognition would bring financial rewards: A license to issue government bonds or lottery loans within Germany.[177] Though this particular idea generated complaints from the German Finance Ministry, the chancellor obligated Germany to work for the recognition of the association by the other powers of Europe.[178] Leopold's tentative request included some very liberal borders, which ran well beyond even the loosest interpretation of the (often forged) maps and treaties Leopold had just submitted for review by the United States.[179] Still, Bismarck, who early on insisted that Leopold's imagined territory was too large, eventually agreed to turn an augmented version of that same fantasy into legal reality.[180] Thus he was not only putting an end to the "almost comical" uncertainty under which the AIA had hitherto existed; he was turning the AIA, on paper, into the master of an estimated fifteen million Africans.[181] This, notwithstanding that the Congo, by Bismarck's own admission, was a "geography I do not know," and that Bismarck privately identified the AIA's intentions toward indigenes as "parasitism."[182] "The rights accorded to the inhabitants," he predicted dryly, "may be very small."[183]

Given that Leopold was surreptitiously making himself the sole authority behind the AIA and that there was no mechanism for enforcing Leopold's free-trade guarantee for Germans, the conversion of Bismarck was no small feat.[184] It has even led some historians to speculate, incorrectly, that Leopold bamboozled the German chancellor.[185] At first glance, this interpretation has merit: Leopold had dangled the prospect of a "German India" in Africa and Bismarck had accepted Leopold's carte blanche border requests in his interest, both as an imitator of Borneo, and as a prospective buyer. Uniquely, Bismark had even consented to turn what had hitherto been advertised as "independent states" (first confederated, then "federated"), into one "independent state."[186] On the other hand, nothing Leopold did irrevocably upset any of Bismarck's plans. First, the effect of the pact between France and Leopold was relatively muted, insofar as France was not exactly an enemy of Bismarck's colonial games in mid- to late 1884. Rather, because France was an enemy of Bismarck's temporary public enemy, Britain, Bismarck was prepared to make small concessions to France in Africa in the interest of tangible European gains.[187] As important, from the perspective of *Innenpolitik* (domestic politics), Bismarck had not quite given up the hope that a German company would acquire or exercise the association's rights.[188] He could also still make great use of Leopold's case for his own domestic popularity. This was a fact pointed out early on by Leopold's man in Berlin, Victor Gantier.[189] It was also a key aspect behind holding a conference about the Congo in Germany's capital. In this context, consider the timeline of Bismarck's recognition of the AIA. In early July, Leopold bragged to the Italian ambassador in Brussels about Germany's "imminent" recognition.[190] By the end of September, with that recognition still in abeyance, Leopold gave into all of Bismarck's demands but still could not get a commitment from Germany.[191] Instead Bismarck scrupulously delayed formal recognition until November 8, 1884—the days immediately preceding the Berlin Conference, and a time highly convenient for him.[192]

At home Bismarck could certainly bend the AIA's case for statehood to his own ends, fitting any German support for the AIA into both his Anglophobic election campaign and the public relations battle for private

German colonies.[193] In May, in a series of newspaper articles commissioned by Bismarck, discussion about the Congo was arranged to shift "the attention of a larger circle" to some problems that had hitherto occupied only "historians and lawyers." These were, Bismarck's mouthpieces said, the issues of "how states are founded," whether "sovereign rights partly or entirely may be sold to private persons," and "whether one can sell independent states."[194] As no formal recognition of the AIA had yet been agreed, the newspaper articles questioned whether the AIA would measure up to such principles. They did not object to the principles as such, however.[195] Nor did they protest when Leopold's propagandists linked his efforts to those undertaken by merchants from Lüderitz's hometown in Bremen.[196]

By virtue of this whole matter going through the election cycle, it would help to bring Bismarck a more pliant majority in parliament, where he saw himself in a continual state of war readiness.[197] "Public opinion in Germany lays so great a stress on our colonial policy," Bismarck declared, "that the Government's position in the country actually depends on its success."[198] Weighed against this success, Leopold's fortunes as an individual hardly mattered so long as the German public continued to favor Bismarck's new path. Even when a delay of the U.S. participation in the Berlin Conference forced postponement of the conference to November—the month after German elections—the German chancellor gladly continued to entwine his own experimental colonial program with the fate of Leopold's Congo.[199] This was true abroad, as when Bismarck would adjoin complaints over Cameroon to pleas for Britain to support the AIA.[200] It was also true at home, even if it was not immediately apparent to foreign diplomats in Berlin or, for that matter, to future generations of historians.[201]

As 1884 ended Bismarck had deeply pragmatic reasons to continue with the policy. To begin, his foray into colonialism—the full dimensions of which were not-so-coincidentally unveiled to the electorate on October 13—had already helped him and his allies in late October 1884.[202] In March 1884, before the colonial initiative, election predictions foresaw Left-Liberals, Social Democrats, and the Catholic Center increasing their support—which, when combined, already constituted a majority of seats.[203] Instead, on October 28, with months of Bismarck's colony-heavy election propaganda behind them, voters went to the polls and cost the Left-Liberals forty-one seats in parliament, with the Center (arguably the least hostile of the bunch toward colonies) also losing one.[204] Bismarck's coalition, in turn, gained enough seats for a workable plurality partly because news of the coups in Africa galvanized younger voters, many of whom helped to ensure a record turnout of 59.3 percent on election day.[205] Some youth, including Max Weber, censured the Left-Liberals for failing to accept what seemed like a moderate, compromise vision of private German empires.[206] Measured separately, Bismarck's individual popularity also reached record highs at this time.[207]

Yet, even after October, the fate of many projects—including Bismarck's longstanding effort to pass a bill subsidizing steamship routes to Samoa and the Far East—still hinged on the popular domestic perception of colonialism generally.[208] Gains in parliamentary seats, though helpful, proved limited enough to let several bills the chancellor supported suffer quick defeats; Social Democrats had picked up a dozen of the slots lost by Left-Liberals, for example, and they hotly contested even a small funding measure to hire an additional director at the Foreign Ministry.[209] Moreover, the nature of administration and "subventions" in Germany's colonies received parliamentary grilling thanks to two new developments.[210] The first, the signing of treaties by Hansemann's agents in Northern New Guinea, did not concern Africa directly but nonetheless looked set to swell the ranks of private governments, and indeed by early November the German flag was flying at the island of New Britain (in today's Papua New Guinea), with thirteen further flag-raisings to follow within a month.[211] The second development was an uprising in Cameroon, where Bismarck had reluctantly consented to send warships for the purpose of smashing resistance to the administration of Adolph Woermann.[212] Here the pertinent debates were to begin as soon as the German emperor opened the Reichstag on November 20, 1884, urging the deputies, in a speech provided by Bismarck, to consider the global implications of "the dispatches regarding the overseas settlements that had been placed under the protection of the German empire."[213] As the emperor also noted, the Berlin Conference started just four days earlier, on November 16.[214] All these events involved the specter of Britain, Bismarck's electoral and foreign policy opponent du jour; all these events involved doubts about whether privately run empires could, or would, emerge as independent governing entities ready to pay colonial bills already running in the hundreds of thousands of marks.[215] Toward year's end there was a swell of opinion, from the Catholic Center to progressives and socialists, "that the colonial policy, as it is currently developing, exceeds the dimensions which the chancellor laid out for us in the sessions of the previous year."[216] Bismarck, in other words, would travel back and forth between the Reichstag and the Palais Radziwill to discuss essentially the same issue, privately run empires, with the same domestic politics at stake, by Bismarck's admission, from November to February, or roughly as long as the duration of the "rising" in Cameroon.[217]

If it was true that this issue was only one of many on the agenda, therefore, it was also undeniable that the recognition by the international community of Leopold's treaties, designs, and "statehood" could bolster Bismarck's tenuous domestic colonial program in which "bold Hanseatic merchants . . . acquired sovereign rights on their own account."[218] Every morsel of information about the AIA's progress that made its way to Berlin—and Leopold's agents fed meals to Bismarck's lieutenants—reinforced Bismarck's vision of privately run German empires.[219] Leaked reports of indigenous uprisings in the Congo coincided with a discussion of setbacks in Cameroon.[220] Newspaper readers in Frankfurt received news of the Berlin Conference alongside published versions of Woermann's treaties with Ndumbé Lobé Bell, as well as excerpts from the British House of Commons concerning the North Borneo Company.[221] Nor were these the only products of expert timing. In the conference's second month, the German government published multiple "White Books" of official documents on the establishment of a colony at Angra Pequeña—a novel bit of transparency for German diplomacy.[222] It also leaked entire files of colonial information to the press.[223] At the same time, Gustav Nachtigal's inspection of German colonial sites publicly included a lengthy rendezvous in the Congo, complete with visits to the installations of the International African Association. Nachtigal spent three weeks inspecting Leopold's handiwork, and three days on Lüderitz's.[224] His journeys into the West African interior also derived on-the-ground intellectual support from the AIA's propagandists.[225]

Considering these links, Bismarck looked less than bamboozled by his Belgian interlocutor.[226] The German chancellor took care to make sure that support for the AIA among the majority of German papers was equated, not with an international spirit, but with German nationalist aims—notably the particular project of private colonialism that he was launching and defending against Left-Liberals in his parliament.[227]

At the conference in Berlin, Bismarck would further enforce this equation by making no distinction between the various types of government being set up by Europeans in Africa—whether "protectorate," "colony," or otherwise.[228] Nationalism aside, however, the guarantee of German free trade in the Congo would also mean economic protection for German merchants with little direct cost to Berlin.[229] Germany proper would have to provide a measure of "consular" protection to its citizens' Congo operations, but that was something Germany already afforded to citizens in any foreign territories. It would simply mean the status quo, with benefits.

As regarded finances, Bismarck would see to it that Leopold's outfit benefitted German traders in particular, with or without Germany's purchase of Leopold's rights. One could even argue that informal preference was better for German merchants than direct German control.[230] That left the question of what the merchants might give Bismarck in return. Part of the answer lay in Berlin, where, toward the end of 1884, Bismarck's plan to shift the onus for "German" colonial expense onto the shoulders of German business was coming under assault just a few months after its introduction.[231] Some of the problem was accidental: A febrile Nachtigal had also gone beyond his mandate in one location—Little Popo—by signing treaties of protection not only with the local "king," Mlapa III, but also with Ewe leaders from other territories as far away as Lomé.[232] As a result, dozens of German flags now attested that the coast of today's Togo lay under the vague control of Germany proper, not privately run empires. This too-broad growth threatened to bring conceptual confusion and spread the Borneo idea thin.

Bismarck had initially conceived his colonial arrangement as being similar to the old German Confederation, even going so far as to describe the arrangement with a term, *Oberherrlichkeit,* that he had once used to describe Prussia's relationship to other confederated North German states in the 1860s.[233] Another analogy was to the Samoan islands, where, as recently as 1880, Bismarck had preferred to have Germany share in sovereignty with Britain, the United States, and Samoans, rather than to claim it exclusively.[234] But as the number of test cases grew, Bismarck's attempt to contextualize the new German colonies met with derision from several important parties.[235] Deputies in the Reichstag questioned the applicability of the Borneo "exemplar" to what was actually happening; "to be frank," one said, "it was only because of it" that they had "declared ourselves inclined to support in a certain measure" the smaller colonial policy Bismarck had inaugurated in June.[236] The Left-Liberal Bamberger complained that the whole system sounded good but had fallen apart upon closer inspection; the conservative Holstein thought Bismarck might be going senile; the socialist Frederick Engels called the Borneo plan "dumb"; and August Reichensperger, a retiring Catholic deputy, told voters he worried about it having brought Germany into "great costs and entanglements."[237] Engels's contemporary, Wilhelm Liebknecht, was only slightly more generous when he called Bismarck's plan a "fata morgana on the sands and swamps of Africa," charging the chancellor with "an unusual dose of naiveté."[238] None of these critics knew how right they were. In October Bismarck was forced to call a hush-hush meeting, at which he told a syndicate of Germans doing business in West Africa—in a retreat from demands he had made just a few weeks earlier, in another closed session—that, should the businessmen collapse, Germany proper was prepared to take on, not just foreign relations in each colony, but justice and military administration as well.[239]

"I am trying," Bismarck eventually told his critics, "to push the governance off on the Hanseatic merchants. It isn't easy."[240] Global finance, for its part, did not help the cause. Starting in May 1884, an acute panic began in America and spread to Europe, meaning even Woermann and his well-connected colleagues had trouble getting loans, whether from the D-Banks, London, or Paris. Accordingly, there was little private appetite for risk overseas precisely when Bismarck most coveted it.[241] Woermann quickly complained that German companies, unlike their counterpart on Borneo, had to keep fair terms for British rivals unless they wanted to risk shutting out foreign traders and experiencing reprisals in foreign territories where the volume of German trade was much larger.[242] By October 1884, while Bismarck spoke of many German empires with "the whole organization of administration" in the hands of merchants, Woermann denied his responsibility for any public expenses: courts, police, customs houses.[243] Then he warned any prospective German emigrants away from Cameroon. "Sovereignty on the part of the businessmen," Woermann later told his colleagues, was a "ridiculous" delusion.[244] Nor could there be any discussion of his governing Cameroon in the long term.[245] Woermann eventually turned to the parliament—where members mocked him as "King" and suggested he form a "Praetorian Guard" of Bismarck loyalists for Cameroon's defense—to deny there had ever been a plan for him to run any government.[246]

As this conjuncture matured, Bismarck weighed requests to send more warships to the Cameroon coast, where a series of violent conflicts erupted among people not consulted in their supposed kings' sale of political rights to Woermann.[247] Woermann was finding it prohibitively expensive to make new treaties and periodically asked for Nachtigal's help.[248] Worse still for Woermann, Africans who had agreed to deals quickly regretted them, and would "gladly reverse the whole event, if they could."[249] King Bell, his subjects having taken up arms against him, was forced to flee Bell Town and, according to missionaries, spent six weeks hiding around a nearby creek.[250] As concerning for a legal theorist, though, were eyewitness reports that the treaties arranged by Woermann had never, even at the moment of sale, achieved a consensus in the affected communities.[251] On the contrary, initial negotiations had aroused such ire among headmen—many of whom preferred an alliance with the British—that German agents had to start conducting talks at night, while the majority of the population slept.[252] In one case, this meant 3 A.M.[253] Simply put, many indigenes, including the son of the man who had allegedly signed over control of a vast territory to Woermann, did not yet recognize overarching German authority.[254] Woermann therefore asked that Bismarck and Germany step in by contributing taxpayer money with which to fund armies and build infrastructure.[255]

In the final months of 1884, with Cameroon's "rising" in view, Bismarck beseeched nearly every party involved in the German colonial movement to do more than profit from free trade in the Congo.[256] Whether in Cameroon or Togo, he urged these men to look at Leopold's Congo as a legal and spiritual model for private governance, even going so far as to forward to Woermann an advance copy of his speech recognizing the Congo as a state.[257] Nor was that all. In the midst of diplomacy that culminated in the Congo Association's Europe-wide recognition, Stanley conducted a tour around Germany, stopping in Cologne, Frankfurt, Wiesbaden, and other cities to give speeches to chapters of the German Colonial Society.[258] The supposed hero of the Congo landed plaudits for his role as an American delegate to the ongoing Berlin Conference—his presence there, and his tour in Germany, only possible via Bismarck's direct authorization.[259] Stanley became a member of both the German African Society and the German Geographical Society.[260] He also received an honorary doctorate from the University of Halle and even won an audience with the German emperor, whom he went on to toast in prominent speeches.[261] Perhaps more intriguingly, though, he remained in close correspondence with key German outlets. In late September, he wrote a published letter to the editor of Munich's largest newspaper opining that perhaps only private societies, and not preexisting European states, could properly conduct Sub-Saharan colonization.[262] Bismarck took some initiative, too, as when he encouraged several of the parties hosting Stanley to take "rejuvenation from his work," and to craft Germany's own policies after the "method used by Stanley" in "peacefully" acquiring and governing territory by private means.[263]

These ranks included the usual suspects from within Germany—dignitaries (Prince Hohenlohe-Langenburg, the Grand Duke of Saxe-Weimar-Eisenach), publicists (Friedrich Fabri), and potential investors (Gerson Bleichöder, Werner von Siemens)—but also a wide array of diplomats from Spain, Portugal, Italy, Brazil, and Japan.[264] At one banquet in Frankfurt, organizers placed the flag of the Congo Association in the middle of a row of flags from the various German provinces.[265] At another, in Berlin, the German Union for Trade Geography explicitly located Stanley's work in the Congo within larger German traditions: anti-French nationalism; German unification; and, not least, the colonial movement of which Bismarck was the "political, intellectual originator."[266] Whether Stanley comprehended the domestic significance of such developments is unclear.[267] "Such kindness as she has shown," remarked Stanley when referring to Germany's reception, "was totally unexpected by me."[268] Yet, after complaints that his duty was only to deliver "platitudes" and "pointless" speeches to German audiences, he did, in any event, identify an ulterior motive in Berlin's depiction of a "special" relationship in which the AIA would favor Germany above other nations.[269] This warm welcome may not necessarily have been a sign, as he later theorized, that German citizens would eventually try to seize the Congo for themselves; though such schemes were still alive by late 1884.[270] Rather, Stanley's German celebration was a tool with which Bismarck hoped to "get" several Congos, each tied just enough to Germany to bring its chancellor glory without major expenditure.

One of the messages sent to the German colonialists honoring Stanley—by Bismarck's design—was that control of, and financial responsibility for, German colonies needed to stay in private hands as much as possible.[271] In other words, the doctrine of protecting German merchants, for which Bismarck had implied blanket acceptance to an enthusiastic electorate before October 1884, actually needed to have limits.[272] This preference became still clearer at a dinner hosted by Bismarck exclusively for Stanley and Woermann on November 24, 1884, just four days after the Reichstag received the first formal request for funding support in the "German" colony of Cameroon.[273] Bismarck began by introducing the two men. He then proceeded, in impeccable English, to "express his amazement that a private man like Stanley could have acquired such an immense territory."[274] Woermann noted that "this fact had positively influenced the decision of Bismarck to acquire colonies for Germany."[275] But there was also an urgency to the matter, for Woermann was at that very moment embroiled in a dispute with Bismarck over the further costs of governance in the fledgling colony of Cameroon: a dispute over who would pay to run prisons, build roads, and maintain a coast guard.[276] A formal request from Woermann on November 20 was the first of many to come, and it came not long after the latest opening of a private German state, in New Guinea.[277] There, too, the hoisting of a German flag—"in the same measure and under the same conditions as the Hanseatic undertakings in Southwest Africa," Bismarck hoped—became known to the public in the middle of debates over the Congo.[278]

Woermann had never wanted to take on the burden of rule—though it is probable that he had misled Bismarck about his intentions to do so from April 1884 through at least September of the same year.[279] Still, Bismarck wanted Woermann's Cameroon regime to copy the men in Borneo sincerely, by shouldering virtually all governmental expenses and perhaps even turning Woermann's considerable logistical and marine apparatuses into an ersatz navy.[280] This wish was only growing in view of indigenous unrest, which was prompting Woermann to barrage Bismarck's office in November 1884 with requests for the dispatch of German naval cruisers and other assistance through direct subsidies.[281] By the end of 1884, reported one journalist, the colonial question was still playing a "lead role" in Reichstag debates, "in newspaper articles, and social conversations" generally; famous economist Wilhelm Roscher even weighed in, concluding that "political trading companies" were "dangerous" to the "long-term fortune" of a subject people, and likely to create "great political and social difficulties."[282] For now, Bismarck wanted Woermann to act in step with Borneo's biggest imitator: Leopold. Woermann and German businessmen, who had so far not been giving "sufficient support" to Bismarck's Borneo plan, would do well to witness the success that was coming with "ease" to the Congo enterprise toward the end of 1884.[283] Bismarck, after all, controlled the fate of both, and he would continue to insist on private governance well into 1885.[284]

The German chancellor told the American ambassador as much in November 1884.[285] Bismarck understood, a German admirer wrote, "how to make the affair of the Belgian King into one of his own."[286] What support for Leopold would look like was another, initially hazy matter.[287] In part it consisted of Germany's official recognition of the Congo State, finally extended on November 15. Another aspect was to invite Leopold's agents to meetings of German colonialists—Lüderitz and company—in order to give each party an "excellent occasion" to "make influential friends."[288] But the majority of the picture became clear at the so-called Berlin Conference, a notorious gathering of diplomats held in Berlin from November 15 through early 1885.[289]

TO THIS DAY there is much myth surrounding the affair, which also went by other names among its participants: "Congo Conference," "West African Conference," and, more simply, the "African Conference."[290] The future Wilhelm II, the son of the German crown prince, characterized the conference as a gathering of powers united against England.[291] He was perhaps half right.[292] An agreement to host the conference in Berlin, not London—announced to the public around two weeks before the German elections, within twenty-four hours of when Bismarck unveiled his full German colonial program—did look like a swipe at Britain.[293] The *Morning Post* went so far as to call it "the most cruel, the most contemptuous, and the most dangerous blow ever dealt to the reputation and influence of the English Government."[294] And British public opinion was so panicked by the prospect of the Franco-German fleets' outnumbering Britain's that parliament agreed on a vast peacetime increase in funding for warship construction.[295]

Certainly, Britain did stand to lose from the formalization of rules for territorial acquisitions in the Congo and Africa generally, given London's preference to maintain an informal hegemony.[296] The German government did much to play up that point through early November, both in the press and in symbolism, such as the decision to replace London-made maps with German ones in the conference meeting hall.[297] Bismarck even declared that the proceedings would take place without Britain if necessary, despite Britain's having promptly agreed to participate.[298]

That said, some diplomats correctly predicted the Franco-German entente—really more of a détente—would not escape the conference untarnished.[299] By November France was not inclined to antagonize Britain in African affairs, having been obliquely strong-armed by Lord Lyons from his office in London; Ferry's grip on power was also weakening, his cabinet entering an acute phase of conflict in Indochina that would spell his downfall.[300] The notion of a Franco-German alliance had, unsurprisingly, proven distasteful to the French public.[301] Likewise, with German elections ending after October 28, Bismarck could relax his anti-British posturing.[302] Germany accordingly did not remain united with France during the Berlin Conference, with much of its activity there running counter to French ambitions, and some of it—such as placating the U.S. delegates—occurring with direct British assists.[303]

One piece of this work comprised German recognition of the AIA's chosen frontiers, which partly overlapped with those claimed by the French, in conjunction with the opening of ceremonies. If this ostensible German generosity was a surprise that offended French preferences for a much smaller zone, it was also a check to France's momentum in its side negotiations with the AIA over territorial boundaries, and an unfavorable precedent so far as other nations were concerned.[304] From the summer of 1884 through early 1885, French agents had signed a number of treaties in territories disputed by the AIA in order to add bargaining chips; they even threw up French flags and houses on AIA station grounds.[305] So concerted was this effort that, immediately prior to the conference, Leopold's agents admitted internally that they had accomplished "nothing" with France and did "not think it likely" they would do so, absent some intervention.[306]

Bismarck forced a different outcome. In various ways he protested against what he perceived as French aggression "at the center of Africa," going, as he put it, "truly as far as he knew how to go" without irreparably damaging Franco-German relations.[307] Throughout the proceedings, he supported Stanley, a man Ferry wanted cashiered, at the expense of Brazza's proxy and former comrade in exploration, the French physician Noël Ballay.[308] The French, having refused an agreement allowing the AIA to build a railway in the Lower Congo, ran up against German opposition.[309] Upset by what it regarded as Leopold's intrigues, France's team sought to delay proceedings so as to hasten the association's financial collapse, or "suicide," as Leopold called it.[310] By contrast, Bismarck repeatedly insisted that France quickly settle its borders around the Congo via concurrent negotiations with the AIA, prompting Ferry to threaten to walk away and flirt with the idea of a Portuguese alliance.[311] Alphonse Chodron de Courcel of the French delegation speculated that Bismarck was profiting by his zealous support of the association, "perhaps in Africa, perhaps in Europe," but he admitted to not comprehending how.[312] By January, with several meetings already postponed as a result of the German foreign minister's illness, France would push for yet another extension of the conference's timetable, despite Bismarck's support for an immediate deal favorable to the AIA.[313] The French press had already turned heavily against Berlin.[314]

So much for the Franco-German entente. More approximately, a number of historians have vilified the Berlin Conference as a gathering that laid down rules for carving up the African continent. Such a finding is understandable, for the public's image of the conference at the time consisted of European aristocrats, seated at a horseshoe-shaped table between marble walls, drawing lines on a fourteen-foot-tall wall map of Africa.[315] Just two months after it ended, an Italian parliamentarian would look back at the conference and accuse it of facilitating the conquest of Africa by its participants.[316] Carl Schmitt reinforced this impression in his 1950 tome *Nomos of the Earth,* writing of an international congress, clear and consistent in its purpose, which aimed to appropriate all the land in Africa.[317] In truth, though, the gathering was an odd hybrid.

On the one hand, it was understood by its participants, in the moment, as certain to have "far reaching effects" and to become "one of the most important [events] in history."[318] The conference, so predicted the German crown princess, was to arrange Africa's future.[319] And, to be sure, some attendees did just that, as when Woermann, on behalf of

Germany, unilaterally negotiated with the Spanish delegate to accept certain wild Spanish claims to rule along the Río Campo, in exchange for Madrid's compliance with German claims opposite the Bight of Biafra.[320] On the other hand, the conference only addressed certain parts of Africa, and its official agenda did not so much authorize new colonization as approve colonization that had already gotten underway. Besides, far from orchestrating grand designs with precision, its participants looked downright unorganized. They hastily crammed information in the lead-up to the opening.[321] Thereafter, they met only in afternoons, only for a few hours at a time, and only at irregular intervals, with notifications of postponements frequently arriving at delegates' hotel rooms the evening before an appointment.[322] Of these last instances, perhaps the most egregious derived from the British ambassador's failure to decipher his telegraphic instructions in time for a scheduled session.[323] Compounding such time troubles, most delegates at the conference felt cramped for space. They lacked typewriters and had to rely on their respective embassies in Berlin for logistical support just to record everything under discussion at meetings.[324] Even the hall they met in looked overcrowded: For much of December, it housed a towering Christmas tree and gifts in addition to the horseshoe-shaped conference table.[325]

Another reason historians struggle with the conference is that its legal significance is tough to evaluate. Those who believe its resolutions carried out the partition of Africa surely exaggerate.[326] But those who dismiss it as meaningless also go too far.[327] Such analysis, however critical or respectful, overlooks that Bismarck partly convened the conference to rubber-stamp certain partitions that had already occurred: those of his private German empires. The hidden beneficiaries of the conference's imprimatur were Bismarck's German colonial experiment and the Borneo precedent on which it relied.[328] This outcome may seem obvious in hindsight; it was not so in the summer of 1884, when Britain, to quote Foreign Secretary Lord Granville, agreed to the conference with the erroneous understanding "that it was only about the Congo."[329] Though Bismarck had his own agenda, very few others had more than a vague advance sense of what would occur during the conference. "All in fact is in obscurity as to what will be done tomorrow," American delegate Henry Sanford wrote to his wife the night before proceedings began.[330]

By the end of 1884 various lesser powers with and without direct colonial ambitions in Africa accepted invitations to the conference. Spain and the Ottoman Empire harbored immediate agendas in regard to Morocco and the Egyptian Sudan, respectively.[331] As for the rest, historians generally find it easy to overlook their presence, but that is to miss an important aspect of Bismarck's plan.[332] When asked about the Austrian delegation's remit, Count Kálnoky, the foreign minister, assured his colleagues that they had no interest whatsoever in the proceedings.[333] Such talk was bombast, however.[334] Behind closed doors at the conference, Austrian and Swedish officials expressed a desire to securing favorable long-term trade access; Austria, for one, had been exporting Maria Theresa *thaler* to Africa profitably for over a century, to the extent that the coins became de facto standards in many East African settings.[335] Italy believed inclusion in such commercial opportunities in West Africa would prove popular at home, if perhaps not immediately.[336] Still other attending powers, such as the Netherlands, admitted to having a different stake in the outcome when worrying over whether the Congo matter would establish precedents that might prove binding for non-African colonial realms.[337] Even Russia, seemingly the power least relevant to Africa, had strong religious ties to Ethiopia in the 1880s and meddled heavily in that empire's complicated affairs, which already included steady supplies of firearms from French and Italian dealers.[338]

One needs to keep this set of interests in mind when evaluating that, from Germany's perspective, the point of inviting a wide array of powers to the Berlin Conference was to create an impression of broad multilateral consensus such as had been achieved at the Congress of Vienna in 1815 and the Berlin congress on Ottoman affairs in 1878, as well as in river conventions for the Danube in 1856, 1878, and 1883.[339] This assessment is accurate but misses part of the picture. Bismarck himself mused that the greater the variety of ceremonial delegates, the greater the impression of global legitimacy—especially insofar as the conference ostensibly concerned two international rivers.[340] But Dutch officials, for example, knew that the court of international opinion had been packed partly through their attendance.[341] It all worked because of a quid pro quo: In exchange for attendance and some concessions, the lesser powers mostly agreed to "play the mute duck role," as the Italian delegate put it, thus giving Bismarck an overwhelming mandate for his colonial vision, when and in what manner he needed it.[342]

The corollary of this approach was that it positioned Germany as a better internationalist than Britain, which roughly contemporaneously refused to invite more than six powers to conferences concerning the Suez and Egypt.[343] Bismarck welcomed the United States, invited Sweden-Norway and Denmark so they would not feel "left out," and granted the Ottomans' and Italians' late requests for invitations; Britain appeared indifferent to each proposition.[344] Hence, too, Germany's wish to implement considerable pomp and circumstance at the conference, even to the point of last-minute rearrangements of seating charts.[345] Undeterred by a series of cold and dreary days with high winds, the German organizers made sure they prepared a sumptuous spread of meats, fish *en mayonnaise,* fried lobster, wine, and tea in the parlors adjoining the council room; they staged supposedly spontaneous procolonial demonstrations outside the meeting hall; they even put on dozens of evening balls held by German nobility—"imperial tediousness," as the Americans complained.[346]

Aware of the potential public-relations benefits, Bismarck initially proposed two conferences: the first, to include only the directly involved major powers; the second, to include "other maritime powers whose agreement would seem desirable": Austria-Hungary, Italy, Russia, Sweden-Norway.[347] Although Bismarck ultimately abandoned that scheme, the single conference still looked a lot like two, with delegates from "backbench" powers not only being marginalized during the most important negotiations, but even being seated in a way that visualized their lesser rank.[348] Viewed as a spectrum, the number of official speeches confirmed such disparities. Germany's delegates took the floor a staggering 142 times between them, while their French, British, Belgian, and Portuguese counterparts each registered totals in the forties and sixties. Denmark and Sweden-Norway only made a single nonprocedural comment, and at one point the Ottoman delegate was told to remain silent or risk ostracism from future conferences.[349] Add to this the secrets, open even before the conference began, that Italy would indefatigably support the AIA and that Austria would do Germany's bidding—having done just that in discussions on Egypt a few months earlier.[350] Still, it is worth noting, notwithstanding such discrepancies, that Bismarck's public relations effort proved successful, in part because each power formally claimed just one vote in resolutions.[351]

Able to act with French backing in November 1884, Bismarck opened the conference to an audience of perhaps thirty delegates.[352] Insiders who predicted that the "first question to be brought up will be the Congo" soon proved correct. For at least the next month, as one joke ran, the Congo became "the dinner on all menus" for diplomats; and even Berlin socialites complained that the Congo was all anyone seemed to talk about.[353] In fact the Congo determined the conference's entire trajectory, with its final day arriving only when the AIA had secured its last letter of diplomatic recognition.[354] Choosing to forget everything that he had gleaned about Leopold's duplicity—and some of what other delegates already suspected—Bismarck stressed the humanitarian aims of the latter's organization.[355] The takeaway from Bismarck's speech was that all delegates should support Leopold's philanthropic efforts and, more controversially, should agree to the proposition that the rights acquired by treaty had made the AIA into a state. Though the conference ostensibly excluded all territorial questions from its deliberations, Bismarck—put forward for presidency of the conference by the pliant Italian delegate—ensured that the AIA's recognition occurred in simultaneous shadow sittings, "an ingenious method of settling such questions extramurally."[356]

In a little over a week's time, most European powers moved to realize Bismarck's wishes for the AIA, though doubts remained about the exact manner of recognition. The AIA's lobbyists in Europe quickly drafted a sample treaty in which delegates would sign off on the "decisions of the African Conference of Berlin" while simultaneously "recognizing" the Association of the Congo as a "new state."[357] Of course, unless this draft was to remain hypothetical, the new "État indépendant du Congo," appropriately taking the acronym of the old East India Company (EIC), needed to see "its boundaries be fixed and declared."[358] It needed, as well, to produce some "simple Bill of Rights and Constitution defining rights and duties but leaving the details of carrying them out to the local authorities" and to have either a plenipotentiary or "the Governor General of the Independent State of the Congo present" at Berlin to sign treaties with representatives of the other powers.[359] Nonetheless, "affairs of the Congo," as Leopold assured Belgium's prime minister, now looked "very well" because of Germany's support.[360] The conference in some cases froze time in the association's battles with Portugal and France on the ground.[361] European leaders would contemporaneously order their navies in the gulf of the Congo to avoid "any act that would affect the status quo" until "all things concerning the river" could be decided in Berlin.[362] Alternatively, agents of the association convinced French rivals to fly both parties' flags in front of indigenous populations until a Berlin verdict materialized.[363] Thus it was not enough to say, as an American delegate did, that the association had been "re-energized now by Germany" and was "*much* stronger today than with our recognition alone."[364] A more apt description was probably the one offered later by a Belgian advisor, who remarked that Bismarck had become Leopold's "lucky star."[365]

Bismarck certainly provided considerable assistance to agents that Leopold had planted within and around the conference's meetings.[366] He extended official welcomes to all of them and assisted them in lobbying Austria-Hungary, even when their diplomatic credentials had not arrived.[367] At a court dinner, he sat the association's lobbyists near the German emperor and crown prince so that the latter could all "be more acquainted with" their organization.[368] The association's attendees included the Belgian statesman François Auguste, Baron Lambermont; Henry Morton Stanley; Henry Sanford; Sir Travis Twiss; and Émile Banning, all delegates working unofficially on Leopold's behalf; as well as Maximilien Strauch, the nominal head of the *Comité*, Liévin van de Velde, and Belgian state minister Eudore Pirmez, "imported person[s]" who made visits to Berlin from November 13 to carry on their work somewhat less prominently, in the gardens and corridors adjoining Bismarck's residence.[369] Owing to this lobbying group, and in part to widespread ignorance about Africa, most delegates not in Leopold's employ proved ready to overlook the disparity between his territorial claims and geographical reality.[370] "Knowledge is power," Sanford observed laconically.[371]

It was later reported, albeit without acknowledgement of the presence of dozens of informal hangers-on (including missionaries) familiar with African affairs, that only two delegates at the conference had ever been in Africa.[372] Nearly all of them relied on Stanley's assistance with African maps—"after him, there was nothing to say by anybody"—or perused "books, brochures, and maps" selectively provided by the German Foreign Ministry to familiarize them with "all the latest."[373] As if it were not enough that this collection heavily favored Leopold's propaganda, there was a periodic blurring of the lines between Leopold's unofficial lobbyists and those formally sent by the Belgian government.[374] Leopold had Sanford, Stanley, and Strauch stay in a different hotel from the Belgian delegation proper; Sanford even paid his own expenses.[375] Strauch, however, was going "around in his grand uniform" as a Belgian colonel to make "official visits" at various embassies, even though he was actually, like his master, a half-rogue.[376]

Of the major powers, Britain arguably carried the most weight in relation to the AIA's hopes; on its decision hinged also the fate of Portuguese obstruction, and the surrender of the latter position would allow Italy—afraid of antagonizing Lisbon, but predisposed to support Leopold's "work"—an opportunity to finalize its recognition of the AIA.[377] Several officials in London had peered through Leopold's smokescreens, only to find greed and piracy without the sanction of any preexisting government. Residents in the vicinity of Sette Cama, a site hotly contested between French and association claims, had complained to British businessmen that the AIA was trying to inflate the terms agreed on in its treaties—in particular, by pretending that an agreement to make roads amounted to a sale of the country.[378] British officials also understood that, in Bismarck's view, an endorsement of Leopold would also entail an endorsement of the fledgling German empires overseas.[379] Virtually all of the latter territories conflicted with English claims, particularly regarding Cameroon, and, collectively, the German territories were already being viewed by some English commentators as an "ignominious chapter in the colonial history of England."[380] Either way, Britain, said one of its delegates early in the process, could never extend diplomatic recognition to Leopold's organization.[381] After all, besides any concerns about Leopold's motives, lawyers examining the Congo in the Foreign Office believed there was no way for the AIA "to prove its title," let alone find a legal precedent allowing it to buy the status of a state.[382] Even if it could, Sir Thomas Villiers Lister, assistant under-secretary for foreign affairs, insisted that "we are bound to commit ourselves against the filibustering of an irresponsible Association of no nationality, which cheats the natives out of their lands and sovereign rights and establishes monopolies in order to sell them to the highest bidder."[383]

Bismarck begged to differ, dangling a withdrawal of his tentative support for British supremacy in the lower Niger River Basin, as well as in Egypt, unless he got his way.[384] Whitehall's first instinct was to bristle at the demand.[385] Still, the British government had reasons to take any threat over the Niger quite seriously. To begin, the threat of a Brazza-inspired French penetration of the Niger had been perceived since 1882, and it was only reinforced by Ferry's insistence on including the Niger in the discussions at Berlin.[386] Second, there was a major, and growing, German presence in the Niger Delta at the time, with Eduard Flegel, an explorer and member of the German Colonial Society, suggesting that Bismarck authorize a colony on the Benué, the Niger's main tributary.[387] British and French trade with the area had tripled from 1879 to 1884, and Germans could win a share.[388] Equally significant, Flegel was in Berlin during the conference and closely advised Bismarck on colonial affairs.[389]

Although no Africans were present at the conference formally, Flegel had developed intimate relations with several African communities along the Benué, to the extent that indigenous navigators joined him for an extended sojourn in Berlin starting in late October 1884.[390] With these navigators figuring among the unofficial circles surrounding the delegates, and in view of Bismarck's colonial turn, it was easy for the British and French to imagine a scenario in which the Germans went on to contest various contracts and treaties signed by British merchants in regard to the Niger interior, perhaps even by producing their own.[391] French generals already knew such tactics well, contemporaneously hosting Timbuktu's ambassador at the Grand Hôtel du Louvre to upstage rivals in Western Sudan.[392] London took Flegel's entourage seriously enough to commission an inquiry into his influence among Niger elites and to prepare a report explaining why their subjects' claims were superior to those of the Germans.[393] In the event, in early December 1884, Bismarck told Britain he wanted to keep open the possibility of expanding northward the German holdings in Cameroon; Nachtigal had already gestured in this direction.[394] Precisely as Bismarck made his threat, Flegel partnered with the firm of Jantzen & Thormählen, which had recently bought sovereign rights in Cameroon, to found a separate "German Niger Company" dedicated to Benué trade.[395] Add to this that, by the time Flegel's "black friends" made it to Berlin, they went from being identified as "caravan-leaders" to being advertised as nothing less than princes.[396]

A final, related motive for a British volte-face regarding the Congo was that the architects of British Niger policy had close ties to the Borneo precedent.[397] Among them was Sir Travers Twiss, a disgraced Oxford professor now acting as a legal advisor to the British delegation. Twiss had developed close personal ties to Sanford—the two met daily during their time in Berlin—and had already written several pamphlets in support of the association's statehood prior to arriving at the conference, motivated in large part by the recent events in Borneo (see Epilogue).[398] Twiss's favorable disposition agreed with that of the Scottish industrialist William Mackinnon, another of Leopold's friends; Mackinnon produced a memorandum for the Foreign Office recommending Britain support a series of African ventures "on the lines of the North Borneo Company."[399] A final contributor to the détente was Julian Pauncefote, permanent undersecretary in the Foreign Office and, as mentioned, a close confidante and early defender of the British North Borneo Company.[400]

Pauncefote, known to have greatly influenced Gladstone's decision to grant the North Borneo charter in 1881, viewed Leopold's enterprise "with great interest" while keeping tabs on the conference back in London.[401] He granted confidential lobbying visits to Strauch's associates, such that Stanley thought him the "most sympathetic" Foreign Office member toward the association.[402] "Why," asked Pauncefote in a formulation very consistent with Leopold's propaganda, "should we not recognize the political existence of the Free States of the Congo and make a Treaty with their chosen Chief, the Association?"[403] Britain, Pauncefote noted, had already recognized the right of African states to transfer political control in exchange for money; Pauncefote had confirmed as much when reviewing correspondence on his government's recognition of Lüderitzland.[404] One of Britain's own subjects, George Goldie Taubman, had just claimed to conclude several treaties on precisely this basis in the lower Niger River area.[405] And what about Western states generally?[406] A memorandum produced for the conference by the Colonial Office argued that, for some time now, they all had been paying valuable sums for political control over Africans by means of treaty.[407] Leopold's propagandists were thus correct when they argued that their method of getting "sovereign rights was not inferior to the titles relied upon by the European powers in the course of their colonial expansion" so far.[408] This history's most recent entry, as Brazza would attest, came in the form of the *makoko* treaties.[409]

Against this backdrop Bismarck threatened to withdraw his support for British plans in Egypt as well as the lower Niger—unless Britain recognized Leopold's Congo state.[410] Although Bismarck's opposition to Britain had more to do with German domestic policy than with intrinsic interest in Egypt or the Niger, archived correspondence suggests that Bismarck's threat still disturbed London. Partly this was sheer annoyance: Germany had consented when Britain conditioned its participation in the conference on the basis that, in the Niger, its subjects' "agreements made with the native chiefs . . . will be respected."[411] Regarding Egypt, Bismarck also seems to have timed some of his protests to coincide with Britain's issuance of new suggestions for debt resolution.[412] A more serious cause for consternation was that the methods behind expansion in the Niger and in the Congo looked virtually identical.[413] The foundation of Taubman's incipient control in the lower Niger was not vague claims about occupation; it was a private company that had been signing treaties purporting to buy "powers of government over the region where it traded."[414] Thirty-seven such documents would make their way into the cabinet's hands by February 1885, when Taubman made formal a longstanding proposal that the lower Niger "might be governed" by this company, "somewhat as Rajah Brooke was governing Borneo," or, alternatively, somewhat as the North Borneo Company was allegedly doing.[415] In this same vein, the lawyer handling Taubman's negotiations with the British government had long been pitching his client's holdings as analogues to those acquired by Brooke and Alfred Dent, scion of the North Borneo Company.[416] Pauncefote did not champion Taubman's cause so resolutely as he had championed Dent's years earlier; in particular, Pauncefote objected to irregularities in Taubman's treaties.[417] But Taubman drew heavy support from the Manchester Chamber of Commerce, which also rallied behind Leopold in the Congo.[418]

Borneo, to this extent, was the linchpin of multiple designs toward the end of 1884. British officials had been disinclined through mid-1884 to support Taubman with "protection," fearing bloodshed and costs to the taxpayer; consequently, London would turn down four of his requests for a charter in as many years.[419] By the end of 1884, though, pessimists could invert the equation: With Taubman having just bought out the last of his rivals in October, weeks before delegates convened at Berlin, a failure to issue a charter and win international approval for

Taubman's shaky regime might leave costly direct administration by London as the only option to keep British trade in the Niger from collapse—especially if Taubman followed through on periodic threats to sell out to "foreign" interests.[420] More than one bureaucrat in Whitehall now wondered whether the Niger Company were "taking such properties and occupying such a position in these vast and distant regions as to impose the absolute necessity of a stronger organization than they possess as a mere commercial association."[421] For some the answer seemed simple: Britain needed to recognize that the company was a state, then give this state a charter and bring it under as much loose oversight as existed in the case of Borneo. There would be utility in such a course: It would save Britain money and keep trade along the lower Niger free from any protectionism by French rivals, as well as from the looming threat from Germans in Cameroon and other neighboring areas.[422] A strong stance on West Africa could, in turn, yield positive publicity for Gladstone's cabinet, already weakened by a host of factors: electoral reform legislation; tumult in Egypt; ongoing crisis in Ireland; near-war with Russia over Afghanistan; and, as of late January 1885, the failure of Garnet Wolseley's expedition to save Gordon at Khartoum.[423]

Again, though, one must remember that the legality of a potential privately held sovereignty in the lower Niger was a controversial matter—especially since it dovetailed with the international uncertainty surrounding the Congo.[424] Some politicians agreed with Taubman's assessment, made in 1882, that several of Britain's African problems could "be solved only by Chartered Companies."[425] But the British foreign secretary, for one, admitted he still did not understand the legal implications of this course, even if it came with caution and—as of November 1884—with a wink from himself.[426] A top British lawyer counseled that a "charter ought not be granted" by Britain because the "alleged" cessions made to Taubman's company were, like those credited to Leopold, more than likely not "rightful and legitimate transactions."[427] The treaties signed by Taubman's company did not, another critic noted, have the bona fides of the East India Company, or even of the North Borneo Company.[428] Rather, Taubman's company faced familiar charges of having "negotiated" with African political figures whom they in some cases deliberately misidentified as kings. It was said by some that these figures were unfamiliar with the concept of sovereignty. Nor, in many cases, did the figures wield power commensurate with the concept or understand the wording of the contracts Taubman's agents placed before them.[429] Taubman's company, therefore—which for years would not even attempt to extend its writ beyond the immediate vicinity of the Niger—had at this time what could only be described as a series of paper claims.[430] This was true even if these same claims were vast and included criminal jurisdiction, control of customs and taxes, and military rights.

Ultimately, however, the lower Niger met the Congo, just as the Congo met German Southwest Africa and Cameroon. British officials agreed to recognize that Taubman's treaties had much in common with the recent German and Belgian treaties, in that several European parties all purported to copy the perceived example set on Borneo.[431] With Britons themselves having established the latter precedent, "it would not be consistent" for Britain to deny Leopold, or the Germans, or any other private party their recognition in 1884 and 1885.[432] In part this conclusion was assisted by the advice of Taubman himself, who, like Lüderitz, Woermann, and a coterie of Dutch and English merchants invested in Africa, was personally present at the conference in Berlin as a so-called technical expert.[433] Somewhat over the objections of colleagues at the Colonial Office, the British foreign secretary also presumed—wrongly, as it turned out—that finding ways to agree with Bismarck's demands for the Congo would win Bismarck's ongoing support in Egypt.[434]

Either way, with Pauncefote in the ascendant, Britain officially took a pragmatic view of Congo negotiations by December 4, 1884 at the latest. The proposition to recognize the AIA as a state, declared one of Pauncefote's lieutenants, "comes at a very useful moment for us in the Conference, as it assures us the cooperation of the German representatives in securing what we desire with regard to the Niger."[435] Along with Taubman and his fellow British "experts," to whom much of the real work fell, the German businessmen moving in and around the conference gave their unanimous support to the idea of a private state in the Congo.[436] Bismarck, accordingly, got his way, and Britain, which only weeks earlier had insisted it could not recognize Leopold, did just the opposite mere weeks into the Berlin Conference, on December 16, 1884.[437] Pauncefote delivered the news to Stanley and Mackinnon personally, saying "all that you wanted is done," and implying that the Foreign Office would henceforth "follow every initiative of Germany which favors the Association."[438] To be fair, this was not such a simple gesture as the British taking "compensation," as Italy's delegate saw it.[439] Along with the other delegates, Britain resolved to attach certain guarantees to the protocol issued by the Berlin Conference: legal commitments to rights of free trade, duty-free imports, freedom of movement, and consular protection for Anglo-Europeans in the Congo. Through these guarantees, the Berlin Conference appeared—at least to some observers—to have turned the Independent State of the Congo into another object of Bismarck and England's newfound fixation: a chartered company.[440]

There was a final dimension to consider. In the background of this wrangling, the issue of Borneo was again bubbling up, though not officially within the confines of the Berlin Conference. Precisely as he negotiated with European states over the legitimacy of German colonies and the Independent State of the Congo, Bismarck turned to finalize a long-delayed protocol with England and Spain concerning disputed rights in the northern part of the island of Borneo.[441] The protocol in question involved Spain's agreeing that northeastern Borneo fell exclusively under sovereignty that had been acquired by the North Borneo Company. Historians have often struggled to explain why Germany, which was a bit player regionally, moved to validate that protocol only in June 1884, after years of holding up the process, especially because it gained nothing in Asia by so doing.[442] The answer may well be found in chronological overlap: Germany's validation occurred just as a separate protocol, that concerning the Congo, was undergoing British scrutiny—and just as that very protocol was relying on the positive example of the North Borneo Company. Principles concerning Borneo traveled to Berlin, but also from it, radiating outward with renewed strength.[443]

Writing a history of Borneo in the 1950s, Graham Irwin referred to the 1880s as a "Scramble for Brunei," likening the once-vast empire's near-dismemberment by Sarawak and the British North Borneo Company to Africa's rapid partition by Europe.[444] Another scholar estimates that competition around Brunei peaked in December 1884.[445] In numerous respects, the two Scrambles blended together. Consider the pace of the Brunei partition, which accelerated from the early 1880s before culminating in 1888 with Britain's declaration of protectorate status for Brunei, Sarawak, and Sabah. A major catalyst for the chartering of the British North Borneo Company around 1881 was fear of foreign takeovers of the company's rights, with Germany and Belgium as prime suspects. A few years later, the new catalyst was fear that one of these powers might import their private colonial systems, which had partly been born out of the rush for northern Borneo, from Africa to Southeast Asia—perhaps by targeting the financially vulnerable polities of Brunei, Sarawak, and Sabah for purchase.[446] One Scramble reinforced the other in a sort of feedback loop.

In any event, with Britain's indirect authorization assured, Leopold gradually won the recognition of most other powers by February 1885, with the completion of this process and France's stalling not only dragging the Berlin Conference past tentative deadline after deadline—including New Year's—but essentially determining when it ended.[447] Taking Germany's letter of recognition as their template, other powers such as Italy recognized the AIA's chosen borders, even when these conflicted with France's claims, thus placing further pressure on Ferry to close a deal.[448] Some powers pretended to take inspiration from Britain's declaration of recognition, with Italy excusing itself to Portugal by saying it could not abstain from following Britain's lead days before Britain had finalized the ink on the declaration in the first place.[449]

Meanwhile the king's Congo operations, for the first time, broadly took the formal title of "state." To be sure, it took Leopold a while to vanquish the remaining qualms of the French and the Portuguese, whom Britain had gradually abandoned since February 1884.[450] In particular, he sought in vain to win a right of way for a proposed railroad running through French territory, and to secure international authorization for his recruitment of laborers from Portuguese Cabinda to the Congo.[451] Nonetheless, with Britain and Germany pressurizing his rivals, Leopold proceeded to pay off both Lisbon and Paris with territorial concessions near the mouth of the Congo—some in exchange for a French capital infusion needed to retire Leopold's debts to the Rothschilds and other bankers.[452] Paris received at least ten stations and appeared pleased enough that Courcel even turned to do some "work for the Association, after being its greatest enemy"—helping it to mediate its remaining problems with Portugal.[453] Brazza was recalled to France in early 1885, his mission having officially ended as a direct result of the Berlin Conference's termination.[454] Soon the Ottoman Empire joined the queue to recognize the flag of the Independent State. So, too, did Sweden-Norway, the Netherlands, and Austria-Hungary—the last of which had tacitly agreed before the conference to do as Germany asked.[455] Finally, there was Italy, which had begun to make its own imperial incision into the East African coast, in what is now Eritrea.[456]

Italy's motives were not exactly altruistic; it had added incentive to approve the Congo project because of weaknesses identified in its own colonial treaties, and because Leopold's most formidable foe, France, had made gains in Tunisia that troubled what Rome deemed a North African equilibrium.[457] The Italian claim to govern at East Africa's Assab Bay rested partly on abortive consular appointments there by Britain, but more generally on a series of dubious agreements transferring land from the Afar people to an Italian company, and thence to the Italian government itself.[458] The Italian parliament had approved this scheme, after years of confusion and debate, in June 1882—promptly attracting a first run of skepticism from distinguished institutions such as the Royal Geographical Society.[459] As of late 1884, Rome also planned on sending in an army to occupy Massawa, the bay's largest port.[460]

Italy essentially contemplated the same trick as Lüderitz and Leopold, pretending that some purchases of land by private individuals amounted to purchases of territory and sovereignty. This sleight of hand won Italian favor just after Britain brought events in Borneo to public attention, and just after Leopold hatched his scheme to imitate the Borneo adventurers in the Congo.[461] In Rome, some explorers published letters calling for similar maneuvers in Tripoli, Benghazi, and other places in North Africa.[462] In August 1884, the Italian foreign minister even commissioned a legal inquiry on the question of privately held sovereignty.[463] Hence, while the travails of the Berlin Conference did little to impress the British public, they did have the effect of tempering resistance to Italy's colonial claims, such as that being weighed by the central government of the Ottoman Empire.[464] It was fitting that Italy's "technical expert" at the conference was Christopher Negri, an economist present at the AIA's genesis.[465]

The near-universal agreement emerging from the conference pleased Bismarck. Admittedly, he did complain in January 1885 that he had he grown bored with the day-to-day, not least because the French were dragging proceedings on longer than planned; the British cabinet also wondered why he did not take a greater interest in the association's side-negotiations with France.[466] Still, even as Bismarck skipped most sessions at the conference to oversee debates in the Reichstag, Bismarck's domestic agenda received a boost.[467] In the wake of the 1884 elections and the attendant Berlin Conference, Stanley's book on the founding of the Congo was becoming a bestseller in Germany, prompting one observer to call it "*the* great book of the year."[468] Accordingly, Bismarck's privately run colonies remained "a source of inexhaustible interest for the Germans," prompting the chancellor to confess privately in January that colonial questions had proven a "matter of life or death" for his government.[469] Readers of the *Allgemeine Zeitung*, one of Germany's top newspapers, digested no less than thirty-two articles tying Lüderitz to the conference over its duration, or about one every third day.[470] And while average voters in Berlin may not have followed the minutiae of the conference as regarded the Congo, they perceived the conference as an endorsement of German colonialism and could be heard "singing Cameroon songs on the streets and alleyways" of the city.[471] The crown princess complained that the nation was "really like a child, delighted with a new toy."[472] Into mid-1885, that toy continued to amuse the electorate and to distract from whispers of a "colonial swindle" among a minority opposition in parliament.[473] Bismarck, however precariously, continued to ride the momentum.

Lawyers in Leipzig, the seat of the Imperial Supreme Court, could read all about how Bismarck had woven German colonial questions, starting with Lüderitz's, into the fabric of an international conference ostensibly devoted to solving Belgian and English questions in Africa.[474] Reviewing the action of the conference, for example, a British delegate in attendance now took Lüderitz's "sovereign rights" for granted.[475] Contemporaneously, confidantes of Leopold sensed they were being used by Germany's government as much as using it, writing that Bismarck's facilitation "appeared to be bound up with the fulfillment" of some inscrutable agenda.[476] Even at the time, other observers saw this tactic clearly, with Austria's ambassador and Sweden's King Oscar II alleging that Germany had won recognition for her private empires by convening the conference, and to some extent by supporting the AIA.[477]

Leopold may not have minded being used by Bismarck.[478] Pageantry surrounding the Berlin Conference did not negate that by February 1885, insiders found the International Association's finances alarming.[479] The operation's survival depended on winning Berlin's international recognition, then leveraging the same to overcome opposition at home. For some time, liberals in the Belgian parliament had insisted their king could not act as the head of two separate states, in accordance with Article 62 of the country's constitution.[480] The Congo enterprise, so the party line ran from 1876 on, was nothing more than a commercial venture in which Leopold was investing as a private citizen, and care needed to be taken to ensure that his expenses were not charged to Belgium in the event of a collapse.[481] Throughout the Berlin Conference, this debate was holding up the payment of Leopold's bills because a plan he had developed to raise a Belgian loan remained in limbo until Belgium could sort out its own stance.[482]

Beginning in the summer of 1884, Leopold tried to get around his problems at home by replacing cabinet ministers with loyal servants.[483] In another moment of creativity, he even suggested signing over all his rights in the Congo to his wife.[484] After the Berlin Conference, however, Leopold and his Belgian allies had their most potent weapon yet: an endorsement from Europe's greatest powers of all his Congo treaties.[485] The Independent State of the Congo already existed, according to Britain, Germany, and—as of late February 1885—the Belgian Foreign Ministry.[486] By September 1885 France would formally launch its own diplomatic exchange, as the United States modified its qualified recognition into something more absolute.[487] "Just as the philosopher of old demonstrated the principle of movement by walking," bragged one of the king's associates, Leopold could now demonstrate his new state's existence.[488] Thus, so the thinking went, unless the Belgian parliament wanted to contradict the great powers and risk incoherence, it had no choice but to sanction the fait accompli by an overwhelming vote in favor of Leopold.[489] His pretensions to being the "suzerain of the Congo" ridiculed by Belgium's minister of foreign affairs as recently as one year earlier, Leopold now was beginning to merit his later reputation as "the cleverest—and wickedest—man living."[490]

Admittedly, some doubts would soon emerge from distant diplomatic quarters, with future U.S. secretary of state James Blaine, once he got a closer look at Leopold's treaties, asking "to know the truth, the whole truth and nothing but the truth, respecting the Independent State of the Congo."[491] Yet, within Belgium itself, only a handful of deputies bothered to mention the uncomfortable fact that Leopold's "state" as presented in early 1885 appeared ramshackle. Rather like Prussia in 1815, this territory consisted of patches of land that did not link up, even according to the most generously fraudulent maps provided by the royal staff. "I find it difficult," remarked one liberal member of parliament in Brussels, "to reconcile the existence of the treaties with the empty spaces that constitute 9 / 10 of the map of the new state."[492] When another observer joked that Leopold's mapmaker would have mixed up the Rhine and the Rhône, had he been looking at Europe instead of Central Africa, the remark was not hyperbolic.[493] At one point Leopold suggested switching the name of Kabinda so as to appease a Portuguese request for its transfer to Lisbon's control. "We could easily change the name of Kabinda," he wrote, "and call that place something else and give a few places between the Tchibango and Lanoume the name of Kabinda or New Kabinda."[494] Furthermore, the supposed legitimacy of Leopold's new state rested not on actual governance administered on the ground—it would not even try to implement a court system until 1887, and then only as far as Leopoldville (Kinshasa)—but rather on paper treaties signed with the taint of duress on indigenes, when signed by the latter at all.[495] Stanley confidentially recoiled at the immense boundaries sought by Leopold, to whom he attributed "an enormous voracity to swallow a million of square miles with a gullet that will not take in a herring."[496]

Had it not been for a prevailing silence among many close to the monarchy, the public in Brussels might have seen that the text of these same dubious treaties appeared rife with contradictions, including instances in which only a few parcels of land, rather than any political privileges, passed to Leopold's group through sale. At any rate, Belgium may have had no choice but to follow Europe's great powers in approving Leopold's move; as of late 1885, as many as six consuls were seeking accreditation to and from the AIA.[497] In the bargain, though, Belgium was proving indifferent to the legitimacy of the new state in the eyes of Congolese, as well as undermining the rule of law in Brussels, where Leopold spent the early months of 1885 broadly soliciting advice on how to introduce his already-sanctioned government and its departments to most of the Congo.[498] His response to skeptics would only augment their doubts: In order to create "harmonious" rule of the AIA's "vast" and often unconnected territories, he planned to tell governments abroad that he would transfer sovereignty from the AIA directly to himself, with the mere stroke of a pen.[499] The AIA would quietly die just as it entered the world in the European public's eye.[500]

In 1884 and 1885, Belgium's diplomats joined to legitimate the private group calling itself a state in the Congo, as well as, indirectly,

Bismarck's and England's "private" schemes for colonialism. A few whispers in London papers about treaty "fraud" and "swindlers" did not quite change the equation.[501] Nor did protests from Central Africa itself, where Leopold's talk of being "very busy preparing the political charters and the fundamental laws for the new state" looked disingenuous, to say the least.[502] During the Berlin Conference Leopold had covenanted to introduce "modern principles" of government to the Congo, including "numerous contributions made to the legislation of the United States, England, and Austria."[503] That was not how matters looked up close, especially for indigenous peoples of "Banana Island." In July, the Independent State's first governor general, Sir Francis de Winton, invited European traders and a series of leaders from Banana, to Boma.[504] The Congo and its residents, he announced from a throne covered in lion pelts and encircled by animal heads, were now to come under the exclusive control of a "new white prince," thanks in part, he said, to the "decisions" of the Berlin Conference.[505] De Winton, sitting in front of a colossal banner with the logo of the AIA, was going to serve as the new prince's proxy, issuing fresh laws effective January 1, 1886 and having final say in every case of African conflict, whether internecine or with foreigners.[506] This was less a modern system by European standards than it was an absolute monarchy. It was also, as the throne's ostentation suggested, a regime more apt to project signs of supremacy than to build consensus.[507] Some of the gifts laid out on a veranda for attending African dignitaries remained untouched, as attendance proved noticeably less than expected.[508]

Fittingly, the most significant of de Winton's early acts had nothing to do with courts or welfare: It was to annul all preexisting contracts in the Congo Basin and to convert allegedly "vacant" or "undeveloped" lands into public—that is association—property.[509] By 1892, this *régime domanial* multiplied to include virtually all land.[510] That escalation, along with usurpation and rapid expansion of the Congo's money supply, a "rubber miracle," and the forced labor of Congolese taxed by a *corvée* system, helped Leopold make at least the inflation-adjusted equivalent of hundreds of millions of dollars and become, as one observer put it, the "king of money" as much as "of the Belgians" or Congolese.[511] "The world," an anonymous voice in Accra wrote toward the close of the Berlin Conference, had "perhaps never witnessed until now such high handed a robbery on so large a scale."[512] But it was a mere preview.

Across the continent, the German and British East Africa companies more or less duplicated the scheme, and soon the world would also find out what atrocities could result when Leopold's will—which, according to the Congo's heavily delayed and long-obscured constitution, trumped the rule of law—remained free of any checks or balances.[513] Leopold's position as a despot allowed him to embrace policies that led to so many deaths—ultimately estimated at ten million—that one Belgian official privately speculated about a future without black Congolese.[514] And all this in a country where a single province amounted to an area fifteen times to size of Leopold's home, Belgium; and where anthropologists estimated that there had been some two hundred distinct polities on the eve of European colonization.[515]

For now, the most immediate diplomatic fallout of Leopold's ascendancy lay in Europe, where the approval of "private" states left the door open to all sorts of confusion. A legal skeptic could say that the existence of these rogue empires undermined international law. A moral skeptic could decry how they placed indigenous peoples completely at the caprice of Europeans, so far as Europe was concerned. Finally, an economics-minded skeptic could argue that places like Lüderitzland, if they bankrupted, would leave "home" states like Germany responsible for bills. Diplomats had proven willing to put each consideration aside. In short order, though, some of the adventurers behind "private" states would hold certain European powers hostage by threatening to sell "control" over overseas territories to rivals.[516] Bismarck would accordingly find it hard to put his colonial genie back in the bottle.

But first, just as the Berlin Conference was coming to an end, Bismark found himself confronted with a host of questions concerning the new German empires. By March 1885 the intoxicating prospect of a colonial triumph was still attracting German youth to Bismarck's policies, but it was also producing skepticism within a vocal minority.[517] Challenged by deputies in the Reichstag to explain what sort of legal system would emerge in colonial locations where private parties owned sovereign rights, Bismarck initially had to confess his own ignorance—much like his contemporary, Leopold II, who early on "intend[ed] to avoid all public discussion of the details" of his Independent State's constitution because he had little idea what to put in it.[518]

In June 1884, in the middle of his Borneo-fueled public relations offensive, Bismarck suggested reserving to the Reichstag the option, but not the obligation, to exercise jurisdiction over Europeans living in the colonies.[519] Into 1885, however, "regarding those conditions for justice that will take hold in these colonies later on," Bismarck admitted, "I have so far not been able to establish any kind of firm view—a view that I would be committed to maintaining."[520] Legal advisors in Berlin hoped to import the British colonial system from North Borneo to "German" Africa, but the idea fizzled; British colleagues correctly noted major deficits in Bismarck's planning.[521] Germany would have to improvise, for example, in Cameroon, where representatives from the supposed new king, Woermann, provisionally told British officials, who had been maintaining courts of equity there since 1856, that they did not have a plan for jurisdiction yet.[522] Even the borders of the area where they might adjudicate remained uncertain.[523] All Bismarck really knew was that he wanted his "system" for economic and political reasons. The actual justice it administered would be deferred, only to witness thereafter a number of abortive iterations beginning in 1886.[524] Skeptics seized on the uncertainty, with one Bavarian jurist complaining to a crowd in Nuremberg that the problems started with the popular term "colonial politics" *(Kolonialpolitik)*: Everyone said they were for it. No one bothered to agree what it meant.[525]

Bismarck's experiment only concerned a hundred German citizens directly at the beginning of 1885: estimates counted twenty Germans living in Lüderitzland, twenty in Cameroon, and so forth, along with zero in what was soon to be "German New Guinea." Yet, in what was an unfortunate turn of events for many, the experiment's scope was to grow far larger, for by early 1885 the reluctance of businessmen was prompting suggestions that Germany directly manage colonial jurisdiction over Africans and Europeans alike: that is, "over the whole population" of what were supposed to be privately governed territories. *Pace* Bismarck, this move would necessitate putting expensive infrastructure in place to try cases involving "the negroes in Cameroon and the Hottentots in Angra Pequeña." Both places required installations such as jailhouses—none of which the businessmen had deigned to build.[526] All of this was not to mention other potential embarrassments for Berlin, not least the enforcement of an oath Woermann had made to certain "negro kings" in Cameroon to respect the institutions of slavery and polygamy. In the event, a constitutional clarification of colonial law would not arrive until 1886, and even this step brought more questions surrounding citizenship, flags, and the degree of Reichstag oversight.[527]

The scope of Bismarck's already-inflated experiment increased still more in early 1885, thanks to new "purchases" of an estimated 156,000 square miles of territory in East Africa.[528] The author of these supposed acquisitions—which, incredibly, involved even less pretense of negotiation than had Leopold's or Taubman's—was Carl Peters, another Borneo devotee with ambitions to replicate what he called "the creations of Lord Clive and Warren Hastings."[529] Early on Bismarck wanted nothing to do with Peters, whom he dismissed, more than a little hypocritically, as a filibuster.[530] Bismarck believed that the German business community had already gotten enough of Africa to digest, and he had refused support when Peters asked to replicate Lüderitz's feat in September 1884.[531]

Thereafter, with Kusserow's help, Peters resolved to force the issue. By year's end he showed up on the East African coast, toting hundreds of "sale" treaties purporting to deliver him complete jurisdiction over a vast swath of lands. There was a patina of legitimacy to each treaty, which saw Peters assure alleged sultans "that slaves would no longer be dragged away from the area" for sale in the Indian Ocean trade.[532] This tactic had, after all, worked for Leopold II in certain instances. The bigger problem was that although everyone surmised that Peters's documents were at least partly fraudulent—not least because Peters himself labeled them fiction—his claims for protection were not verifiably less worthy in the public eye than those underscoring German involvement in the Cameroons and Southwest Africa.[533] The Sultan of Zanzibar, himself a man with imperial ambitions, protested that the purported treaties infringed upon lands falling under his own jurisdiction—and that Peters had only been able to meet with certain political figures after having produced the sultan's letter of recommendation.[534] Bismarck, aware of such inconsistencies, later joked that "acquisition of land is a very easy matter in East Africa." "For a pair of rifles," he remarked, "one can obtain a paper with some negroes' crosses."[535] But things soon got more serious for Bismarck when Peters took these same papers and envisioned selling them to Leopold.[536] The latter, looking for additional ground on which to base a second "kingdom," was already putting his energy into other negotiations. He went on to haggle with Spain and British merchants for a share of their holdings in eastern and western Morocco, respectively.[537] He even pondered colonial syndicates in the Amazonian rainforest.[538] But his most realistic sight was set on East Africa, likely in the awareness that cloves, one of the area's main exports, had been

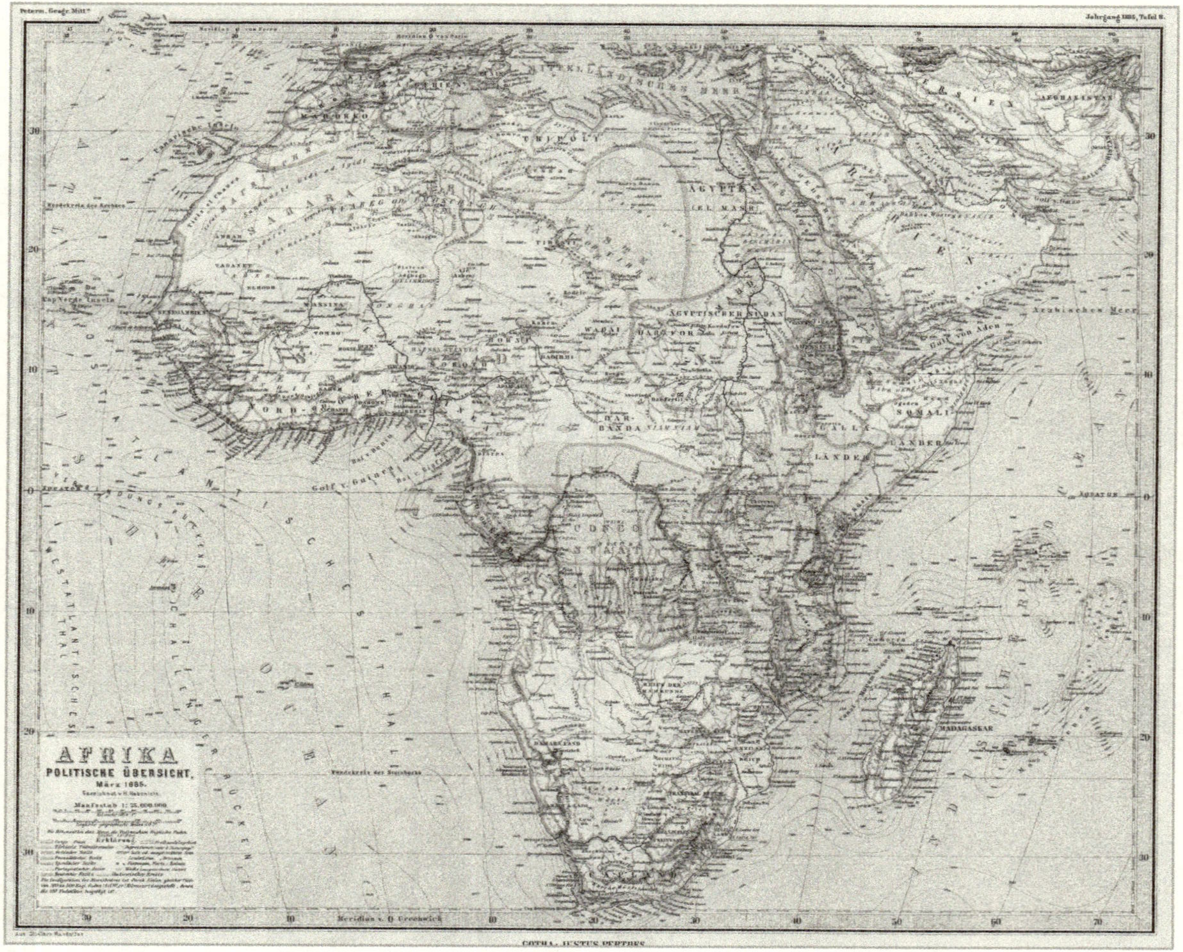

Map 4 Political Divisions in Africa, March 1885, immediately following the Berlin Conference. Note the enclosures of Leopold's Congo state, Lüderitzland, and Peters's East Africa. Above all, note the absence of firm political boundaries in most of the continent's interior. Private states along the Niger and Cameroon rivers—crucially referred to as the "property" of their home countries, but not as colonies—are indicated by shaded lines at the coast. *Source:* Hermann Habenicht, "Afrika Politische Übersicht, März 1885," *Petermanns Geographische Mitteilungen,* vol. 31 (Gotha 1885). Courtesy of University Library, University of Illinois at Urbana-Champaign.

seeing a rise in prices despite the deflationary pressures on most other commodities.[539]

Bismarck had just put the finishing touches on Leopold's new Congo kingdom, which sat right next to the territories Peters had supposedly acquired in the span of a mere five weeks.[540] For this help Leopold was particularly grateful to Kusserow, whose influence in winning over Bismarck was attested by Leopold's prompt wish to give him the highest medal of honor in Belgium.[541] Still, there would be no guarantee of friendly treatment for German traders in Peters's "new" territory, if it were sold to Leopold; this, although Peters's official contact along the East African coast was the German consul, Gerhard Rohlfs, otherwise known as Leopold's lobbyist in Germany. At the same time, German trade with East Africa was increasing rapidly such that its exports there rivaled only Britain's in volume.[542] Thus, on February 27, 1885, just as the Berlin Conference was ending and eight days after Kusserow was given a major promotion, the German government reluctantly granted a charter for Peters's enterprise.[543]

In accordance with the model Kusserow had envisaged for the rest of Germany's young overseas "empire," Peters's state was acknowledged by Bismarck, quite hastily, as possessing all territorial rights, including jurisdiction over Africans. It was also advertised to the German emperor as a descendant of the "model" North Borneo Company.[544] In fact, assuming one viewed the Peters treaties as genuine, Bismarck could tell the emperor that he was doing just what Gladstone and Britain had attempted to do with their original charter for the Borneo Company: to win a very slight measure of regulatory control over an otherwise rogue empire. In this case, though, the stakes were much higher for Germany, for Peters wanted to launch full-on competition with rival British traders, some of whom would also claim to produce cession treaties. If Peters went too far, then Britain would fight back, and Germany would be on the hook for the diplomatic and economic consequences.[545] Bismarck, a British delegate noted, looked at the future with dread on the very day he sanctioned Peters.[546]

In the wake of Bismarck's scheme, the consequences of private sovereignty plans not only endured, they multiplied. To some extent Bismarck anticipated such a multiplication as early as August 1884, but it soon became clear just how much the phenomenon outstretched his expectations.[547] First, the Sultan of Zanzibar boasted about overriding

Peters's treaties and charter with force in mid-1885, whereupon the German chancellor ordered an expensive naval campaign against Zanzibar to avoid losing face. In Spain, a private society of "Africanists" claimed to have signed treaties with eighty indigenous polities to annex fifteen thousand square miles behind the Rio Muni estuary.[548] Finally, there was the case of Cameroon, where, even after the Berlin Conference, Bismarck and the British found themselves at odds over the machinations of one Stefan Rogozinski.[549] Rogozinski, a Polish lieutenant in the Russian navy who decided to visit West Africa on an unauthorized "scientific expedition," claimed to have bought sovereignty over a large island near the Cameroon River—for himself.[550] Rumor had it that this freelancer intended to use his rights to found a colony for his partitioned Polish homeland.[551] The fact was that, by early 1885, Rogozinski was selling his "rights" and influence to Britain in an effort to thwart German settlement.[552] He eventually faded away when Britain abandoned all its claims to govern parts of Cameroon, in exchange for assurances that Bismarck would not challenge British control in the Niger Basin—where, to the east of Lagos, yet another German firm, with the sanction of Nachtigal, had just produced treaties buying governing rights over roughly twenty miles of coastline.[553] Bismarck also found himself obliged to quash similar schemes around the Dubréka River (today's Guinea) and Delagoa Bay (today's Mozambique), with the latter being a place where Adolf Lüderitz had incredibly sought to stake another claim to sovereignty in early 1885.[554]

Legal implications of this course remained firmly in flux, with increasingly unpredictable consequences.[555] Theorists from the continent would soon be forced to take up the matter more earnestly.[556]

EPILOGUE

Afterlives

INSOFAR AS AFRICA'S rogue empires won approval at the Berlin Conference, it is fair to say that Leopold II led the way along with Bismarck, whom one Belgian deputy at the conference rightly labeled a "collaborator in the concept."[1] Between 1886 and 1890, Europe fostered the spirit of Berlin by sanctioning still more "governing merchants" like those who had emerged in Borneo—and who were, via further sovereignty purchases, expanding operations.[2] First came George Goldie Taubman's Royal Niger Company, which won a charter in 1886 partly as a result of its advocate, Hardinge Stanley Giffard, taking office as lord chancellor under Prime Minister Salisbury.[3] Then came the British East Africa Company, hastily cobbled together by William Mackinnon, Leopold's confidante, in response to Carl Peters's aggressive expansion along the Zanzibari coast. The British South Africa Company, as well as Portuguese, Dutch, and Italian chartered ventures, rounded out a litany of schemes, with each group simply following a trail of imitators that preceded them.[4]

One historian estimates that, at one time or another, 75 percent of the British territory acquired in Sub-Saharan Africa after 1880—a massive piece of a massive haul totaling 2.5 million square miles—fell under the aegis of chartered company governments.[5] This statistic may run too low—an early French source pegged the figure at 78 percent.[6] Either finding looks more staggering when viewed together with the German and Leopoldian acquisitions. Contemporary surveys estimated a million square miles of land in the Independent State of the Congo, and a combined 896,000 square miles in Southwest Africa, Togoland, Cameroon, and German East Africa.[7] These portions in the aggregate represented about five times the size of all French colonial holdings in Africa prior to 1884.[8] So while it is wrong to accept that the Berlin Conference had "given away all the territory that is on the map," as one delegate put it, it is fair to see the "gift" as overwhelmingly private: perhaps 30.7 percent of Africa, and 6.2 percent of the world's land.[9]

Why so many nearly identical ventures in Africa came onto the scene simultaneously is a question worth asking, especially since the notion of a private or freelance empire had largely fallen into disrepute by the 1850s. There is evidence that everyday observers themselves began to wonder. As early as 1894, the *New York Times,* trying to account for the sheer variety of political forms under European imperial control, jokingly hypothesized that millions of philatelists had conspired to form "African real and pretended states"; a stamp collector was the only party who "hails with delight the formation of any new independent state, for it means that a new series of stamps is about to be issued."[10] In the scholarly world, however, the search for explanations never fully launched.[11] Looking back on the partition of Africa by largely private means, one historian simply dismissed the process as illogical.[12] Such an argument may hold up in regard to finances. Then again, it may assume too much, since the proliferation of limited-liability companies, depressed returns on European capital at home, and political strictures on great powers' colonial spending all indirectly encouraged investment in—or sanction of—rogue empires overseas.[13]

A careful etiology reveals that each instance of a rogue empire after 1883 not only occurred thanks to a considerable swell of opinion in Europe.[14] Each instance also, as eyewitness Charles Dilke observed, "closely followed the lines of" the original charter given by Britain to Borneo in late 1881.[15] Some contemporaries correctly posited an even longer lineage. In Germany, looking forward to the day when the history of German colonialism would be written, a nationalist intellectual society sketched an outline of the key moments, with Overbeck's proposals in the 1870s forming their starting point.[16] In France and Holland, economists plotted a trajectory from Sir James Brooke's ascendancy in Sarawak through to the chartered company resurgence.[17] Borneo had provided a theoretical, if imprecise, blueprint for the private treaty-making in Africa between roughly 1882 and 1890.[18]

Doubtless sheer copycatting also played a major role throughout, inspired partly by the notion that—as with Sarawak—a few dozen

Europeans could successfully govern an entire country of hundreds of thousands.[19] Sir Rutherford Alcock, supporter of the Independent State of the Congo and managing director of the British North Borneo Company, told an audience in 1886 that it was "not unworthy of note" that Bismarck and so many other colonizers sought to impose on Africa "exactly the same course" as they thought Britain had agreed upon in Borneo.[20] German newspaper editorials confirmed as much.[21] In a curious ricochet, British officials even encouraged each other to "remember the new principles Bismarck ha[d] introduced into colonial politics," lest a German company swoop in and become the government in places under informal British influence such as Brunei—itself the very medium by which rogue empires had traveled from Asia to Africa.[22]

Yet, the concept of copycatting does not suffice as an explanation. In sanctioning rogue empires, a host of European powers did something that had been quite recently dismissed as foolish. Why? One is tempted to ascribe the move to *Torschlusspanik* (fear of a closing door), a medieval idea sometimes used to explain Europe's accelerated partition of Africa in the 1880s. Perhaps Bismarck and others saw the Borneo model being applied so readily that they rushed past the door before it closed, not really knowing what lay beyond, but thinking they could not afford to miss out. Still, too much focus on fear—an emotional response—risks overlooking how many European powerbrokers approached the door rationally. In a sense, the powers authorized rogue empires who were willing to enter the door as less formal, but still not entirely informal and autonomous, proxies. So: Instead of relying on the *Torschlusspanik* concept, we might do better to think of the 1880s as did a contemporary meeting of the British Royal Society of Arts, which surmised that "the ice once broken . . . other charters, not only in this but also in other countries, followed apace."[23] Remarks of this kind suggest the preferability of what economic sociologists call a "threshold model."[24] The more a few European authorities seized on a cult surrounding magical treaties produced in Borneo, the more it felt acceptable, even imperative, for a spate of others to do likewise. A decisive point fell in and around the Berlin Conference, when numerous powers with low thresholds made their move.

In this vein, it starts to cohere that, in the wake of the Berlin Conference, many governing companies entered into a circular series of justifications for their existence. When it came time for Taubman's firm, after much wrangling, to receive its charter, his lawyers penned a hypothetical conversation to the Foreign Office in which they answered criticisms from an *"avvocato del diavolo."* The lawyers bested "A.D.D." not just by reference to Borneo, but also by reference to Bismarck's Africa, where they argued "the circumstances [are] alike."[25] To those skeptics in London who might say that the North Borneo Company was "unprecedented," and that "this is not the 17th but the 19th century"—a point also raised in Germany—Taubman's lawyers celebrated the overwhelming array of recent German examples, whereas Germans were themselves celebrating British precedents to win over skeptics in Berlin.[26] Making an analogy to foreign cases, even if inexact, was perhaps as important a step as any domestic legal evidence Taubman could adduce.[27] For if it was true, as Taubman maintained, that "Her Majesty's Government are only asked to do what the German Government have done by a Charter to a German Company," then to approve the Niger charter was to adhere to a delicate international legal consensus.[28] And that, according to former home secretary Baron Aberdare, would only help to soothe any foreign complications arising in colonial Africa, especially as they related to Germany.[29]

No doubt some of Europe's rogue empires, insofar as they materialized, amounted, in the words of J. A. Hobson, to "little else than private despotism."[30] Thus one Berlin banker could joke, "In the early morning hours, before he came to work, Adolph Hansemann ruled New Guinea."[31] With the benefit of hindsight, we know that such experiments produced a great many disastrous effects: that they stood accused of ruining the country nearly everywhere they operated, and that they generally failed to reward their investors.[32] But to focus solely on what an experiment bungled is to ignore why it occurred. Many institutions in Europe thought, or at least agreed to pretend for a brief moment, that a less traditional kind of governance could have salubrious effects. Nor was this idea ridiculous. On the contrary, there was the example of James Brooke. And then there was the Berlin Conference itself, which, in taking note of the Independent State of the Congo and the German colonies' supposedly independent and "private" sovereignty, lent international approval to such notions in a kind of humanitarian spirit. Whatever the conference achieved, one French consul proved astute when he said it had embedded rogue empires within the fabric of "the rights of men."[33]

Critics may note that both the rationales and the criticisms surrounding these empires in the late nineteenth century look identical to those levied against the British East India Company and other similar firms in an earlier, supposedly quite different time.[34] That said, if it was realistic in the 1880s to think history would eventually repeat itself with a bailout of private empires, then it was also not unrealistic to argue—as at least one prominent French economist did—that the new iterations would prove commercially or strategically beneficial to the West in the meantime, as had their predecessors.[35] The American Colonization Society, founder of Liberia, reinforced that opinion in a public address given shortly after the Berlin Conference.[36] So, too, did John Kasson, one of America's delegates at Berlin. Provided entities like the Independent State of the Congo negotiated favorable trade terms with great powers, the latter's economies could "gain everything which we could gain by owning the country, except the expense of governing it."[37]

On a scale not seen since the heyday of the East India Company, the early to mid-1880s saw a broad, palpable European excitement for rogue empires.[38] One could find proof even among segments of the public in France. The *Société de Géographie* requested translations of British dossiers on the subject through late 1885, and farmers debated Borneo's significance as a precedent.[39] Similar excitement determined the legitimation of the Independent State of the Congo, as well as a host of endeavors that never really took off—both in Germany, where several *compagnies de gouvernement* failed to win charters, and in France, which countenanced several such schemes, including one for the Sahara, albeit with little parliamentary support.[40] Even in Britain, which yielded the best-known ventures, there emerged a series of also-rans. There was, for instance, a plan to convert the Northwest African Company, located along a strip of the Moroccan coast, into another state on the model of North Borneo.[41] Likewise, there were proposals to bring new chartered company governments to places as far afield as Mozambique and the Canadian Yukon.[42]

That the spirit was alive and well outside the official mind was also attested to by multiple economic treatises, including one commissioned by l'Académie des Sciences Morales et Politiques, and one by Leopold II's future secretary, Count Edmond Carton de Wiart.[43] At the Faculté de Droit in Paris, students could attend lectures on the subject.[44] In Italy, Pope Leo XIII evaluated a proposal from one of his cardinals to have the Knights of Malta start their own state east of Lake Tanganyika, on the putative model of Leopold's Congo enterprise; meanwhile, readers devoured Emilio Salgari's adventure stories set on Borneo, with Sandakan and Brooke's private kingdom playing starring roles beginning in 1883.[45] Finally, from Washington, D.C. to Palo Alto, Americans discussed plans to create privately run empires abroad. Liberian devotees hoped that perhaps "a similar association" to Leopold's could emerge in the Sudan, under U.S. stewardship.[46] David Starr Jordan, president of Stanford University, suggested America "find a Rajah Brooke" to colonize the Philippines—an idea he borrowed from the Oxford historian James Froude, who yearned for a similar outcome in the increasingly clamorous British West Indies.[47]

These were hardly the only occasions where Borneo appeared to give Europeans cause for study; for example, starting in the 1870s, colonial officials "on the spot" in the Malay Peninsula looked to Brooke's "resident" system as a model for new regimes of control they had to introduce at the Colonial Office's behest.[48] In the case of Africa, though, the salient point was that governing rights were up for sale to the highest bidder, whether state, man, or company.[49] In the aftermath of 1885, this was a valuable principle that served not just as an inspiration, but also as a template—with Britain, for instance, reviewing stacks of Borneo records to decide how to handle the British East Africa Company as a government.[50] Major powers, stirred to action by the competition of rogue Belgian and German actors, still did not want to take on overseas governing expenses that taxpayers might resent. Instead, European leaders looking to save money but deter rivals went on to embrace what they thought were revivals of the vaunted East India Company, albeit by way of the South China Seas.

Di Rudinì, later the Italian prime minister, spoke accurately when he said Europeans in Africa were staking claims in a spirit of imitation.[51] After 1885 the kind of private treaty-making practiced in Borneo became endemic, essentially taking one of two forms. In the first, less farcical variant, European adventurers and company employees entered authentic negotiations, albeit often with the intention of defrauding their counterparty. In so doing, these Europeans encountered some indigenous leaders who, to quote Frederick Lugard (then an employee of the Royal Niger Company), "understand the nature of a written contract, and consider nothing definitely binding till it is written down."

Such education meant "every claim [was] discussed in all its bearings, sometimes for days," and "words [were] altered" in accordance with points negotiated prior to the transfer of certain governmental rights. Hence, practitioners like Lugard issued assurances that their work could "only by an abuse of language" be likened to the filibustering seen in certain parts of the Congo.[52]

That was not exactly true, for even these practitioners could resemble the infamous American filibustering expeditions of a William Walker. But this first variant at least treated the motions of European law with some respect, and it at least involved Africans who, either because of prior acquaintance with European customs or because of real political ambitions, could act as genuine interlocutors. The Duala rulers of Cameroon, to recall a salient case, appeared to insert so many restrictions into the clauses confirming their transfer of sovereignty to German merchants circa 1884 that one cannot accept the contention that all African partners to colonial treaties failed to grasp the written word's significance.[53]

Then there was the second, and much more common, variant. In it, filibustering via abuse of language was precisely the order of the day, leading to scenes that looked more absurd than what had passed for acceptable behavior decades before, on Borneo. Consider, for example, what Carl Peters did to leaders in Usagara, Useguha, and Nguru: Peters purported to pay them for sovereignty over an estimated sixty thousand square miles of territory, yet many of them quickly denied selling anything, even plots of land.[54] Alternatively, take another look at Lugard's career. He acknowledged to an audience of the Royal Geographical Society in 1892 that in some cases of negotiation, he did not even give a copy of the supposed treaty he was signing to the West Africans who were his supposed counterparties, because written documents meant nothing to them. He merely "put down on paper what was the pith of the contract between us" as discussed orally.[55]

Whatever their bona fides, such parleys inaugurated the age of what is called "indirect rule": a system of protectorates, treaties, split sovereign rights, and legal chaos that allowed European powers vague influence over Africans while limiting European liability. This was a system that partially overlapped with rogue empires, and both were not above dressing up a random villager to impersonate a dead king.[56] As one German columnist noted in 1891, the system saw some indigenous leaders sell the same territory multiple times to different parties.[57] In another instance, the British East Africa Company purchased sovereignty over a certain "Mount Mufumbiro," although it soon transpired that no such mountain existed. Consider, finally, the treaty Adolph Woermann signed on July 24, 1884. In exchange for £70, Woermann acquired sovereignty over an island off the Cameroon coast, only to admit later that the island was a place where "no man, not even a negro," had ever lived.[58] Small wonder that Lord Salisbury later joked that he and his colleagues had been trading mountains, rivers, and lakes to each other without any clue as to their real location or meaning.[59]

Watching from afar, the United States Treasury remarked that the process begun in Borneo seemed "an answer to the question how to recognize the necessity of development and expansion without laying a heavy burden on the present generation of citizens."[60] Here was a means of acquiring influence over foreign territory without taxpayers' incurring risk or red tape.[61] Here, too, was an efficient means of moving capital into developing countries.[62] Or so it seemed, for a brief moment.[63] Optimistic theories held in isolated instances—for instance, in Nigeria, where, strictly speaking, Taubman's company governed at its sole cost through at least 1888. Elsewhere European parliaments tried to force the issue, as when the Reichstag refused to approve any budgetary subsidies for overseas colonies until governing companies signed a declaration saying they, *not the German Empire proper,* would shoulder the expenses of tax collection, policing, and courts.[64] In general such efforts proved futile. It was not long after the rogue empires began operations in 1884 and 1885 that they faltered under the combined weight of financial distress and moral opprobrium, prompting their "home" states to step in for fear of losing face—a common logic at the time.[65]

In Germany's case, slipshod plans for governance crumbled as Adolf Lüderitz, once advertised as the "nephew of and successor to" the Borneo Company, failed miserably.[66] In late 1884 he began a push to sign treaties extending his territory beyond the Namib Desert. Heinrich von Kusserow expected the additions to stretch northward along the coast to Cape Fria, or roughly the bottom of Portuguese claims in Angola.[67] Lüderitzland itself looked relatively secure; Josef Frederiks recognized some of Lüderitz's "rights" as valid, even if he contested their extent, and even if he appeared heavily intoxicated, again, during some of newly appointed consul Vogelsang's visits to Bethanie.[68] The bigger problem—

intractable, as of 1885—was to convince other potent southern Namibian leaders to grant Germans supremacy in their backyard.[69] Rival German firms approached Frederiks's neighbors semiregularly in their own quests to prospect for minerals. Alas, most of those parties wanted little to do with Lüderitz as a governor.

Rather than negotiate with the major Herero or Nama authorities, Lüderitz tasked his viceroy, Vogelsang, and other agents with producing a series of agreements to buy land from lesser figures: the Rehoboth Basters; the Topnaar, a clan of the Nama; and Jan Jonker Afrikaner, the captain of the Orlam Afrikaners.[70] Many of the resultant treaties, signed in haste, explicitly transferred "sovereign rights" to Lüderitz in return for payments. That said, the treaties often looked considerably more implausible than those "made" with Frederiks in 1883.[71] In one case, Lüderitz even had the temerity to offer a sale of territory he did not own—deep to the north of Nama territory, in Hereroland—in exchange for a territory his prospective African counterparty did not control, let alone own.[72]

In a further complication, Lüderitz came under criticism from the Vatican, which received intelligence claiming he intended to ban Catholic missionaries in "his" territory, in a sort of return to the culture wars of the 1870s.[73] Though the report proved erroneous, its circulation represented yet another testament to the spiking valence of rogue empires, and yet another blow to Lüderitzland's credibility.[74] Within a short time, Bismarck would learn that Josef Frederiks, the ruler and alleged seller of Lüderitzland, had never intended to give up sovereign rights over any part of his territory.[75] Already, the German navy had informed Bismarck of some discrepancies between the pretenses of Lüderitz and the actual content of his treaties—discrepancies that some believed Kusserow, known to have political aspirations in Lüderitz's hometown of Bremen, had encouraged.[76] As a result, Bismarck instructed Lüderitz to get his treaties in order, seemingly unaware that each one was too surrounded by fraud to sustain such an effort.[77] Bismarck forbade Kusserow from communicating with Lüderitz after the summer of 1884, but when that embargo failed, Kusserow was given the posting of ambassador to the Hanseatic states.[78] This may have represented a kind of exile; it may also have been a way in which to encourage closer collaboration between heavyweight colonial businessmen in Hamburg and Bremen, and the civil servant who had arguably done the most to support their ambitions.[79] Either way, the German Foreign Ministry twinned Kusserow and the Hanseatic kings *manqué* indefinitely.

Despite, or perhaps because of, his misgivings, Bismarck had Nachtigal negotiate separate "protection" treaties on behalf of the German government with Frederiks and Lüderitz's other partners beginning in late October 1884.[80] Still, by late 1885, Lüderitz had insufficient funds to run government operations in "his" empire, much less the new areas where Germany was signing fresh "protection" contracts with indigenous groups. A silver strike in the bay around Angra Pequeña turned out to have been a mirage; there was little water for agriculture; cattle trading operations lost money; supply ships wrecked on the African coast; and it proved too expensive to export what little copper had been found in the interior.[81] Lüderitz lost well over a half-million marks in 1884 alone.[82] In late 1885 he went rogue again, threatening to sell out his remaining "sovereign rights" to the highest bidder—likely Rhodes or another magnate at the British Cape.[83] Lüderitz's agents did not have the money or muscle even to begin a push into the Herero territory, where official German agents had been attempting to sign protection contracts. Whether Bismarck had the will was also an open question.

Calling in favors, Bismarck hastily brought together a group of German financiers: Deutsche Bank and Dresdner Bank, but also such heavy hitters as Adolph von Hansemann, Werner von Siemens, Guido Henckel von Donnersmarck, and Gerson von Bleichröder.[84] This consortium purchased Lüderitz's rights and control over the territory formerly known as Lüderitzland, where surveyors estimated an average of one inhabitant for every three square kilometers of earth.[85] Thereafter, the consortium entered into negotiations with the German government proper over how to handle the contracts signed by Germany with indigenous groups.[86] Germany, as noted, had agreed to "protection" not only with Josef Frederiks's community, but also with other, more isolated peoples, in exchange for some as-yet-theoretical rights of supremacy in the latter's vassal states. Now, Bismarck proposed that the consortium lease these same rights from Germany and more or less run a state on their own.[87] But by 1887 this plan, too, would be dismissed by one Berlin law professor as "not executable."[88] As for Lüderitz, he died in 1886, having drowned along the Namib's Skeleton Coast according to a testimonial by Frederiks.[89]

Meanwhile, in Cameroon and the vicinity of the Niger, German businessmen nominally in charge of running their own empires simply forewent the option to govern and sold their rights to Germany proper, or, in the latter case, to England.[90] One company's lawyer asked whether a governing company should enter sovereign rights into its ledger as an asset or a liability.[91] Overall, despite Bismarck's talk about protecting German economic interests through the introduction of a colonial system, the volume of German trade generated by South-West Africa and its ilk never rose higher than the volume of German trade in neighboring French and English colonies, let alone in more important foreign markets such as Brazil.[92] (A nearly 50 percent decline in the price of palm oil between 1884 and 1886 added plenty of downward pressure on exports from Togo and Cameroon.[93]) Such numbers ensured that a trickle of dissent turned into a deluge by the late 1880s, when Left-Liberals published a primer on "colonial politics" charging that there had been no broad public agitation for colonies on behalf of Germany, let alone on behalf of German businessmen, prior to 1884.[94]

The balance sheet looked more auspicious in East Africa, but only briefly.[95] By 1887 the dominance of Indian and Arab traders dashed German hopes of exporting elephant ivory profitably, leaving the Deutsch Ostafrikanische Gesellschaft (DOAG) unable to attract large investors, desperate for loans from the Prussian state bank, and without Bismarck's support for more military expeditions that might expand their tax base in the interior.[96] By the early 1890s the DOAG—which, for a time, had expanded to govern portions of Wituland—had bungled so much, and fomented such indigenous hatred, that Germany was forced again to step in and relieve another rogue empire from the burden of government.[97] First, though, Germany had to pay millions of marks as "compensation" for the DOAG's sovereign rights.[98] Half a world away, a similar fate emerged for Hansemann's company in New Guinea.[99] Although reasonably competent, its management consistently bickered over how much sovereignty it wished to retain before deciding to sell off all its governing rights in the 1890s, in the interest of keeping profit margins high.[100] Being the government, Hansemann complained, did not pay.[101]

Britain's record looked more mixed, at least from a financial standpoint. Rhodes, drawing on his legendary personal fortune, turned the British South Africa Company into a behemoth governing areas that now comprise Zambia and Zimbabwe. As for the Royal Niger Company, Taubman proved an efficient, if oft-callous, administrator. Not only did the company pay dividends of 6.5 percent per annum through century's end.[102] It also consistently increased exports and—unlike most neighboring governments—placed efficacious restrictions on the flow of alcohol. So successful did Taubman's organization look that, for a time, some colonial officials proposed letting it take over governmental responsibilities in a foreign territory: Britain's own Oil Rivers Protectorate.[103] Nonetheless, contemporary observers generally recognized that neither Taubman nor Rhodes could compete with the resources of the British treasury as the stakes of colonial policy—and the ascendancy of Joseph Chamberlain, an advocate for British imperial expansion as Colonial Secretary—grew more pronounced in the 1890s.[104] Excessive expenses or setbacks seemed to come with each attempt to occupy territory farther into the interior, even as Britain proper continually pushed for further penetration. Besides, at least in Taubman's case, the private model looked much less viable by 1895, when the coastal Nembe polity overpowered the company's fortified headquarters at Akassa, then briefly won the sympathy of the British public by publishing a litany of economic grievances.[105]

Both Rhodes's and Taubman's ventures eventually arranged the sale of their rights to Britain, with the Royal Niger Company's shareholders netting £444,300 in their bargain—off an overall sale price three times as large as the company's physical assets.[106] This process involved delicate approaches and negotiation, not dicta.[107] The end came more swiftly for the Imperial British East Africa Company, run by Leopold II's friend and supporter William Mackinnon.[108] In 1895, with the company struggling to acquire capital from risk-averse investors fearful of developing markets, it had invested just ten shillings, on average, in each of the fifty thousand square miles of territory under its control.[109] That same year, Britain bought out the Imperial British East Africa Company's governing rights, thus landing itself in precisely the situation it had sought to avoid: a mountain of debt and an obligation to administer justice directly in unassimilated areas.[110]

Joseph Thomson, the celebrated explorer, joined Taubman in lamenting that when one "compared Downing Street versus chartered companies" as a means to develop territory, the latter would always achieve better results.[111] Maybe the problem, agreed a Foreign Office clerk, was that the companies had worse material to work with than did traditional European powers.[112] It would not be wrong to say that a sizeable contingent of intellectuals shared his opinion.[113] For example, Auguste Beernaert, Belgium's prime minister during the first ten years of Leopold's Independent State of the Congo, speculated about the advantages of "autocratic enterprises" when compared to traditional public governments.[114] Obviously this sentiment found a warm welcome with speculators such as Overbeck, who once boasted that when it came to a private regime and a traditional nation-state, society ought to opt in favor of the former.[115] But the truth looked more complicated, for even the British Anti-Slavery Society endorsed for-profit government by company, at least when the only remaining alternative was Portugal.[116] Leopold, for his part, did not waver either, suggesting, as late as 1898, that he form a company to lease sovereignty over the Philippines from Spain, and that he take a controlling interest in the British North Borneo Company, should its shareholders grow discouraged by ongoing bills related to fighting the Mat Salleh resistance.[117] Around 1901 a New York syndicate tied to Leopold even resolved to pay Bolivia for police and court powers over its rubber-rich land around Acre.[118]

Of course, plenty of prominent figures disagreed vehemently. A former Belgian minister of the interior, writing in 1889, probably spoke for the majority when he concluded that such companies, "preoccupied above all with assuring strong dividend payments to their shareholders," had "responded poorly to the greater exigencies of our time," namely, "considerations of the law and of humanity."[119] A clerk with the Berlin state supreme court agreed, saying the systematic failure grew evident to his colleagues by 1890.[120] "A company of shareholders," added a sympathetic French law professor, "is the worst of sovereigns, for it has only one organ: its cash register."[121]

Belgian officials, whatever their views on "the policy of creating reigning companies," as *The Economist* called it, had their own hands full with the Congo by century's end.[122] Ferry's pledge to pay the Independent State for some border territory remained suspended through 1887, partly because of lingering hostility toward what Ferry called "an establishment neither of commercial purpose nor of recognized public utility."[123] France's parliament voted hundreds of thousands of francs less than Leopold had agreed to during the Berlin Conference, and when even this abbreviated payment proved slow in arriving, Swiss banks began to eye the Belgian king's financial distress as an opportunity for exploitative lending.[124] After a multimillion-franc lottery loan in 1888 failed to repair the budget deficits run up by his government, Leopold suggested that without another complex borrowing operation, he could not maintain the Independent State.[125] In 1889 he drew up a will that would award Belgium the Independent State upon his death (in exchange for payment of certain debts); the parliament in Brussels also voted to inject ten million francs into a struggling railway company in which the Independent State held the controlling interest.[126] Just one year later, Brussels extended the Independent State a 3 percent, ten-year loan of 25 million francs—albeit with little prospect of being repaid for the time being, and in addition to an annual subsidy of perhaps 5 million francs.[127] These moves represented the slow build of a plan meditated by Leopold since 1887: to sell his Congo state to Belgium.[128]

To put that into perspective, consider that the rubber boom that would make Leopold a fortune did not begin until at least 1891—and that the boom culminated in 1895, when Leopold drew yet another loan from Belgium to the Independent State, partly to pay off a smaller loan from an Antwerp banker.[129] Then consider that Congolese subjects still overwhelmingly paid their taxes not in cash, but in kind and labor; that a loan of 25 million francs amounted to roughly twelve times the Independent State's budget of 2.1 million francs in 1886; and that Leopold at one point tried, albeit unsuccessfully, to raise as much as 150 million francs from the Rothschilds.[130] The takeaway was that, into the early 1890s, Leopold was saddling himself with debts imposing enough to make Hubert-Jean van Neuss, his director of Congo finances, warn of a catastrophe.[131] Domestic industrialists might well have joined in his complaint, since Belgian exports to the Independent State—advertised as a potential benefit to both countries—never exceeded a 1 percent share in Belgium's global total.[132] At any rate, by 1908 the situation looked remarkably similar to that prevailing in the British and German cases. Belgium essentially had to purchase the rights of a governing company and take over its responsibilities. Leopold died roughly a year later in ignominy—the finances of the outgoing king's empire still in many senses unknown to Belgian statisticians because of record-burning he had overseen.[133]

Last and least, there was a smattering of empires to be run by citizens of lesser colonial powers. Italian imitations of Borneo, which had been planned for the Somali coast, never quite got off the ground, despite several dubious purchases.[134] Companies founded by Lisbon for the purpose of running northern Mozambique, as well as an amplification of the prazo system in Angola, did limp into the first decades of the twentieth century, dying only around 1930.[135] But their annals, too, featured mostly a maze of bankruptcies, scandals, and government rescue packages.[136] As for the Russians, their ignominy confined itself to a single, small chapter. Late in 1888 a nobleman, Nicholas Ivanovitch Achinoff, resolved to found his own empire on the Somali coast. Without official authorization, he journeyed to Abyssinia and produced a treaty with the Negus paying for control over an abandoned fort. The French, holding competing claims to the area, eventually demolished Achinoff's "New Moscow," but only after Russia disavowed the undertaking.[137]

From an ethical perspective, one must remember that, insofar as many "treaties" underlying private sovereignty in Africa amounted to theft, their impact was felt most acutely by the indigenous populations they touched. In some cases—for example, in the Namib Desert—that theft later yielded amazing riches for those Europeans who found themselves in possession of ill-gotten claims to political supremacy, however brief their tenure as rulers. The theft also made lasting impacts on international law and boundaries, however, and both of these matters worked to structure African colonial history. To put such relationships into full perspective, it is first necessary to return to the realm of legal theory.

Recovering the Borneo precedent raises a crucial issue: Why deals for private sovereign rights, starting with those in Borneo, had the veneer of legality, if not always respectability. For a good explanation one would do well to return to the firestorm that heated up around the "Congo Question" in 1883 and early 1884, when Leopold's propaganda circulated throughout Europe.[138] Recall that more than one critic, including Jules Ferry, rejected the association's pretensions to statehood on the basis that it was not affiliated with, controlled from, or even protected by, a recognized European government. Recall, also, that several members of the British Foreign Office argued that the recognition of statehood in such a body by Europe's leaders would set a disastrous precedent.[139]

The other side of this debate consisted foremost of men paid by Leopold. His advocates pointed out their opponents' tautology: that the AIA could not become a state because it was not a state already. Many of those opponents were working as lawyers in France—even after the French government made its initial gesture of approval for the AIA.[140] Some of them did concede that, many years earlier, parties like the East India Company had purchased and held governmental powers. At the same time, the French contingent dismissed the idea of private government as impossible because it was not "modern." "It is a principle of law," wrote noted scholar Louis Delavaud, "that states alone may exercise sovereign rights, and that a private company may never have them."[141] Private parties simply could not make the legal jump to sovereignty anymore, no matter how awesome they grew or how weak nearby states became. The reason, wrote another commentator in 1885, was because that kind of activity was symptomatic of Europe's ancien régime, of a time, in other words, when political subjects were treated like chattel and bandied about in dowries and the pragmatic business deals of monarchs.[142]

In the run-up to the Berlin Conference, Leopold employed mercenary lawyers and journalists to use the Borneo precedent to demolish the "strange fallacy" maintained by the French.[143] Borneo was part of a larger picture, for as Leopold's main legal hand, Twiss, put it, history stood with rogue empires.[144] There were precedents dating to the Middle Ages: the Teutonic Knights, the Knights of Malta. Borneo was the latest installment. But the takeaway was that all its acquisitions had been recognized officially by the French government, which said on one occasion—before the Congo affair percolated—that it "did not question the capacity of private individuals or of companies" to act as states.[145] Britain, Germany, Austria-Hungary, and the United States also went on the record with similar statements, and by the mid-1880s international law would recognize Britain's protectorate agreements with Sarawak and Sabah as treaties between foreign states.[146] And so, whatever any French critic might say about the customs of law in theory, European diplomats proved it false several times over.[147]

Twiss presented his arguments at international-law conferences throughout 1883 and 1884, to some acclaim; no one mentioned his earlier doubts about the feasibility of privately held sovereign rights, vocalized in the 1860s when his star reached its zenith.[148] Twiss proceeded to appeal to influential figures around Britain, including ministers of parliament.[149] He found even more receptive audiences in the United

States.[150] The chief justice of New York's Court of Common Pleas, Charles Daly, accepted Twiss's arguments about private sovereignty because he found the Borneo precedents convincing; Senator John Tyler Morgan, equally moved by Twiss's reasoning, even asked Leopold's lobbyists to "get up the instances in our history of the treaties made by those who came to America as private people, not under charters, and made treaties with the Indians."[151]

Other famous professors, each hired by Leopold, supported the proposition by claiming the world was a marketplace for sovereignty.[152] One of these figures was Émile de Laveleye, a recognized expert on the history of property who initially opposed what he called Leopold's "series of adventures," but who later claimed that the association must become a state because Belgium did not own, and would not buy, the association's sovereign rights.[153] A more stalwart defender was the Belgian Égide Arntz, best known as secretary general of the Institute of International Law in Geneva.[154] Leopold's team even won a cameo from John Westlake—arguably Britain's foremost legal mind.[155] In addition to expanding on Twiss's list of examples of acquisition of sovereignty by private individuals or companies, the team collectively broached the subject of sovereignty's capacity to become a commodity when it came to sales among major European powers: France, Britain, Germany, and the like. Arntz, for example, challenged French critics to show a rule *against* the purchase of sovereign rights.[156] (Incidentally, his pamphlet on the subject quickly landed in the hands of Henry Morton Stanley, who made use of it in arguments with rivals in the vicinity of Nokki.[157])

For Arntz and his colleagues—whose arguments showed up with varying attribution not only in the batch of educational material prepared for delegates at Berlin in late 1884, but also in public forums as far afield as the Austrian city of Linz—discussions centering on ethics missed the point.[158] What really mattered was that everyone legally could participate in a worldwide market for sovereignty, be they monarchs, entrepreneurs, or missionaries. Monarchs continued to trade in sovereignty well into the late nineteenth century, just as rich rulers did in earlier ages. Bismarck recalled one such moment during the Berlin Conference: an 1865 deal to purchase Lauenburg from Austria.[159] Meanwhile, his colleagues on the Imperial Supreme Court at Leipzig continued to explore with what implications the individual German states had transferred "sovereignties" as "property" to the new Reich created in 1871.[160] Most famous, though, was the legality of the Russian czar's selling Alaska to the United States—a circumstance Twiss knew well, having been selected by the British cabinet in 1867 to explain the sale's ramifications.[161] Even in 1881, when the Prussian Economic Council initiated legislation to appropriate funds for the purchase of sovereignty over overseas colonies, the bill detractors complained about the idea's inutility, not its legality.[162]

By 1884 no critic could coherently deny an African polity's right to sell some or all of its governing rights. When it came to buying such rights, those working for Leopold—a monarch who did not even pretend to associate with the unwashed—argued that royalty must play by the same rules as other private individuals or groups.[163] As in earlier centuries, so for the nineteenth; as for monarchs, so for commoners; as for Europe, so for such other parts of the world as Africa and Southeast Asia.[164] All buying or selling of sovereignty, it seemed, took place in a vaguely private capacity anyway.[165] In fact, even if a private man or group were to live in one state and take on sovereign powers in another, that private man or group could remain a loyal subject in its home state by virtue of what was, in law, a "double personality." This concept was the very same double personality through which sovereigns could purchase disparate territories and hold them in "personal union."[166]

THE DECADES following the Berlin Conference saw a dramatic shift away from acceptance of rogue empires, owing partly to the passage of time and the spread of skepticism about what the Borneo precedent might mean for states everywhere. "The international law propounded and adopted at Berlin," Verney Lovett Cameron told a British parliamentary committee in late 1886, had "startled a good many," and now they would reevaluate.[167] Cameron—the man whose solo attempt to annex the Congo had foundered a decade earlier—declared he was skeptical about the very notions of "private" sovereignty and "private" governance: "In no case as yet," he wrote, "has the action of any company (save, perhaps, the Borneo Company) been sufficiently known for it to be possible that there should be any adequate public discussion on it, and the [Independent State of the Congo] has also maintained a profound secrecy."[168]

Far from being anomalous, Cameron's was one of several such protests emanating from a variety of European authorities.[169] Some objectors, motivated by philosophical concerns, hoped to demarcate governance from business by opposing the concept of "a state in shares."[170] A small contingent in the British Foreign Office deemed it "a great act of folly" to have tolerated the Independent State of the Congo and its ilk.[171] Other critics intervened less altruistically. These ranks included the usual suspects—France was well-represented—but also newcomers from Germany, where many experts tried to forget how Bismarck had implemented his ill-fated colonial system.[172] The ruling company in North Borneo, complained law professor Conrad Bornhak, turned out to have been "an entirely insignificant exception" in recent history, and should never have been factored into Germany's policy.[173] In September 1888, Gerhard Rohlfs, Germany's most storied living explorer, published an editorial calling for Berlin to dissolve the remaining governing companies.[174] Beyond these attacks, however, there was also a transnational current of professional resentment toward interlopers who had manipulated, even embarrassed, the temple of international law. John Westlake complained about "adventurers . . . who in recent times have led the way to the partition of Africa, [and who] have had a sufficient tincture of the forms and language of international law to hope for an advantage over European competitors, through what have really been travesties of them."[175] More politely, a law professor in Toulouse worried about falling into "the arbitrary and the chaotic" by deviating from centuries of increasing separation between the public and private sectors.[176]

This was only one component in a two-pronged assault. The other emerged in September 1885, when a seven-member commission from the Institut de Droit International met in Brussels to study the question of "effective occupation" by European powers in Africa.[177] Diplomats at the Berlin Conference never defined "effective occupation," though there was a consensus that it meant European powers ought to establish themselves on the ground wherever they held paper claims to rule. Since early 1885, when the conference adjourned, most diplomats agreed that "effective occupation" should henceforth apply to new acquisitions of territory on the African coast, in accordance with the conference's protocol.[178] But no one even agreed on how long it would take to establish such occupation: One insider suggested twenty-five years, while Italy eschewed any limits.[179] What the powers *did* agree on was that any firm rules could threaten their interests, if extended worldwide. Were the Dutch held to "effective occupation" in Southeast Asia, or the Americans on their guano islands, or the British in Egypt and Afghanistan, the world map might transform dramatically.[180] This was why delegates at Berlin—with Bismarck's approval—had included a proviso in their final protocol whereby "protectorates" and other forms of colonial government short of outright annexation would not be held to whatever standard "effective occupation" represented.[181] Crucially, this proviso kept a path open for rogue empires.

The Berlin delegation, by divorcing its heavily diluted concept of effective occupation from "private" acquisitions that had already taken place in the absence of real control—along the Niger, the Congo, or in German colonies—essentially left the commission in Brussels with an impossible task. No diplomat could easily mount a winning challenge to rogue acquisitions made in the run-up to 1885. Nor, significantly, could legal scholars undo Germany's would-be private empires and the popular support they brought Bismarck.[182] Instead, the commission could only debate potential rules for acquisitions at some vague future point. In what further confused the matter, a number of participants in the Berlin Conference did not ratify its protocol by February 1886—the agreed deadline.[183] Finally, in the greatest complication of all, the Berlin Conference's protocol had already pledged that its ambit only extended to indeterminate spots on the coast, as distinct from Africa's vast interior.[184] That left little room for the doctrine of "effective occupation"—even once it was fleshed out by the commission of seven lawyers—to carry much weight.

Nonetheless, in 1887, the commission met and endorsed a report produced by one of its members, Ferdinand von Martitz.[185] Martitz undertook an "examination of the theory" behind the Berlin Conference, but he curiously avoided discussion of rogue empires or their acquisitions of territory—both of which had also won the endorsement of Émile de Laveleye, a founder of the Institut de Droit International and still loyal to Leopold.[186] Martitz recast the Berlin Conference as an affirmation of the doctrine of *"territorium nullius,"* sometimes conflated—mistakenly—with *terra nullius* and *res nullius*.[187] According to Martitz's interpretation, which analogized political control to unclaimed property, when traditional European powers occupied politically backward lands in Africa, they instantly became the governments there.[188] Yes, Martitz conceded, the African territories in question were populated and hardly amounted to blank earth. Yes, some Africans living there even had systems of private property that Martitz recognized as similar to those existing in Europe. Nonetheless, African polities had not developed enough for Martitz to declare them commensurate with the West's; they did not comport with the concept of sovereignty. Hence, although transfers of private property rights by African rulers to Europeans should henceforth be treated as legitimate, African rulers' sales of political control—territorial sovereignty, suzerainty, and so on—were illegitimate and without legal basis.

Here was a significant, if subtle, deviation from the official record that had already sanctioned the establishment of rogue empires in Togo, Cameroon, Southwest Africa, East Africa, the Congo, and Nigeria. While meeting at Berlin in 1885, delegates had taken the position that "native Princes" of Africa had "alienated their rights of sovereignty" through "equitable arrangements" of sale, both to whites individually and to European states.[189] This meant the successful realization of an argument made by Leopold and his ilk, according to which much of Sub-Saharan Africa existed as a series of independent sovereign states.[190] Barons Courcel and Lambermont, two of the most important delegates at the Berlin Conference, had said that, when it came to treaty documents, indigenous populations "certainly ought not to be regarded as outside the pale of international law."[191] To illustrate the point, an American academic, Walter Scaife, wrote that the Berlin Conference represented precisely a disavowal of ideas like *territorium nullius,* and, instead, an endorsement of African treaties that sold sovereignty to private persons and foreign countries. "It can scarcely be denied," he concluded, "that the native chiefs have the right to make these treaties."[192] Hendrik Witbooi, a powerful Nama leader in South-West Africa, understood the Berlin Conference as having confirmed this point.[193] Julian Pauncefote, writing in 1886, produced a like-minded memorandum read by colleagues in the British Foreign Office.[194] Still earlier, Bismarck had rejected British arguments about res nullius in favor of Lüderitz's treaties when it came to South-West Africa: The former arguments, he said, had less basis in international law than did the latter.[195]

Two years after the conference, Martitz conceded that the treaties existed, but he called it "an exaggeration" to insist that they were necessary to justify the exercise of jurisdiction by colonial governments over other Europeans or Africans within the territory.[196] This contradiction divorced Martitz from the architects of 1884–1885, but it did not deny him the concurrence of other prominent international lawyers. One admirer was Alphonse Rivier, the president of the Institute of International Law, Belgium's consul in Switzerland, and finally—if rather incredibly, given that he never visited Africa—Switzerland's consul to the Congo.[197] Rivier endorsed the Martitz report while declaring of treaties like those made in the Congo that "nothing is less serious than they are."[198]

Endorsements also came from Germany, where the failure of Bismarck's colonial schemes was becoming apparent enough that legal experts overwhelmingly did something they had not done in 1884: question chartered company governments per se.[199] Friedrich Fabri, the missionary whose dream for German annexation of the Namib had been deferred in favor of Lüderitzland, now argued that Africans had been incapable of understanding treaties, and that it was doubtful "whether a political order, [that is] a condition of law and security" could be achieved "by individuals and private companies in overseas areas."[200] Robert Adam, a professor in Munich, endorsed a "more humane" course, adding that because the "treaty business" rested only on *Scheinverträge*—documents with the form, but not the substance, of real agreements—the principle justifying European occupation should be that of seizing politically "unoccupied land."[201] While not everyone agreed with this nod to Martitz—Paul Laband, a prominent scholar, insisted that any signed treaties carried moral obligations—the consensus held that it was frivolous to attribute binding effects to such documents.[202]

As the process of sanctioning governments in places like the Congo and Lüderitzland gave way to actual occupation, a large contingent of international observers embraced Martitz's approach and sought to find another basis for the new European governments in Africa. Rather than focus on the often fraudulent documents used to justify rogue empires in 1884 and 1885—or, crucially, on the sometimes considerable commitments Europeans agreed to in them—many in Europe went on either to ignore the documents' existence or to trivialize them as a mere "courtesy."[203] Contemporaneously, lawyers in this same European community began to invent new, and often more explicitly racist, explanations for the occupation of African lands.[204] It is unclear when racism began to inject itself most forcefully into this equation, but its increased presence in legal fora certainly conformed to a wider trend of the 1890s, when scientific racism reached its apogee in terms of acceptance from European institutions.[205]

Take, for example, the Cambridge professor John Westlake, briefly a member of Leopold's propaganda unit.[206] Tasked with addressing the proposition that treaties transferring sovereignty could provide the basis for private European government over Africans, Westlake eventually delivered a resounding no, not because of concerns about fraud, but because he believed all African political systems theoretically acting as counterparties could never be anything more than "transient agglomerations effected by savage Napoleons."[207] Africans, agreed Westlake's Bavarian contemporary Baron von Stengel, did not live in communities resembling nation-states prior to European arrival; therefore, their authority could not have amounted to sovereignty, and, besides, only a European power like Germany could even transfer sovereignty.[208] This view was the legal equivalent to Jules Ferry's notorious declaration that superior races had a right to subjugate inferior ones. (Ferry, too, had refused to recognize a landscape in which indigenous Africans transferred political rights to Europeans by treaty.[209])

That was not to deny that, within the boundaries set by Martitz's broad strokes, confusion prevailed well into the twentieth century. An optimist could hope that "the march of events and the labors of jurists [were] slowly working out a just and rational theory."[210] But attempts at systemization remained in vain.[211] Things already looked hazy in late 1885, when a French parliamentary committee tasked with assessing the findings of the Berlin Conference failed to reach any conclusions.[212] By the time the First Universal Races Conference gathered in London in 1911, attendees could still not agree on what to make of Africa's relationship with the doctrine of *territorium nullius,* which, like rogue empires, failed to win universal acceptance from the 1890s on.[213] In Munich, Professor Emanuel von Ullmann simply prepared a list of confused declarations and unexplored issues left over from the Berlin Conference.[214]

What, for example, was one to make of Europe's existing diplomatic relations with African states? Zanzibar's sovereignty and position as a member of the international system had already been confirmed before it signed onto the protocol of the Berlin Conference; by the late 1870s, it claimed two accredited consuls in France.[215] Germany had long since established diplomatic relations in published conventions with the

Makhzen in Morocco; in 1880, France, Germany, and other major powers signed a convention guaranteeing Moroccan independence.[216] Liberia could claim similar conventions, and, in October 1884, it even participated in an international conference concerning the designation of a prime meridian for navigational and chronological purposes.[217] Further back, in 1862, the French Empire directly recognized the king of Madagscar as the sovereign of an independent Malagasy state, dispatching consuls in the bargain.[218] Finally, Napoleon III conceived of Algeria as an "Arab Kingdom" to which he would offer protection.[219]

The history of treaties did not seem to mesh with Martitz's vision, either. Europeans had been making treaties with Africans periodically since the twelfth century, from Marrakesh to Monrovia and beyond, leading the High Court of Admiralty to remark in 1801 that Africans "long have acquired the character of established governments . . . confirming to them the relations of legal states."[220] One popular type of arrangement explicitly exchanged territory for money and recognized sovereignty as residing in indigenous "kings" and "princes."[221] The French paid off the Guinean "King of Kommenda"; the British haggled on the Sierra Leone River with Pa Samma, "King of North Bulloms"; the Belgian senate ratified a treaty in 1848 that purchased sovereign rights along the Rio Nuñez from "Lamina, supreme boss of the Nalous."[222] In a slightly different vein, from the 1840s on the British had signed at least seventy other trade treaties in which West African "negro princes" pledged to favor no European nation.[223] One such document emerged as late as 1874, during the Third Anglo-Ashanti War.[224]

Given this history, by which criteria should Europeans distinguish such already recognized African polities from those to be designated as lacking sovereignty?[225] No one in the 1880s or 1890s could find clarity. The U.S. ambassador to Portugal would plead that "differences of opinion existed among governments as among individuals and the trite saying was oftentimes applicable: 'circumstances alter cases.' "[226] August Busch, a German diplomat who managed most of the Berlin Conference, "hesitated to express an opinion" on such "delicate questions."[227] So did Bismarck.[228] That, as both men said and as the British preferred, was "a length to which the conference declined to go."[229] Clearly, though, it never seemed consistent to justify European colonialism post-1885 simply by labeling African lands as "backward territory." Nor was it tenable, as Martitz argued, that the occupation of Sub-Saharan Africa had its legal basis in European states levying claims on politically empty territory—especially since the Roman concepts supposedly underpinning this belief also lacked a fixed definition.[230] (Uncertainty of this kind appears to have been a recurring phenomenon in European imperial expansion; a similar set of debates had taken place in the 1770s about official decisions denying North American speculators in their unauthorized attempt to buy "private empires" through contracts signed with Native American rulers.[231])

Yet another problem: To dismiss treaties such as that made by Lüderitz was arguably to impeach the character of Europeans and European states alike. Europe's sovereigns, whether the kaiser, the queen, or the French parliament, had lent their signature to these documents. So too had the United States, in the case of Liberia.[232] When lawyers later argued for the inapplicability of treaties—even going so far as to label African rulers who insisted on observing treaties as "filibusters"—they gave reason to question their home government's imprimatur and implied that great powers had approved a fraudulent venture.[233] Such lawyers also overlooked a host of incidents in which European powers "retroceded" territory to indigenous leaders, thereby confirming the latter's legitimacy as a counterparty.[234] Nonetheless, denials and arguments to the contrary obtained. To judge from international law debates, insofar as "private" treaties for sovereignty were not going to be respected as binding treaties by the majority of experts in international law, the loophole exploited from Borneo to Berlin—the one that allowed private purchases of sovereignty by adventurers and confidence men—effectively looked sealed.[235] And while it was "obvious," as one British Foreign Office lawyer wrote, that the treaties signed to this effect remained at issue, they would be inconsistently respected, and further imitation was also going to prove difficult, since editors of treaty compilations were encouraged to limit the publication of all European-African documents starting in the early 1890s.[236]

Sealing the loophole for rogue empires was just a single stage in Europe's long history of inconsistent respect for treaties.[237] Yet, one could argue that it may have proven beneficial for indigenous welfare. If Europe wanted to view indigenous treaties selling sovereignty as legitimate, then Europe had to recognize that the buyers, whether traditional states or individuals and companies, were endowed with absolute power over their African territories.[238] That posed a problem, because such absolute power arguably did not need to abide by any international oversight—notably the weak humanitarian declarations agreed at Berlin.[239] Taubman evinced no scruples about erecting trade monopolies along the Niger, despite explicit stipulations to the contrary in the charter issued to his company by Britain.[240] Leopold, for his part, behaved similarly when he waited only briefly to abolish freedoms of trade that he had agreed to uphold during the Berlin Conference, under international scrutiny.[241] True, Leopold did make a point of allowing a basket of European currencies to circulate as legal tender in the Congo. But this system actually bolstered his claims to independence by pegging his own fledgling currency to more reliable standards.[242] In 1888, meanwhile, the Independent State signed one of its first international agreements as a recognized, fully independent power. Its object: membership in the Union for the Publication of Customs Tariffs.[243] By then, plans to establish tariffs had gestated for two and a half years.[244]

Leopold's staff maintained that rogue empires in possession of sovereignty had no obligation to accord Africans any rights.[245] To truly understand the Independent State's place in the international system, they claimed, one needed to imagine not necessarily a new East India Company, but a more independent East India Company emancipated from Britain or any third party.[246] Any consideration of international law not explicitly confirmed in the Independent State's constitution, predicted the British judge and Queen's Counsel Francis Jeune, was thus likely to be disregarded.[247] In the event, numerous European businessmen, including Germans, were turned away from the Congo on the grounds that their operations might impair the new state's sovereignty.[248] And Baron Adolphe de Cuvelier, foreign secretary for the Independent State of the Congo, incredibly argued that if his "State were to establish slavery, the other parties to the Berlin Act could not legally interfere."[249] This, despite promises made at the Berlin Conference that Europe would "watch over the preservation of the native tribes" in the Congo, guarantee religious freedoms, abolish slavery, and, however vaguely, "care for the improvement of the conditions of their moral and material well-being."[250] Leopold himself authorized a shift away from obligations as early as February 1885, as meetings at Berlin adjourned. "Everything should be completely forgotten today," he wrote Stanley and Sanford in regard to particular trade concessions made around Europe.[251]

Viewed in this light, it was somewhat advisable for Europe to dismiss "private" treaties as illegitimate.[252] Under this scenario, Europe would turn to *territorium nullius* to justify its presence in most of Africa. Unlike Leopold, the European lawyers espousing the doctrine who spoke of "inferior" Africans—whose polities were allegedly not yet developed enough to sell off their sovereign rights—would pursue some theoretical guarantees of safety for the disenfranchised local populations.[253] A constellation like this one gave Europe as a whole an obligation to civilize Africans.[254] That was why Henri La Fontaine, an ardent internationalist and renowned legal figure, embraced *territorium nullius* when calls mounted to wind down Leopold's abusive Congo regime.[255] Yes, the concept of "civilization" was vague and subject to cynical abuse, often amounting to what is today called "cheap talk."[256] Yes, it placed European powers in the paternalistic role of an "official guardian," to use the words of negotiators at Berlin. Yes, it tended to mean the legitimacy of every power in Africa would consist of a mix of European legal impositions and force, rather than some kind of formal cooperation.[257] But to many lawyers this approach seemed preferable to the path of absolute, unrestrained despotism, such as was instantiated in Leopold's Congo.[258] Besides, the notion of a civilizing mission, notwithstanding its myriad problems and hypocrisies, was one consistently agreed upon by a spate of European powers, from Britain, to France, to Portugal.[259] No such consensus endured in regard to the Borneo principle, which had the additional demerit of destabilizing European understandings of statehood and governmental legitimacy.

Both traditional and rogue empires in Africa went on to break treaties once viewed as sacred. The Germans ruling the colony of South-West Africa (today's Namibia), for instance, unilaterally annulled their treaties with the Nama and Herero on account of putative rebellion.[260] Still, whatever the conclusions of lawyers in the decade after 1885, European powers did not roundly dismiss treaties and principles relating to "private" sovereignty. For example, no state ever challenged Leopold's contention that his acquisitions, made by "treaties with the legitimate Sovereigns," gave him personal control of a chunk of territory extending to Lake Tanganyika.[261] Leopold's rights were "conceded by all to have been indisputable," despite some theoretical checks arguably inserted into the Berlin Act of 1885.[262] Similarly, German bureaucrats structured much of their policy in the former Lüderitzland—even after the late

1880s, when people stopped calling the place by that name—on the basis of the abortive private empire created there.[263] In 1908, when a railway inspector working in the Namib Desert found what was then the largest deposit of diamonds ever discovered, German courts returned to the original Lüderitz treaties in order to justify the closure of an entire desert to outsiders. Claiming Lüderitz had never sold his "mining sovereignty" to the German government, the courts sanctioned a split of sovereign rights between Lüderitz's business successors and the German state proper, thus ensuring that the former had complete autonomy—and still more profits—in matters relating to diamonds. The agreement of 1908 lives on today in the form of social consequences for Namibians, whose diamond wealth has disproportionately flowed to the inheritors of Lüderitz's "private" sovereignty, De Beers.

At present one can observe similar dynamics across Africa, many of whose political boundary lines came about in the brief era of rogue empires.[264] Former Tanzanian president Julius Nyerere had some basis to complain that the Berlin Conference's creation of artificial nations in 1884 was a principal cause of contemporary African struggles.[265] One can, for instance, look to the erstwhile Independent State of the Congo (today's Democratic Republic of the Congo), where Leopold's quest for fortune resulted in a decimation of indigenous peoples that irrevocably altered demographics.[266] Since at least 1891, when the Independent State began to assert itself more forcefully in parts hitherto only nominally under its sway, this area's mineral and energy resources have almost always fallen into the hands of foreign companies—chiefly, though not exclusively, Belgian. All such companies operate in a territory whose property rights, boundaries, and climate of corruption saw formative years, if not birth, under the policies of the Independent State and the early *"concessionnaires"* established and part-owned by the government.[267]

Of course, it is perhaps too convenient to assume that the quality of private governance by a rogue empire was fundamentally different from that of traditional colonial powers. Germany's genocidal campaign against the Herero and Nama, launched well after Lüderitz's rogue empire had dissolved, certainly rivaled the worst abuses of Leopold's system in the Congo, which fell under scrutiny more or less contemporaneously. Still, bearing in mind that the distinction between the two types of empire *did* exist in the minds of Europeans gives cause for some more

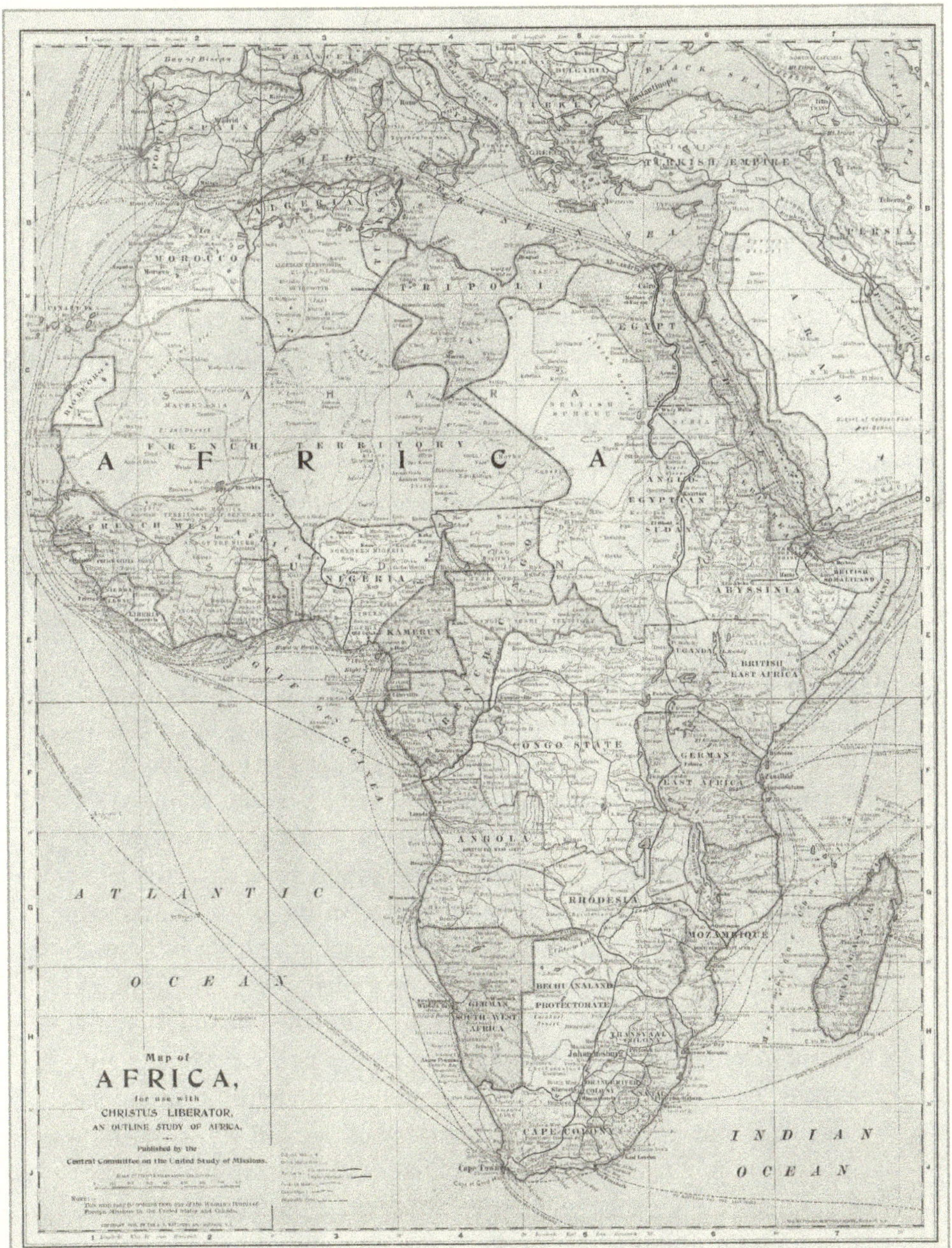

Map 5 Political Divisions in Africa, 1905. Just twenty years removed from the Berlin Conference, Europeans had nearly completed the partition. Note the continued independence of Leopold's Congo State. Stark changes are reflected not only in demarcated boundaries throughout the continent's interior, but also in dotted and straight lines tracing a proliferation of railroad, shipping, and telegraph cable routes. *Source:* Central Committee on the United Study of Missions, *Map of Africa, for Use with Christus Liberator, an Outline Study of Africa* (Buffalo 1905). Courtesy of Yale University Library Map Collection.

counterfactuals. For one, history would have looked different had there been a public check on the King of the Belgians' power early on, if for no other reason than that more parties would have demanded a slice of profits and thus diluted his authority.[268] A wider set of stakeholders would not have permitted one man to claim eminent domain over a country as huge as the Congo. Nor, in turn, would the resultant struggle to control land have remained quiet enough—even in a European climate rife with hypocrisy and racism—to allow for a policy whereby African subjects annually owed the state 310 days in forced labor.[269] A final point concerns size: Without the megalomania of a Leopoldian empire, colonization of the Congo may well have taken on more modest contours, thus sparing some pockets of territory the fate of interaction with European colonialism, if only for a time.

What if, more broadly, the Borneo model had never come to Africa? And what if, absent this inspiration, Europe had never sanctioned a host of rogue empires? One could argue that the broad outlines of African partition would not have changed.[270] Given advances in steamships, breech-loading rifles, quinine, missionary work, the Suez Canal, Ottoman decline, the increasing integration of West Africa into international markets, and the encroachment of Britain on the Transvaal, it is easy to conclude that Africa's partition by Europe was overdetermined, even inevitable.[271] But the partition would not have accelerated dramatically in 1884–1885 without Borneo. On the contrary: In this aspect it looks like an indispensable piece of a subpuzzle, for without it (1) Leopold could not have won his own Congo state; (2) Bismarck would likely not have ventured into colonialism when he did, if at all; (3) Bismarck would likely not have worked against a Portuguese-dominated Congo with the same vigor; and (4) the Berlin Conference would likely not have convened when it did, or with the same outcome, thus removing from European imperial history one of its seminal moments. Evidence that Borneo accelerated the rate of partition can be found in the text of several "protectorate" treaties circa 1884, including the very first one made by Germans in Togo, whereby King Mlapa pledged not to transfer sovereign rights over any part of his territory "to a foreign power or person."[272] True, even irrespective of such developments, Britain would probably still have come to dominate South Africa, Southwest Africa, a chunk of East Africa, and, indirectly, Portugal's territories in Mozambique, Angola, and the Congo Basin.[273]

Likewise, France still would have brought a very substantial portion of West Africa under its sway, including a piece of the Congo. Even in France, however, the Borneo connection altered the nature of partition. The infamous concessionary companies unveiled by colonial authorities to develop their portion of the Congo in the late 1890s—the cornerstones of an era known as *la mise en valeur* (economic exploitation) of the Congo—would almost certainly not have run so far, if at all, without the example recently ushered in by the rogues.[274]

East Africa's counterfactual fate would seem harder to predict. Perhaps Britain and France, or even Italy, would have split the region between them. But it is certain that each power would have done so at a much slower rate if Carl Peters, having had no model on which to base his "government," had never pressured Germany into increasing its involvement.[275] Any such delay would also have allowed room for the exercise of greater autonomy by the Zanzibari Empire, which arguably served as another driver in the African partition from the 1870s on.[276] Retaining the emphasis on East African actors, one can imagine that the absence of the Borneo model, and the probably attendant inaction of Germany and Leopold, might also have hastened, or even emboldened, the aims of Muhammad Ahmed's Mahdist jihād in the Sudan.[277] That knock-on effect, in turn, would suggest different paths for the Egyptian khedive's imperial agenda; Britain's (non-)intervention in the Sudan; and, not least, the eventual interaction between the Khalifa, Ahmed's successor, and the embattled neighboring state in Ethiopia.[278]

So much for virtual history and its consequences in Africa. But one must not overlook how indelibly the rogue empires and their ideas interacted with the European continent proper. To the European mind, rogue empires put more at stake than just conflicts or history in far-flung locales: They endorsed a particular view of territory as a simple commodity, and this view resembled, and even reinforced, patrimonial conceptions of Western statehood.[279] To this extent the empires were, to borrow a phrase from the late Arno Mayer, a sign of the persistence of the old regime: one in which kings, queens, and princes willfully traded their control over subjects in dowries or for debt relief.[280] That kind of persistence certainly looked incongruous with dominant themes of the nineteenth century: expanded civil freedoms, democratization, nationalism, parliamentarization. It tested key narratives of European history even as major scholars were writing them.

Paradoxically, however, it was also possible to read rogue empires as a threat to the old regime. By 1885, a typical European intellectual knew that individual Europeans were claiming to acquire governing powers in Africa through leases, sales, and even stock shares. He or she would soon learn that international lawyers, diplomats, and scientists did not quite know how to process this trend. As years passed, it would become fashionable to dismiss what happened in Africa as unique to supposedly "backward" lands and peoples. Colonial Africa and Europe played by different rules, one might claim. Not so the rogues, who persisted in arguing that the world was still a marketplace for state territory and rights of government—a place where a pack of common speculators, or a deluded adventurer, could start their own states by citing inchoate customs and precedents of law. That landscape sounded a lot like the early modern period—the vestiges of which were just being shed by consolidated nation-states. On the other hand, it also looked like a brave new world in which the playing field for political control had been leveled. Perhaps the bourgeois order of capitalism had conquered yet another arena of life: titles to rule and claims to supreme political authority.

The old regime acquitted itself well at the Berlin Conference in 1885. Leopold's Congo schemes received the seal of formal recognition, not with approval from European parliaments, but from monarchs like Italy's Umberto I and Germany's William I, the embodiment of an institution that had openly treated European territory as patrimony through the nineteenth century. Still, it is not enough to say that the concept of a free market in territory helped to carry the Berlin Conference by appealing to old-regime instincts.[281] Contemporaneously, the concept of a sovereignty market was hardly confined to elite circles and circulated in at least seven different languages via the immensely successful, worldwide, and simultaneous publication of Stanley's two-volume study, *The Congo and the Founding of Its Free State*.[282] Such circumstances suggest that, by 1885, the "old regime" had seen one of its key tenets popularized and accepted by diverse social strata—thanks partly to the machinations of rogues from Borneo to Africa.

Here as elsewhere, the rogue empires challenged nineteenth-century Europeans to rethink certain familiar dichotomies: between European metropoles and colonies, between states and companies, between private property and political control, between early modern and modern. This intellectual exercise hardly seems irrelevant today. For ours is not only a landscape with cases of privatized governance—think of the Internet Corporation for Assigned Names and Numbers—but also a time in which De Beers has merged its mining companies with the Namibian and Botswanan governments; in which Honduras has agreed to establish a foreign, chartered company-run city at its coast; and in which PetroChina, a state-owned firm, has hired mercenary armies to police its oil fields in South Sudan.

Notes

Abbreviations

AHR	*American Historical Review*
AMAE	Archives of French Foreign Ministry
APR	Archives du Palais Royal
BEA	*Bismarck, Europe, and Africa: the Berlin Africa Conference 1884–1885 and the onset of partition*, ed. Stig Förster, Ronald Robinson, Wolfgang J. Mommsen (Oxford: Oxford University Press, 1988).
BMJ	*Brunei Museum Journal*
BMSA	Baptist Missionary Society Archives
CFFS	Henry Morton Stanley. *The Congo and the founding of its free state: a story of work and exploration* (New York: Harper, 1885).
DDF	*Documents diplomatiques français*
DDI	*I Documenti Diplomatici Italiani*
DFB	Despatches from U.S. Consuls in Brunai
DFHK	Despatches from U.S. Consuls in Hong Kong
DFS	Despatches from U.S. Consuls in Singapore
EHR	*Economic History Review*
FRUS	*Foreign Relations of the United States*
HAU	*Journal of Ethnographic Theory*
JAH	*Journal of African History*
JICH	*Journal of Imperial and Commonwealth History*
JMBRAS	*Journal of Malaysian Branch of Royal Asiatic Society*
JMH	*Journal of Modern History*
JSEAS	*Journal of Southeast Asian Studies*
JTMP	John Tyler Morgan Papers
LII	Leopold II

LOC	Library of Congress
LVP	Liévin van de Velde Papers
MAS	*Modern Asian Studies*
NAW	Namibian Archives, Windhoek
NYT	*New York Times*
PAAA	Politisches Archiv des Auswärtigen Amts
RDI	*Revue de Droit International*
RGS	*Proceedings of the Royal Geographical Society*
RMCA	Royal Museum for Central Africa
SAN	Sanford Papers
SMJ	*Sarawak Museum Journal*
SPAR	Sparhawk Papers, British Library
STAN	Stanley Papers
USNA	United States National Archives

Introduction

1. George Washington Williams, "Report on the Congo-State," in John Hope Franklin, *George Washington Williams: A Biography* (Durham, NC: Duke University Press, 1998), 269.
2. Williams to Henry Shelton Sanford, October 31, 1889, Henry Shelton Sanford Papers (hereafter SAN), Box 22, Folder 5.
3. Jesse Siddall Reeves, *The International Beginnings of the Congo Free State* (Baltimore: Johns Hopkins University, 1894), 70; William Edward Hall, *A Treatise on International Law* (Oxford: Clarendon Press, 1890), 88.
4. Edouard Rolin-Jaequemyns, "L'Annee 1888," *Revue de Droit International* (hereafter *RDI*) 21 (1889): 181.
5. Congo Reform Association, *Conditions in the Congo State* (Washington, D.C.: Judge and Deyweiler, 1904), 5.
6. "Congo," *New York Tribune*, December 7, 1884.
7. Paul de Borchgrave to Sanford, September 2, 1884, SAN, Box 25, Folder 16.
8. Henry Wack, *The Story of the Congo Free State: Social, Political, and Economic Aspects of the Belgian System of Government in Central Africa* (New York: Putnam's, 1905), 552.
9. Williams to Sanford, October 31, 1889, SAN, Box 22, Folder 5.
10. Williams to Sanford, February 12, 1890, SAN, Box 28, Folder 19.
11. Rolin-Jaequemyns, "L'Annee 1888," 182.
12. Congo Reform Association, *Conditions in Congo*, 13.
13. William Holman Bentley to Alfred Henry Baynes, October 31, 1888, Baptist Missionary Society Archives (hereafter BMSA) (Microfilm), Reel 32.
14. Franklin, *George Washington Williams*, 201–221.
15. Kevin Grant, "Christian critics of empire: Missionaries, Lantern lectures, and the Congo Reform Campaign in Britain," *Journal of Imperial and Commonwealth History* (hereafter *JICH*) 29 (2001): 27.

16. Willard Tisdel to John Tyler Morgan, November 25, 1884, John Tyler Morgan Papers (hereafter JTMP), Box 1, Library of Congress (hereafter LOC). Friedrich Johann von Alvensleben to Otto von Bismarck, August 13, 1885, Politisches Archiv des Auswärtigen Amts (hereafter PAAA), London 388.
17. Tisdel to Frederick Frelinghuysen, November 25, 1884, JTMP, Box 1.
18. Richard von Schmidthals to Bismarck, May 14, 1885, PAAA, London 388.
19. Jean-Luc Vellut, "La violence armée dans l'État Indépendant du Congo," *Culture et Développement* 16 (1984): 671.
20. "Article 6, Decree of 17th April 1887," BMSA, Reel 32.
21. Richard Raab, *Der alte und der neue Kongostaat* (Hamburg: J.F. Richter, 1892), 33.
22. Jules Devaux to Sanford, January 29, 1884, SAN, Box 25, Folder 19.
23. Raab, *Kongostaat,* 34.
24. But see George Grenfell to Sanford, November 23, 1889, SAN, Box 24, Folder 19.
25. Congo Reform Association, *Conditions in Congo,* 5.
26. David Northrup, *Beyond the Bend in the River: African Labor in Eastern Zaire, 1865–1940* (Athens: Ohio University Press, 1988), 29–36.
27. Alfred Zimmermann, "Kongo," *Preußische Jahrbücher,* vol. 60 (Berlin 1887), 309. For evidence of slow pace, see the flowery take by an American, Henry Phillips, "An Account of the Congo Independent State," *Proceedings of the American Philosophical Society,* vol. 26 (Philadelphia 1889), 459.
28. Bernard Porter, "Imperialism and the Scramble," *JICH* 9 (1980): 76.
29. See Elizabeth Colson, "African Society," in *Colonialism in Africa: 1870–1960,* vol. 1, ed. L. H. Gann and Peter Duignan (London: Cambridge University Press, 1969), 27.
30. Henri Brunschwig, "'Scramble' et 'Course au Clocher,'" *Journal of African History* (hereafter *JAH*) 12 (1971): 139.
31. See David Kenneth Fieldhouse, *Economics and Empire 1830–1914* (London: Macmillan, 1984), 467.
32. Edward Keene, "The Treaty-Making Revolution of the Nineteenth Century," *International History Review* 34 (2012): 491.
33. Henri Brunschwig, *Le Partage de l'Afrique noire* (Paris: Flammarion, 1971), 84.
34. Rowland Aderemi Adeleye, *Power and Diplomacy in Northern Nigeria, 1804–1906: The Sokoto Caliphate and its Enemies* (New York: Humanities Press, 1971), 132.
35. Frederick Lugard, *The Dual Mandate in British Tropical Africa* (Edinburgh: W. Blackwood and Sons, 1922), 15.
36. Alexandre N'dumbe, *L'Afrique et l'Allemagne de la colonisation à la coopération, 1884–1986: le cas du Cameroun* (Yaoundé: AfricAvenir, 1986), 42–68.

37. Wolfgang J. Mommsen, *Das Zeitalter des Imperialismus* (Frankfurt am Main: Fischer Bücherei, 1969), 154.
38. John L. Comaroff, "Colonialism, Culture, and the Law," *Law and Social Inquiry* 26 (2001): 306; Malcolm N. Shaw, *Title to Territory in Africa: International Legal Issues* (Oxford: Clarendon Press, 1986), 37.
39. Paul Reichard, *Deutsch-Ostafrika: Das Land und seine Bewohner* (Leipzig: Otto Spamer, 1892), 8.
40. Lamar Middleton, *The Rape of Africa* (London: Robert Hale, 1936), 116.
41. Friedrich Fabri, *Fünf Jahre deutscher Kolonialpolitik* (Gotha: Perthes, 1889), 20, 64.
42. Margery Perham and Mary Bull, eds., *The Diaries of Lord Lugard,* vol. 1 (Evanston, IL: Northwestern University Press, 1959), 318.
43. Lugard, *Dual Mandate,* 15.
44. Jeffrey Herbst, "The creation and maintenance of national boundaries in Africa," *International Organization* 43 (1989): 673.
45. Martti Koskenniemi, *From Apology to Utopia: The Structure of International Legal Argument* (Cambridge: Cambridge University Press, 2005), 176.
46. Taslim Olawale Elias, *Africa and the Development of International Law* (Dordrecht: Martinus Nijhoff Publishers, 1988), 19.
47. Edward Keene, "The Treaty-Making Revolution," 478, 496.
48. Edward Keene, "A Case Study of the Construction of International Hierarchy: British Treaty-Making Against the Slave Trade in the Early Nineteenth Century," *International Organization* 61 (2007): 311–339. Alfred P. Rubin, *Law of Piracy* (Newport: Naval War College Press, 1988), 207.
49. Edward Keene, "The Treaty-Making Revolution," 484.
50. Saadia Touval, "Treaties, Borders, and the Partition of Africa" *JAH* 7 (1966): 280.
51. Anonymous, "Do ut Des," *Asiatic Quarterly Review,* vol. 9 (London 1890), 384. See Gambetta, *The Sicilian Mafia: The Business of Protection* (Cambridge, MA: Harvard University Press, 1993).
52. Jürgen Osterhammel, *The Transformation of the World: A Global History of the Nineteenth Century* (Princeton, NJ: Princeton University Press, 2014), 444. John Darwin, *After Tamerlane: The Global History of Empire Since 1405* (New York: Bloomsbury, 2008), 314, 54.
53. Albert Wirz and Andreas Eckert, "The Scramble for Africa: Icon and Idiom of Modernity," *Slave Trade to Empire,* ed. Olivier Pétré-Grenouilleau (New York: Routledge, 2004), 137. George Neville Sanderson, "The European Partition of Africa: Coincidence or Conjuncture?" *JICH* 3 (1974): 1.
54. Ronald Robinson and John Gallagher, *Africa and the Victorians* (London: Macmillan, 1965), 163, 465. Gallagher and Robinson, "Imperialism," *Economic History Review* (hereafter *EHR*) 6 (1953): 1–15.
55. Compare Martti Koskenniemi, *The Gentle Civilizer of Nations: The Rise and Fall of International Law 1870–1960* (Cambridge: Cambridge University Press, 2001).

56. "Of Pirates, Empire, and Terror," *Humanity: An International Journal of Human Rights, Humanitarianism, and Development* 2 (2011): 75.
57. Christopher A. Bayly, *The Birth of the Modern World, 1780–1914* (Malden, MA: Blackwell Publishers, 2004), 86.
58. Peter J. Cain, *Hobson and Imperialism: Radicalism, New Liberalism, and Finance 1887–1938* (Oxford: Oxford University Press, 2002), 54.
59. Bernard Porter, "The Berlin West Africa Conference of 1884–85 Revisited: A Report," *JICH* 14 (1985): 92.
60. Robert D. Jackson, "Resistance to the German Invasion of the Tanganyika Coast, 1888–1891," in *Protest and Power in Black Africa,* ed. Robert I. Rotberg and Ali Mazrui (New York: Oxford University Press, 1970), 43.

Chapter 1: The Man Who Bought a Country

1. I have relied on the following sources for analysis of Brooke's ascendancy as it relates to Dayaks: Robert Pringle, *Rajahs and Rebels: the Ibans of Sarawak Under Brooke Rule, 1841–1941* (Ithaca, NY: Cornell University Press, 1970); and John H. Walker, *Power and Prowess: The Origins of Brooke Kingship in Sarawak* (Honolulu: University of Hawai'i Press, 2002). A list of Brooke's many biographies includes some early accounts by contemporaries: Hugh Low, *Sarawak* (London: Bentley, 1848); Henry Keppel, *The Expedition to Borneo of H.M.S. Dido for the Suppression of Piracy* (New York: Harper, 1848); Rodney Mundy, *Narrative of Events in Borneo and Celebes, down to the occupation of Labuan* (London: John Murray, 1848); Spenser St. John, *The Life of Sir James Brooke, Rajah of Sarawak* (Edinburgh: W. Blackwood and Sons, 1879). For the most thorough historical account, see Nicholas Tarling, *The Burthen, the Risk, and the Glory: A Biography of Sir James Brooke* (Oxford: Oxford University Press, 1982).
2. Joseph Balestier, "Mr. Brooke, of Sarawack," *Merchants' Magazine and Commercial Review,* vol. 18 (1848), 56.
3. Anonymous, "A White Rajah," *Eclectic Magazine,* vol. 31 (1880), 481.
4. Elihu Doty and William Pohlman, "Tour in Borneo," *Chinese Repository,* vol. 8 (1839), 283.
5. See Christopher A. Bayly, *Imperial Meridian: The British Empire and the World 1780–1830* (London: Longman, 1989).
6. St. John, *Life of Brooke,* 10.
7. Marshall Sahlins, "On the culture of material value and the cosmography of riches," *HAU: Journal of Ethnographic Theory* 3 (2013): 183.
8. Graham Saunders, *A History of Brunei* (Kuala Lumpur: Oxford University Press, 1994), 73, 33.
9. See D. E. Brown, *Brunei: The Structure and History of a Bornean Malay Sultanate* (Brunei: Brunei Museum, 1970).
10. Jane Kate Leonard, *Wei Yuan and China's Rediscovery of the Maritime World* (Cambridge, MA: Harvard University Press, 1984), 123.

11. Matassim Jibah, "Pengiran Indera Mahkota Shahbandar Mohammad Salleh and James Brooke in the History of Brunei," *Brunei Museum Journal* (hereafter *BMJ*) 4 (1979): 38.
12. Marshall Sahlins, "Alterity and autochthony: Austronesian cosmographies of the marvelous," *HAU: Journal of Ethnographic Theory* 2 (2012): 144.
13. Sabine Baring-Gould, *A History of Sarawak under its Two White Rajahs* (London: Sotheran, 1909), 207.
14. Saunders, *History of Brunei*, 74.
15. George T. Lay, *Notes made during the Voyage of the Himmaleh in the Malay Archipelago* (New York: French, 1839). Carl A. Gibson-Hill, "George Samuel Windsor Earl," *Journal of Malaysian Branch of Royal Asiatic Society* (hereafter *JMBRAS*) 32 (1962): 105.
16. Tarling, *Piracy and politics in the Malay world: a study of British imperialism in nineteenth-century Southeast Asia* (Melbourne: Cheshire, 1963), 115.
17. Baring-Gould, 69.
18. C.C. Brown, "Sejarah Melayu," *JMBRAS* 25 (1952): 1. Hugh Low, "Selesilah," *JMBRAS* 5 (1880): 2.
19. Virunha, "Perceptions," *Thai South and Malay North: Ethnic Interactions on a Plural Peninsula*, eds. Michael Montesano and Patrick Jory (Singapore: National University of Singapore Press, 2008), 68.
20. See H.R. Hughes-Hallett, "Brunei," *BMJ* 5 (1981): 18.
21. Sahlins, "Alterity," 147.
22. Gertrude Johan Resink, *Indonesia's History Between the Myths* (Hague: van Hoeve, 1968), 322.
23. Philip J. Stern, *The Company-State: Corporate Sovereignty and the Early Modern Foundations of the British Empire in India* (Oxford: Oxford University Press, 2011), 179.
24. Carl A. Gibson-Hill, "Raffles," *JMBRAS* 28 (1955): 184. Andrew F. Smith, "New Light on Alexander Hare," *Borneo Research Bulletin*, vol. 44 (2013): 100.
25. Stern, *Company-State*, 181.
26. Carl Bock, *The Head-Hunters of Borneo* (London: Low, 1882), 172.
27. Graham Saunders, "Seekers of Kingdoms: British Adventurers in the Malay Archipelago," *BMJ* 4 (1980): 138. William John Hocking, *Catalogue of the coins, medals, dies, and seals in the museum of the Royal Mint*, vol. 1 (London: His Majesty's Stationery Office, 1906), 291.
28. Excerpted in Gertrude Jacob, *Raja of Saráwak*, vol. 1 (London: Macmillan, 1876), 96.
29. Etienne Denis, *Bordeaux et la Cochinchine sous la Restauration et le Second Empire* (Paris: Imprimerie Delmas, 1965), 132. Craig A. Lockard, "The Evolution of Urban Government in Southeast Asian Cities: Kuching under the Brookes," *Modern Asian Studies* (hereafter *MAS*), vol. 12 (1978): 245.
30. Joseph Conrad to Margaret Alice Lily, July 15, 1920, *Letters of Joseph Conrad*, vol. 7, ed. Laurence Davies (Cambridge: Cambridge University Press, 2005), 137.

31. Baring-Gould, 73.
32. Joseph Hume to Earl of Malmesbury, April 7, 1852, *Further Correspondence Respecting Piracy* (London: Harrison and Son, 1853), 4. Jacob, *Raja*, vol. 1, 166.
33. Brooke to John Templer, September 25th, 1841, *The private letters of Sir James Brooke, K.C.B., Rajah of Sarawak: narrating the events of his life, from 1838 to the present time*, vol. 1 (London: Richard Bentley, 1853), 113–117.
34. "Transfer by Pangeran Muda Hassim of Government of Sarawak," dated 1841 (in translation), *Treaties and engagements affecting the Malay States and Borneo*, ed. William Maxwell and William Gibson (London: Truscott, 1924), 184.
35. "Appointment by Sultan of Brunei of James Brooke to Govern as His Representative," dated 1842 (in translation), *Treaties and Engagements*, 185.
36. E. Parnell, "The Tribute Paid in Former Days by the Then Dependent Provinces of Sarawak," *Sarawak Museum Journal* (hereafter *SMJ*) 1 (1911): 130.
37. Graham Saunders, "James Brooke's Visit to Brunei in 1844: A Reappraisal," *SMJ* 17 (1969): 305.
38. Saunders, *History*, 76.
39. Barbara Andaya, "Political Development between the Sixteenth and Eighteenth Centuries," *Cambridge History of Southeast Asia*, ed. Nicholas Tarling, vol. 1, part 2 (Cambridge: Cambridge University Press, 1999), 67.
40. William Treacher, *British Borneo* (Singapore: Government Printing Department, 1891), 14.
41. Alfred Russel Wallace, *Australasia* (London: E. Stanford, 1888), 377.
42. Brooke to Lord Derby, December 4th, 1858, *Rajah Brooke & Baroness Burdett Coutts*, ed. Owen Rutter (London: Hutchinson, 1935), 51.
43. Spenser St. John, *Life in the Forests of the Far East*, vol. 1 (London: Smith, Elder & Co., 1863), 96.
44. Keppel, *Expedition*, 203.
45. Keppel, *Expedition*, 359, postscript to second edition, June 6, 1846.
46. Foreign Office to Brooke, January 25, 1847, United Kingdom National Archives (hereafter UKNA) FO 12 / 5.
47. Rodney Mundy to Thomas Cochrane, January 12, 1847, CO 144 / 2, treaty dated May 27, 1847, FO 93 / 16(2).
48. The Royal Archives, Queen Victoria's Journals, RA VIC / MAIN / QVJ (W) 29 March 1845 (Princess Beatrice's copies).
49. Treaty of May 27, 1847, UKNA FO 93 / 16.
50. Grant by Sultan Omar Ali, August 2, 1846 (in translation), *Treaties and Engagements*, 186.
51. Joan Rawlins, *Sarawak* (London: Macmillan, 1965), 24.
52. Grant by Sultan Omar Ali, 186.
53. Various grants of 1855, *Treaties and Engagements*, 189.

54. Harriette McDougall, *Sketches of our Life at Sarawak* (London: Society for Promoting Christian Knowledge, 1886), 9.
55. Hume's speech, July 10, 1851, *Hansard's Parliamentary Debates,* vol. 118 (London 1851), 449.
56. Joseph Balestier to Arthur Crookshank, May 27, 1850, FO 12/8.
57. Robert Stafford, *Scientist of Empire: Sir Roderick Murchison, Scientific Exploration and Victorian Imperialism* (Cambridge: Cambridge University Press, 1989), 149.
58. James T. Costa, *Wallace, Darwin, and the Origin of Species* (Cambridge, MA: Harvard University Press, 2014), 29.
59. Harry Ricketts, *Rudyard Kipling: A Life* (New York: Da Capo, 2001), 3. Henry Walker, "The State of North Borneo," *Journal of the Society for Arts* 51 (1903): 516.
60. Coutts to Thomas Fairbairn, September 1866, Rutter, *Brooke & Coutts,* 271.
61. But see Eric Tagliacozzo, "Trafficking Human Subjects in the Malay World, 1850–1910," *Global Human Smuggling,* ed. David Kyle and Rey Koslowski (Baltimore: Johns Hopkins University Press, 2011), 87.
62. Craig A. Lockard, "The Early Development of Kuching 1820–57," *JMBRAS* 49 (1976): 111.
63. "Derby on Limits," *The Economist,* December 4, 1858, 1345.
64. Keat Gin Ooi, *Of free trade and native interests: The Brookes and the economic development of Sarawak, 1841–1941* (Oxford: Oxford University Press, 1997), 113.
65. Kees van Dijk, "From Raja to Prime Minister," *Moussons* 12 (2008): 105.
66. Baring-Gould, 78. Pringle, 15.
67. Brooke's letter, October 1842, Papers of the Brookes of Sarawak, MSS Pac. s 83, vol. 38, Bodleian Library, Oxford.
68. Lockard, "The Evolution," 247.
69. See Alex Middleton, "Rajah Brooke and the Victorians," *Historical Journal* 53 (2010): 381.
70. See Rajat Kanta Ray, "Asian Capital in the Age of European Domination: The Rise of the Bazaar, 1800–1914," *MAS* 29 (1995): 449.
71. *The Economist,* August 26, 1848, 974.
72. William Gladstone, "Piracy in Borneo," *Contemporary Review* 30 (July 1877): 186.
73. van Dijk, 105.
74. Walker, *Power,* 186, 116. Compare O. W. Wolters, *History, Culture, and Region in Southeast Asian Perspectives* (Ithaca, NY: Cornell University Press, 1999), 112.
75. Marshall Sahlins, "The Stranger-King," *Indonesia and the Malay World* 36 (2008): 193.
76. Sahlins, "Alterity," 144.
77. Travers Twiss to Julian Pauncefote, December 27, 1884, FO 403/48.

78. John Macgregor to Robert Peel, September 26, 1844, Papers of Prime Ministers, British Library, MS 40551.
79. James Brooke, *A vindication of his character and proceedings in reply to the statements privately printed and circulated by Joseph Hume* (London: Ridgway, 1853), 5.
80. Financial Reform Association, *Speech of Molesworth* (London: Simpkin, 1849), 10.
81. John Ingleson, *Expanding the Empire: James Brooke and the Sarawak Lobby, 1839–1868* (Perth: Centre for SSEA Studies, 1979), 81.
82. "Virtus in Medio," *Hongkong Times*, September 22, 1875; "Ethics of Filibusterism," *The Times* (London), April 28, 1857.
83. Kipling, *The Man Who Would Be King* (New York: Doubleday, 1899), 34, 97. See Ben Macintyre, *The Man Who Would Be King: The First American in Afghanistan* (New York: Farrar, Straus and Giroux, 2005), 5.
84. Benedict Sandin, *The Sea Dayaks of Borneo before White Rajah Rule* (London: Macmillan, 1967), 61.
85. Gladstone, "Piracy in Borneo," 185.
86. Sebastian Evans, "Rajah Brooke," *Macmillan's Magazine*, vol. 36 (London 1877), 146.
87. Tarling, *Burthen*, 170.
88. Hume to Malmesbury, December 10, 1852, *Correspondence Respecting Piracy* (London 1853), 29.
89. Anonymous, "Indian Archipelago," *Eclectic Review*, vol. 1 (London 1857), 283.
90. Chamerovzow, *Borneo Facts versus Borneo Fallacies* (London: Gilpin, 1851).
91. See Lauren Benton and Lisa Ford, *Rage for Order* (Cambridge, MA: Harvard University Press, 2016), chapter 5.
92. Nicholas Tarling, *British Policy in the Malay Peninsula and Archipelago, 1824–1871* (Kuala Lumpur: Malayan Branch of Royal Asiatic Society, 1957), 195. Alfred P. Rubin, *Law of Piracy* (Newport: Naval War College Press, 1988), 206, 231.
93. Middleton, "Brooke," 391.
94. Tarling, *Piracy*, 121, 144.
95. See Benton and Ford.
96. RA VIC/MAIN/QVJ (W) 25 October 1847 (Princess Beatrice's copies).
97. Ingleson, *Expanding*, 127.
98. David Hannell, "Lord Palmerston and the 'Don Pacifico Affair' of 1850: The Ionian Connection," *European History Quarterly* 19 (1989): 495.
99. Robert Cochrane, *The Treasury of British Eloquence* (London: Nimmo, 1877), 353.
100. Memorandum of January 26, 1855, *Parliamentary Papers 1854–1855*, vol. 29, 1–12.
101. Chew, *Chinese pioneers on the Sarawak frontier, 1841–1941* (Singapore: Oxford University Press, 1990), 18–38. Craig A. Lockard, "The 1857 Chinese

Rebellion in Sarawak: A Reappraisal," *Journal of Southeast Asian Studies* (hereafter *JSEAS*) 9 (1978): 85.

102. James Brooke to Earl of Clarendon, February 4, 1858, UKNA FO 12/25. Ooi, 90, 107.
103. Lockard, "1857," 93.
104. Sahlins, "Alterity," 144. Emily Hahn, *James Brooke of Sarawak* (London: Barker, 1953), 223.
105. Brooke Brooke's original name was John Brooke Johnson. He changed his last name to Brooke when he arrived in Borneo c. 1848, with the expectation of succeeding his uncle.
106. Rutter, *Brooke & Coutts,* 247. Spenser St. John to Charles Brooke, November 10, 1858, Correspondence and papers of the Brooke Family, MSS Pac. s 90, vol. 15, Bodleian Library, Oxford.
107. "British North Borneo Company," *Nautical Magazine,* vol. 51 (London 1883), 42.
108. Edward Hertslet's memo, December 29, 1876, FO 12/51. Graham Irwin, *Nineteenth-Century Borneo: A Study in Diplomatic Rivalry* (Singapore: D. Moore, 1955), 101.
109. Brooke to Edward Lytton, August 1858, in Jacob, *Raja,* vol. 2, 270.
110. "Sarawak," *The Times* (London), December 1, 1858.
111. Frederick Boyle, "Rajah Brooke," *Temple Bar,* vol. 24 (November 1868), 215.
112. Confirmation by Sultan Abdul Momin, August 24, 1853, *Treaties and Engagements,* 187.
113. RA VIC/MAIN/QVJ (W) 25 October 1847 (Princess Beatrice's copies).
114. Hardinge Giffard, *The laws of England: A complete statement of the whole law of England,* vol. 6 (London: Butterworth, 1909), 422. Arthur Berriedale Keith, *The constitution, administration and laws of the Empire* (London: Collins, 1924), 289.
115. George Bowyer, *Commentaries on the constitutional law of England* (London: Richards, 1846), 47.
116. Law Officers (LO) to Clarendon, November 17, 1854, in *International Law Opinions,* ed. McNair, vol. 1 (Cambridge: Cambridge University Press, 1956), 26. LO to Clarendon, January 9, 1854, FO 83/2292. LO to FO, January 19, 1856 and February 15, 1856, FO 83/2235. Clarendon to St. John, April 9, 1856, FO 12/23.
117. James Taylor, *Creating Capitalism: Joint-Stock Enterprise in British Politics and Culture 1800–1870* (Cornwall: Boydell Press, 2006), 3.
118. Sanjay Subrahmanyam, *The Portuguese Empire in Asia, 1500–1700* (London: Longman, 1993).
119. See K. N. Chaudhuri, "Treasure and Trade Balances: the East India Company's Export Trade, 1660–1720," *EHR* 21 (1968): 480. See most recently Emily Erikson, *Between Monopoly and Free Trade: The English East India Company, 1600–1757* (Princeton, NJ: Princeton University Press, 2014).

120. John H. Elliott, *Empires of the Atlantic World* (New Haven, CT: Yale University Press, 2007), 118. Ann M. Carlos and Stephen Nicholas, "'Giants of an Earlier Capitalism': The Chartered Trading Companies as Modern Multinationals," *Business History Review* 62 (1988): 410.
121. Charles H. Alexandrowicz, *An Introduction to the History of the Law of Nations in the East Indies* (Oxford: Clarendon Press, 1967), 39, 59. David Armitage, "The Scottish vision of empire: intellectual origins of the Darien venture," *A Union for Empire: Political Thought and the British Union of 1707,* ed. John Robertson (Cambridge: Cambridge University Press, 1995), 97.
122. Compare "Charter of Province of Georgia," in *A digest of the English statutes in force in the* state of Georgia, ed. William Schley (Philadelphia: J. Maxwell, 1826), 435. See Philip J. Stern, "British Asia and the British Atlantic: comparisons and connections," *William and Mary Quarterly* 63 (2006): 693.
123. Anthony Pagden, *Lords of all the World: Ideologies of Empire in Spain, Britain and France c.1500–c.1800* (New Haven, CT: Yale University Press, 1995), 130.
124. William Howard Russell, *My Diary in India,* vol. 1 (London: Routledge, 1860), 52.
125. Samuel Purchas, *Hakluytus Posthumus,* vol. 2 (Glasgow: James MacLehose, 1905), 366. Arthur Berriedale Keith, *A Constitutional History of India, 1600–1935* (London: Methuen, 1936), 6.
126. Stern, *Company-State,* 12, 47.
127. Nicholas B. Dirks, *The Scandal of Empire: India and the Creation of Imperial Britain* (Cambridge, MA: Harvard University Press, 2006), 316.
128. Entry for May 17, 1818, *The Private Journal of the Marquess of Hastings,* ed. Marchioness of Bute, vol. 2 (London: Saunders, 1858), 326.
129. Anthony Pagden, "The Struggle for Legitimacy and the Image of Empire in the Atlantic to c. 1700," *Oxford History of British Empire,* ed. Nicholas Canny, vol. 1 (Oxford: Oxford University Press, 2001), 38.
130. Alexandrowicz, *Law of Nations,* 14–31.
131. Stern, *Company-State.* 47–60.
132. Arnold A. Sherman, "Pressure from Leadenhall: The East India Company Lobby, 1660–1678," *Business History Review* 50 (1976): 329.
133. Stern, *Company-State,* 38, 68, 152.
134. Farhat Hasan, "Indigenous Cooperation and the Birth of a Colonial City: Calcutta, c. 1698–1750," *MAS* 26 (1992): 65. I. B. Watson, "Fortifications and the Idea of Force in the Early East India Company," *Past and Present* 88 (1980): 70.
135. East India Company, *Memoir on the affairs of the East-India company* (London: J. L. Cox, 1830), 51.
136. For document, dated December 24, 1757, see Francis Russell, *A Short History of the East India Company* (London: Sewell, 1793), 11. Huw V. Bowen,

Revenue and Reform: The Indian Problem in British Politics 1757–1773 (Cambridge: Cambridge University Press, 1991), 54.

137. Stern, *Company-State,* 58.
138. See P. J. Marshall, "Empire and authority in the later eighteenth century," *JICH,* vol. 15 (1987), 105.
139. Sudipta Sen, *Empire of Free Trade: The East India Company and the Making of the Colonial Marketplace* (Philadelphia: University of Pennsylvania Press, 1998), 5.
140. Christopher A. Bayly, "The British Military-Fiscal State and Indigenous Resistance: India 1750–1820," in *An Imperial State at War: Britain from 1689 to 1815,* ed. Lawrence Stone (London: Routledge, 1994), 322.
141. Bowen, *Revenue,* 51.
142. Mahabir Prashad Jain, *Outlines of Indian legal history* (Bombay: Tripathi, 1966), 52.
143. P. J. Marshall, "Indian Officials under the East India Company in Eighteenth-Century Bengal," *Bengal Past and Present* 84 (1965): 95.
144. Edward John Thompson, *The Making of the Indian Princes* (Oxford: Oxford University Press, 1943), 137.
145. C. U. Aitchison, *A Collection of Treaties, Engagements and Sunnuds relating to India and the Neighboring Countries,* vol. 2, (Calcutta: Cutter, 1876), 33, 35, 76, 3.
146. William Miller, *Outline of the Case of His Highness Prince Azeem Jah* (London: Adam Burn, 1859), 11. Alexandrowicz, *Law of Nations,* 8.
147. Huw V. Bowen, "British India, 1765–1813: The Metropolitan Context," *The Oxford History of the British Empire,* vol. 2, ed. P. J. Marshall (Oxford: Oxford University Press, 1998), 547.
148. Huw V. Bowen, "A question of Sovereignty? The Bengal land revenue issue, 1765–67," *JICH* 16 (1998): 155. See H. H. Dodwell, "The Development of Sovereignty in British India," *Cambridge History of India,* ed. H. H. Dodwell, vol. 5 (Cambridge: Cambridge University Press, 1929), 589.
149. Dodwell, 596.
150. Thompson, 281.
151. C. H. Philips, "The East India Company 'Interest' and the English Government, 1783–4," *Transactions of the Royal Historical Society,* vol. 20 (1937), 83. On climate of corruption: Erikson, 107.
152. William Bolts, *Considerations on India Affairs,* vol. 1 (London: Almon, 1772), ix, 49, 210.
153. P. J. Marshall, "The Personal Fortune of Warren Hastings," *EHR,* vol. 17 (1964), 284.
154. Mithi Mukherjee, "Justice, War, and the Imperium," *Law and History Review* 23 (2005): 589.
155. Edmund Burke, *The works of the Right Hon. Edmund Burke,* vol. 1 (London: Holdsworth and Ball, 1834), 191. See Jennifer Pitts, *A Turn to Empire: The*

Rise of Imperial Liberalism in Britain and France (Princeton, NJ: Princeton University Press, 2005), 259.

156. Neil Sen, "Warren Hastings and British Sovereign Authority in Bengal, 1774–80," *JICH* 25 (1997): 81.
157. East India Company, *The preliminary debate at the East-India House on 5th January, 1813, on the negotiation with His Majesty's ministers relative to a renewal of the Charter* (London: Black, Parry, and Co., 1813), 1121.
158. Frederick A. Mann, "The Law Governing State Contracts," *British Yearbook of International Law* 21 (1944): 27.
159. "Nabob of Carnatic," *Reports of cases argued and determined in the High Court of Chancery*, ed. Francis Vesey, vol. 1 (London: S. Brooke, 1827), 370.
160. Michael William Jacobs, *A Treatise on the Law of Domicil* (Boston: Little, Brown, and Company, 1887), 222.
161. Alfred Simonides (ed.), *Borneo Question* (Singapore: Simonides, 1854), 3.
162. Bowen, *Business of Empire*, 252.
163. Benjamin Disraeli to Sarah Disraeli, June 8, 1852, *Disraeli: Letters*, ed. John Alexander Gunn, vol. 6 (Toronto: University of Toronto Press, 1997), 77.
164. Boyle, 205.
165. Alexandrowicz, *Law of Nations*, 12. "General Henningsen," *New York Herald*, January 5, 1858. F. W. Newman, "English Rule in India," *Westminster Review* 69 (1858): 112.
166. Christopher A. Bayly, *Indian Society and the Making of the British Empire* (Cambridge: Cambridge University Press, 1988), 134.
167. Eric Stokes, *The Peasant and the Raj: Studies in Agrarian Society and Peasant Rebellion in Colonial India* (Cambridge: Cambridge University Press, 1978), 159–205.
168. John Bright, *Speech on Legislation and Policy for India* (London: Stanford, 1858), 3.
169. Henry Tremenheere, "How Is India to Be Governed?" *Bentley's Miscellany*, vol. 43 (London 1858), 116.
170. Taylor, *Creating Capitalism*, 154, 211.
171. Ronald J. Jensen, *The Alaska Purchase and Russian-American Relations* (Seattle: University of Washington Press, 1975), 14.
172. Benjamin Disraeli to Sarah Brydges Willyams, December 28, 1857, *Disraeli: Letters*, vol. 7, 107.
173. RA VIC / MAIN / QVJ (W) 1 November 1857 (Princess Beatrice's copies).
174. Romesh Dutt, *India in the Victorian Age* (London: K. Paul, 1904), 230.
175. See Jan Martin Lemnitzer, *Power, Law and the End of Privateering* (New York: Palgrave Macmillan, 2014).
176. Karl Marx, "Indian Bill," *New-York Daily Tribune*, July 24, 1858.
177. "Review of Year," *Daily News*, December 31, 1857.
178. Sultan of Brunei to Brooke, August 23, 1846, FO 12 / 8. Ooi, 121.
179. Amarjit Kaur, "The Babbling Brookes: Economic Change in Sarawak 1841–1941," *MAS* 29 (1995): 73.

180. Joseph Hume, *Letter to the Earl of Malmesbury* (London: Robson, 1853), 7.
181. Spring Rice's memo, January 7, 1859, FO 12/35.
182. Denis, 137.
183. David Todd, "A French Imperial Meridian, 1814—1870," *Past and Present* 210 (2011): 179.
184. Rawson W. Rawson, *British and Foreign Colonies* (London: Stanford, 1884) 16.
185. Nicholas Tarling, *Imperialism in Southeast Asia* (London: Routledge, 2001), 115.
186. Wagener, "Bornéo et les Anglais," *L'Isthme de Suez: Journal de l'Union des deux Mers,* vol. 3 (Paris 1858), 231, 254.
187. See J. P. Daughton, *An Empire Divided: Religion, Republicanism, and the Making of French Colonialism, 1880–1914* (Oxford: Oxford University Press, 2006), 6, 13.
188. Austen Layard's memo, January 2, 1862, FO 12/35. 165.
189. L. H. Gann and Peter Duignan, *Burden of Empire. An Appraisal of Western Colonialism in Africa South of the Sahara* (New York: Praeger, 1967), chapter 2.
190. Figure taken from Barbara N. Ramusack, *The Indian Princes and their States* (Cambridge: Cambridge University Press, 2004), 53.
191. Lauren Benton, "From International Law to Imperial Constitutions: The Problem of Quasi-Sovereignty, 1870—1900," *Law and History Review* 26 (2008): 601.
192. Benton, "From International Law to Imperial Constitutions," 598.
193. John Russell to Brooke Brooke, October 7, 1859, FO 12/35.
194. Boyle, 214.
195. This process began in 1856. James Murray's memo, November 16, 1865, FO 12/32.
196. *The Economist,* August 21, 1858, 925.
197. Ingleson, *Expanding,* 109.
198. Charles Sumner, *Our Foreign Relations* (Boston: Wright and Potter, 1863), 50.
199. Frederick Gibbs, *Recognition: A Chapter from the History of the North American & South American States* (London: M'Dowall, 1863), 6.
200. See Hersch Lauterpacht, *Recognition in International Law* (Cambridge: Cambridge University Press, 1947), 90.
201. Compare Owen Rutter, *British North Borneo* (London: Constable and Company, 1922), 128.
202. John Russell's memo, August 23, 1863, FO 12/31.
203. Compare Gibbs, *Recognition,* 22–23.
204. John Bassett Moore, *Digest of International Law,* vol. 1 (Washington, D.C.: Government Printing Office, 1906), 90. Herbert Smith, *Great Britain and the Law of Nations,* vol. 1 (London: P. S. King & Son, 1932), 107.
205. Richard Lyons to William Mure, December 24, 1860, FO 414/17.
206. See Carl A. Trocki, *Prince of Pirates: The Temenggongs and the Development of Johor and Singapore 1784–1885* (Singapore: NUS Press, 2007), 100.

207. "Sarawak," *The Times* (London), December 1, 1858.
208. Anonymous, "North Borneo Company," *Calcutta Review*, vol. 76 (Calcutta 1883), 196.
209. Peter McQuhae, "A visit to Rajah Brooke at Sarawak," *Bentley's Miscellany*, vol. 23 (London 1848), 65.
210. James Murray's memo, November 16, 1865, FO 12/32.
211. "Trade with Foreign Nations," *Morning Post* (London), April 6, 1865.
212. Earl of Clarendon to Brooke, May 26, 1869, FO 12/35.
213. Elliott Marten to Earl Granville, December 1, 1871, *Reports Relative to Consular Establishments*, vol. 4 (London 1872), 212.
214. Boyle, 215.
215. W. H. Chaloner, "Currency Problems of the British Empire 1814–1914," *Great Britain and Her World, 1750–1914: Essays in Honour of W. O. Henderson*, ed. Barrie M. Ratcliffe (Manchester: Manchester University Press, 1975), 195.
216. FO 12/28, Spenser St. John to John Russell, March 8, 1861.
217. James Brooke to Brooke Brooke, September 2, 1859, Basil Brooke Papers, MSS Pac. s 90, vol. 2B.
218. CO 144/26, Admiralty to CO, January 4, 1867.
219. Baring-Gould, 242.
220. Fairbairn to Coutts, September 9, 1866, in Rutter, *Rajah Brooke*, 273.
221. Memo by Edward Hertslet, December 28, 1878, FO 881/3991. See Ooi Keat Gin, "For Want of Rice: Sarawak's Attempts at Rice Self-Sufficiency during the Period of Brooke Rule, 1841–1941," *JSEAS* 29 (1998): 9.
222. "Sarawak and Its Rajah," *Straits Times*, November 13, 1875, 4.
223. Moses to W. H. Seward, July 29, 1864, United States National Archives (hereafter USNA), RG 59, Despatches from U.S. Consuls in Brunai (hereafter DFB). A pioneering, though not exhaustive, treatment of this episode was produced by Kennedy Gordon Tregonning, "American Activity in North Borneo, 1865–1881," *Pacific Historical Review* 23 (1954): 357.
224. Anson Francis to F. W. Seward, September 1, 1862, DFB.
225. Moses to W. H. Seward, July 4, 1864, DFB.
226. *The Rebellion Record: A Diary of American Events*, ed. Frank Moore, vol. 1 (New York: Putnam, 1861), 132.
227. T. F. Callaghan to Earl of Clarendon, January 29, 1866, FO 12/33.
228. "The Paris Duel," *New York Times* (hereafter *NYT*), October 8, 1861. Credit to Lois Fonseca for her suspicion that Moses suffered head trauma.
229. "Friday, Oct. 27th," *Straits Times*, October 27, 1865.
230. G. T. Ricketts to John Russell, October 12, 1865, FO 12/32.
231. Moses to W. H. Seward, August 10, 1865, DFB.
232. Moses to W. H. Seward, July 30, 1866.
233. Adolph Studer to F. W. Seward, September 17, 1878, USNA, Despatches from U.S. Consuls in Singapore (hereafter DFS), vol. 13.
234. Ricketts to Russell, October 12, 1865, FO 12/32.

235. Saunders, *History*, 83.
236. Lease from Pangeran Tumongong to Moses, August 11, 1865, CO 874/2.
237. Henry Keppel, *A Sailor's Life under Four Sovereigns*, vol. 3 (London: Macmillan, 1899), 127.
238. U.S. State Department, *United States Consul's Manual* (Washington, D.C.: Government Printing Office, 1863), 132.
239. Sultan of Brunei to President Andrew Johnson, August 1866, UKNA FO 12/33.
240. Charles Wilkes, *Narrative of the United States Exploring Expedition*, vol. 5 (Philadelphia: Blanchard, 1849), 359.
241. Hunter Miller (ed.), *Treaties and other international acts of the United States of America* (Washington, D.C.: Government Printing Office, 1937), 819.
242. Compare Mark Lindley, *The Acquisition and Government of Backward Territory in International Law* (London: Longman, 1926), 286.
243. Moses to W. H. Seward, December 31, 1865, DFB.
244. I leave it to future researchers to consider this question from the perspective of gender, both for Moses and for the rest of the adventurers coming under scrutiny. See Heather Streets, *Martial Races: The Military, Race and Masculinity in British Imperial Culture, 1857–1914* (Manchester: Manchester University Press, 2004). See also Graham Dawson, *Soldier Heroes: British Adventure, Empire and the Imagining of Masculinities* (New York: Routledge, 1994).
245. W. H. Seward to Moses, March 2, 1866, DFB.
246. Agreement between Moses, Torrey, and others, September 9, 1865, CO 874/3.
247. Lease of Banguey, November 29, 1865, CO 874/6. Proclamation of Torrey, December 21, 1865, UKNA FO 12/33.
248. See Herbert Smith, *Britain and the Law of Nations*, vol. 1, 255.
249. Torrey to President Andrew Johnson, November 30, 1865, DFB.
250. Moses to W. H. Seward, July 30, 1866, DFB.
251. "Death of Mr. J. W. Torrey," *Hong Kong Daily Press*, August 8, 1885.
252. Studer to F. W. Seward, September 17, 1878, DFS, vol. 13.
253. David Sickels to Mosby Campbell, September 13, 1877, USNA, Despatches from U.S. Consuls in Bangkok, vol. 6.
254. I. J. Allen to F. W. Seward, USNA, Despatches from U.S. Consuls in Hong Kong, vol. 5 (DFHK). Moses to Seward, July 30, 1866, DFB.
255. For example, his close friend William Emerson Baker. Credit to Gloria Greis of Needham Historical Society.
256. Sickels to State Department, October 5, 1880, Despatches from U.S. Consuls in Bangkok, vol. 6. Studer to F. W. Seward, July 1, 1880, DFS, vol. 13.
257. Mosby to Peter Smith, March 6, 1879, DFHK, vol. 12. Mosby to William Rogers, May 19, 1879, quoted in James Ramage, *Gray Ghost: The Life of Col. John Singleton Mosby* (Lexington: University of Kentucky Press, 1999), 294, 392.

258. Frederic C. Torrey, *Torrey Families*, vol. 1 (Lakehurst, NJ: Frederic Torrey, 1924), 81. Luther Farnham, *A discourse delivered in the First Congregational Church, West Newbury, Mass.: on Thanksgiving Day, November 25th, 1852* (Boston: J. G. Torrey, 1853), 2.
259. Studer to F. W. Seward, July 1, 1880, DFS, vol. 13.
260. Studer to F. W. Seward, November 27, 1879, DFS, vol. 13.
261. Articles of Partnership, October 25, 1865, CO 874 / 4.
262. Carl T. Smith, *Chinese Christians: Elites, Middlemen, and the Church in Hong Kong* (Hong Kong: HKU Press, 2005), 118. Elizabeth Sinn, *Pacific Crossing: California Gold, Chinese Migration, and the Making of Hong Kong* (Hong Kong: HKU Press, 2013), 111.
263. Tarling, *Piracy*, 145.
264. Henry Bulwer to Granville, August 17, 1872, CO 144 / 37.
265. Carl A. Trocki, "Singapore," *Connecting Seas and Connected Ocean Rims: Indian, Atlantic, and Pacific Oceans and China Seas Migrations from the 1830s to the 1930s*, ed. Donna Gabaccia (Leiden: Brill, 2011), 223. Government of India, *Papers Relating to Opium Question* (Calcutta: Office of Government Printing, 1870), 66.
266. Moses to W. H. Seward, January 1, 1866, DFB. Carlo Racchia to S. Riboty, June 2, 1872, in *I Documenti Diplomatici Italiani* (hereafter *DDI*), 2nd series, vol. 3 (Rome: Istituto poligrafico dello stato, 1969), 562.
267. Torrey to W. H. Seward, January 5, 1866, DFB.
268. T. S. Dobree, *Report on the country in the northern portion of Borneo, lately ceded to Messrs. Dent and Overbeck* (London: Dobree, 1879), 9.
269. Callaghan to FO, January 9, 1866, FO 12 / 33.
270. "An Interesting Case," *London and China Telegraph*, March 7, 1866.
271. Moses to W. H. Seward, July 30, 1866, DFB.
272. "American Trade in Borneo," *Hong Kong Daily Press*, February 6, 1866.
273. Basil Lubbock, *The Opium Clippers* (Boston: Lauriat, 1933), 371.
274. Allen to W. H. Seward, March 31, 1867, DFHK, vol. 6.
275. Moses to W. H. Seward, July 30, 1866, DFB.
276. Tarling, *Piracy*, 185.
277. Moses to W. H. Seward, October 1, 1866, DFB.
278. "Hong Kong," *London and China Telegraph*, May 28, 1866.
279. Compare Amity A. Doolittle, *Property and Politics in Sabah, Malaysia: Native Struggles over Land Rights* (Seattle: University of Washington Press, 2005), 180.
280. Torrey to W. H. Seward, January 5, 1866, DFB.
281. David Armitage, *The Declaration of Independence: A Global History* (Cambridge, MA: Harvard University Press, 2007), 36.
282. John Lind, *An Answer to Declaration of the American Congress* (London: Sewell, 1776), 95.
283. Charles Wesley, "The Struggle for Recognition of Haiti and Liberia as Independent Republics," *Journal of Negro History* 2 (1917): 369.

284. Studer's report, July 1, 1880, DFS, vol. 13.
285. Torrey to W. H. Seward, January 5, 1866, DFB.
286. Moses to W. H. Seward, December 31, 1865, DFB.
287. Moses to W. H. Seward, July 30, 1866, DFB.
288. Torrey to Callaghan, May 8, 1866, FO 12 / 33.
289. Moses to W. H. Seward, October 1, 1866, DFB.
290. Ferry de Goey, *Consuls and the Institutions of Global Capitalism, 1783–1914* (New York: Routledge, 2016), 17.
291. Inche Mahomet to Callaghan, April 16, 1866, FO 12 / 33.
292. But see Brooke to Foreign Office, March 10, 1852, FO 12 / 12.
293. Colin Crisswell, *Rajah Charles Brooke: Monarch of All He Surveyed* (Kuala Lumpur: Oxford University Press, 1978), 158.
294. "Sarawak," *Straits Times*, November 13, 1875, 4.
295. "Friday, Oct. 27th," *Straits Times*, October 27, 1865, 2.
296. St. John, *Life of Brooke*, 363.
297. Pretyman's diary entry of January 3, 1879, in Harrisson (ed.), "Diary of Pretyman (II)," *SMJ* 8 (1957): 214.
298. FO to Low, April 2, 1867, FO 12 / 33.
299. FO to Callaghan, November 18, 1865, FO 12 / 32.
300. Moses to W. H. Seward, July 13, 1867, DFB.
301. Moses to W. H. Seward, September 9, 1866, DFB. Allen to W. H. Seward, March 31, 1867, DFHK, vol. 6.
302. Inche Mahomet to Low, March 25, 1867, FO 12 / 33.
303. Moses to W. H. Seward, July 13, 1867, DFB.
304. Bradford to W. H. Seward, March 16, 1868, DFB.
305. Keppel, *Sailor's Life*, vol. 3, 127. Torrey to W. H. Seward, March 27, 1867, DFHK, vol. 6. Inche Mahomet to J. Pope-Hennessy, March 7, 1868, FO 12 / 34.
306. W. H. Seward to President Andrew Johnson, December 31, 1867, *The Papers of Andrew Johnson*, ed. Paul Bergeron, vol. 13 (Knoxville: University of Tennessee Press, 1996), 400.
307. Torrey to W. H. Seward, March 27, 1867, DFHK.
308. "American Trading Company of Borneo," *Hong Kong Daily Press*, September 13, 1866.
309. Kennedy Gordon Tregonning, *A History of Modern Sabah* (Singapore: University of Singapore, 1965), 5.
310. FO to Callaghan, September 18, 1866, FO 12 / 33.
311. O. F. Bradford to W. H. Seward, March 16, 1868, DFB.
312. Torrey to W. H. Seward, October 22, 1867, USNA RG 59, General Records of Department of State, Miscellaneous Letters, October, Part II, 1867.
313. N. A. McDonald to W. H. Seward, August 13, 1869, Despatches from Bangkok, vol. 6.
314. Moses Pariente to Jesse McMath, October 27, 1863, *Papers Relating to Foreign Relations of United States, 1864* (Washington, D.C.: Government Printing Office, 1865), 417.

315. Bishop of Natal to George Grey, June 14, 1854, CO 879 / 1 / 23.
316. Anonymous, *The Rajahate of Sarawak* (Brighton: Tower Press, 1875), 1.
317. "Dutch India," *Manchester Guardian*, April 12, 1858.
318. *Speech of Molesworth*, 11.
319. R. Andree, "Araukanerstaat," *Ergänzungsblätter zur Kenntniß der Gegenwart*, vol. 2 (Hildburghausen: Verlag des Bibliographischen Instituts, 1870), 269.
320. Edmond Smith, *The Araucanians* (New York: Harper, 1855).
321. "Chronique Américaine," *Revue orientale et américaine*, vol. 5 (Paris 1861), 394.
322. Boyle, 215.
323. Jules Verne, *Les Enfants du Capitaine Grant* (Paris: Hetzel, 1868), 78.
324. Palmer, *Letter to Clayton* (Washington 1849), 10. Buchanan, *Letter from Secretary of State, Relative to . . . Oriental Nations* (Washington 1847), 14.
325. Robert E. May, *Manifest Destiny's Underworld: Filibustering in Antebellum America* (Chapel Hill: University of North Carolina Press, 2002).
326. "A British Walker," *Harper's Weekly*, vol. 1 (1857), 346. "Criminality of American Filibusters," *Cincinnati Daily Enquirer*, May 28, 1857. George Train, *Young America abroad in Europe, Asia and Australia* (London: S. Low, 1857), 139.
327. "Our London Correspondence," *New York Herald*, May 17, 1857.
328. "Henningsen," *New York Herald*, January 5, 1858. "Ethics of Filibusterism," *The Times* (London), Tuesday, April 28, 1857.
329. George Train, *Spread-Eagleism* (New York: Derby and Jackson, 1859), 134.
330. But compare May, *Underworld*, 62.
331. Richard Cobden to George Moffatt, June 1, 1856, *The Letters of Richard Cobden*, vol. 3, ed. Anthony Howe and Simon Morgan (Oxford: Oxford University Press, 2012), 213. "Nicaragua," *Manchester Guardian*, March 5, 1857.
332. May, *Underworld*, 1.
333. Anonymous, "Rajah Brooke," *Gentleman's Magazine*, vol. 1 (London 1868), 268.
334. Elsbeth Locher-Sholten, *Sumatran Sultanate and Colonial State* (Ithaca, NY: Cornell University Press, 2004), 101.
335. "Fast and Loose," *Dundee Courier*, March 26, 1851.
336. Charles Fenwick, *The Neutrality Laws of the United States* (Washington, D.C.: Carnegie Endowment, 1913), 15–48.
337. Inche Mahomet to Low, June 22, 1875, UKNA FO 12 / 41.
338. Law Officers to Clarendon, January 9, 1854, UKNA FO 83 / 2292.
339. William Krause, *American Interests in Borneo* (San Francisco: Bancroft, 1867), 22.
340. Torrey to W. H. Seward, October 22, 1867. USNA RG 59, Miscellaneous Letters, October, Part II, 1867.
341. "White Rajahs of Borneo," *NYT*, November 17, 1867.
342. Fenwick, 50.
343. "New York Legislature," *New York Tribune*, March 28, 1868.

344. "Arrival of 'Colorado'," *Daily Alta California*, September 15, 1867.
345. Joseph Torrey, *American Trading Company of Borneo* (New York: William C. Bryant, 1868). The Universiteitsbibliotheek Leiden's copy is numbered 2024.
346. Torrey, *American Trading Company of Borneo*, 6.
347. "Irrepressible Yankee," *Hartford Daily Courant*, December 31, 1867. "American Rajah," *Milwaukee Daily Sentinel*, January 18, 1868.
348. Krause, *Borneo*, 37.
349. "Irrepressible Yankee," *Daily Cleveland Herald*, January 3, 1868.
350. T. J. Thurlow's Report, July 1, 1868, *Reports by Her Majesty's secretaries of embassy and legation on the manufactures, commerce, etc. of the countries in which they reside* (London: Harrison and Sons, 1869), 433.
351. Torrey to Sultan of Brunei, February 13, 1867, UKNA FO 12/41.
352. Train, *Young America*, 139.
353. Train to W. H. Seward, February 11, 1867, USNA RG 59, Miscellaneous Letters, October, Part I, 1867.
354. Racchia to Riboty, March 20, 1870, *DDI*, 2nd series, vol. 3 (Rome 1969), 552.
355. "By Telegraph," *Sacramento Daily Union*, November 21, 1867.
356. "Arrivals," *San Francisco Daily Alta Californian*, April 3, 1868.
357. "Foreign," *Pacific Appeal*, December 28, 1867.
358. Torrey to Examiner of Claims, March 27, 1867, USNA RG 59, Miscellaneous Letters, October, Part II, 1867. "An American Rajah in Borneo," *Sacramento Daily Union*, January 31, 1868.
359. Joseph Wheelwright to Moses, August 18, 1866, DFB.
360. Pengiran Temenggung Hasyim Sahibul Bahar to Wheelwright, May 29, 1869, Cambridge University Library, Or. 847 (3).
361. Low to Stanley, December 1, 1866, CO 144/25.
362. Henry Pease to U.S. Naval Command, March 19, 1867, USNA, Letters Received by Secretary of Navy from Commanding Officers of Squadrons, 1841–1886: Asiatic Squadron, 1865–1885, File Microcopies: No. 89, Roll 252.
363. Reynolds, "Borneo," *Atlantic Monthly*, vol. 18 (1866), 667.
364. McDonald to W. H. Seward, August 13, 1869, Despatches from Bangkok, vol. 6.
365. "Entry," *Hong Kong Government Gazette*, July 17, 1869.

Chapter 2: The Emergence of an Idea

1. Mortgage between Torrey and Overbeck, undated, c. 1870, CO 874/10. "Government Notification," *Hong Kong Government Gazette*, July 16, 1870.
2. Assignment by Torrey and Sarah Harris to Baron de Overbeck, undated, CO 874/9. Agreement of sale between Torrey and Overbeck, January 19, 1875, CO 874/12.
3. Adolph Studer to F. W. Seward, July 1, 1880, USNA, Despatches from U.S. Consuls in Singapore (hereafter DFS), vol. 13.

4. Adolph Studer to F. W. Seward, September 17, 1878, DFS, vol. 13. "Hongkong," *North-China Herald,* February 13, 1873.
5. See jury roll in *Hong Kong Government Gazette,* March 1, 1873. "Hong Kong Chamber of Commerce," *North-China Herald,* September 22, 1871. Entry for July 18, 1871, *David McLean Letterbooks,* vol. 4, 364, School of Oriental and African Studies London.
6. See *Hong Kong Government Gazette,* March 1, 1873. "Russia, Germany," *London and China Telegraph,* April 29, 1867. Overbeck's file at the Secret State Archives Prussian Cultural Heritage Berlin III. HA, II Nr. 722.
7. Overbeck's Austrian file: Austrian State Archive, AT-OeStA / HHStA MdÄ AR F4–242–9.
8. Studer to F. W. Seward, September 17, 1878, DFS, vol. 13.
9. Max von Brandt, *Dreiunddreissig Jahre in Ostasien: Erinnerungen eines deutschen Diplomaten,* vol. 1 (Leipzig: Wigand, 1901), 232.
10. Algernon Redesdale, *Memories,* vol. 1 (London: Hutchinson, 1915), 340; vol. 2 (1916), 640. "Locales," *Wiener Abendpost,* July 18, 1881.
11. Madeleine Dahlgren (ed.), *Memoir of John A. Dahlgren* (Boston: Osgood, 1882), 644. "Hof—und Personalnachrichten," *Morgen-Post* (Vienna), May 26, 1870.
12. McLane Tilton to Nan Tilton, January 22, 1872, Folder 3, McLane Tilton Papers, Marine Corps Museum, Quantico, Virginia.
13. "Death of Torrey," *Boston Evening Transcript,* June 22, 1885. "Rajah Torrey," *NYT,* July 5, 1885.
14. Studer to F. W. Seward, September 17, 1878, DFS, vol. 13. "Shanghai Silk Shippers," *London and China Telegraph,* February 24, 1873.
15. *Ischler Cur-Liste,* no. 16, August 8, 1873. "Aus Hongkong," *Das Vaterland,* August 7, 1872. "Es dürfte allgemein interessieren," *Berliner Börsenzeitung,* June 3, 1880. Henry May, *Notes on Pony and Horse Racing* (Hong Kong: Noronha 1909), 17, 27. Josef Hafenbredl, *A Ramble Round the World,* vol. 2 (London: Macmillan 1874), 371.
16. *Congressional Record* (Senate), August 10, 1876, 5405. Brandt, vol. 1, 232.
17. Agreement dated July 11, 1874, CO 874 / 14.
18. Ernst Friedel, *Die Gründung preußisch-deutscher Colonien im Indischen und Großen Ozean mit besonderer Rücksicht auf das östliche Asien* (Berlin: Eichhoff, 1867), 100. On Assab Bay: Edward Hertslet, *Map of Africa,* vol. 2 (London: His Majesty's Stationery Office, 1909), 446.
19. Allen, "Memoranda," 43.
20. Redesdale, vol. 2, 642.
21. Jacob, *Raja of Saráwak,* vol. 2 (London 1876), 343. See May, *Underworld* (Chapel Hill, NC 2002), 61.
22. J. Pope-Hennessy to Lord Granville, April 11, 1870, CO 144 / 31. "Tagesbericht," *Wiener Abendpost,* September 2, 1872.
23. Diary entry for October 27, 1894, in Raleigh Trevelyan, *Princes Under the Volcano* (New York: William Morrow, 1973), 289.

24. Angela Burdett-Coutts to James Lacaita, February 5, 1867, in Rutter, *Brooke & Coutts*, 292. *Overland China Mail*, February 20, 1873.
25. Pope-Hennessy to Foreign Office, April 21, 1870, UKNA FO 12/36. Carlo Racchia to S. Riboty, March 20, 1870, *DDI*, vol. 3, 552.
26. Racchia to Riboty, June 2, 1872, *DDI*, vol. 3, 562.
27. S. Riboty to Marquis Visconti-Venosta, May 26, 1872, *DDI*, vol. 3, 551. Henry Bulwer to Earl of Kimberley, January 15 and April 14, 1873, CO 144/40.
28. Max von Brandt to Foreign Ministry, May 24, 1873, German Federal Archive Berlin-Lichterfelde, R1001/7157. Entry for May 12, 1878, Harrisson (ed.), "Diary of Pretyman (I)," *SMJ*, vol. 7 (1956), 347.
29. Quoted in Sergio Angelini, "Il tentativo italiano per una colonia nel Borneo," *Rivista di Studi Politici Internazionali*, vol. 33 (Florence: F. le Monnier, 1966), 546.
30. Studer to F. W. Seward, September 17, 1878, DFS, vol. 13.
31. Robert E. Johnson, *Far China Station: The U.S. Navy in Asian Waters, 1800–1898* (Annapolis: Naval Institute Press, 1979), 127.
32. Allen to W. Seward, April 7, 1867, DFHK, vol. 6.
33. "News of Week," *Straits Times*, July 13, 1872.
34. *Hong Kong Daily Press*, February 10, 1873. Felice Giordano, "Una esplorazione a Borneo," *Bollettino della Società Geografica Italiana*, vol. 11 (Rome: Civelli, 1874), 187. Angelini, 548.
35. Compare "Samarang," *De Locomotief*, April 30, 1869.
36. "Government Notification," *Hong Kong Government Gazette*, May 3, 1873, 211. Overbeck to Gyula Andrássy, March 5, 1873, Austrian State Archives, AT-OeStA/HHStA SB NL Braun 7–2–17.
37. "Ritter von Overbeck," *Wiener Weltausstellungs-Zeitung*, February 19, 1873. "Handelspolitische Streifzüge," *Die Reform*, vol. 11 (Vienna 1872) 405.
38. "Weltausstellung," *Tages-Post* (Linz), June 20, 1873. Gustav von Overbeck, *Special-Catalog der chinesischen Ausstellung, III. Abteilung* (Prague: Skrejsovsky, 1873), 3.
39. Heinrich Benedikt, *Wirtschaftliche Entwicklung* (Vienna: Herold, 1958), 109. "Austrian Version," *Straits Times*, July 6, 1878.
40. Walter Sauer, "Habsburg Colonial: Austria-Hungary's Role in European Overseas Expansion Reconsidered," *Austrian Studies*, vol. 20 (2012), 16.
41. "Deutschland," *Altonaer Nachrichten*, May 22, 1880.
42. Overbeck to Andrássy, September 8, 1875, Austrian State Archives, AT-OeStA/HHStA SB NL Braun 34–32. See Stephen Gwynn, *The Life of the Right Hon. Sir Charles Dilke*, vol. 1 (New York: Macmillan, 1917), 227.
43. Heinrich Lutz, "Zur Wende der Österreichisch-ungarischen Außenpolitik," *Mitteilungen des österreichischen Staatsarchivs*, vol. 25 (1972), 169.
44. John S. Galbraith, "The 'Turbulent Frontier' as a Factor in British Expansion," *Comparative Studies in Society and History* 2 (1960): 156. Ira Klein, "British Expansion in Malaya, 1897–1902," *Journal of Southeast Asian History* 9 (1968): 53.

45. Hugh Low to Derby, May 30, 1875, FO 12/41.
46. Low to Earl of Carnarvon, May 23, 1875, CO 144/44.
47. "Kampf mit Seeräubern," *Linzer Volksblatt,* July 23, 1875. "Von Corvette 'Friedrich,'" *Linzer Volksblatt,* July 24, 1875.
48. Low to Derby, June 1, 1875, FO 12/41.
49. "Asiatic Squadron," *NYT,* June 4, 1867.
50. Johnson, *China Station,* 127.
51. Sir Ernest Mason Satow's diary entry, February 13, 1903, *The Diaries of Sir Ernest Satow, British Envoy in Peking (1900–06),* vol. 1, ed. Ian C. Ruxton (Morrisville, NC: Lulu Press, 2006), 318. "Eine ebenso interessante," *Berliner Tageblatt,* May 22, 1880.
52. Low to Carnarvon, July 6, 1875, CO 144/44.
53. Studer to F. W. Seward, September 17, 1878, DFS, vol. 13.
54. Pengiran Temenggung Hasyim Sahibul Bahar to Wheelwright, May 29, 1869, Cambridge University Library, Or.847 (3).
55. James Warren, *The Sulu Zone, 1768–1898: The Dynamics of External Trade, Slavery and Ethnicity in the Transformation of a Southeast Asian Maritime State* (Singapore: Singapore University Press, 1981), 105.
56. "Schurman on . . . Sulus," *Los Angeles Herald,* November 1, 1899. See Thomas Kiefer, *The Tausug: Violence and Law in a Philippine Moslem Society* (New York: Holt, 1972).
57. "America's Great Shame," *Virginian-Pilot,* September 16, 1900.
58. Warren, 152. Tarling, *Piracy* (Melbourne 1963), 154.
59. George H. Shibley, *Momentous Issues: Competition in Business, Stable Price Level, Prosperity and Republic* (Chicago: Rural Press, 1900), 178.
60. Tarling, *Piracy,* 148. John Ingleson, *Expanding the Empire: James Brooke and the Sarawak Lobby, 1839–1868* (Perth: Centre for SSEA Studies, 1979), 50, 55.
61. Najeeb Saleeby, *The History of Sulu* (Manila: Bureau of Printing, 1908), 177.
62. Warren, 116.
63. Eric Tagliacozzo, "A Necklace of Fins: Marine Goods Trading in Maritime Southeast Asia, 1780–1860," *International Journal of Asian Studies* 1 (2004): 32. Warren, 64.
64. Studer to F. W. Seward, September 17, 1878, DFS, vol. 13. Warren, 117.
65. See Michael Montemayor, *Captain Herman Leopold Schück: The Saga of a German Sea Captain in 19th Century Sulu-Sulawesi Seas* (Manila: University of the Philippines Press, 2005).
66. Stefan Rohde-Enslin, *Östlich des Horizonts* (Münster: Wurf, 1992), 30.
67. Volker Schult, "Sultans and Adventurers: German Blockade-runners in the Sulu Archipelago," *Philippine Studies* 50 (2002): 395.
68. Georg zu Münster to Granville, January 19, 1874, CO 144/40.
69. Emrys Chew, *Arming the Periphery: The Arms Trade in the Indian Ocean during the Age of Global Empire* (New York: Palgrave, 2012), 272n170.
70. See Cesar Majul, "Political and Historical Notes on the Old Sulu Sultanate," *JMBRAS* 28 (1965): 40.

71. Sultan of Sulu to William I, September 1866, Bundesarchiv Berlin Lichterfelde, R1001 / 7154; Robert Noelke to Baron Carlowitz, October 26, 1866.
72. Tagliacozzo, "Necklace," 33.
73. Heinrich von Mühler to Bismarck, December 27, 1866, Bundesarchiv Berlin Lichterfelde, R1001 / 7154.
74. T. F. Callaghan to FO, January 29, 1866, FO 12 / 33. Commander Buckle to Alfred Ryder, February 28, 1875, *Papers Relating to Sulu and Borneo,* vol. 1 (London 1882), 46.
75. Ulrich van der Heyden, *Der Rote Adler an Afrikas Küste: die brandenburgisch-preussische Kolonie Grossfriedrichsburg in Westafrika* (Berlin: Selignow, 2001).
76. Helmuth Stoecker, *Deutschland und China* (Berlin: Rütten, 1958), 49; Rudolf Delbrück to Albrecht von Stosch, February 16, 1872, Bundesarchiv Berlin Lichterfelde, R901 / 11497.
77. Wolfgang Petter, *Stützpunktpolitik* (Freiburg: University of Freiburg, 1975), 213. Warren, 114.
78. Tarling, *Piracy,* 185.
79. See Warren, 114.
80. Lemke to Bismarck, December 1, 1875, Bundesarchiv Berlin Lichterfelde, R1001 / 7158.
81. Volker Schult, "Kampong German," *SMJ* 83 (2006): 63.
82. Dobree, *North Borneo* (London 1879), 10; Tagliacozzo, "Trafficking," in *Global Human Smuggling,* ed. David Kyle and Rey Koslowski (Baltimore: Johns Hopkins University Press, 2011), 104.
83. Treacher, *Borneo* (Singapore: Government Printing Department, 1891), 105.
84. Carl A. Trocki, *Opium, Empire and the Global Political Economy* (New York: Routledge, 1999), 170.
85. Buckle's report, June 3, 1873, CO 144 / 45.
86. See "Jury List for 1874," *Hong Kong Government Gazette,* February 21, 1874, 83.
87. Owen Rutter, *British North Borneo* (London: Constable and Company, 1922), 117. Cowie, "North Borneo," *London and China Express,* November 27, 1908.
88. Torrey to Cowie, September 23, 1876, "W. Clark Cowie," *Singapore Free Press and Mercantile Advertiser,* August 9, 1895.
89. Tom Harrisson, *The Prehistory of Borneo* (Kota Kinabalu: Sabah Society, 1971), 30.
90. James P. Ongkili, "Pre-Western Brunei, Sarawak and Sabah," *SMJ* 20 (1972): 15.
91. Brock Short, "Brunei, Sulu and Sabah: An Analysis of Rival Claims," *BMJ* 1 (1969): 134.
92. "Cowie," *Singapore Free Press and Mercantile Advertiser,* September 19, 1910.
93. Anonymous, *Memoire über die Stellung Oesterreich-Ungarns zum Welthandel* (Vienna: Staatsdruckerei, 1877).

94. Franz von le Monnier, "Borneo," *Mittheilungen der K.K. Geographischen Gesellschaft in Wien,* vol. 26 (Vienna 1883), 523.
95. See "Overbeck and Mr. Dent," *Straits Times,* September 28, 1878, 1.
96. Overend, Gurney & Company was a London bank that collapsed in 1866, prompting the failure of 200 other banks across England and a brief global financial crisis.
97. "In Supreme Court," *Hong Kong Government Gazette,* December 21, 1867.
98. Basil Lubbock, *The Opium Clippers* (Boston: Lauriat, 1933), 373.
99. W. R. Williams, *Parliamentary History of the Principality of Wales* (Brecknock: Davies, 1895), 166.
100. Anonymous, *Memoire über die Stellung,* 20. Grant by Torrey to Overbeck, January 19, 1875, CO 874/11.
101. "Borneo Company," *Straits Times Overland Journal,* April 4, 1878.
102. "Austrian Version."
103. See the many records of UKNA folder marked CO 874/184.
104. Treacher to Derby, January 2, 1878, CO 144/50.
105. Ada Pryer, *Decade in Borneo* (London: Hutchinson 1894), 12.
106. "New Cession," *Straits Times Overland Journal,* May 4, 1878.
107. But see "Sarawak News," *Straits Times Overland Journal,* May 4, 1878.
108. Inche Mahomet to Low, June 22, 1875, FO 12/41. In the interim, the sultan had not scrupled when negotiating further leases of governing rights in Sabah, including, in 1877, the farming to a Chinese of tax-collection rights along an important river corridor. Nicholas Tarling, *Britain, the Brookes, and Brunei* (Kuala Lumpur: Oxford University Press, 1971), 282.
109. Studer to F. W. Seward, September 17, 1878, DFS, vol. 13.
110. Memorandum of May 28, 1881, CO 874/195.
111. Entry of May 3, 1878, in Harrisson, ed., "Diary of Pretyman (II)," *SMJ* 8 (1957): 339.
112. Studer to F. W. Seward, September 17, 1878, DFS, vol. 13.
113. Treacher to Derby, January 22, 1878, FO 12/53.
114. "Borneo," *North-China Herald,* April 4, 1878.
115. I. D. Black, "The Ending of Brunei Rule in Sabah 1878–1902," *JMBRAS* 41 (1968): 178.
116. "Austrian Version," 2. CO 874/185.
117. Tarling, *Imperialism* (London 2001), 66.
118. Charles Brooke to FO, April 11, 1878, FO 12/53. Edith Simcox, *Natural Law* (Boston: Osgood, 1877), 329.
119. Tarling, *Britain, the Brookes, and Brunei,* 240, 262.
120. "Borneo-Maatschappij," *Leeuwarder Courant,* August 16, 1878.
121. Kenneth Gordon Tregonning, "William Pryer," *JMBRAS* 27 (1954): 35.
122. Treacher to Derby, February 2, 1878, FO 12/53.
123. Pollock to Pryer, March 4, 1881, FO 12/56.
124. Pryer, *Decade,* 46.

125. Tregonning, "William Pryer," 37.
126. Entry of August 15, 1878, Harrisson, "Diary of Pretyman (II)," 378.
127. Low to Derby, July 6, 1875, FO 12/41.
128. Law Officers to Granville, September 17, 1880, FO 12/56.
129. "Overbeck and Mr. Dent," 1.
130. Anthony Pagden, *Lords of All the World: Ideologies of Empire in Spain, Britain and France c. 1500–c. 1800* (New Haven, CT: Yale University Press, 1995), 127.
131. G. V. Scammell, *The World Encompassed: The First European Maritime Empires c. 800–1650* (Berkeley: University of California Press, 1981), 316.
132. John H. Elliott, *Empires of the Atlantic World* (New Haven, CT: Yale University Press, 2007), 35. Pagden, *Lords,* 128.
133. Henry Tremenheere, "How Is India to Be Governed?" *Bentley's Miscellany,* vol. 43 (London 1858), 119.
134. Law Officers to Granville, September 17, 1880, FO 12/56.
135. Granville to CO, June 13, 1881, FO 12/56.
136. Entry of November 3, 1878, Harrisson, "Diary of Pretyman (II)," 402.
137. Entry of September 13, 1878, Harrisson, "Diary of Pretyman (II)," 378.
138. Entry of August 16, 1878, Harrisson, "Diary of Pretyman (II)," 378.
139. "Borneo Cession," *Straits Times Overland Journal,* June 29, 1878.
140. Black, "Ending of Brunei Rule," 180. Compare David Henley, "Conflict, Justice, and the Stranger-King: Indigenous Roots of Colonial Rule in Indonesia and Elsewhere," *MAS* 38 (2004): 87.
141. Patricia Seed, *Ceremonies of Possession: Europe's Conquest of the New World, 1492–1640* (Cambridge: Cambridge University Press, 1995), 69.
142. Treacher to FO, September 24, 1878, FO 71/14.
143. "Seventh General Meeting," *Proceedings of Royal Colonial Institute,* vol. 16 (London 1885), 294. Treacher, *Borneo,* 130.
144. William Pryer to Lees, December 24, 1880, FO 12/56.
145. Pryer to C. C. Lees, January 19, 1881, FO 12/56.
146. Count Bylandt to Granville, April 8, 1881, FO 12/56. "Europe centrale," *Indépendance Belge,* October 23, 1879.
147. Locher-Sholten, "Imperialism," *Liberal Imperialism,* ed. Fitzpatrick (New York 2012), 38.
148. "Invasie van vreemde macht," March 26, 1879, *De Standaard* (Amsterdam). "Buitenland," June 14, 1879, *De Standaard.*
149. Pryer to C. Wickes, July 4, 1880, FO 12/86.
150. Entry of May 3, 1878, Harrisson, "Diary of Pretyman (II),"339. Everett to Sultan of Brunei, March 5, 1881, FO 12/56.
151. Entries for May 16 and July 7, 1878, Harrisson, "Diary of Pretyman (II)," 349, 364.
152. Entry of May 5, 1878, Harrisson, "Diary of Pretyman (II)," 341. A. H. Everett to Sultan of Brunei, March 5, 1881, FO 12/56.
153. "Borneo El Dorado," *Straits Times Overland Journal,* May 25, 1878, 2. "News of Week," *Straits Times,* October 12, 1878, 4.

154. Entry of September 5, 1878, Harrisson, "Diary of Pretyman (II)," 382. Everett to Sultan of Brunei, March 5, 1881, FO 12/56.
155. J. G. Mead to Lees, April 29, 1881, FO 12/56.
156. H. Pollock to Pryer, March 4, 1881, FO 12/56.
157. Dobree, preface to *North Borneo.*
158. Tarling, *Piracy,* 185.
159. Lees to Granville, April 29, 1881, FO 12/56.
160. Entry of May 9, 1878, Harrisson, "Diary of Pretyman (II),"346.
161. Everett to Sultan of Brunei, March 5, 1881, FO 12/56.
162. *Hansard Lords Debates,* March 17, 1882, 1193. http://hansard.millbanksystems.com/commons/1882/mar/17/british-north-borneo-company-chapter.
163. John Gallagher, "The Decline, Revival and Fall of the British Empire," *Ford Lectures,* ed. Anil Seal (Cambridge: Cambridge University Press, 1982), 75.
164. Dent to Pryer, March 19, 1879, CO 874/27.
165. Treacher to Derby, January 2, 1878, FO 12/53.
166. Granville's memo, August 15, 1881, FO 12/56.
167. See "Der österreichisch-ungarische General-Konsul," *Berliner Tageblatt,* June 24, 1879.
168. "Cession of Territory," *Straits Times,* June 1, 1878.
169. J. Fergusson to Earl of Kimberley, March 11, 1874, New Zealand General Assembly, *Parliamentary Debates,* vol. 119 (Wellington 1901), 669. But see Tarling, *Imperialism,* 76.
170. Entry of August 18, 1878, Harrisson, "Diary of Pretyman (II),"379.
171. "Overbeck and Mr. Dent," 1.
172. Application draft, undated, is contained in CO 874/163.
173. Dent to Read, November 5, 1880, CO 874/27.
174. Dent to Lees, September 10, 1880, CO 874/27.
175. Entry for May 15 and June 21, 1879, *Alexander von Siebold: Die Tagebücher,* vol. 1, ed. Vera Schmidt (Wiesbaden: Harrassowitz, 1999), 167, 172.
176. Vera Schmidt, "Eine japanische Kolonie in Nord-Borneo: Alexander von Siebolds Memorandum," *Jahrbuch zur Ostasienforschung,* vol. 20 (Bochum 1996), 20.
177. Max von Brandt to Bismarck, November 21, 1875, Bundesarchiv Berlin Lichterfelde, R1001/7158.
178. Agreement between Torrey, Overbeck, Dent, January 15, 1881, CO 874/29.
179. Agreement between Montgelas, Overbeck, Dent, September 1, 1880, CO 874/27.
180. "In den letzten Tagen," *Berliner Börsenzeitung,* April 12, 1882.
181. Dent to Julian Pauncefote, October 8, 1879, FO 12/54.
182. Robert Herbert to Pauncefote, April 15, 1881, FO 12/56.
183. Henry Keppel to Lord Salisbury, October 8, 1879, FO 12/54.
184. For more on this, see the files of CO 874/163.

185. U.S. Treasury, *Colonial administration, 1800–1900: methods of government and development adopted by the principal colonizing nations in their control of tropical and other colonies and dependencies* (Washington, D.C.: Government Printing Office, 1903), 2676.
186. Adam Smith, *An inquiry into the nature and causes of the wealth of nations* (Edinburgh: Nelson, 1843), 234.
187. Thompson, "The Article on . . . British India," *Westminster Review,* October 1829 (London 1830), 31.
188. Benjamin Sullivan, *A prospectus for forming a British colony on the island of New Caledonia* (Sydney: Kemp, 1842). "London, Saturday," *Daily News* (London), January 16, 1847. "Social Science Congress," *British Friend,* vol. 34 (Glasgow 1876), 284.
189. Christopher Lloyd, *Mr. Barrow of the Admiralty, 1764–1848* (London: Collins 1970), 167.
190. Memo by Duke of Buckingham and Chandos, January 25, 1868, CO 880/4.
191. "Business Notes," *The Economist,* November 19, 1881, 1428.
192. Paul Knaplund, *Gladstone's Foreign Policy* (New York: Harper, 1935), 116.
193. "New Cession," *Straits Times Overland Journal,* May 4, 1878.
194. Granville to Kimberley, June 13, 1881, FO 12/56.
195. Bylandt to Granville, April 8, 1881, FO 12/56.
196. "London, 13. Juni," *Berliner Börsenzeitung,* June 15, 1879. Francis B. Harrison to Elpidio Quirino, February 27, 1947, http://www.gov.ph/1947/02/27/letter-of-francis-b-harrison-to-vice-president-and-secretary-of-foreign-affairs-elpidio-quirino/.
197. Earl of Carnarvon, *Hansard Lords Debates,* 13 March 1882, vol. 267, 719.
198. "Annexation of Borneo," *Herald of Peace,* January 2, 1882, 6.
199. Alexander Baillie-Cochrane in *Hansard Lords Debates,* 13 March 1882, vol. 267, 708–713.
200. "Annexation of Borneo," 6.
201. Studer to F. W. Seward, September 17, 1878, DFS, vol. 13.
202. Overbeck to Treacher, April 7, 1878, CO 144/50. *Japan Weekly Mail,* March 11, 1882.
203. Salisbury to Brooke, June 3, 1878, CO 144/51.
204. "Sarawak News," *Straits Times Overland Journal,* May 4, 1878.
205. Pauncefote's memo, April 11, 1878, FO 12/53.
206. Granville memo, August 15, 1881, FO 12/56.
207. M. Kuitenbrouwer, *The Netherlands and the Rise of Modern Imperialism: Colonies and Foreign Policy 1850–1902* (New York: Berg, 1991), 128.
208. Caroline Wakeman, *British Foreign Policy 1880–1895* (Madison: University of Wisconsin, 1917), 8.
209. George Neville Sanderson, "The European Partition of Africa: Coincidence or Conjuncture?" *JICH* 3 (1974): 25.

210. Dent to Pauncefote, October 8, 1879, FO 12/54.
211. Salisbury's memo, October 11, 1879, FO 12/54.
212. "Cession of Territory," *Straits Times,* June 1, 1878.
213. "Borneo Cession," *Straits Times Overland Journal,* June 29, 1878. For context: Peter J. Cain, "Radicalism, Gladstone, and the liberal critique of Disraelian 'imperialism'," in *Victorian Visions of Global Order: Empire and International Relations in Nineteenth-Century Political Thought,* ed. Duncan Bell (Cambridge: Cambridge University Press, 2007), 219.
214. *Hansard,* March 17, 1882, 1185. http://hansard.millbanksystems.com/commons/1882/mar/17/british-north-borneo-company-chapter.
215. Cain, "Radicalism, Gladstone, and the liberal critique," 220–225.
216. Bell and Acqua to Gladstone, November 6, 1881, *Correspondence respecting affairs in the Cameroons* (London: Harrison, 1885), 1.
217. See *The Annual Register,* vol. 80, ed. Edmund Burke (London: Rivington, 1839), 151.
218. Alexander Baillie-Cochrane to Lords, March 13, 1882, *Hansard's Parliamentary Debates,* vol. 267, 712.
219. "East India Company," *Star* (Christchurch), May 28, 1874.
220. Secretary of State for India v. Bha'nji, April 28, 1882, *Commonwealth International Law Cases,* eds. Clive Parry and J. A. Hopkins, vol. 1 (Dobbs Ferry, NY: Oceana, 1974), 93.
221. Charles Dilke, *Problems of Greater Britain,* vol. 2 (London: Macmillan, 1890), 166.
222. *Hansard,* March 17, 1882, 1191. http://hansard.millbanksystems.com/commons/1882/mar/17/british-north-borneo-company-chapter.
223. "North Borneo Company," *The Times* (London), August 19, 1902, 8.
224. Thus James to Commons, March 17, 1882, excerpted in Égide Arntz, *Can Independent Chiefs . . .* (London 1884), 14.
225. "Annexation of Borneo," 6.
226. *Hansard,* March 17, 1882, 1193. http://hansard.millbanksystems.com/commons/1882/mar/17/british-north-borneo-company-chapter.
227. Ibid., 1191.
228. Ibid., 1195.
229. See Mark Lindley, *The Acquisition and Government of Backward Territory in International Law* (London: Longman, 1926), 286, 288.
230. Compare F. Pedler, "British Planning," *Colonialism in Africa,* ed. Peter Duignan and L.H. Gann, vol. 4 (New York 1975), 97.
231. "Annexation of Borneo," 7.
232. *Hansard,* March 17, 1882, 1191–1192. http://hansard.millbanksystems.com/commons/1882/mar/17/british-north-borneo-company-chapter.
233. Arntz, 14.
234. James Taylor, *Creating Capitalism: Joint-Stock Enterprise in British Politics and Culture 1800–1870* (Cornwall: Boydell Press, 2006), 142.

235. Knaplund, *Gladstone* (London 1927), 202.
236. See Sarvepalli Gopal, *British Policy in India 1858–1905* (Cambridge: Cambridge University Press, 1965), 129.
237. Bernard Porter, *Critics of Empire: British Radicals and the Imperial Challenge* (London: Tauris, 2008), xxx. On context of British liberalism, see Casper Sylvest, *British Liberal Internationalism, 1880–1930: Making Progress?* (Manchester: Manchester University Press, 2009), 43.
238. On Basutoland, see Sandra B. Burman, *Chiefdom Politics and Alien Law: Basutoland under Cape Rule, 1871–1884* (London: Macmillan, 1981).
239. On India, see Lauren Benton, "From International Law to Imperial Constitutions: The Problem of Quasi-Sovereignty, 1870–1900," *Law and History Review* 26 (2008): 603, 613.
240. W. H. Chaloner, "Currency Problems of the British Empire 1814–1914," *Great Britain and Her World, 1750–1914: Essays in Honour of W. O. Henderson*, ed. Barrie M. Ratcliffe (Manchester: Manchester University Press, 1975), 195.
241. William Treacher, *British Borneo* (Singapore: Government Printing Department, 1891), 166. William John Hocking, *Catalogue of the coins, medals, dies, and seals in the museum of the Royal Mint*, vol. 1 (London: His Majesty's Stationery Office, 1906), 255.
242. Entry for November 27, 1882, *McLean Letterbooks*, vol. 7, 157.
243. Torrey to Sickels, August 18, 1880, Despatches from Bangkok, vol. 6. Entries for April 14–16, 1879, *The Papers of Ulysses S. Grant*, ed. John Y. Simon, vol. 29 (Carbondale: Southern Illinois University Press, 2008), 121. "Torrey," *Appleton Encyclopedia of American Biography*, vol. 6 (New York: Appleton, 1889), 139.
244. *Hansard*, March 17, 1882, 1149. http://hansard.millbanksystems.com/commons/1882/mar/17/british-north-borneo-company-chapter.
245. "Destiny and Responsibility," *Pall Mall Gazette*, October 11, 1884.
246. *Hansard*, March 17, 1882, 1196. http://hansard.millbanksystems.com/commons/1882/mar/17/british-north-borneo-company-chapter.
247. "Seventh General Meeting," 299.
248. Meeting of October 8, 1885, *First Report of Royal Commission* (London 1886), 26.
249. Kipling to Margaret Burne-Jones, November 28, 1885, *The Letters of Rudyard Kipling*, ed. Thomas Pinney, vol. 1 (New York: Palgrave Macmillan, 1990), 110.
250. "Liberal Jingoism," *New York Tribune*, March 29, 1882.
251. Marsh, *Bargaining* (New Haven 1999), 57. *Hansard*, March 17, 1882, 1197. http://hansard.millbanksystems.com/commons/1882/mar/17/british-north-borneo-company-chapter.
252. CO memo, January 17, 1879, CO 144/52.
253. Herschell's Memo, October 1893, FO 881/6401. *Japan Weekly Mail*, March 11, 1882.

254. Agatha Ramm, *The political correspondence of Gladstone and Lord Granville 1876–1886*, vol. 1 (Oxford: Clarendon Press, 1962), 336.
255. "Malamine," *The Times* (London), August 14, 1902.
256. "Angleterre," *Le Devoir*, April 9, 1882, 215.
257. Franz von le Monnier, 523.
258. Benton, "From International Law to Imperial Constitutions," 613–615. See Edward Tyas Cook, *Rights and Wrongs of the Transvaal War* (London: Arnold, 1901), 154.
259. Hewett to Granville, January 14, 1882, *Correspondence Respecting Cameroons*, 2. An extract of charter appeared in *London Gazette*, November 8, 1881.
260. See Frederick Parsons, *The origins of the Morocco question, 1880–1900* (London: Duckworth, 1976), 164.
261. Henry Walker, "State of North Borneo," *Journal of Society of Arts* 51 (April 17, 1903): 516.
262. Kenneth Gordon Tregonning, "Steps in the Acquisition of North Borneo," *Historical Studies* 5 (1952): 242.
263. "How Nigeria Was Won," *Mataura Ensign*, May 5, 1898.
264. Martin Lynn, *Commerce and Economic Change in West Africa: The Palm Oil Trade in the Nineteenth Century* (Cambridge: Cambridge University Press, 1997), 112.
265. Allan McPhee, *The Economic Revolution in British West Africa* (London: Routledge, 1926), 35.
266. Taubman to Anderson, November 1, 1884, FO 84/1814.
267. C. J. Gertzel, "Commercial Organisation on the Niger Coast, 1852–1891," *Proceedings of the Leverhulme Intercollegiate History Conference* (Salisbury 1960), 1.
268. "North Borneo Company," *The Times* (London), August 22, 1902, 6.
269. James S. Coleman, *Nigeria: Background to Nationalism* (Berkeley: University of California Press, 1958), 438. John E. Flint, *Sir George Goldie and the Making of Nigeria* (London: Oxford University Press, 1960), 80.
270. Flint, *Goldie*, 42.
271. List of Treaties, August 1893, FO 881/6425. Macdonald's Report, March 1890, FO 881/5913.
272. Northbrooke's Memo, March 4, 1885, FO 84/1879.
273. John Darwin, *The Empire Project: The Rise and Fall of the British World System, 1830–1970* (Cambridge: Cambridge University Press, 2009), 80.
274. Meeting Notes, July 16, 1897, FO 403/249.
275. Aberdare to Granville, February 23, 1883, CO 879/20.

Chapter 3: King Leopold's Borneo

1. Memo by Leopold II (hereafter LII), May 20, 1865, Léon Lefebve de Vivy, *Documents d'histoire précoloniale belge (1861–1865). Les idees coloniales de Léopold*

duc de Brabant (Brussels: Académie royale des sciences d'outre-mer, 1955), 35. Bismarck to Robert von der Goltz, August 8, 1866, Hermann Oncken, *Die Rheinpolitik Kaiser Napoleons III von 1863 bis 1870*, vol. 2 (Stuttgart: Deutsche Verlags-Anstalt, 1926), 35.

2. T. G. Otte, *The Foreign Office Mind: The Making of British Foreign Policy, 1865–1914* (Cambridge: Cambridge University Press, 2011), 48.
3. Jan Vandersmissen, "The king's most eloquent campaigner: Emile de Laveleye, Leopold II and the creation of the Congo Free State," *Revue belge d'Histoire contemporaine* 41 (2011): 7.
4. See Jan-Frederik Abbeloos, "Belgium's Expansionist History between 1870 and 1930," in *Europe and its Empires*, ed. Mary Harris and Csaba Lévai (Pisa: Plus-Pisa, 2008), 105.
5. Albert Duchesne, "La pensée expansionniste du duc de Brabant," *L'expansion belge sous Léopold Ier (1831–1865)* (Brussels: Académie royale des Sciences d'Outre-Mer, 1965), 741.
6. Jean Stengers, "La genèse d'une pensée coloniale: Léopold II et le modèle hollandais," *Tijdschrift voor Geschiedenis* 90 (1977): 46.
7. But see Vincent Viaene, "King Leopold's Imperialism and the Origins of the Belgian Colonial Party, 1860–1905," *Journal of Modern History* (hereafter *JMH*) 80 (2008): 741.
8. But see Henri Nicolai, " Le Mouvement Géographique, un journal et un géographe au service de la colonisation du Congo," *Civilisations* 41 (1993): 257.
9. Strauch to William Mackinnon, November 19, 1881, Mackinnon Papers, File 226, Reel 19, SOAS, London. Jean Stengers, "L'anticolonialisme," *Bulletin des Séances, Académie Royale des Sciences d'Outre-Mer* (Brussels 1965), 481.
10. Roderick Braithwaite, "Rio Nunez," *Revue française d'histoire d'outre-mer* 83 (1996): 25.
11. Anonymous, *Sir Travers Twiss et le Congo: réponse à la Revue de Droit international et de Législation comparée et au Law Magazine and Review* (Brussels: Lebègue, 1884), 6.
12. Adam Hochschild, *King Leopold's Ghost* (Boston: Houghton Mifflin, 1998), 39.
13. Political Archive of the German Foreign Ministry (hereafter PAAA) Botschaft Brüssel, R4345. Ludwig Bauer, *Leopold, the Unloved: King of the Belgians and of Wealth* (Boston: Little, Brown, and Co., 1935), 10.
14. A. J. Wauters, *Histoire politique du Congo Belge* (Brussels: Pierre Van Fleteren, 1911), 8.
15. W. F. Vande Walle, "Belgian Treaties," in *The History of the Relations Between the Low Countries and China in the Qing Era (1644–1911)* (Leuven: Leuven University Press, 2003), 430.
16. Jean Stengers, "Leopold II entre L'Extreme Orient et L'Afrique (1875–76)," in *La Conference de Geographie de 1876* (Brussels: Académie royale des

sciences d'Outre-Mer, 1976) 326. LII to Jules Greindl, April 25, 1874, Léopold Greindl, *À la Recherche d'un État indépendent: Léopold II et les Philippines* (Brussels: Académie royale des Sciences d'Outre-Mer, 1962), 330.

17. Duke's journal entry, May 26, 1861, Archives de Palais Royal (hereafter APR), Fonds Goffinet.
18. Gustave Stinglhamber, *Léopold II au travail* (Brussels: Éditions du Sablon, 1945), 72.
19. James Brooke to Brooke Brooke, August 26, 1862, Basil Brooke Papers, vol. 3.
20. Baron du Jardin to Adrien Goffinet, May 1, 1861; du Jardin to LII, undated (late 1861), Stinglhamber, 68 and 75. See Pety de Thozée, *Théories de la colonisation* (Brussels: Hayez, 1902), 162.
21. James Brooke to Brooke Brooke, September 6, 1862; Spenser St. John to Brooke Brooke, September 7, 1862, Basil Brooke Papers, vols. 3 and 15.
22. James Brooke to Brooke Brooke, August 9, 1862, Basil Brooke Papers, vol. 3.
23. Brooke to Coutts, February 22, 1862, in *Rajah Brooke & Baroness Burdett Coutts,* ed. Owen Rutter (London: Hutchinson, 1935), 137.
24. LII to Baron du Jardin, December 4, 1861, Stinglhamber, 76–77.
25. Brooke to Coutts, February 22, 1862, in *Rajah Brooke,* 137.
26. Rutter, *Rajah Brooke,* 153. See R. H. W. Reece, "A 'Suitable Population': Charles Brooke and Race-Mixing in Sarawak," *Itinerario* 9 (1985): 67.
27. Stinglhamber, 79.
28. Stengers, "Leopold II entre," 326n54.
29. Henry Shelton Sanford's memo, undated, SAN, Box 104, Folder 10.
30. Louis de Lichtervelde, *Léopold II* (Brussels: Dewit, 1926), 71.
31. See M. de Ramaix, *La question sociale en Belgique et le Congo* (Brussels: Lebègue, 1891).
32. Auguste Roeykens, *Léopold II et la Conférence géographique de Bruxelles, 1876* (Brussels: Académie royale des sciences coloniales, 1956), 64.
33. Viaene, 756.
34. James Brooke to Brooke Brooke, August 26, 1862, Basil Brooke Papers, vol. 3.
35. Jean Stengers, "King Leopold's Imperialism," in *Studies in the Theory of Imperialism,* ed. R. Owen and R. Sutcliffe (London: Longman, 1972), 268.
36. LII's memo, May 1873, in Léopold Greindl, 66.
37. Neal Ascherson, *The King Incorporated: Leopold II in the Age of Trusts* (London: Allen and Unwin, 1963), 55.
38. LII to Auguste Lambermont, August 22, 1875, in Auguste Roeykens, *Les débuts de l'œuvre africaine de Léopold II, 1875–1879* (Brussels: Académie royale des sciences colonials, 1955), 96.
39. Louis van Herwijnen to Count van Bylandt, October 8, 1872, in *Bescheiden Betreffende de Buitenlandse Politiek,* part. 2, vol. 1 (Gravenhage: Nijhoff, 1972), 398.

40. Inche Mahomet to Hugh Low, June 27, 1875, FO 12/41.
41. James Money, *Java,* 2 vols. (London: Hurst, 1861).
42. Louis van Herwijnen to Dutch ambassador at Vienna, June 26, 1874, in *Buitelandse Politiek,* 728.
43. LII to Jules Greindl, April 25, 1874, in Léopold Greindl, 330.
44. Jules Greindl to LII, February 23, 1875, in Auguste Roeykens, *L'initiative africaine de Léopold II et l'opinion publique belge,* vol. 1 (Brussels: Académie royale des sciences d'outre-mer, 1963), 195.
45. Stengers, "Leopold II entre," 328.
46. Queen Victoria's Journals, United Kingdom Royal Archives, RA VIC/MAIN/QVJ (W) 7 June 1876 (Princess Beatrice's copies).
47. Stengers, "Leopold II entre," 328.
48. Edmund Monson to Earl of Rosebery, January 28, 1893, FO 403/188.
49. See Jan Vandersmissen, "The geographical societies of Brussels and Antwerp, and their focus on Africa in the period preceding the Berlin Conference (1876–1885)," in *L'Afrique belge aux XIXe et XXe siècles: Nouvelles recherches et perspectives en histoire coloniale,* ed. Patricia van Schuylenbergh (Brussels: Peter Lang, 2014), 101. See A. Roeykens, *Léopold II et l'Afrique, 1855–1880* (Brussels: Académie Royale des Sciences Coloniales, 1958), 53.
50. On Cameron: Dane Kennedy, *The Last Blank Spaces: Exploring Africa and Australia* (Cambridge, MA: Harvard University Press, 2013), 66, 70.
51. See Georg Tams, *Die portugiesischen Besitzungen in Süd-West-Afrika* (Hamburg: Kittler, 1845), 30.
52. See Marcel Luwel, " Verney Lovett Cameron ou l'échec d'un concurrent de Stanley," *La Conférence de Géographie* (Brussels 1976), 57.
53. Johannes Fabian, *Out of Our Minds: Reason and Madness in the Exploration of Central Africa* (Berkeley: University of California Press, 2000), 3, 9, 62.
54. "Lieut. Cameron's Journey," *Proceedings of the Royal Geographical Society* (hereafter *RGS*), vol. 20 (London 1876), 117. Kennedy, 80.
55. FO to CO, February 8, 1876, FO 84/1459.
56. Cameron to Earl of Derby, Nov. 29, 1875, quoted in Edmond Fitzmaurice, *Life of Granville,* vol. 2 (London: Longmans, 1905), 343.
57. Newbury, "Trade and authority in West Africa from 1850 to 1880," *Colonialism in Africa,* vol. 1, 93.
58. Cameron to Henry Rawlinson, November 22, 1875, "Lieut. Cameron's Journey," 118.
59. Joseph Conrad, *Heart of Darkness and Other Tales* (Oxford: Oxford University Press, 2008), 108.
60. Grant Elliott to Adolphe van de Velde, March 11, 1885, Liévin van de Velde Papers, Oregon University (hereafter LVP).
61. Tim Butcher, *Blood River* (New York: Grove Press, 2009), 9.
62. Andrew Jampoler, *Congo: The Miserable Expeditions and Dreadful Death of Lt. Emory Taunt, USN* (Annapolis: Naval Institute Press, 2013), 5.

63. Kajsa E. Friedmann, *Catastrophe and Creation: The Transformation of an African Culture* (Amsterdam: Harwood, 1996), 124.
64. "Rebels Accused," *Michigan Daily*, September 22, 2002.
65. Cecile Fromont, *The Art of Conversion: Christian Visual Culture in the Kingdom of Kongo* (Chapel Hill: University of North Carolina Press, 2014), 217.
66. Fabian, 89.
67. Anonymous, "Commercial Future of Congo State," *Friends' Review*, vol. 38 (Philadelphia 1885), 701.
68. See cover of Anonymous, *The Operations of Association Internationale Africaine and of the Comité d'Études du Haut Congo* (London: Spon, 1883).
69. Kennedy, 40, 54, 59.
70. Henri Nicolai, "L'image de l'Afrique centrale au moment de la création de l'EIC," *Centenaire de l'État Indépendant du Congo*, ed. Jean-Jacques Symoens and Jean Stengers (Brussels: ARSOM, 1988), 13.
71. Queen Victoria's Journals, RA VIC / MAIN / QVJ (W) 13 May 1876 (Princess Beatrice's copies).
72. Roeykens, *Léopold II et la Conférence*, 19.
73. Roeykens, *Les débuts*, 122.
74. Barbara Emerson, *Leopold II of the Belgians: King of Colonialism* (London: Weidenfeld, 1979), 74. FO to CO, February 8, 1876, FO 84 / 1459.
75. CO to FO, undated, FO 84 / 1459.
76. Arthur Berriedale Keith, *The Belgian Congo and the Berlin Act* (Oxford: Clarendon Press, 1919), 27.
77. Charles Dilke in Commons, May 20, 1903, *Parliamentary Debates*, fourth series, vol. 122 (London 1903), 1300.
78. W. F. W. Owen, *Narrative of Voyages to Explore the Shores of Africa, Arabia, and Madagascar* (New York: Harper, 1833), 53, 158.
79. CO to FO, February 1876 (undated), FO 84 / 1459.
80. Kennedy, 120, 123.
81. Frank McLynn, *Stanley: Sorcerer's Apprentice* (London: Constable, 1991), 18.
82. See Roger Anstey, *Britain and the Congo in the Nineteenth Century* (Oxford: Clarendon Press, 1962), 37–56.
83. RA VIC / MAIN / QVJ (W) 10 September 1838 (Lord Esher's typescripts). See Lauren Benton, "Abolition and Imperial Law, 1790–1820," *JICH* 39 (2011): 355.
84. For example, the treaty of August 6, 1861, in George Stallard and Edward Richards (eds.), *Ordinances, and orders and rules thereunder, in force in the Colony of Lagos on December 31st, 1893* (London: Stevens, 1894), 962.
85. Robert W. Shufeldt to Richard Thompson, June 3, 1879, Robert W. Shufeldt Papers, Box 22, LOC.
86. Edward Keene, "A Case Study of the Construction of International Hierarchy: British Treaty-Making Against the Slave Trade in the Early Nineteenth Century," *International Organization* 61 (2007): 328.

87. Anonymous, "Les Grandes Compagnies Coloniales," *Journal des Économistes* 49 (Paris 1902): 276.
88. "Engagement" of March 27, 1876, Lewis Hertslet (ed.), *A complete collection of the treaties and conventions, and reciprocal regulations, at present subsisting between Great Britain and foreign powers,* vol. 14 (London: Butterworths, 1880), 36.
89. LII to Henri Solvyns, January 12, 1876, APR, Fonds Goffinet.
90. RA VIC / MAIN / QVJ (W) 25 and 28 April 1876 (Princess Beatrice's copies).
91. Cameron, *A travers l'Afrique: Voyage de Zanzibar à Benguela.* (Paris: Hachette, 1878), 530.
92. Consul Hopkins to Derby, June 12, 1877, *British Documents on Foreign Affairs,* ed. Kenneth Bourne et al., part 1, series G, vol. 23 (Frederick, MD: University Publications of America, 1997), 17.
93. Bismarck to Georg zu Münster, December 17, 1876, Otto von Bismarck, *Gesammelte Werke,* vol. 2, ed. Rainer Bendick (Paderborn: Schöningh, 2005), 670.
94. See Linda M. Heywood, "Slavery and Its Transformation in the Kingdom of Kongo: 1491–1800," *Journal of African History* (hereafter *JAH*) 50 (2009): 22.
95. *Sir Travers Twiss et le Congo,* 17. Gervase Clarence-Smith and R. Moorsom, "Underdevelopment and Class Formation in Ovamboland, 1845–1915," *JAH,* vol. 16 (1975), 372. See Leslie Bethell, "The Mixed Commissions for the Suppression of the Transatlantic Slave Trade in the Nineteenth Century," *JAH* 7 (1966): 83.
96. Consul Hopkins to Derby, June 12, 1877, 16.
97. Compare Miguel Bandeira Jerónimo, *The "Civilising Mission" of Portuguese Colonialism, 1870–1930* (New York: Palgrave Macmillan, 2015), 27.
98. Paul E. Lovejoy, *Transformations in Slavery: A History of Slavery in Africa* (Cambridge: Cambridge University Press, 1983), 136. See Matthew S. Hopper, *Slaves of One Master: Globalization and Slavery in Arabia in the Age of Empire* (New Haven, CT: Yale University Press, 2015).
99. See Frederick Cooper, "The Problem of Slavery in African Studies," *JAH* 20 (1979): 103. See Igor Kopytoff and Suzanne Miers, "African 'Slavery' as an Institution of Marginality," in *Slavery in Africa: Historical and Anthropological Perspectives,* ed. Igor Kopytoff and Suzanne Miers (Madison: University of Wisconsin Press, 1977), 17.
100. Janet J. Ewald, "Slavery in Africa and the Slave Trades from Africa," *AHR* 97 (1992): 466; R. W. Beachey, "The Arms Trade in East Africa in the Late Nineteenth Century," *JAH* 3 (1962): 451.
101. "Congo Treaty and Portugal," March 27, 1884, BMSA, Reel 32.
102. R. W. Beachey, *The Slave Trade of Eastern Africa* (New York: Barnes & Noble, 1976), 262.
103. Daniel Laqua, "The Tensions of Internationalism: Transnational Anti-Slavery in the 1880s and 1890s," *International History Review* 33 (2011): 707.

104. Roeykens, *Léopold II et la Conférence géographique de Bruxelles*, 29.
105. Law to Jules Devaux, February 19, 1883, APR, Fonds Congo, File 1.
106. Henry Shelton Sanford to John Latrobe, July 30, 1877, SAN, Box 29, Folder 10.
107. Commission Internationale de l'Association Africaine, *Session de juin 1877* (Brussels: Hayez, 1877), 17.
108. A. Vandeplas, "À propos," in *Revue Congolaise*, vol. 11 (Brussels 1957), 737.
109. Coutts to LII, May 31, 1885, APR, Fonds Congo, File 24.
110. Sanford to John Tyler Morgan, March 24, 1884, SAN, Box 26, Folder 5.
111. See Anonymous, *Les points sur les I de l'Association internationale africaine* (Brussels: Vanderauwera, 1882), 7.
112. Robert Stanley Thomson, *Fondation de l'État Indépendant du Congo: Un chapitre de l'histoire du partage de l'Afrique* (Brussels: Lebègue, 1933), 52. Bismarck to Münster, December 17, 1876, *Gesammelte Werke*, vol. 2, 671.
113. Augustus Sparhawk to Stanley, November 6, 1881, Augustus Sparhawk Papers, British Library (hereafter SPAR).
114. A. Vandeplas, "La fondation," *Revue Congolaise*, vol. 14 (Brussels 1960), 81. Sanford to Latrobe, July 30, 1877, SAN, Box 29, Folder 10.
115. Jules Greindl to Sanford, December 10, 1878, SAN, Box 24, Folder 18. Strauch to Charles Daly, April 23, 1884, *Journal of American Geographical Society*, vol. 16 (New York 1884), 151. Strauch to van de Velde, December 7, 1882, LVP.
116. LII's memo, circa November 1878, cited in R. J. Cornet, "Rapport sur les dossiers," *Bulletin des Séances: Institut Royal Colonial*, vol. 25 (Brussels 1954), 591.
117. Mackinnon to Sanford, April 14, 1879, SAN, Box 127, Folder 2.
118. Latrobe to Sanford, September 22, 1877, SAN, Box 25, Folder 8. Compare L. Guebels, "Rapport sur le dossier," *Bulletin des Séances*, vol. 24 (Brussels 1953), 34.
119. Henry Morton Stanley, *The Congo and the founding of its free state: a story of work and exploration*, vol. 1 (hereafter *CFFS*) (New York: Harper, 1885), 27.
120. Henk L. Wesseling, "The Netherlands and the Partition of Africa," *JAH* 22 (1981): 499.
121. LII to Burdett-Coutts, February 6, 1879, Angela Burdett-Coutts Papers, MS 85276, British Library.
122. Archives of Staffordshire Record Office, Staffordshire, United Kingdom, D593/P/26/5.
123. Robert Stanley Thomson, "Léopold II et le Congo révélés par les notes privées de Henry S. Sanford," *Congo: revue générale*, vol. 12 (Brussels 1931), 168. Strauch to Mackinnon, October 24, 1884, Mackinnon Papers, File 226, Reel 19.
124. Emerson, 88.
125. "Stanley und Brazza," *Berliner Tageblatt*, December 23, 1884.
126. Stanley, *CFFS*, vol. 1, 21.

127. Sanford to James Bennett, undated, SAN, Box 29, Folder 2; Jules Greindl to Sanford, June 11, 1878, SAN, Box 24, Folder 18.
128. Charles George Gordon to FO, March 10, 1880, FO 84/1585.
129. Strauch to Sanford, November 15, 1883, SAN, Box 31, Folder 3.
130. Latrobe to Sanford, September 22, 1877, SAN, Box 25, Folder 8.
131. Travers Twiss, *The law of nations considered as independent political communities* (Oxford: Clarendon Press, 1884), xvi.
132. E. van Grieken, "H. M. Stanley," *Bulletin des Séances,* vol. 25 (Brussels 1954), 1124.
133. Entry for August 1879, Stanley's Congo Journal, Stanley Papers (hereafter STAN), RP2435, I, Box 4.
134. Albert Adu Boahen, *African Perspectives on Colonialism* (Baltimore: Johns Hopkins University Press, 1987), 4.
135. J. Forbes Munro, *Africa and the International Economy, 1800–1960* (London: Dent, 1976), 74.
136. Dilke to Edward Grey, April 13, 1908, Charles Dilke Papers, British Library, MS 43897.
137. Stengers, "Leopold II and the Association Internationale du Congo," in *Bismarck, Europe, and Africa: the Berlin Africa Conference 1884–1885 and the onset of partition* (hereafter *BEA*), ed. Stig Förster, Ronald Robinson, Wolfgang J. Mommsen (Oxford: Oxford University Press, 1988), 238.
138. LII's undated memo, cited in Roeykens, *Les débuts,* 398. Latrobe to Sanford, March 6, 1884, SAN, Box 25, Folder 8.
139. Marshall Sahlins, "The Stranger-King," *Indonesia and the Malay World* 36 (2008): 177.
140. Georges Balandier, *Daily Life in the Kingdom of the Kongo* (New York: George Allen, 1968), 36.
141. Sahlins, "The Stranger-King," 183. J. Cuvelier, *L'ancien royaume de Congo* (Brussels: de Brouwer, 1946).
142. Alexander Bortolot, "Luba and Lunda," in *Heilbrunn Timeline of Art History* (New York: Metropolitan Museum of Art, 2000). See Jan Vansina, *Kingdoms of the Savanna* (Madison: University of Wisconsin Press, 1966).
143. See M. L. Bastin, *Tshibinda Ilunga: héros civilisateur* (Brussels: Mimeograph, 1966).
144. Tim Jeal, *Stanley: the Impossible Life of Africa's Greatest Explorer* (New Haven, CT: Yale University Press, 2007), 259, 280–289.
145. Thomson, "Léopold II et le Congo révélés," 179.
146. Count Chotek to Count Kálnoky, June 9, 1884, Austrian State Archives, AT-OeStA/HHStA *Diplomatie und Außenpolitik* 1848–1918 GKA GsA Berlin 189–183.
147. Strauch to Sparhawk, June 1, 1879, SPAR. Sanford to LII, June 1, 1879, SAN, Box 29, Folder 12. Ascherson, 117. Strauch to van de Velde, August 30, 1883, LVP.

148. Wesseling, "The Netherlands and the Partition of Africa," 499.
149. Stanley to van de Velde, January 29, 1883; Strauch to van de Velde, June 1, 1883; Chief of Vivi Station to R. Philipps, July 26, 1883, LVP. Otto Lindner to Sparhawk, November 8, 1881, SPAR.
150. Latrobe to Sanford, April 24, 1884, SAN, Box 25, Folder 8.
151. Chief of Manyanga Station to Stanley, January 5, 1883, LVP. Daninas, Berand, & Co. to Sparhawk, July 12, 1879, SPAR.
152. See Journal entry, May 18, 1884 in Dundas Museum and Archives, Ontario, Canada, Lesslie Family Fonds, Box 2, Folder 20.
153. Stanley, *CFFS*, vol. 1, 133.
154. Fabian, 3.
155. Sparhawk to Stanley, March 8, 1881, SPAR.
156. Sparhawk to Stanley, March 8, 1881, SPAR.
157. Sparhawk to Stanley, March 8, 1881, SPAR. But see Jeal, 241.
158. Compare Allen Godbey, *Stanley in Africa: The Paladin of the Nineteenth Century* (Chicago: Donohue, 1889), 229, 475; Lugard, "Treaty Making in Africa," *Geographical Journal*, vol. 1 (London 1893), 53; Robert Felkin, *Uganda and Egyptian Soudan*, vol. 2 (London: Sampson Low, 1882), 41.
159. Francis de Winton to LII, September 18, 1884, de Winton Papers, Archives of Royal Museum for Central Africa (hereafter RMCA) RG 840.
160. Francis Drake to Shufeldt, June 2, 1879, USNA, RG 45, Cruise of Ticonderoga, vol. 2.
161. Mumbanza Mwa Bawele, "Afro-European Relations in the Western Congo Basin, c. 1884–1885," in *BEA*, 474.
162. H. Johnston, *George Grenfell and the Congo* (London: Hutchinson, 1908): vol. 1, 113; vol. 2, 687.
163. See James L. Newman, *Imperial Footprints: Henry Morton Stanley's African Journeys* (Washington, D.C.: Potomac Books, 2004), 190.
164. Phyllis M. Martin, "Power, Cloth and Currency on the Loango Coast," *African Economic History*, vol. 15 (1986), 1. Jan Vansina, "Raffia Cloth in West Central Africa, 1500–1800," in *Textiles: Production, Trade, and Demand*, ed. Maureen Mazzaoui (Aldershot, UK: Ashgate, 1998), 263. Edouard Mambu ma Khenzu, *A Modern History of Monetary and Financial Systems of Congo, 1885–1995* (Lewiston: Edwin Mellen, 2006), 2, 21.
165. Alexandre Delcommune, *Vingt années de Vie africaine*, vol. 1 (Brussels: Larcier, 1922), 48. Camille Coquilhat, *Sur le Haut-Congo* (Paris: Lebegue, 1888), 270.
166. Robert W. Harms, *River of Wealth, River of Sorrow: The Central Zaire Basin in the Era of the Slave and Ivory Trade, 1500–1891* (New Haven, CT: Yale University Press, 1981), 222. See Khenzu, 23.
167. Sanford to LII, December 10, 1884, SAN, Box 29, Folder 2.
168. Stanley, *Through the Dark Continent*, vol. 2 (New York: Harper, 1878), 448. See entry for August 14, 1880 in Augustus Sparhawk's memoranda book, Massachusetts Historical Society, Ms. SBd-112.

169. William Holman Bentley, *Pioneering on the Congo*, vol. 1 (New York: Revell, 1900), 72; William Hornaday, *Free Rum on the Congo* (Chicago: Woman's Temperance Publication Association, 1887), 72. Daniel Rankin, "Peoples and Commercial Prospects of the Zambesi Basin," *Scottish Geographical Magazine*, vol. 9 (1893), 225.
170. Charles Jeannest, *Quatre années au Congo* (Paris: Charpentier, 1883), 25–33.
171. Louis Weber de Treunfels to Sanford, August 14, 1886, SAN, Box 23, Folder 8.
172. Exploring Expedition Reports, 1886, SAN, Box 32, Folder 8.
173. Sparhawk to Stanley, November 6, 1881, SPAR.
174. Compare Karl E. Laman, *The Kongo*, vol. 1 (Uppsala: Studia Ethnographia Upsaliensa, 1953), 135.
175. Diary entry, October 21, 1881, SPAR.
176. Entry of June 28, 1884, Lesslie Family Fonds, Box 2, Folder 20.
177. Strauch to Stanley, STAN, #925. See Antonin Deloume, "Le droit des gens," *Bulletin de la société de géographie*, vol. 2 (Toulouse 1883), 456.
178. Sanford to Paul de Borchgrave (undated), SAN, Box 29, Folder 12.
179. John K. Thornton, "The Development of an African Catholic Church in the Kingdom of Kongo, 1483–1750," *JAH* 25 (1984): 147; John K. Thornton, "Afro-Christian Syncretism in the Kingdom of Kongo," *JAH* 54 (2013): 53. "Congo," *Missionary Herald*, October 1, 1879. Sanford to Latrobe, July 30, 1877, SAN, Box 29, Folder 10. Stanley, *Cinq années* (Paris 1885), 12.
180. See Susan Broadhead, "Beyond Decline: The Kingdom of the Kongo in the Eighteenth and Nineteenth Centuries," *International Journal of African Historical Studies* 12 (1979): 615.
181. Gustave Moynier, *La fondation de l'état indépendant du Congo au point de vue juridique* (Paris: Alphonse Picard, 1887), 25.
182. Jan Vansina, *Oral Tradition as History* (Madison: University of Wisconsin Press, 1985), 24, 117.
183. But see "Nouvelles et informations," *Mouvement Géographique*, March 22, 1885.
184. van de Velde, "Région," *Société Royale Belge de Géographie*, vol. 10 (Brussels 1886), 354.
185. Jeannest, 34.
186. Sparhawk to Stanley, November 6, 1881, SPAR.
187. Jesse Siddall Reeves, *The International Beginnings of the Congo Free State* (Baltimore: Johns Hopkins University Press, 1894), 23.
188. Anstey, 28.
189. See Paul Güssfeldt, *Die Loango-expedition ausgesandt von der Deutschen Gesellschaft zur Erforschung Aequatorial-Africas, 1873–1876* (Leipzig: Baldamus, 1888), 90.
190. Phyllis M. Martin, *The External Trade of the Loango Coast 1576–1870: The Effects of Changing Commercial Relations on the Vili Kingdom of Loango* (Oxford:

Oxford University Press, 1972), 156. "Le Port de Banana," *Mouvement Géographique*, March 22, 1885.

191. Compare Henri Wauwermans, *Les prémices de l'œuvre d'émanicipation africaine* (Brussels: Institut national de géographie, 1885), 47.
192. LII to Frère-Orban, February 21, 1880, *Léopold II et le cabinet Frère-Orban (1878–1884): correspondance entre le roi et ses ministres*, ed. Nadine Lubelski-Bernard, vol. 1 (Leuven: Nauwelaerts, 1983), 130.
193. Reeves, *Beginnings*, 25.
194. Frederic Goldsmid, "Congo," *RGS*, vol. 6 (London 1884), 178.
195. Geoffroy Chodron de Courcel, "Berlin Act of 26 February 1885," *BEA*, 247.
196. Thus Auguste Lambermont, cited in *Léopold II et le cabinet Frère-Orban*, vol. 1, 71.
197. Devaux to Sanford, May 28, 1883, SAN, Box 25, Folder 19.
198. Newman, *Imperial Footprints*, 192. Jeal, 282.
199. Strauch to van de Velde, December 7, 1882; Stanley to van de Velde, January 29, 1883, LVP.
200. Strauch to Lindner (undated), Marcel Luwel, *Otto Lindner, 1852–1945: ein weinig bekend medewerker van Leopold II in Afrika* (Brussels: Académie royale des sciences coloniales, 1959), 215.
201. Strauch to Lindner, January 15, 1882, Luwel, *Lindner*, 125.
202. Strauch's convention template, undated, STAN, # 4778.
203. Strauch to van de Velde, December 7, 1882, LVP.
204. "Congo Mission," *Missionary Herald*, March 1, 1883.
205. "Central Africa," *Missionary Herald*, November 1879. Bentley, *Pioneering*, vol. 1, 342.
206. Pierre Legrand to Paul-Armand Challemel-Lacour, July 18, 1883, Archives of the French Foreign Ministry (hereafter AMAE) 1md / 88.
207. Pauncefote's memo, May 13, 1880, FO 84 / 1585.
208. Eric Axelson, *Portugal and the Scramble for Africa, 1875–1891* (Johannesburg: Witwatersrand University Press, 1967), 38.
209. Reeves, *Beginnings*, 24.
210. H. R. Wallis, *Report on the Trade of Tete and District for the year 1901* (London: His Majesty's Stationery Office, 1902) 5. Francois Bontinck, " Les makuta dans le passe," *Zaïre* 27 (1987): 357.
211. John K. Thornton, "Master or Dupe? The Reign of Pedro V of Kongo," *Portuguese Studies Review* 19 (2011): 115.
212. Jerónimo, *The "Civilising Mission" of Portuguese Colonialism*, 25.
213. John Russell's memo, October 13, 1860, Thomas Tomlinson, *Congo Treaty* (London: Stanford, 1884), 31.
214. Sociéte de Geographie de Lisbonne, *La question du Zaire* (Lisbonne: Lallemant frères, 1883), 9. Antonio Galvano, *The discoveries of the world, from their first original unto the year of our Lord 1555* (London: Hakluyt Society, 1862), 76. See John K. Thornton, "Early Kongo-Portuguese Relations: A New Interpretation," *History in Africa* 8 (1981): 183.

215. Richard James Hammond, *Portugal and Africa 1815–1910: A Study in Uneconomic Imperialism* (Stanford, CA: Stanford University Press, 1966), 49. Anstey, 47.
216. Thomson, *Fondation*, 98.
217. But see A. J. Wauters, *Le Congo & Les Portugais: réponse au memorandum de la Société de géographie de Lisbonne* (Brussels: Vanderauwera, 1883), 52.
218. Kintamba Treaty of January 1, 1882, STAN, #6908.
219. Bentley to Baynes, November 17, 1882, BMSA, Reel 31.
220. Miguel Martins d'Antas to Granville, August 4, 1884, FO 403 / 39.
221. Carlos de Magalhães, *Le Zaire et les contrats de l'Association internationale* (Lisbonne: Adolpho, Modesto & Co., 1884), 31.
222. Sparhawk to Stanley, November 6, 1881, SPAR.
223. Sanford to Frederick Frelinghuysen, December 30, 1882, SAN, Box 29, Folder 9.
224. LII to Frère-Orban, July 15, 1880, *Léopold II et le cabinet Frère-Orban*, vol. 1, 145.
225. Anonymous, *Aus den Archiven des belgischen Kolonialministeriums*, vol. 1 (Berlin: Mittler, 1918), 62.
226. Francois Bontinck, *Aux origines de l'État Indépendant du Congo* (Paris: Nauwelaerts, 1966), 101.
227. Brazza's report, August 28, 1882, Henri Brunschwig, *Brazza Explorateur:Les Traités Makoko, 1880–1882* (Paris: Mouton, 1972), 273.
228. Brazza to Lanessan, March 24, 1901, in Henri Brunschwig, *L'avènement de l'Afrique Noire du XIXe siècle à nos jours* (Paris: Colin, 1963), 143.
229. Compare entry for November 12, 1880, Sparhawk's memoranda book.
230. Henri Brunschwig, "La négociation du traité Makoko," *Cahiers d'Études Africaines* 5 (1967): 9.
231. Entry for December 31, 1881, Sparhawk's diary, SPAR.
232. Treaty of October 3, 1880, printed as "convention" in *Journal du droit international privé et de la jurisprudence comparée*, vol. 9 (Paris: Billard, 1882), 668.
233. See Jan Vansina, *The Tio Kingdom of the Middle Congo, 1880–1892* (Oxford: Oxford University Press, 1973), 396–410.
234. Mary Kingsley, *Travels in West Africa, Congo Français, Corisco and Cameroons* (London: Macmillan, 1897), 360.
235. Levi P. Morton to Frelinghuysen, December 6, 1882, *Papers Relating to the Foreign Relations of the United States* (Washington, D.C.: Government Printing Office, 1884), 259.
236. Jules Herbette to Bernard Jauréguiberry, July 7, 1882, AMAE 1md / 59.
237. Anonymous, *Les points sur les I de l'Association internationale africaine*, 23.
238. Treaty in *Journal du Droit International Privé*, vol. 9 (Paris 1882), 668.
239. Brazza's report, August 28, 1882, 268. But see Edward Berenson, *Heroes of Empire: Five Charismatic Men and the Conquest of Africa* (Berkeley: University of California Press, 2011), 66.

240. See Jelmer Vos, *Kongo in the Age of Empire, 1860–1913: The Breakdown of a Moral Order* (Madison: University of Wisconsin Press, 2015).
241. Anonymous, "Future of Congo," *Edinburgh Review* 160 (Edinburgh 1884): 175.
242. Jan Vansina, "The Kingdom of the Great Makoko," *Western African History*, ed. Daniel F. McCall, vol. 4 (New York: Praeger, 1969), 20.
243. Treaty in *Journal du Droit International Privé*, vol. 9, 668.
244. Brunschwig, *L'avènement*, 148.
245. Henk Wesseling, *Divide and Rule: The Partition of Africa, 1880–1914* (Westport: Praeger, 1996), 95.
246. Compare Bulama arbitration of January 13, 1869, in John Bassett Moore, *History and Digest of the International Arbitrations*, vol. 2 (Washington, D.C.: Government Printing Office, 1898), 1909.
247. Antony Allott, "The changing legal status of boundaries in Africa: a diachronic view," in *Foreign Relations of African States*, ed. Kenneth Ingham (London: Butterworths, 1974), 116.
248. Joseph Chavanne, *Reisen und Forschungen im alten und neuen Kongostaate* (Jena: Costenoble, 1887), 114. Compare Édouard Viard, *Explorations Africaines* (Paris: Guérin, 1885), 10.
249. Richard Burton, *Two trips to gorilla land and the cataracts of the Congo*, vol. 2 (London: S. Low, 1876), 109.
250. See Adda B. Bozeman, *Conflict in Africa: Concepts and Realities* (Princeton, NJ: Princeton University Press, 1976), 122.
251. Peter Cutt Lloyd, *Yoruba Land Law* (Ibadan: Oxford University Press, 1962), 62.
252. Maurice Flory, "La notion de territoire arabe," *Annuaire français du droit international* 3 (1957): 79.
253. Vansina, *Kingdoms of the Savanna*, 4, 247. Compare David Birmingham, *Central Africa to 1870* (Cambridge: Cambridge University Press, 1981), 109.
254. Edwin Scott Haydon, *Law and Justice in Buganda* (London: Butterworths, 1960), 127. Burton, 109.
255. Richard Edward Dennett, "The Congo," *Journal of the Manchester Geographical Society* 2 (1886): 298.
256. Chlodwig zu Hohenlohe-Schillingsfürst to Bismarck, October 5, 1882, R1001 / 9039.
257. Viewable at http://www.brazza.culture.fr/en/missions/sejour_mbe_arch1.htm.
258. "Documents Internationaux," *Journal du droit international privé*, vol. 9 (Paris 1882), 668.
259. Various treaties, *The Consolidated Treaty Series*, ed. Clive Parry, vol. 161 (Dobbs Ferry, NY: Oceana, 1978), 238, 227, 212.
260. C. M. Andrew and A. S. Kanya-Forstner, "The French 'Colonial Party': Its Composition, Aims and Influence, 1885–1914," *Historical Journal* 14 (1971): 99.

261. Paul Leroy-Beaulieu, *De la colonisation chez les peuples modernes* (Paris: Librairie Guillaumin et Cie, 1898).
262. "Par la force," *Le Temps* (Paris), March 12, 1885. See Alice L. Conklin, *A Mission to Civilize: The Republican Idea of Empire in France and West Africa, 1895–1930* (Stanford, CA: Stanford University Press, 1997).
263. Thomson, *Fondation*, 81.
264. Napoléon Ney, *Conférences et lettres de P. Savorgnan de Brazza sur ses trois explorations dans l'ouest africain de 1875 à 1886* (Paris: Dreyfous, 1887), 415. Brunschwig, *L'avènement*, 150.
265. Brazza's report, August 28, 1882, 274.
266. Ibid., 269.
267. Vansina, *Tio Kingdom*, 396–410.
268. Brunschwig, *L'avènement*, 164.
269. See Thomson, *Fondation*, 113–114.
270. Fernando d'Azevedo to António de Serpa Pimentel, November 24, 1882, in Ministère des Affaires Étrangères, *Affaires du Congo* (Paris: Imprimerie Nationale, 1884), 37.
271. "Nouvelles du Jour" *Le Temps*, December 4, 1882.
272. Brunschwig, *L'avènement*, 159. Jean Stengers, " L'impérialisme colonial de la fin du XIXe siècle: Mythe ou Réalité," *JAH* 3 (1962): 475.
273. Gabriel Hanotaux and Alfred Martineau, *Historie des colonies françaises et de l'expansion de la France dans le monde*, vol. 4 (Paris: Plon, 1929), 409.
274. Rosaline Eredapa Nwoye, *The public image of Pierre Savorgnan de Brazza and the establishment of French imperialism in the Congo, 1875–1885* (Aberdeen: Aberdeen University African Studies Group, 1981), 16.
275. Robert McLane to Thomas Bayard, October 20, 1886, *Papers Relating to the Foreign Relations of the United States* (Washington, D.C.: Government Printing Office, 1888), 272.
276. "Friendship pact, December 14th, 1882," *Nouveau Recueil General de Traites*, ed. Martens, series 2, vol. 9 (Göttingen 1884), 216.
277. Compare Peter Duignan and L.H. Gann, *The United States and Africa: A History* (Cambridge: Cambridge University Press, 1987), 123.
278. Yves Gonjo, "Le *'plan Freycinet,'* 1878–1882," *Revue historique*, vol. 248 (1972), 49–86.
279. Devaux to Sanford, January 19, 1884, SAN, Box 25, Folder 9.
280. Sanford to Frelinghuysen, December 30, 1882, SAN, Box 29, Folder 9.
281. Émile Banning, *Le partage politique de l'Afrique d'après les transactions internationales les plus récentes* (Brussels: Muquardt, 1888), 98.
282. LII to Jules van Praet, July 8, 1882, in *Léopold II et le cabinet*, vol. 2, 1191.
283. John H. Weeks, *Among the Primitive Bakongo* (London: Seeley, 1914), 206.
284. See Anstey, 20–32.
285. Catherine Coquery-Vidrovitch, *Brazza et la prise de possession du Congo francais, 1883–85* (Paris: Mouton, 1969), 91.

286. Jean Stengers, "Léopold II et Brazza," *Revue Française d'Histoire Outre-Mer* 63 (1976): 105.
287. Jean Stengers, "Léopold II et la fixation," *Flambeau*, vol. 46 (1963), 160. Brazza to Jules Ferry, June 12, 1883, AMAE 1md/88.
288. M. Cordier to Lucien Brun, March 14, 1883, AMAE 1md/87.
289. Challemel-Lacour to Alphonse de Courcel, May 1, 1883, in Louis Renault (ed.), *Archives Diplomatiques*, 2nd series, vol. 11 (Paris: Welter, 1884), 289.
290. Charles Duclerc to LII, October 16, 1882, *Affaires du Congo* (1884), 1. Marquis de Montebello to Duclerc, January 3, 1883, *Documents diplomatiques français* (hereafter *DDF)*, vol. 4 (Paris: Imprimerie Nationale, 1922), 570.
291. LII to Queen Victoria, October 15, 1882, in *Letters of Queen Victoria*, vol. 3 (London 1928), 350.
292. Albert Maurice, *H. M. Stanley: Unpublished Letters* (New York: Philosophical Library, 1957), 161.
293. Sanford to LII, undated, SAN, Box 29, Folder 12; Sanford to Frelinghuysen, December 30, 1882, SAN, Box 29, Folder 9.
294. "Central Africa," *The Times* (London), May 8, 1875.
295. Dennett, "Congo," 298. "Brazza," *The Times* (London), December 24, 1886. Kingsley, 360.
296. Strauch to Lindner, November 30, 1881, in Luwel, *Lindner*, 215.
297. Strauch to Stanley, STAN, #924.
298. Frère-Orban's memo, circa December 1882, in *Léopold II et le cabinet*, vol. 1, 274.
299. Ascherson, 122; Jeal, 258; Emerson, 98.
300. "Parliamentary Intelligence," *The Times* (London), March 18, 1882.
301. LII's memo, March 13, 1882, excerpted in Cornet, 561.
302. Gordon to Horace Waller, April 4, 1880, Horace Waller Papers, Bodleian Library, University of Oxford, vol. 2, Folder 126–127. Compare undated memorandum, STAN, #4788.
303. Strauch to Stanley, March 27, 1882, STAN, #902.
304. J. Savile Lumley to Granville, November 25, 1882, FO 403/14.
305. See Charles Salomon, *L'occupation des territoires sans maître* (Paris: Giard, 1889), 147.
306. Goldsmid to Devaux, March 6, 1884, Lambermont Papers, Archives of Ministry of Foreign Affairs, Belgium. Compare Strauch's convention template, undated, STAN #4778.
307. Pauncefote's memos: May 13, 1880, FO 84/1585; April 11, 1878, FO 12/53.
308. Maurice Jametel, "Une Nouvelle Colonie," *L'Économiste français*, vol. 11 (Paris 1883), 136; "Angleterre," *Le Temps* (Paris), March 15, 1882; Ludwig Geßner, " Zur Neutralisirung des Congo," *Die Gegenwart*, vol. 24 (Berlin 1883), 50. Rutherford B. Hayes to Sultan of Brunei, March 8, 1880, FO 12/55.
309. Willem Frederik Rochussen to Taalman Kip, February 27, 1883, *Bescheiden betreffende*, part 2, vol. 3 (Gravenhage 1967), 402.

310. Wauwermans, 71.
311. Devaux to Sanford, December 12, 1883, SAN, Box 25, Folder 19.
312. Strauch to Stanley, April 2, 1883, STAN, #929.
313. Strauch to Stanley, March 27, 1882, STAN, #902.
314. Stinglhamber, 73.
315. Stanley to Strauch, June 23, 1881, Maurice, *Stanley,* 85.
316. Charles Adolphe Marie Liebrechts, *Léopold II, fondateur d'empire* (Brussels: Office de publicité 1932), 20.
317. Strauch to Stanley, March 27, 1882, STAN #902.
318. J. Peltzer, "Bornéo," *Société belge de géographie: Bulletin,* vol. 5 (Brussels 1881), 297.
319. "Séance du 6 Novembre 1885," *Compte rendu des séances de la Société de géographie* (Paris 1885), 515. "Geographischer Bericht," *Mittheilungen der Kais. Königl. Geographischen Gesellschaft,* vol. 28 (Vienna 1885), 358.
320. Adrien Goffinet to LII, June 19, 1883, APR, Fonds Goffinet.
321. Strauch to Stanley, March 27, 1882, STAN, #902.
322. "North Borneo Company," *The Times* (London), March 25, 1882, 6.
323. Moritz Busch, *Tagebuchblätter,* vol. 3 (Leipzig: Grunow, 1899), 192.
324. Strauch to Stanley, March 27, 1882, STAN, #902.
325. Herbert Ward, *Five years with the Congo cannibals* (London: Chatto, 1891), 27.
326. See Jeal, *Stanley.*
327. Stanley to LII, August 1883, STAN, #35.
328. "Stanley on Congo," *The Times* (London), September 25, 1883. Sanford to Frelinghuysen, December 30, 1882, SAN, Box 29, Folder 9.
329. Strauch to Stanley, March 27, 1882, STAN, #902.
330. Strauch to Eduard Pechuël-Loesche, September 14, 1882, Eduard Pechuël-Loesche, *Kongoland* (Jena: Costenoble, 1887), 17.
331. LII to Strauch, October 16, 1882, Maurice, *Stanley,* 161.
332. Strauch to Stanley, November 1, 1882, STAN, #4777.
333. Strauch to Pechuel-Loesche, October 12, 1882, STAN, #1010.
334. Strauch to Stanley, November 1, 1882, STAN, #4777. Compare undated form attached to Strauch to Lindner, November 30, 1881 by Luwel, *Otto Lindner,* 215.
335. Pechuël-Loesche, *Kongoland,* 17.
336. "Tableau du personnel blanc," *Mouvement Géographique,* April 6, 1884.
337. LII to Frère-Orban, July 15, 1880, in *Léopold II et le cabinet,* vol. 1, 144. LII to Devaux, May 5, 1883, APR, Fonds Congo, File 2. Grant Elliott, "Kwilou-Niadi," *Société Royale Belge de Géographie: Bulletin,* vol. 10 (Brussels 1886), 109.
338. Frédéric Orban to Stanley, February 22, 1883, Orban Papers, RG 644, RMCA.
339. Magalhães, 24. Diary entry of June 28, 1884 in Lesslie Family Fonds, Box 2, Folder 20.

340. Excerpted in Christine Denuit-Somerhausen, "Les traités de Stanley et de ses collaborateurs avec les chefs africains, 1880–1885," *Centenaire de l'État Indépendant,* 86.
341. Bogumil Jewsiewicki, "Notes," *Études d'Histoire Africaine* 3 (1972): 200.
342. Strauch to Sanford, November 15, 1883, SAN, Box 31, Folder 3.
343. But see Jean Stengers, "King Leopold and Anglo-French Rivalry," in *France and Britain in Africa,* ed. Prosser Gifford and William Roger Louis (New Haven, CT: Yale University Press, 1978), 142.
344. Strauch to Stanley, March 27, 1882, STAN, #902.
345. Thomas Comber to Baynes, September 5, 1882, BMSA, Reel 31. Strauch to Stanley, February 5, 1883, STAN, #924. Strauch to Stanley, March 6, 1883, STAN, #925.
346. Charles de Chavannes, *Avec Brazza* (Paris: Plon, 1935), 191.
347. Thomas Comber, "Project of Contract," BMSA, Reel 32. Compare Stengers, "King Leopold and Anglo-French Rivalry," 143.
348. Minutes of Society, November 21, 1882, BMSA, Reel 4. "French Expedition to Congo," March 5, 1883, BMSA, Reel 32. Baynes to Strauch, November 17, 1882, BMSA, Reel 31.
349. Minutes of Society, June 17, 1884, BMSA, Reel 4.
350. Strauch to van de Velde, January 18, 1883 (letter fragment), LVP.
351. Strauch to Stanley, STAN, #924.
352. d'Antas to Granville, August 4, 1884, FO 403 / 39.
353. Frère-Orban to Jules Devaux, November 30, 1883, in *Léopold II et le cabinet,* vol. 1, 345.
354. William Parminter to van de Velde, August 21, 1884, excerpted in Jean-Luc Vellut, " Les traités de l'Association internationale du Congo dans le bas-fleuve Zaïre," *Un siècle de documentation africaine (1885–1985)* (Brussels: Bibliothèque africaine, 1985), 24–34n23.
355. "Affairs on Congo," *Manchester Guardian,* September 26, 1884. Coquilhat, *Sur le Haut-Congo,* 103.
356. Report of British Consul at Luanda, November 6, 1883, excerpted in Henry Richard Fox Bourne, *Civilisation in Congoland* (London: P.S. King, 1903), 44.
357. Delcommune, *Vingt années,* vol. 1, 165. Chavanne, *Reisen und Forschungen,* 135. Contract of April 19, 1884, Portugal, *Les droits du Portugal au Congo* (Lisbonne: Imprimerie Nationale, 1884), 45.
358. Declarations of May 16, 1884, *Les droits du Portugal,* 48.
359. d'Antas to Granville, August 4, 1884, FO 403 / 39.
360. Letter to van de Velde, July 17, 1883, LVP.
361. Godbey, *Stanley in Africa,* 405.
362. Chavanne, *Reisen und Forschungen,* 114.
363. d'Antas to Granville, August 4, 1884, FO 403 / 39.
364. Strauch to van de Velde, December 7, 1882, LVP.
365. Stanley to van de Velde, January 29, 1883, LVP. Compare Bourne, 45.

366. Osama W. Abi-Mershed, *Apostles of Modernity: Saint-Simonians and the Civilizing Mission in Algeria* (Stanford, CA: Stanford University Press, 2010), 102.
367. Édouard Descamps, *New Africa: an essay on government civilization in new countries, and on the foundation, organization and administration of the Congo Free State* (London: S. Low, 1903), 36.
368. Sir Robert Reid to Commons, January 31, 1900, *Parliamentary Debates*, fourth series, vol. 78 (London 1900), 213. John Fisher, *Paul Kruger: His Life and Times* (London: Secker and Warburg, 1974), 118.
369. Brunschwig, "La négociation du traité Makoko," 12.
370. Compare Philip Wodehouse to Hercules Robinson, March 31, 1881, Transvaal Royal Commission, *Reports from Commissioners*, vol. 28 (London 1882), 7. Compare Julian Pauncefote's memo, November 25, 1886, FO 64/1152.
371. For example, the treaty made at Palaballa on April 19, 1884. French copy in Magalhães, 26.
372. "Affairs on Congo," *Manchester Guardian*, September 26, 1884.
373. See F. W. Buckler, "India and the Far East 1848–1858," *The Cambridge History of British Foreign Policy 1783–1919*, ed. Adolphus W. Ward and George P. Gooch, vol. 2 (Cambridge: Cambridge University Press, 1923), 404. See *The Gladstone Diaries: With Cabinet Minutes and Prime-Ministerial Correspondence*, ed. H. C. G. Matthew, vol. 10 (Oxford: Clarendon Press, 1990), lxxxvii.
374. "With His Usual Energy," *Manchester Guardian*, September 27, 1884.
375. But see Stengers, "King Leopold and Anglo-French Rivalry," 141.
376. W. P. B. Shepheard, "Suzerainty," *Journal of Society of Comparative Legislation* 1 (1899): 437.
377. Stengers, "King Leopold's Imperialism," 273. Stengers, "King Leopold and Anglo-French Rivalry," 142.
378. Jeal, 251, 285.
379. Delcommune, *Vingt années*, vol. 1, 165.
380. Edmond Hanssens, "Lettres inédites du capitaine Hanssens," in *Le Congo illustré*, ed. A. J. Wauters, vol. 1 (Brussels 1892), 47.
381. For a copy of first treaty, January 7, 1883, see *Consolidated Treaty Series*, vol. 161, 297.
382. Edward Hertslet (ed.), *The Map of Africa by Treaty*, vol. 1 (London: His Majesty's Stationery Office, 1894), 200.
383. Sparhawk to Stanley, March 8, 1881, SPAR.
384. Devaux to Sanford, March 13, 1884, SAN, Box 25, Folder 19.
385. Cordier to Brun, June 30, 1883, AMAE 1md/88.
386. Frère-Orban, undated memo, in *Léopold II et le cabinet*, vol. 1, 275. *Comité* to French Foreign Ministry, November 20, 1882, AMAE 1md/91.
387. Entry for Sunday, June 13, 1880, "Personal Account," SPAR.
388. Sparhawk to Strauch, November 13, 1881, SPAR.
389. Ferry to Brazza, June 26, 1883, AMAE 1md/88.

390. Richard West, *Brazza of the Congo: European exploration and exploitation in French Equatorial Africa* (London: Jonathan Cape, 1972), 160.
391. William Roger Louis, "The Berlin Congo Conference," in *France and Britain in Africa,* 182.
392. "Le général Strauch," *Mouvement géographique,* vol. 28 (Brussels 1911), 310. Roeykens, *Les débuts,* 415.
393. Alfred Zimmermann, "Der Kongo und der Kongostaat," *Preußische Jahrbücher,* vol. 60 (Berlin 1887), 306. Strauch to Pechuël-Loesche, November 5, 1882, STAN #1010.
394. "Das Utopien am Kongo," *Deutsche Kolonialzeitung,* vol. 2 (Berlin 1885), 730.
395. "Kürzere Mittheilungen," *Globus,* vol. 48 (Braunschweig 1885), 366.
396. Strauch to Pechuël-Loesche, September 14, 1882, *Kongoland,* 17.
397. Jeal, 263.
398. Journal entries, March–April 1883, STAN, #35. Decree of February 5, 1883, AMAE 1md / 87. Paul Robiquet, *Discours et opinions de Jules Ferry,* vol. 5 (Paris: Colin, 1897), 141.
399. "Goldsmid," *The Times* (London), Jan 13, 1908.
400. "Report of the Proceedings at a Public Dinner," *The private letters of Sir James Brooke, K.C.B., Rajah of Sarawak: narrating the events of his life, from 1838 to the present time,* vol. 3 (London: Richard Bentley, 1853), 301.
401. Strauch to Stanley, July 23, 1883, STAN, #936.
402. Goldsmid, "My Recent Visit to Congo," *Proceedings of the Royal Geographical Society,* vol. 6 (Apr. 1884), 178.
403. Strauch to Mackinnon, November 30, 1883, Mackinnon Papers, File 232 Reel 19.
404. "Goldsmid," *The Times* (London), Jan 13, 1908.
405. Frédéric Orban to H. Johnston, December 9, 1883, Orban Papers, RG 644, RMCA.
406. Anonymous, *Aus den Archiven,* 58–62.
407. See H. H. Johnston, "A Visit to Mr. Stanley's Stations," *RGS,* vol. 5 (Oct. 1883), 569.
408. Frelinghuysen to John Tyler Morgan, March 13, 1884, SAN, Box 24, Folder 11.
409. Devaux to Sanford, March 13, 1884, SAN, Box 25, Folder 19.
410. Compare Devaux to Sanford, March 13, 1884, SAN, Box 25, Folder 19.
411. "Sir Frederick Goldsmid's Mission," *The Times* (London), January 5, 1884, 8.
412. Goldsmid to Jules Devaux, May 20, 1884, APR, Fonds Congo, File 2.
413. d'Antas to Granville, August 4, 1884, FO 403 / 39.
414. LII's memo, circa December 1883, APR, Fonds Congo, File 2.
415. Elliott, "Kwilou-Niadi," 110. See treaty (tellingly undated) in Henry Wack, *The Story of the Congo Free State; social, political, and economic aspects of the Belgian system of government in Central Africa* (New York: Putnam's, 1905), 490.
416. "Discussion," *Journal of Anthropological Institute of Great Britain and Ireland* 17 (1888): 234.

417. d'Antas to Granville, August 4, 1884, FO 403/39.
418. Devaux to Sanford, April 27, 1884, SAN, Box 25, Folder 19.
419. Descamps, 30.
420. Teobaldo Filesi, "Preludio alla Conferenza di Berlino," *Africa: Rivista trimestrale di studi e documentazione dell'Istituto italiano per l'Africa e l'Oriente* 39 (1984): 537.
421. See Georges Blanchard, *Étude sur la formation & la constitution politique de l'État indépendant du Congo* (Paris: Pedone, 1899), 57.
422. Devaux to Sanford, December 12, 1883, SAN, Box 25, Folder 19.
423. Lyons to Granville, December 2, 1884, FO 881/5051. Edouard Rolin-Jaequemyns, "L'Annee 1888," *Revue de Droit International* 21 (1889): 182.
424. Sanford to Mackinnon, December 24, 1884, 1884, SAN, Box 127, Folder 10.
425. Frère-Orban, memo, circa December 1882, in *Léopold II et le cabinet,* vol. 1, 274. Jean Stengers, "Léopold II et le cabinet Malou," in *1884: un tournant politique en Belgique,* ed. Emiel Lamberts and Jacques Lory (Brussels: Publications des Facultés universitaires Saint-Louis, 1986), 165, 199. LII to Sanford, January 31, 1885, SAN, unindexed.
426. Meeting protocol, June 9, 1883, AMAE 1md/88.
427. Joachim von Holtzendorff to Bismarck, October 26, 1883, R1001/4108.
428. Sanford to Gertrude Sanford, November 27, 1883, Box 83, Folder 7; Daly to Sanford, January 9, 1884, SAN, Box 24, Folder 8. Joseph Tritton to Alfred Baynes, March 5, 1883, BMSA, Reel 32.
429. Message of December 4, 1883, in James D. Richardson (ed.), *A Compilation of the Messages and Papers of the Presidents,* vol. 8 (Washington, D.C.: Government Printing Office, 1898), 175.

Chapter 4: Bismarck's Borneo

1. Henri Brunschwig, *L'expansion allemande outre-mer du XVe siècle à nos jours* (Paris: Presses universitaires de France, 1957), 45.
2. Théophile Gautier, "Une visite au Comte Bismarck," *Revue de Paris,* August 1903, 786.
3. Various proposals can be found in the German Federal Archive (Bundesarchiv) Berlin-Lichterfelde, R1001/7155–7158.
4. John Stonham (ed.), *Official Year Book of the Commonwealth of Australia,* no. 15 (Melbourne: Green, 1922), 961.
5. Frank Lorenz Müller, "Imperialist Ambitions in Vormärz and Revolutionary Germany," *German History* 17 (1999): 346. Hans Fenske, " Imperialistische Tendenzen in Deutschland vor 1866," *Historisches Jahrbuch,* vol. 97 (1978), 336. See Matthew P. Fitzpatrick, *Liberal Imperialism in Germany: Expansionism and Nationalism, 1848–1884* (New York: Berghahn, 2008), 25. See, finally, Hermann Hiery, "Der Kaiser, das Reich und der Kolonialismus: Anmerkungen zur Entstehung des deutschen Imperialismus im 19.

Jahrhundert," *Imperium—Empire—Reich*, ed. Franz Bosbach and Hermann Hiery (Munich: Saur, 1999), 165.

6. Justus B. Westerkamp, *Über die Reichsverfassung* (Hannover: Rümpler, 1873), 50. See Hartmut Pogge von Strandmann, *Imperialismus vom Grünen Tisch* (Berlin: Christoph Links, 2009), 33.
7. Peter Hampe, *Die 'ökonomische Imperialismustheorie': Kritische Untersuchungen* (Munich: Beck, 1976).
8. Hans Rosenberg, *Grosse Depression und Bismarckzeit* (Berlin: de Gruyter, 1967).
9. Mary E. Townsend, *The Rise and Fall of Germany's Colonial Empire, 1844–1918* (New York: Fertig, 1966), 66.
10. Klaus J. Bade, *Friedrich Fabri und der Imperialismus in der Bismarckzeit: Revolution, Depression, Expansion* (Freiburg: Atlantis, 1975), 359.
11. William Otto Henderson, *Studies in German Colonial History* (London: Cass, 1962), 12.
12. Dan S. White, *The Splintered Party: National Liberalism in Hessen and the Reich, 1867–1918* (Cambridge, MA: Harvard University Press, 1976), 57.
13. Stanley Zucker, *Ludwig Bamberger: German liberal politician and social critic, 1823–1899* (Pittsburgh: University of Pittsburgh Press, 1975), 212.
14. J. D. Hargreaves, "Towards a History of the Partition of Africa," *JAH* 1 (1960): 102. André Villard, *Histoire du Sénégal* (Dakar: Viale, 1943), 90.
15. George Peabody Gooch, *Franco-German relations, 1871–1914* (London: Longmans, 1923), 21.
16. Teobaldo Filesi, "Preludio alla Conferenza di Berlino," *Africa: Rivista trimestrale di studi e documentazione dell'Istituto italiano per l'Africa e l'Oriente* 39 (1984): 531.
17. Hans-Ulrich Wehler, *Bismarck und der Imperialismus* (Cologne: Kiepenheuer & Witsch, 1969), 161–172; 298–332.
18. Mack Walker, *Germany and the emigration, 1816–1885* (Cambridge, MA: Harvard University Press, 1964), 221.
19. William Osgood Aydelotte, *Bismarck and British colonial policy: the problem of South West Africa, 1883–1885* (Philadelphia: University of Pennsylvania Press, 1937), 21.
20. Erwin Wiskemann, *Hamburg und die Welthandelspolitik* (Hamburg: Friederichsen, 1929), 222.
21. Hartmut Pogge von Strandmann, "Domestic Origins of Germany's Colonial Expansion under Bismarck," *Past and Present* 42 (1969): 148. See Helmut Washausen, *Hamburg und die Kolonialpolitik des Deutschen Reiches 1880 bis 1890* (Hamburg: Christians, 1968), 26.
22. Frank Lorenz Müller, *Our Fritz: Emperor Frederick III and the political culture of imperial Germany* (Cambridge, MA: Harvard University Press, 2011), 175. Ina Susanne Lorenz, *Eugen Richter: Der entschiedene Liberalismus in wilhelminischer Zeit 1871 bis 1906* (Husum, Germany: Matthiesen, 1981), 100.

23. Strandmann, "Domestic Origins," 148. Hans-Peter Jaeck, "Die deutsche Annexion," *Kamerun unter deutscher Kolonialherrschaft*, ed. Helmuth Stoecker (Berlin: Rütten and Loening, 1960), 60.
24. Crispi's note, June 17, 1882, in *The Memoirs of Francesco Crispi*, vol. 2 (London: Hodder and Stoughton, 1912), 132. Italics mine.
25. A. J. P. Taylor, *Germany's First Bid for Colonies, 1884–1885: A Move in Bismarck's European Policy* (London: Macmillan, 1938), 6.
26. "Es dürfte allgemein interessieren," *Berliner Börsenzeitung*, June 3, 1880.
27. Speech of Eugen Richter, *Stenographische Berichte*, February 4, 1885, 1083.
28. "Der 'Köln. Ztg.' geht ein Telegramm," *Hamburger Nachrichten*, May 23, 1880. "Kolonisationsversuche," *Altonaer Nachrichten*, May 30, 1880.
29. Volker Schult, *Wunsch und Wirklichkeit: deutsch-philippinische Beziehungen im Kontext globaler Verflechtungen 1860–1945* (Berlin: Logos, 2008), 59.
30. Livesay to Tom Harrisson, February 26, 1956, Harrisson (ed.), "Diary of Pretyman (I)," *SMJ* 7 (1956): 336.
31. Emil Deckert, *Die Colonialreiche und Colonisationsobjecte der Gegenwart* (Leipzig: Paul Frohberg, 1885), 61.
32. Ernst von der Brüggen, "Auswanderung, Kolonisation und Zweikindersystem," *Preußische Jahrbücher*, vol. 49 (Berlin 1882), 314. See, for example, Louis Schneider to Bismarck, February 23, 1867, German Federal Archive, R1001 / 7154; Wilhelm Koner, "Der Suluh-Archipel," *Zeitschrift der Gesellschaft für Erdkunde zu Berlin*, vol. 2 (Berlin 1867), 141.
33. Adolf Lüderitz to Heinrich Vogelsang, March 26, 1884, *Die Erschließung von Deutsch-Südwest-Afrika durch Adolf Lüderitz: Akten, Briefe und Denkschriften*, ed. C.A. Lüderitz (Oldenburg: Gerhard Stalling, 1945), 88.
34. Lüderitz to Foreign Ministry, November 16 and 23, 1882, R1001 / 1994.
35. See Antony Anghie, "Finding the Peripheries: Sovereignty and Colonialism in Nineteenth-Century International Law," *Harvard International Law Journal* 40 (1999): 57. See Mary Dewhurst Lewis, "Geographies of Power: The Tunisian Civic Order, Jurisdictional Politics, and Imperial Rivalry in the Mediterranean, 1881–1935," *JMH* 80 (2008): 791.
36. Westerkamp, 50. Müller, "Imperialist Ambitions," 365.
37. Anna Maria Helena Vermeer-Künzli, *The protection of individuals by means of diplomatic protection: diplomatic protection as a human rights instrument* (Leiden: Department of Public International Law, Faculty of Law, Leiden University, 2007), 13.
38. Anonymous, "Zur Geschichte der deutschen Erwerbung," *Deutsche Kolonialzeitung*, vol. 1 (Frankfurt 1884), 314.
39. See Richard V. Pierard, *The German Colonial Society, 1882–1914* (Iowa City: University of Iowa, 1964). M. de Pina de Saint-Didier to Jules Ferry, October 19, 1884, AMAE 1CPC / 11.
40. Lüderitz to Foreign Ministry, November 23, 1882.

41. William Otto Henderson, *The Zollverein* (Cambridge: Cambridge University Press, 1939), 335. Otto Pflanze, *Bismarck and the Development of Germany*, vol. 3 (Princeton, NJ: Princeton University Press, 1990), 121.
42. de Pina de Saint-Didier to Ferry, October 19, 1884, AMAE 1CPC / 11. Compare Waldemar Belck, "Lüderitzland?" *Deutsche Kolonialzeitung*, vol. 2 (Berlin 1885), 132.
43. Adolph Woermann to Heinrich von Kusserow, March 3, 1884, R1001 / 9039.
44. de Pina de Saint-Didier to Ferry, October 19, 1884, AMAE 1CPC / 11.
45. "Deutsche Kolonialpolitik," *Die Grenzboten*, vol. 43, part 3 (Leipzig 1884), 163.
46. Brunschwig, *L'expansion allemande*, 99.
47. Lüderitz to Foreign Ministry, November 23, 1882.
48. Albert Harding Ganz, *The Role of the Imperial German Navy in Colonial Affairs* (Columbus: Ohio State University, 1972), 2.
49. Hans Schinz to Julie Schinz-Voegeli, November 19, 1884, in Dag Henrichsen (ed.), *Hans Schinz: Bruchstücke: Forschungsreisen in Deutsch-Südwestafrika* (Basel: Carl Schlettwein Stiftung, 2012), 20.
50. Frederick Carruthers Cornell, *The glamour of prospecting: wanderings of a South African prospector in search of copper, gold, emeralds, and diamonds* (London: Fisher, 1920), 42.
51. Compare Edward Crankshaw, *Bismarck* (New York: Viking, 1981), 386.
52. Schinz to Schinz-Voegeli, December 16, 1884, in Henrichsen, *Schinz*, 25.
53. Compare Eugen Wolf, *Vom Fürsten Bismarck und seinem Haus: Tagebuchblätter* (Berlin: Fleischel, 1904), 16.
54. Herbert Bismarck to Wilhelm Bismarck, September 1, 1884, *Staatssekretär Graf Herbert von Bismarck: Aus seiner politischen Privatkorrespondenz*, ed. Walter Bussmann (Göttingen: Vandenhoeck & Ruprecht, 1964), 259. Lothar Gall, *Bismarck: der weiße Revolutionär* (Berlin: Propyläen, 1980), 620. Klaus Hildebrand, *Deutsche Außenpolitik 1871–1918* (Munich: Oldenbourg, 2008), 132. But see Henry Ashby Turner, "Bismarck's Imperialist Venture: Anti-British in Origin?," in *Britain and Germany in Africa*, ed. Prosser Gifford and William Roger Louis (New Haven, CT: Yale University Press, 1967), 47.
55. T. G. Otte, *The Foreign Office Mind: The Making of British Foreign Policy, 1865–1914* (Cambridge: Cambridge University Press, 2011), 144.
56. Wilhelm I to Bismarck, May 7, 1884, *Kaiser Wilhelms des Großen: Briefe, Reden und Schriften* (Berlin: Mittler, 1906), 403. "Bismarck's Vast Schemes," *New York Times*, January 25, 1885. For a comprehensive argument, see Axel T. G. Riehl, *Der "Tanz um den Äquator": Bismarcks antienglische Kolonialpolitik und die Erwartung des Thronwechsels in Deutschland 1883 bis 1885* (Berlin: Duncker & Humblot, 1993).
57. Crown Princess to Lady Mary Elizabeth Ponsonby, October 17, 1884, *Letters of Empress Frederick*, ed. Frederick Ponsonby (London: Macmillan, 1928), 194.

58. But see Karina Urbach, *Bismarck's Favourite Englishman: Lord Odo Russell's Mission to Berlin* (London: I. B. Tauris, 1999), 202.
59. Wilhelm Liebknecht's speech, March 4, 1885, *Stenographische Berichte,* 1540.
60. Odo Russell to Granville, August 2, 1884, in *Letters from the Berlin Embassy, 1871–1874, 1880–1885,* ed. Paul Knaplund, vol. 2 (Washington, D.C.: Government Printing Office, 1944), 339. See Wehler.
61. Bismarck to Clemens August Busch, August 30, 1884 and Wolfram von Rotenhan to Bismarck, October 3, 1884, in *Die Große Politik der europäischen Kabinette 1871–1914,* vol. 3 (Berlin: Deutsche Verlagsgesellschaft für Politik und Geschichte, 1922), 424, 431.
62. Adolf Coppius, *Hamburgs Bedeutung auf dem Gebiete der deutschen Kolonialpolitik* (Berlin: Heymanns, 1905), 62.
63. Anthony Gerald Hopkins, *An economic history of West Africa* (London: Longman, 1975), 130. Klaus J. Bade, "Imperial Germany and West Africa," *BEA,* 142.
64. M. d'Azincourt to Ferry, March 26, 1885, AMAE 1CPC / 11.
65. Heinrich Drießler, *Die Rheinische Mission in Südwestafrika* (Gütersloh: Bertelsmann, 1932), 19. Carl Gotthilf Büttner, *Das Hinterland von Walfischbai und Angra Pequeña: Eine Übersicht der Kulturarbeit deutscher Missionare und der seitherigen Entwicklung des deutschen Handels in Südwestafrika* (Heidelberg 1884), 68. See Brigitte Lau, "The Origins of Colonial Conquest: Namibia 1863–1870," *Hundert Jahre Einmischung in Afrika,* ed. E. Bruchhaus and L. Harding (Hamburg 1986), 115.
66. Kusserow's memo, November 4, 1880, R1001 / 2098.
67. Erich Prager, *Die deutsche Kolonialgesellschaft* (Berlin: Reimer, 1908).
68. Taylor, *Germany's First Bid,* 4.
69. Strandmann, *Imperialismus,* 59.
70. Compare Strandmann, "Domestic Origins," 140. See Elfi Bendikat, *Organisierte Kolonialbewegung in der Bismarck-Ära* (Heidelberg: Kivouvou, 1984).
71. Heinrich von Göring to Bismarck, March 31, 1883, R1001 / 4188.
72. Foreign Ministry to Wilhelm Delius, November 27, 1882. R1001 / 1994.
73. See Jörg Schildknecht, *Bismarck, Südwestafrika und die Kongokonferenz: die völkerrechtlichen Grundlagen der effektiven Okkupation und ihre Nebenpflichten am Beispiel des Erwerbs der ersten deutschen Kolonie* (Hamburg: LIT, 1999), 10.
74. See Lüderitz, *Die Erschließung von Deutsch-Südwest-Afrika durch Adolf Lüderitz,* title page.
75. "Unterredung mit Lüderitz," *Berliner Tageblatt,* January 5, 1885.
76. Lüderitz to Richard Lesser, October 11, 1884, in Lüderitz, *Erschließung,* 12.
77. James Leasor, *Rhodes and Barnato: The Premier and the Prancer* (London: Cooper, 1997), 157.
78. Lüderitz to Bismarck, December 25, 1884, R1001 / 1983.
79. Lüderitz to Foreign Ministry, November 23, 1882, R1001/1994.

80. Schüssler, *Adolf Lüderitz: ein deutscher Kampf um Südafrika 1883–1886* (Bremen: Schünemann, 1936), 93.
81. Franz Michael Zahn, "Branntweinhandel," *Allgemeine Missions-Zeitschrift*, vol. 13 (Gütersloh 1886), 35.
82. Heinrich Vogelsang, "Die ersten Schritte zur Erwerbung von Südwestafrika," *Zeitschrift für Kolonialpolitik, Kolonialrecht und Kolonialwirtschaft*, vol. 8 (Berlin 1906), 37. Friedrich Prüser, "Bremer Kaufleute als Wegbereiter Deutschlands in Übersee," *Koloniale Rundschau*, vol. 33 (Leipzig 1942), 86.
83. Johannes Warneck, "Zur Abwehr," *Allgemeine Missions-Zeitschrift*, vol. 1 (1884), 476.
84. Vogelsang, "Schritte," 38. Bismarck to Münster, June 10, 1884, R1001 / 1996.
85. On Hahn: George McCall Theal, *History and Ethnography of Africa South of the Zambesi*, vol. 1 (Cambridge: Cambridge University Press, 1910), 46.
86. Warneck, "Zur Abwehr," 476. Johannes Olpp, *Erlebnisse im Hinterlande von Angra-Pequeña: dem Volke erzählt* (Barmen: Verlag der Rheinischen Missions-Gesellschaft, 1886), 5.
87. Eric Axelson, *The Dias Voyage, 1487–1488: Toponymy and Padrões* (Coimbra: Universidade de Coimbra, 1988), 46.
88. Roger Webster, *At the Fireside: True South African Stories*, vol. 3 (Cape Town: New Africa Books, 2005), 53.
89. Vogelsang, "Schritte," 38.
90. Axelson, 51. B. Walker to W. G. Romaine, November 17, 1863, in United States Department of State, *Papers Relating to Foreign Affairs, 1864*, vol. 1 (Washington, D.C.: Government Printing Office, 1865), 258.
91. Schüssler, *Lüderitz*, 49.
92. Heinrich Vedder, *South West Africa in Early Times: Being the Story of South West Africa Up to the Date of Maharero's Death in 1890* (Oxford: Oxford University Press, 1938), 450. See Dag Henrichsen, "Pastoral Modernity, Territoriality and Colonial Transformations in Central Namibia, 1860s to 1904," in *Grappling with the beast: indigenous southern African responses to colonialism, 1840–1930*, ed. Peter Limb, Norman Etherington, and Peter Midgley (Leiden: Brill, 2010), 87.
93. Ernst von Weber's memo, May 7, 1873, R1001 / 7157.
94. Lüderitz to Vogelsang, March 26, 1884, in *Erschließung*, 86.
95. Bismarck to Georg zu Münster, June 14, 1884, R1001 / 1996.
96. "Äußerung des Reichskanzlers über Kolonialpläne," May 13, 1880, R1001 / 2098.
97. Anonymous, "Nord-Borneo Company," *Deutsche Geographische Blätter*, vol. 7 (Bremen 1884), 377.
98. Treaty between Hasenclever's representative and Jan Jonker Afrikaner, August 4, 1883, Namibian National Archives at Windhoek (hereafter NAW), ZBU, 1853, UIVbIbd1, August 15, 1883.

99. Carl Hoepfner, "Die Kupfererzlagerstätten von Südwest-Africa," *Berg—und Hüttenmännische Zeitung*, vol. 43 (Leipzig 1884), 81.
100. "Tagebuch der Expedition," *Erschließung*, 16–57.
101. Aydelotte, 38.
102. Delius to Foreign Ministry, November 29, 1882, R1001 / 1994.
103. Vogelsang, "Schritte," 38.
104. Hahn to Vogelsang, March 31, 1883, NAW, ZBU, AIa1bd1, 71.
105. Schinz to Schinz-Voegeli, March 13, 1885, in Henrichsen, *Schinz*, 41.
106. Vogelsang, "Schritte," 39.
107. Deposition of July 25, 1910, NAW, ZBU 1860, UIVc5bd1, 21.
108. Vogelsang, "Schritte," 40, 44.
109. Tilman Dedering, *Hate the Old and Follow the New: Khoekhoe and Missionaries in Early Nineteenth-Century Namibia* (Stuttgart: Steiner, 1997), 9.
110. Alvin Kienetz, "The key role of the Orlam migrations in the early Europeanization of South West Africa," *International Journal of African Historical Studies* 10 (1977): 570.
111. Warneck, "Zur Abwehr," 478.
112. Lüderitz to Foreign Ministry, November 23, 1882.
113. Vogelsang, "Schritte," 41.
114. Diary entry, April 26, 1883, *Erschließung*, 25.
115. See Andreas Vogt, *National Monuments in Namibia: An Inventory of Proclaimed National Monuments in the Republic of Namibia* (Windhoek: Gamsberg Macmillan, 2004), 195.
116. Schinz to Schinz-Voegeli, March 13, 1885, in Henrichsen, *Schinz*, 41. Theodor Leutwein, *Deutsch-Süd-West-Afrika* (Berlin: Reimer, 1898), 5.
117. Brigitte Lau, "Conflict and Power in Nineteenth-Century Namibia," *JAH* (1986): 29.
118. Jon M. Bridgman, *The Revolt of the Hereros* (Berkeley: University of California Press, 1981), 24. Kienetz, 553, 560.
119. Isaac Schapera, *The Khoisan Peoples of South Africa* (London: Routledge, 1930), 49.
120. But compare Leonhard Harding, *Geschichte Afrikas im 19. und 20. Jahrhundert* (Munich: Oldenbourg, 1999), 134.
121. Gesine Krüger, "Das goldene Zeitalter der Viehzüchter: Namibia im 19. Jahrhundert," *Völkermord in Deutsch-Südwestafrika: Der Kolonialkrieg (1904–1908) in Namibia und seine Folgen*, ed. Jürgen Zimmerer and Joachim Zeller (Berlin: Links, 2003), 19.
122. Brigitte Lau, *Southern and Central Namibia in Jonker Afrikaner's time* (Windhoek: Namibian National Archives, 1987), 143.
123. Lau, "Namibia," 32. Lau, *Jonker*, 148.
124. de Pina de Saint-Didier to Ferry, July 16, 1884, AMAE 1CPC / 11.
125. "Erklärung des Häuptlings Josef Fredriks und seines Rates," December 31, 1883, R1001 / 2010.

126. Lau, *Jonker,* 144. Kristin Kjaeret and Kristian Stokke, "Rehoboth Baster, Namibian or Namibian Baster? An analysis of national discourses in Rehoboth, Namibia," *Nations and Nationalism,* vol. 9 (2003), 584.
127. L. Smyth to Lord Derby, November 6, 1883, CO 48 / 507.
128. "German African Expedition," *The Economist,* May 23, 1885, 629.
129. Vogelsang, "Schritte," 45.
130. Lüderitz to Vogelsang, April 21, 1884, *Erschließung,* 88. Townsend, *Rise and Fall,* 128.
131. Copy in Namibian National Archives, NAW, ZBU, 1854, UIVc1bd1, 60; R1001 / 9325.
132. Lüderitz to Theodor von Holleben, July 12, 25, and 27, and August 2, 1883; Viktor von Bojanowski's memos, August 8, August 12, August 15, 1883, R1001 / 1994.
133. *The Holstein Papers,* vol. 2, ed. Norman Rich and M. H. Fisher (Cambridge: Cambridge University Press, 1957), 163. Anton Hellwig's memo, April 12, 1884, R1001 / 1995. J. H. Esterhuyse, *South West Africa, 1880–1894: the establishment of German authority in South West Africa* (Cape Town: Struik, 1968), 37. Compare Robert Cornevin, *Histoire de la colonisation allemande* (Paris: Presses universitaires de France, 1969), 42.
134. Diary of Vogelsang, May 12, 1883, *Erschließung,* 35.
135. Names for the area remained contested for some time. See Birthe Kundrus, *Moderne Imperialisten: das Kaiserreich im Spiegel seiner Kolonien* (Cologne: Böhlau, 2003), 185.
136. Diary entry of Schinz, late November 1884, excerpted in Henrichsen, *Schinz,* 134.
137. *Lagos Observer,* September 27, 1883, 3.
138. *Deutsche Kolonialzeitung,* vol. 1 (Frankfurt 1884), 448. Lüderitz's letter, August 7, 1884, in *Angra Pequeña: Further Correspondence Respecting the Settlement at Angra Pequeña on the South-West Coast of Africa* (London: Eyre and Spottiswoode, 1884), 60.
139. Daniel de Pass to Colonial Office, June 26, 1884, in *Das Staatsarchiv: Sammlung der offiziellen Aktenstücke zur Aussenpolitik der Gegenwart,* vol. 44 (Leipzig: Akademische Verlagsgesellschaft, 1885), 107.
140. Raymond Walter Bixler, *Anglo-German Imperialism in South Africa, 1880–1900* (Columbus: The Ohio State University Press, 1932), 9.
141. Percy Ernst Schramm, *Deutschland und Übersee* (Braunschweig: Westermann, 1950), 312.
142. John Holland Rose, *The Origins of the War, 1871–1914* (Cambridge: Cambridge University Press, 1915), 190.
143. Oskar Lenz, "Monatsbericht," *Mittheilungen des Kais. Königl. Geographischen Gesellschaft in Wien,* vol. 27 (Vienna 1884), 564.
144. "India and Colonies," *Pall Mall Budget,* September 26, 1884, 3.
145. Basil Williams, *Cecil Rhodes* (New York: Holt, 1921), 72.

146. Moritz Busch, *Tagebuchblätter,* vol. 3 (Leipzig: Grunow, 1899), 172.
147. Schüssler, *Lüderitz,* 141.
148. W. Roglie to Heinrich von Kusserow, November 7, 1884, excerpted in Heinrich von Poschinger, "Zur Geschichte," *Deutsche Kolonialzeitung,* vol. 23 (Berlin 1906), 343.
149. Anonymous, "Bechuanaland," in *Encyclopedia Britannica,* vol. 26 (London 1902), 188.
150. Lieutenant Sanders' memo, September 10, 1883, NAW, ZBU, 1860, UIVc5bd1.
151. Anonymous, "Zur Geschichte der deutschen Erwerbung," *Deutsche Kolonialzeitung,* vol. 1 (Frankfurt 1884), 313.
152. Israel Goldblatt, *History of South-West Africa from the Beginning of the Nineteenth Century* (Cape Town: Juta, 1971), 101.
153. Statement by Josef Frederiks, November 24, 1883, NAW, ZBU, 1854, UIVc1bd1, 62. Heinrich Bam's translation of a second declaration by Frederiks, made at Bethanie, December 31, 1883, *Staatsarchiv,* vol. 44 (Leipzig 1885), 141.
154. Anonymous, "Zur Geschichte der deutschen Erwerbung," *Deutsche Kolonialzeitung,* vol. 1, 313.
155. Consul Lippert to Foreign Ministry, September 25, 1883, R1001 / 1994.
156. Lüderitz to Emmy Lüderitz, October 28, 1883, *Erschließung,* 60.
157. "Der 'Daily News'" *Vossische Zeitung,* October 25, 1883.
158. But see "Angra Pequeña," *Cape Argus,* November 3, 1883.
159. E. Walt Wegner, *Aus Deutsch-Afrika!: Tagebuch-Briefe eines jungen Deutschen aus Angra Pequeña (1882–1884)* (Leipzig: Schloemp, 1885), 6.
160. Foreign Ministry to German Colonial Society for Southwest Africa, December 2, 1887, R1001 / 1538.
161. Heinrich von Poschinger, *Stunden bei Bismarck,* vol. 3 (Vienna: Konegen, 1910), 295.
162. Paul von Hatzfeldt to Münster, April 16, 1883, *Weißbuch,* vol. 2 (Berlin 1885), 38.
163. *Holstein Papers,* vol. 2, 163.
164. "Angra Pequeña," *St. James Gazette,* December 31, 1884.
165. Consul Lippert to Foreign Ministry, September 25, 1883, R1001 / 1994.
166. Namibian National Archives at Windhoek, NAW, ZBU, 1854, UIVc1bd1, 61.
167. Heinrich von Göring to Bismarck, September 15, 1887, R1001 / 1538.
168. Anonymous, "Zur Geschichte der deutschen Erwerbung," 313.
169. Schinz to Schinz-Voegeli, December 16, 1884, in Henrichsen, *Schinz,* 25.
170. Gustav Nachtigal to Bismarck, December 9, 1884, R1001 / 1537.
171. Nils Ole Oermann, *Mission, Church, and State Relations in South West Africa under German Rule (1884–1915)* (Stuttgart: Steiner, 1999), 59.
172. Lüderitz to Vogelsang, March 26, 1884, *Erschließung,* 87.
173. Paul Rohrbach, *Dernburg und die Südwestafrikaner* (Berlin: Kolonialverlag, 1911), 46.

174. Schinz to Schinz-Voegeli, December 16, 1884, in Henrichsen, *Schinz*, 25. Compare de Pina de Saint-Didier to Ferry, October 19, 1884, AMAE 1CPC / 11.
175. Sieghard Rost, *Bismarcks Kolonialpolitik im Spiegel der fränkischen Presse* (Erlangen: Friedrich-Alexander-Universität Erlangen, 1956).
176. Lüderitz to Vogelsang, March 26, 1884, *Erschließung*, 87.
177. Bismarck's marginalia to Kusserow's memo, April 8, 1884, R1001 / 1995. For more on spelling, see Bismarck to Nachtigal, May 24, 1884, R1001 / 4194.
178. Kusserow's memo, April 8, 1884, R1001 / 1995. Bojanowski's memo, April 26, 1883, R1001 / 1994.
179. Paul Vasili, *La Société de Berlin* (Paris: Nouvelle revue, 1884), 29.
180. John Richard Seeley, *The expansion of England: two courses of lectures* (Boston: Roberts, 1883), 8.
181. Max Quarck, "Kolonisationsfrage," *Die neue Zeit*, vol. 2 (Stuttgart 1884), 26.
182. "Kolonial-Unternehmungen," *Globus*, vol. 44 (Hildburghausen 1883), 253.
183. Bismarck's memo, August 17, 1883, R1001 / 1994.
184. Diary entry for September 23, 1884, *Holstein Papers*, vol. 2, 163.
185. Bade, *Fabri*, 234.
186. Ronald Robinson, "Imperial Problems in British Politics, 1880–1895," in *The Cambridge History of the British Empire*, ed. E. A. Benians, James Butler, and C. E. Carrington (Cambridge: Cambridge University Press, 1959), 174.
187. Owen Philipps, "Germany and the Palm Kernel Trade," *Journal of African Society*, vol. 14 (1915), 193.
188. K. Onwuka Dike, *Trade and Politics in the Niger Delta, 1830–1885* (Oxford: Clarendon Press, 1956), 97.
189. John E. Flint, *Sir George Goldie and the Making of Nigeria* (London: Oxford University Press, 1960), 11.
190. Hatzfeldt to Richard Wentzel, December 22, 1883, in *Staatsarchiv*, vol. 43, 244.
191. Bismarck to Nachtigal, May 19, 1884, in *Staatsarchiv*, vol. 43, 248.
192. John Bramston to Granville, October 7, 1884, in *Staatsarchiv*, vol. 44, 131.
193. "Kolonisation an der Westküste von Afrika," R1001 / 4192.
194. "Die Borneo-Frage," *Allgemeine Zeitung*, June 21, 1878.
195. E. Brass, "Erwerbung," *Geographische Nachrichten*, vol. 1 (Berlin 1879), 344. Karl August Zehden, "Gedanken," *Deutsche Rundschau*, vol. 5 (Vienna 1883), 85. Adolf Bastian, *Zwei Worte über Colonial-Weisheit von jemandem, dem dieselbe versagt ist* (Berlin: Dümmler, 1883), 13.
196. Carl von Scherzer, *Die deutsche Arbeit in fremden Erdtheilen* (Leipzig: Maier, 1880).
197. R. Allen Lott, *From Paris to Peoria: How European Piano Virtuosos Brought Classical Music to the American Heartland* (Oxford: Oxford University Press, 2003), 259.

198. "Vor längerer Zeit," *Berliner Börsenzeitung,* August 27, 1881. Hans von Lenke to Bismarck, December 1, 1875, R1001 / 7158. "Nouvelles des Pays-Bays," *Indépendance Belge,* May 28, 1880.
199. "Das nördliche Borneo," *Allgemeine Zeitung,* October 4, 1879. Anonymous, "Pflichten des Reiches," *Die Grenzboten,* vol. 42 (Leipzig 1883), 116.
200. Hübbe-Schleiden, *Ethiopien* (Hamburg: Friederichsen, 1879), 340. Hübbe-Schleiden, *Überseeische Politik* (Hamburg: Friederichsen, 1881), 69, 103. Hübbe-Schleiden, *Motive zur Begründung einer Guinea-Companie* (unprinted, December 1882), Niedersächsische Staats—und Universitätsbibliothek Göttingen, Nachlass Hübbe-Schleiden, Cod MS 904, 14.
201. Bade, *Fabri,* 170.
202. Emil Zimmermann, *Unsere Kolonien* (Berlin: Ullstein, 1912), 14.
203. Kusserow to Bismarck, January 9, 1882, PAAA Personalakten 8.384.
204. Heinrich von Poschinger, "Kusserow," *Deutsche Revue,* vol. 33 (Stuttgart 1908), 193. *Holstein Papers,* vol. 2, 159. Helmut Steinsdorfer, *Die Liberale Reichspartei (LRP) von 1871* (Stuttgart: Steiner, 2000), 459. Wehler, *Bismarck,* 437.
205. Hartmut Pogge von Strandmann, "Consequences of the Foundation of the German Empire: Colonial Expansion and the Process of Political-Economic Rationalization," *BEA,* 119.
206. John Martin Kleeberg, *The Disconto-Gesellschaft and German industrialization: a critical examination of the career of a German universal bank 1851–1914* (Oxford: St. Catherine's College, 1988), 181.
207. Heinrich von Kusserow, "Kolonialpolitik," *Deutsche Kolonialzeitung,* vol. 15 (Berlin 1898), 297.
208. Brandt to Bismarck, November 21–23, 1875, R1001 / 7158.
209. John Dill Ross, *Sixty Years: Life and Adventure in the Far East* (London: Hutchinson, 1911), 169.
210. Alan Walker, *Hans von Bülow: A Life and Times* (Oxford: Oxford University Press, 2010), 228.
211. Heinrich von Poschinger, "Zur deutschen Colonial-Politik," *Neue Freie Presse,* December 3, 1899.
212. Alexander von Siebold's diary entries, April 14 and 24, 1879, in *Alexander von Siebold,* vol. 1, 165.
213. "Eine ebenso interessante als überraschende Nachricht," *Berliner Tageblatt,* May 22, 1880. "Deutschland," *Altonaer Nachrichten,* May 22, 1880.
214. G. Schuster, "Von 1878 bis zum Ausscheiden Bismarcks," *Gebhardts Handbuch* (Stuttgart 1890), 793.
215. Bade, *Fabri,* 359n30.
216. "Kolonisation an der Westküste von Afrika," R1001 / 4192.
217. "Deutsches Reich," *Hamburger Nachrichten,* February 13, 1884.
218. F. Sievert, "Kriegsflotte," *Deutsche Kolonialzeitung,* vol. 2 (Berlin 1885), 616. Harry Koenig, *Heiß Flagge!: Deutsche Kolonialgründungen durch SMS 'Elisabeth'* (Leipzig: Voigtländer, 1934), 54. Rutherford Alcock to William Treacher, May 23, 1884, CO 874 / 294.

219. Alfred Zimmermann, *Geschichte der Deutschen Kolonialpolitik* (Berlin: Mittler, 1914), 15.
220. See Hübbe-Schleiden, "British North-Borneo Company," *Colonisations-Politik und Colonisations-Technik*, vol. 1 (Hamburg 1883). Hübbe-Schleiden, *Die Vorbereitung und Entwicklung der British North Borneo Company* (unprinted 1882), Nachlass Hübbe-Schleiden, Cod MS 907, 6.
221. See Bismarck to Adolf von Scholz, January 1, 1880, in *Gesammelte Werke*, vol. 4, ed. Andrea Hopp (Paderborn: Schöningh, 2008), 287.
222. Lothar Bucher to Kusserow, September 27, 1884, in Heinrich von Poschinger, "Kusserow," *Deutsche Revue*, vol. 33 (Stuttgart 1908), 270.
223. Bismarck to Münster, June 10, 1884, R1001 / 1996.
224. Memo of April 8, 1884, R1001 / 1995.
225. Karl von Stengel, "Deutsches Kolonialstaatsrecht," *Annalen des Deutschen Reichs für Gesetzgebung* (Munich 1887), 813.
226. See "Kolonialfrage," *Germania*, May 30, 1884.
227. Viktor Rintelen's speech, March 13, 1885, in *Stenographische Berichte*, 1798. Horst Kohl (ed.), *Die politischen Reden des Fürsten Bismarck*, vol. 1 (Stuttgart: Cotta, 1894), 72. See "Wahlaufruf," Felix Salomon, *Die deutschen Parteiprogramme*, vol. 2 (Leipzig: Teubner, 1912), 42. Wilhelm I to Bismarck, May 7, 1884, *Kaiser Wilhelms des Großen: Briefe, Reden und Schriften* (Berlin: Mittler, 1906), 403.
228. Busch, *Tagebuchblätter*, vol. 1, 103.
229. Anonymous, *Einige Blätter zur Kolonial-Frage* (Berlin: Dümmlers, 1884), 5.
230. Bismarck's speeches on March 2 and 13, 1885, in Kohl, *Die politischen Reden*, vol. 1, 65, 84.
231. Bismarck's note, August 7, 1884; Kusserow to Holstein, August 10, 1884, PAAA Personalakten 8.384.
232. Kusserow to Gerhard Rohlfs, August 14, 1884, *Erschließung*, 73.
233. Lüderitz to Vogelsang, March 26, 1884, *Erschließung*, 87.
234. Bismarck's marginalia on Herbert Bismarck to Otto von Bismarck, June 16, 1884, *Große Politik*, vol. 4, 67.
235. Lüderitz to Vogelsang, April 21, 1884, *Erschließung*, 88.
236. Lüderitz to Foreign Ministry, April 22, 1884, *Erschließung*, 66.
237. Memorandum dated April 8, 1884, R1001 / 1995.
238. J. S. Lumley to Granville, March 31, 1883, *Correspondence Respecting New Guinea* (London 1883), 130.
239. Bill Metcalf, "Utopian Fraud: The Marquis de Rays and La Nouvelle-France," *Utopian Studies* 22 (2011): 104.
240. New Guinea Company to Bismarck, November 18, 1887, R1001 / 2978.
241. New Guinea Company to Bismarck, March 21, 1885, R1001 / 2800.
242. L. H. Gann, "Economic Development," *Colonialism in Africa*, ed. Peter Duignan and L. H. Gann, vol. 4 (New York 1975), 221.
243. Adolf Woermann, *Mission und Branntwein-Handel* (Hamburg: Meißner, 1886). Martin Lynn, *Commerce and Economic Change in West Africa: The Palm*

Oil Trade in the Nineteenth Century (Cambridge: Cambridge University Press, 2002), 123. Hornaday, *Free Rum*, 78. Zahn, 10. Bade, *Fabri*, 187.

244. Max Buchner, *Aurora colonialis: Bruchstücke eines Tagebuchs aus dem ersten Beginn unserer Kolonialpolitik 1884/85* (Munich: Piloty & Loehle, 1914), 4. Günther Jantzen, "Adolph Woermann: Ein politischer Kaufmann in den Wandlungen und Spannungen der imperialistischen Epoche des Reiches," *Europa und Übersee: Festschrift für Egmont Zechlin*, ed. Otto Brunner and Dietrich Gerhard (Hamburg: Hans Bredov-Institut, 1961), 171.
245. Washausen, 70.
246. Woermann to Foreign Ministry, March 1, 1883, R1001 / 4188.
247. See Ralph A. Austen, "Slavery and Slave Trade on the Atlantic Coast: The Duala of the Littoral," *Paideuma* 41 (1995): 128.
248. Compare "Liste des Factoreries Allemandes," April 20, 1885, AMAE 1CPC / 11.
249. For more on Duala, see Ralph A. Austen and Jonathan Derrick, *Middlemen of the Cameroons Rivers: the Duala and their Hinterland, c. 1600–c. 1960* (Cambridge: Cambridge University Press, 1999), 6.
250. Edward Hyde Hewett to Granville, January 14, 1882, *Correspondence Respecting Affairs in Cameroons* (London 1885), 2. Adamou Ndam Njoya, *Le Cameroun dans les relations internationales* (Paris: Librairie générale de droit et de jurisprudence, 1976), 30.
251. Wilhelm Jantzen and Johannes Thormählen, "Vorschläge," *Staatsarchiv*, vol. 43, February 5, 1884, 245. Hans-Georg Wolf, *English in Cameroon* (New York: de Gruyter, 2001), 51.
252. Woermann to Eduard Schmidt, May 6, 1884, R1001 / 4447. Treaty between Bell and Woermann, July 12, 1884; treaty between Dido and Woermann, July 11, 1884; accession of twelve subchiefs to treaty of July 12, 1884, July 15, 1884, R1001 / 9325. See Andreas Eckert, *Grundbesitz, Landkonflikte und kolonialer Wandel: Douala 1880 bis 1960.* (Stuttgart: Steiner, 1999), 71.
253. Kusserow's speech, *Stenographische Berichte*, March 2, 1885, 1501.
254. Bismarck to Wilhelm I, May 20, 1884, R1001 / 4194.
255. Lynn, 63.
256. Overview in Albert Adu Boahen, *African Perspectives on Colonialism* (Baltimore: Johns Hopkins University Press, 1987), 5.
257. Also called "coomie" or "kumi." Hugo Zöller, *Die deutsche Colonie Kamerun*, vol. 2 (Berlin: Spemann, 1885), 127.
258. Julius von Soden to Bismarck, August 29, 1885, R1001 / 3826.
259. Dike, *Trade and Politics*, 68, 157.
260. Johannes Thormählen, "Mittheilungen," October 2, 1884, *Mittheilungen der Geographischen Gesellschaft*, ed. Ludwig Friederichsen (Hamburg 1885), 329.
261. Thormählen, "Mittheilungen," 333.
262. Hewett to Granville, January 14, 1882, in *Correspondence Respecting Affairs in Cameroons*, 2. A. Hemming to Robert Meade, March 8, 1882, CO 879 / 20.
263. Johannes Thormählen to Ernst Bieber, September 18, 1884, R1001 / 4202.

264. Woermann to Schmidt, May 6, 1884, R1001/4447. See Andreas Eckert, "Land Rights, Land Use and Conflicts in Colonial Cameroon: The Case of Douala," in *Our Laws, Their Lands: Land Laws and Land Use in Modern Colonial Societies*, ed. Jap de Moor and Dietmar Rothermund (Münster: LIT, 1994), 25.
265. Ulrike Schaper, *Koloniale Verhandlungen: Gerichtsbarkeit, Verwaltung und Herrschaft in Kamerun 1884–1916* (Frankfurt: Campus, 2012), 42. See Verkijika G. Fanso, "Background to the Annexation of Cameroon 1875–1885," *Abbia*, vol. 30 (1975), 231. See also Eckert, *Grundbesitz*, 93.
266. Hewett to Granville, July 30, 1884, in *Correspondence Respecting Cameroons* (London 1885), 30.
267. Schüssler, 112. Heinrich von Poschinger, *Bismarck und seine Hamburger Freunde* (Hamburg: Verlagsanstalt, 1903), 102. Friedrich Fabri, *Fünf Jahre deutscher Kolonialpolitik* (Gotha: Perthes, 1889), 17.
268. Bohner, *Die Woermanns: Vom Werden deutscher Größe* (Berlin: Die Brücke zur Heimat, 1935), 142.
269. Ibid., 144.
270. Karl Radek, *In den Reihen der deutschen Revolution, 1909–1919* (Munich: Wolff, 1921), 80.
271. Bohner, 143.
272. Koschitzky, *Deutsche Colonialgeschichte*, vol. 2 (Leipzig: Baldamus, 1888), 228.
273. Woermann to Bismarck, April 29, 1884; Bismarck to Wilhelm I, May 20, 1884, R1001/4194.
274. Lüderitz to Foreign Ministry, May 1, 1884, *Erschließung*, 70.
275. Poschinger, *Stunden*, 295. Bismarck to Wilhelm I, May 19, 1884, R1001/4194.
276. Kusserow to Nachtigal, March 29, 1884, R1001/4192. Instructions of April 16, 1884, R1001/4193. Bohner, 143.
277. M. d'Azincourt to Charles de Freycinet, April 23, 1885, AMAE 1CPC/11.
278. Bismarck to Nachtigal, May 19, 1884, *Staatsarchiv*, vol. 43, 246. Treaty of July 13, 1884; Treaty of July 10, 1884, R1001/3403.
279. Bismarck to Nachtigal, May 24, 1884, R1001/9325, R1001/4194.
280. Nachtigal to Foreign Ministry, July 9, 1884, R1001/3403. Edoardo de Launay to Pasquale Stanislao Mancini, July 12, 1884, *I Documenti Diplomatici Italiani* (hereafter *DDI*), vol. 17 (Rome: Istituto poligrafico dello stato, 1994), 289.
281. de Pina de Saint-Didier to Ferry, May 8, 1884, AMAE 1CPC/11.
282. "Angra Pequeña," *Berliner Tageblatt*, May 28, 1884.
283. "Angra Pequeña," *Münchner Neueste Nachrichten*, May 31, 1884.
284. "Reichstagsbericht," *Münchner Neueste Nachrichten*, June 28, 1884.
285. de Pina de Saint-Didier to Ferry, May 8, 1884, AMAE 1CPC/11.
286. Zucker, 190.
287. Buchner, *Aurora Colonialis*, 2.

288. Bismarck to Münster, May 5, 1884, *Grosse Politik*, vol. 4, 50.
289. Bismarck's conversation with Odo Russell, June 9, 1884, Heinrich von Poschinger, *Fürst Bismarck und die Diplomaten, 1852–1890* (Hamburg: Verlagsanstalt, 1900), 422.
290. Herbert Bismarck to Bismarck, June 14, 1884, R1001 / 1995.
291. "Angra Pequeña Affair," *Otago Daily Times*, March 21, 1885.
292. Zucker, 190.
293. Herbert Bismarck to Otto von Bismarck, June 18, 1884, *Staatssekretär*, 239. Ronald Robinson and John Gallagher, *Africa and Victorians* (London: Macmillan, 1965), 207. Odo Russell to Hatzfeldt, July 19, 1884, R1001 / 1997.
294. Mary E. Townsend, *Origins of modern German colonialism, 1871–1885* (New York: Columbia University Press, 1921), 178.
295. *Münchner Neueste Nachrichten*, October 2, 1884. de Pina de Saint-Didier to Ferry, October 2, 1884, AMAE 1CPC / 11.
296. "Aus der Rede des Reichskanzlers," *Staatsarchiv*, vol. 43 (Leipzig 1885), 361. de Pina de Saint-Didier to Ferry, June 19, 1884, AMAE 1CPC / 11.
297. Walker, *Germany and the emigration*, 235. "Parlamentarisches," *Norddeutsche Allgemeine Zeitung*, June 27, 1884.
298. "London," *Norddeutsche Allgemeine Zeitung*, June 26, 1884.
299. "Aus der Rede des Reichskanzlers," 364.
300. Poschinger, *Hamburger*, 102.
301. Compare "Konsul," *Meyer's Konversations-Lexikon*, vol. 10 (Leipzig 1896), 503. See Georg Meyer, *Die Staatsrechtliche Stellung der deutschen Schutzgebiete* (Leipzig: Duncker & Humblot, 1888), 174.
302. "Aus der Rede des Reichskanzlers," 364.
303. Bismarck's speech, April 1, 1895, in *Die gesammelten Werke*, vol. 13 (Berlin 1935), 320.
304. See "Deutsche Südseekolonien," *Deutsche Kolonialzeitung*, vol. 2 (1885), 374.
305. *Stenographische Berichte*, June 26, 1884, 1063. Carl Gotthilf Büttner, "Südafrika," *Deutsche Kolonialzeitung*, vol. 4 (Berlin 1887), 659.
306. See Robert C. Holub, "Imagination," in *The Imperialist Imagination*, ed. Sara Friedrichsmeyer, Sara Lennox, and Susanne Zantop (Ann Arbor: University of Michigan Press, 1998), 33.
307. White, *The Splintered Party*, 119.
308. "Generalversammlung," *Berliner Tageblatt*, September 22, 1884.
309. "German Colonial," *The Times* (London), June 26, 1884, 5.
310. Speech of Eugen Richter, February 4, 1885, in *Stenographische Berichte*, 1083. "Deutscher Reichstag," *Allgemeine Zeitung*, February 6, 1885.
311. *Stenographische Berichte*, June 26, 1884, 1062.
312. "Telegramme," *Allgemeine Zeitung*, February 13, 1885.
313. Proclamation of August 7, 1884, Koenig, *Heiß Flagge!*, 48.

Chapter 5: The Berlin Conference

1. Anonymous, *Aus den Archiven des belgischen Kolonialministeriums*, vol. 1 (Berlin: Mittler, 1918), 64.
2. Maximilien Strauch to William Mackinnon, November 19, 1881, Mackinnon Papers, Reel 19, File 226.
3. Jules Ferry to Edmond van Eetvelde, July 21, 1885, Archives of French Foreign Ministry (hereafter AMAE), 1md/93.
4. Ferry to Brazza, June 26, 1883, AMAE 1md/88.
5. Stanley to Mackinnon, May 10, 1884, Mackinnon Papers, Reel 18, File 217.
6. Dermot Bourke, *De Rebus Africanis* (London: Allen, 1883), 63.
7. Thomas Tomlinson, *Congo Treaty* (London: Stanford, 1884), 9.
8. "Possibilities of Trade," *New York Globe*, August 9, 1884.
9. Strauch to Stanley, February 5, 1883, STAN, #924.
10. Robert Stanley Thomson, *Fondation de l'État Indépendant du Congo: Un chapitre de l'histoire du partage de l'Afrique* (Brussels: Lebègue, 1933), 274.
11. Richard James Hammond, *Portugal and Africa 1815–1910: A Study in Uneconomic Imperialism.* (Stanford, CA: Stanford University Press, 1966), 79.
12. John M. Francis to Frederick Frelinghuysen, May 2, 1884, United States National Archives, RG 59, Despatches from Portugal, vol. 32.
13. Richard Harding Davis, *The Congo and Coasts of Africa* (New York: Scribner's, 1907), 112. Édouard Descamps, *New Africa: an essay on government civilization in new countries, and on the foundation, organization and administration of the Congo Free State* (London: S. Low, 1903), 36.
14. Stanley to Mackinnon, May 10, 1884, Mackinnon Papers, Reel 18, File 217.
15. Bourke, 61.
16. Charles Lennox Wyke to Granville, February 2, 1884, FO 403/37.
17. Compare Strauch to Stanley, March 6, 1883, STAN, #925.
18. M. Cordier to Lucien Brun, August 8, 1883, AMAE 1md/88.
19. Jules Greindl to Jules Devaux, June 1, 2, 1883, Archives du Palais Royal, Brussels (hereafter APR), Fonds Congo, File 2.
20. Chameriau to Paul-Armand Challemel-Lacour, July 2, 1883, AMAE 1md/88.
21. Grant Elliott to Jean-Marie Bayol, January 8, 1885, AMAE 1md/93. See Jelmer Vos, *Kongo in the Age of Empire, 1860–1913: The Breakdown of a Moral Order* (Madison: University of Wisconsin Press, 2015), 89.
22. Meeting protocol, June 9, 1883, AMAE 1md/88.
23. Cordier to Brun, August 8, 1883, AMAE 1md/88.
24. Augustus Sparhawk to Stanley, November 6, 1881, SPAR.
25. Devaux to Sanford, March 27, 1884, SAN, Box 25, Folder 19. J. du Fief, *La question du Congo: depuis son origine jusqu'aujourd'hui* (Brussels 1885), 17.

"Congo Free State," *Scottish Review*, vol. 6 (London 1885), 125. Frederic Goldsmid, "Association," *The Times* (London), January 8, 1884.

26. Anthony Pagden, *Lords of All the World: Ideologies of Empire in Spain, Britain and France* (New Haven, CT: Yale University Press, 1995), 86. Compare Edward Berenson, *Heroes of Empire: Five Charismatic Men and the Conquest of Africa* (Berkeley: University of California Press, 2011), 56.
27. Anonymous, *The Operations of the Association internationale africaine and of the Comité d'études du Haut Congo, from December 1877 to October 1882* (London: Spon, 1883), 25. E. F. G. Law, "International Rivalries in Central Africa," *Fortnightly Review*, vol. 35 (London 1884), 820.
28. Sparhawk to Camille Janssen, October 11, 1881, SPAR.
29. Charles Lennox Wyke to Granville, February 2, 1884.
30. Marquis of Lavradio, *Portugal em África depois de 1851* (Lisbon: Divisão de Publicações e Biblioteca, 1936), 92.
31. Jean Stengers, "King Leopold and Anglo-French Rivalry," in *France and Britain in Africa*, ed. Prosser Gifford and William Roger Louis (New Haven, CT: Yale University Press, 1978), 155.
32. François Bontinck, "L'entente entre la France et l'Association internationale du Congo à la lumière des premières négociations," *Études d'Histoire*, vol. 2 (Kinshasa: Nauwelaerts, 1971), 66.
33. Compare "Notizen," *Das Ausland*, November 19, 1883.
34. Devaux to LII, November 1, 1883, APR, Fonds Congo, File 2.
35. LII to Auguste Beernaert, November 10, 1884, in *Léopold II et Beernaert: d'après leur correspondance inédite de 1884 à 1894*, ed. Édouard van der Smissen, vol. 1 (Brussels: Goemaere, 1920), 113. See P. Ceulemans, "Les tentatives de Leopold II pour engager le Colonel Charles Gordon au service de l'Association Internationale Africaine," *Zaïre* 12 (1958): 251.
36. Strauch to Stanley, October 15, 1884, STAN, #969.
37. Marcel Luwel, *Sir Francis de Winton; administrateur général du Congo, 1884–1886* (Tervuren: Musée royal de l'Afrique centrale, 1964), 163.
38. Jan S. Hogendorn, "Economic Initiative and African Cash Farming: Pre-Colonial Origins and Early Colonial Developments," in *Colonialism in Africa, 1870–1960*, ed. Peter Duignan and L.H. Gann, vol. 4 (London: Cambridge University Press, 1975), 311.
39. Charles Lardy to Emil Welti, October 20, 1884, in *Documents diplomatiques suisses*, vol. 3 (Bern: Benteli, 1987), 578.
40. See Rande W. Kostal, *A Jurisprudence of Power: Victorian Empire and the Rule of Law* (Oxford: Oxford University Press, 2008).
41. Harry Rudin, *Germans in the Cameroons: A Case Study in Modern Imperialism* (New Haven, CT: Yale University Press, 1938), 17.
42. A. Hemming's minute, March 19, 1882, CO 879/20.
43. A. Hemming to Earl of Kimberley, March 9, 1882, CO 879/20. But see C. W. Newbury, "Victorians, Republicans and the Partition of West Africa," *Journal of African History* (hereafter *JAH*) 3 (1962): 493.

44. James Cotton, *Colonies and Dependencies* (London: Macmillan, 1883), 114.
45. J. E. Flint, "Chartered Companies and the Scramble for Africa," in *Africa in the Nineteenth and Twentieth Centuries*, ed. Joseph C. Anene and Godfrey N. Brown (Lagos: Ibadan University Press, 1970), 75.
46. G. N. Sanderson, "British Informal Empire, Imperial Ambitions, Defensive Strategies, and the Anglo-Portuguese Treaty of February 1884" in *Bismarck, Europe, and Africa: the Berlin Africa Conference 1884–1885 and the Onset of Partition* (hereafter *BEA*), ed. Stig Förster, Ronald Robinson, Wolfgang J. Mommsen (Oxford: Oxford University Press, 1988), 212.
47. Strauch to Mackinnon, December 18, 1884, Mackinnon Papers, Reel 18, File 217. "Wie ein uns . . .", *Vossische Zeitung*, November 1, 1883.
48. Stanley to LII, December 29, 1884, STAN, #663.
49. Francis de Winton's memo, March 27, 1884, in Luwel, *Sir Francis*, 217.
50. Devaux to LII, October 25, 1883, APR, Fonds Congo, File 2.
51. Granville to LII, February 4, 1883, APR, Fonds Congo, File 2.
52. French Ambassador at Portugal to Ferry, March 15, 1884, in Ministère des Affaires Étrangères, *Affaires du Congo: 1884–1887* (Paris: Imprimerie nationale, 1890), 30. James Gething to John Bright, March 10, 1884, in *A correspondence on fair trade between Mr. James Gething, Hon. Sec to the Birmingham Fair Trade Union, and the Rt. Hon. John Bright, M.P* (Birmingham: Drew, 1884), 4. Ruth Slade, "Congo Protestant Missions and European Powers before 1885," *Baptist Quarterly*, vol. 16 (1956), 270.
53. Devaux to LII, October 27, 1883, APR, Fonds Congo, File 2.
54. John D. Hargreaves, *West Africa Partitioned*, vol. 1 (Madison: University of Wisconsin Press, 1974), 1.
55. Imre Széchényi to Gustav Kálnoky, June 21, 1884, AT-OeStA/HHStA Diplomatie und Außenpolitik 1848–1918 GKA GsA Berlin 189-3.
56. *Aus den Archiven*, vol. 1, 69, 74. Bismarck to Münster, December 17, 1876, in *Gesammelte Werke*, vol. 2, ed. Rainer Bendick (Paderborn: Schöningh, 2005), 672.
57. Bismarck to Wilhelm I, January 14, 1877, in *Gesammelte Werke*, vol. 3, ed. Michael Epkenhans and Erik Lommatzsch (Paderborn: Schöningh, 2008), 9.
58. Baron von Schmidthals' report, May 13, 1884, in *Aus den Archiven*, vol. 1, 76.
59. Edoardo de Launay to Pasquale Stanislao Mancini, *I Documenti Diplomatici Italiani* (hereafter *DDI*), vol. 17 (Rome: Istituto poligrafico dello stato, 1994), 79. Courcel to Ferry, December 3, 1884, *Documents diplomatiques français* (hereafter *DDF*), vol. 5, 501.
60. Solingen Chamber of Commerce to Bismarck, April 1, 1884, R1001/9039. Münster to Bismarck, March 5, 1884, R1001/9039.
61. Invitation for August 31, 1884, Bleichröder Papers, Baker Business Library, Folder 2, Box 34. Enrico Levi Catellani, *Le colonie e la Conferenza di Berlino* (Turin: Unione tipografico-editrice, 1885), 522.

62. J. Schnakenburg's report, March 5, 1863, PAAA Personalakten 8.380. Kusserow, "Les Devoirs d'un gouvernement neutre," *Revue de Droit International* 6 (1874): 64–77.
63. de Launay to Mancini, March 26, 1884, *DDI,* 121.
64. António de Serpa Pimentel to João de Andrade Corvo, August 20, 1883, AMAE 1md / 88.
65. Kusserow's memo, April 10, 1884, R1001 / 9039. Compare Bismarck's marginalia, April 10, 1884, R1001 / 4108.
66. Bismarck's note, August 7, 1884, PAAA Personalakten 8.384.
67. Edward Malet to Granville, November 13, 1884, FO 84 / 1814. "Colonialpolitik," April 10, 1884, R1001 / 9039. Bleichröder to LII, May 6, 1884, APR, Fonds Congo File 117.
68. Kusserow to Holstein, August 10, 1884, PAAA Personalakten 8.384.
69. Paul von Hatzfeldt to Hohenlohe-Schillingsfürst, April 17, 1884, *Das Staatsarchiv: Sammlung der officiellen Actenstücke zur Geschichte der Gegenwart,* ed. Ernst Delbrück, vol. 45 (Leipzig: Duncker & Humblot, 1886), 4.
70. Ferry to ambassadors, March 15, 1884, *DDF,* vol. 5, 235. Kusserow's memo, April 10, 1884, R1001 / 9039.
71. Paul von Hatzfeldt to Baron von Schmidthals, April 18, 1884, *Das Staatsarchiv,* vol. 45, 6.
72. Kusserow's memo, May 6, 1884, R1001 / 9041. Bismarck's memo, May 29, 1884, R1001 / 9043.
73. Bismarck to Bernhard von Bülow, May 29, 1884, in *Gesammelte Werke,* vol. 6, ed. ed. Ulrich Lappenküper (Paderborn: Schöningh, 2011), 184.
74. Ferry's note, August 22, 1884, *DDF,* vol. 5, 380.
75. Münster to Bismarck, April 29, 1884, *Die Große Politik der europäischen Kabinette 1871–1914,* vol. 4 (Berlin: Deutsche Verlagsgesellschaft, 1922), 50. Compare Ronald Robinson's afterword to *Africa and the Victorians: The Official Mind of Imperialism* (London: Macmillan, 1981), 478.
76. Barbara Emerson, *Leopold II of the Belgians: King of Colonialism* (New York: St. Martin's Press, 1979), 107.
77. G. K. Anton and Christian von Bornhaupt, *Kongostaat und Kongoreform: Zwei Studien über die Entwicklung des Kongostaates* (Leipzig: Duncker & Humblot, 1911), 10. Norman Dwight Harris, *Intervention and Colonization in Africa* (Boston: Houghton Mifflin, 1914), 26.
78. Woermann to Bismarck, October 28, 1884, R1001 / 4197.
79. Woermann to Kusserow, March 3, 1884, R1001 / 9039.
80. Münster to Bismarck, March 21, 1884, R1001 / 9039.
81. Charles Lowe, *Prince Bismarck,* vol. 2 (London: Cassell, 1885), 168.
82. "The Possibilities of Trade," *New York Globe,* August 9, 1884.
83. LII to Bleichröder, July 21, 1884, Bleichröder Papers, Box 34, Folder 1.
84. "England on Congo River," *New York Globe,* April 26, 1884, 2.
85. E. Struck, "Die Weltwirtschaft und die deutsche Volkswirtschaft in den Jahren 1881/1883," *Schmollers Jahrbuch für Gesetzgebung, Verwaltung und*

Volkswirtschaft im Deutschen Reich, vol. 9 (Leipzig: Duncker & Humblot, 1885), 1289.

86. Odo Russell to Granville, April 10, 1884, in Paul Knaplund, *Letters from the Berlin embassy: selections from the private correspondence of British representatives at Berlin and Foreign Secretary Lord Granville: 1871–1874, 1880–1885* (Washington, D.C.: Government Printing Office, 1944), 322.
87. Compare Alphonse de Courcel's meeting with Hatzfeldt, "Mitte April, 1884," in Poschinger, *Bismarck und die Diplomaten*, 421; Courcel to Ferry, April 18, 1884, *DDF*, vol. 5, 258.
88. See Jean Darcy, *L'équilibre africain au XXe siècle* (Paris: Perrin, 1900), 42.
89. LII to Bleichröder, May 4, 1883, APR, Fonds Congo File 2.
90. LII to Bleichröder, May 15, 1884, Bleichröder Papers, Box 34, Folder 1.
91. Gerhard Rohlfs's diary entry, May 11, 1884, in Konrad Guenther, *Gerhard Rohlfs* (Freiburg: Fehsenfeld, 1912), 327. Arthur Stevens to Ferry, January 24, 1884, AMAE 1md / 89.
92. Courcel to Ferry, April 25, 1884, *DDF*, vol. 5, 269.
93. Bismarck to Courcel, September 21, 1884, in *The Scramble for Africa: Documents on the Berlin West African Conference and Related Subjects*, ed. R. J. Gavin and J. A. Betley (Ibadan: Ibadan University Press, 1973), 340. Courcel to Ferry, September 21, 1884, *DDF*, vol. 5, 418.
94. Elfi Bendikat, "The Berlin Conference in the German, French, and British Press," *BEA*, 393.
95. Anonymous, *Sir Travers Twiss et le Congo: réponse à la Revue de Droit international et de Législation comparée et au Law Magazine and Review* (Brussels: Lebègue, 1884), 38.
96. Münster to Bismarck, May 12, 1884, R1001 / 9041. Victor Gantier to Kusserow, May 27, 1884, in Thomson, *Fondation*, 321–326. See also Georg Königk, *Die Berliner Kongo-Konferenz, 1884–1885: ein Beitrag zur Kolonialpolitik Bismarcks* (Essen: Essener Verlagsanstalt, 1938), 78.
97. Bleichröder to LII, May 29, 1884, APR, Fonds Congo File 117.
98. See Sanford to William Mackinnon, February 15, 1885, cited in J. Forbes Munro, *Maritime Enterprise and Empire: Sir William Mackinnon and His Business Empire, 1823–1893* (Suffolk: Boydell, 2003), 368.
99. Count Brandenburg to Bismarck, April 27, 1884, R1001 / 9040. Carl Alexander to Lüderitz, December 8, 1884, *Die Erschließung von Deutsch-Südwest-Afrika durch Adolf Lüderitz: Akten, Briefe und Denkschriften*, ed. C. A. Lüderitz (Oldenburg: Gerhard Stalling, 1945), 80.
100. W. R. Firminger, "How Germany Came into East Africa," *Calcutta Review*, vol. 115 (1902), 303.
101. See John A. Kasson's speech, cited in E. D. Morel's "Address," *Official report of the thirteenth Universal peace congress, held at Boston, Massachusetts, U.S.A.* (Boston: The Peace Congress Committee, 1904), 230.
102. Josef Edmund Jörg, *Historisch-Politische Blätter für das katholische Deutschland*, vol. 94 (Munich: Commission der Literarisch-artistischen Anstalt, 1884),

439, 443. Liselotte Saur, *Die Stellungnahme der Münchner Presse zur Bismarck'schen Kolonialpolitik* (Würzburg: Triltsch, 1940), 49.

103. Émile Weyl, *Le Congo devant l'Europe* (Paris: Dreyfous, 1884), 20.
104. "Auf die Bemerkungen," *Norddeutsche Allgemeine Zeitung*, May 21, 1884.
105. Compare Edward Hertslet's memo, October 18, 1884, FO 84 / 1813. Ferry to Courcel, September 20, 1884, *DDF*, vol. 5, 415.
106. Note, undated (c. June 23, 1884), APR, Fonds Congo, File 135.
107. Bismarck to Münster, May 5, 1884, in *Die große Politik*, vol. 4, 50.
108. Kusserow to Friedrich von Alvensleben, April 24, 1884, R1001 / 9040.
109. Lothar Bucher to Kusserow, September 28, 1884, excerpted in Heinrich von Poschinger, "Zur Geschichte," *Deutsche Kolonialzeitung*, vol. 23 (Berlin 1906), 342.
110. Sanford to Gertrude Sanford, November 16, 1884, SAN, Box 84, Folder 11.
111. See Frederick V. Parsons, *The Origins of the Morocco Question, 1880–1900* (London: Duckworth, 1976), 150. M. de Pina de Saint-Didier to Ferry, October 2, 1884, AMAE 1CPC / 11.
112. See Pierre van Zuylen, *L'Échiquier congolais, ou le Secret du Roi* (Brussels: Dessart, 1959), 61.
113. Bendikat, "The Berlin Conference," 393.
114. Joachim von Holtzendorff's remarks in "Die auswärtige Politik," *Münchner Neueste Nachrichten*, November 15, 1884.
115. Bismarck to Münster, January 25, 1885, *Die große Politik*, vol. 4, 96.
116. W. Bismarck to Holstein, September 1, 1884, *Holstein Papers*, vol. 3, 130. W. Bismarck to Stanley, November 1884, STAN, #3112.
117. LII's memo, STAN, #4788.
118. Gantier to Émile de Borchgrave, May 31, 1884, APR, Fonds Congo File 56. Ferry to Courcel, September 19, 1884, *DDF*, vol. 5, 415.
119. Bismarck and Courcel's conversation, August 28, 1884, in Poschinger, *Bismarck und die Diplomaten*, 423.
120. "Angra Pequeña," *Germania*, May 15 and 30, 1884.
121. Meeting report, June 23, 1884, *RGS* 6: 477.
122. Paul Graf Wolff Metternich to Bismarck, September 3, 1884, R1001 / 9039. Compare Bismarck's letter, May 12, 1884, in Tomlinson, 24.
123. Rohlfs's diary entry, May 11, 1884, in Guenther, *Rohlfs*, 327.
124. Richard Lyons to Granville, December 2, 1884, FO 881 / 5051.
125. "Deutschland und Angra Pequeña," *Deutsche Kolonialzeitung*, vol. 1 (Frankfurt 1884), 303.
126. Kusserow's memo, April 8, 1884, R1001 / 1995. Compare "Angra Pequeña," *Hansa: Zeitschrift für Seewesen*, vol. 21, no. 14 (Hamburg 1884), 111.
127. Harry Hamilton Johnston, *George Grenfell and the Congo*, vol. 1 (London: Hutchinson, 1908), 83.
128. Slade, "Congo Protestant Missions," 212.
129. "Angra Pequeña," *Germania*, May 15, 1884.
130. Strauch to Eduard Pechuël-Loesche, November 1882, STAN, #1010.

131. W. N. Lockington, "General Notes," *The American Naturalist,* vol. 17 (Philadelphia 1883), 1149.
132. Anonymous, "Die afrikanische Gesellschaft," *Wissenschaftliche Beilage der Leipziger Zeitung* (Leipzig 1881), 262.
133. Franz-Josef Schulte-Althoff, *Studien zur politischen Wissenschaftsgeschichte der deutschen Geographie im Zeitalter des Imperialismus* (Paderborn: Schöningh, 1971), 72.
134. Theodor Bohner, *Die Woermanns: vom Werden deutscher Größe* (Berlin: Die Brücke zur Heimat, 1935), 140, 143.
135. Thomson, *Fondation,* 51.
136. "Westafrika," *Münchner Neueste Nachrichten,* August 22, 1884.
137. Descamps, 30.
138. Excerpted in Lyons to Granville, December 2, 1884, FO 881 / 5051.
139. Mancini to de Launay, c. November 15, 1884, *DDI,* 475.
140. de Launay to Mancini, July 12, 1884, *DDI,* 290.
141. Bismarck's memo, July 9, 1884, R1001 / 9044.
142. Kusserow to Holstein, August 10, 1884, PAAA Personalakten 8.384.
143. See Courcel to Ferry, December 14, 1884, AMAE 3md / 173.
144. Sanford to Mackinnon, December 24, SAN, 1884, Box 127, Folder 10. Compare "The Congo Country," *New York Times* (hereafter *NYT*), November 7, 1884; M. d'Azincourt to Charles de Freycinet, May 27, 1885, AMAE 1CPC / 11.
145. See Heinrich von Poschinger, "Kusserow," *Deutsche Revue,* vol. 33 (Stuttgart 1908), 272.
146. Alexander von Schleinitz to Bismarck, June 18, 1884, R1001 / 4194. "Congo Expedition," *Proceedings of RGS,* vol. 8 (1886), 634. Max von Koschitzky, *Deutsche Colonialgeschichte,* vol. 2 (Leipzig: Baldamus, 1888), 323.
147. Anonymous, "Obituary: Dr. Paul Pogge," *Africa,* vol. 7, no. 19 (London 1884), 163. A. T. Brooke to Nowell Salmon, September 30, 1884, in Great Britain, *Correspondence Respecting Affairs in the Cameroons* (London: Harrison, 1885), 53.
148. J. S. Lumley to Granville, November 25, 1882, FO 403 / 14.
149. Bancroft Davis to Sanford, April 22, 1884, SAN, Box 22, Folder 2; Sanford to Nachtigal, May 13, 1884, SAN, Box 29, Folder 14. Hohenlohe-Schillingsfürst to Bismarck, April 26, 1884, R1001 / 9040.
150. Compare Courcel to Ferry, September 21, 1884, *DDF,* vol. 5, 418; Brandenburg to Bismarck, April 25, 1884, R1001 / 9040; May 5, 1884, R1001 / 9041. "Berlin," *National-Zeitung,* April 30, 1884.
151. Alvensleben to Bismarck, May 14, 1884, R1001 / 9041.
152. Excerpts appeared in Law, "International Rivalries," 822. Mancini to de Launay, c. November 15, 1884, *DDI,* 473.
153. See Hertslet's memo, February 1893, FO 403 / 192. See also LII to Jules Ferry, April 19, 1884; Strauch to Ferry, April 23, 1884; Ferry to Strauch, April 24, 1884, all of which are in APR, Fonds Congo, File 2; File 136.

154. Courcel to Ferry, February 3, 1885, *DDF*, vol. 5, 583. R. J. Cornet, "Rapport sur les dossiers," *Bulletin des Séances: Institut Royal Colonial*, vol. 25 (Brussels: Librairie Falk fils, 1954), 564.
155. Ferry to General Appert, December 1, 1884, AMAE 1md / 91. Bleichröder to LII, September 25, 1884, APR, Fonds Congo File 117. Compare Sybil Eyre Crowe, *The Berlin West Africa Conference: 1884–1885* (London: Longmans, 1942), 81.
156. Unsigned memorandum, December 12, 1899, AMAE 1md / 92. Ferry to Count de Montebello, April 28, 1884, *DDF*, vol. 5, 273.
157. Draft of convention between France and AIA, January 1885, AMAE 1md / 92; Ferry to Edmond van Eetvelde, July 21, 1885, AMAE 1md / 93.
158. LII to de Winton, May 26, 1884, in Luwel, *Sir Francis*, 216.
159. Hence the rumor in "The Congo Discussions," *NYT*, December 31, 1884.
160. LII to Bleichröder, July 21, 1884, Bleichröder Papers, Box 34, Folder 1.
161. Devaux to Sanford, April 10, 1884, SAN, Box 25, Folder 19.
162. Bismarck to Münster, June 7, 1884, FO 84 / 1811. Liane Ranieri, *Les relations entre l'État indépendant du Congo et l'Italie* (Brussels: Académie royale des sciences coloniales, 1959), 25.
163. Brandenburg to Bismarck, June 28, 1884, paraphrased in *Aus den Archiven*, 136.
164. Camille Coquilhat, *Sur le Haut-Congo* (Paris: Lebegue, 1888), 403.
165. LII to Brandenburg, June 27, 1884, in Cornet, 593. de Winton's memo, March 27, 1884, Luwel, *Sir Francis*, 217. de Winton to Stanley, May 5, 1884, STAN, #1036.
166. Journal entry, May 6, 1884 in Dundas Museum and Archives, Lesslie Family Fonds, Box 2, Folder 20.
167. Thomson, *Fondation*, 181.
168. LII to Bleichröder, July 21, 1884, Bleichröder Papers, Box 34, Folder 1.
169. Bismarck to LII, July 2, 1884, R1001 / 9044. Thomas Villiers Lister's memo, July 17, 1884, FO 403 / 39.
170. Gerson Bleichröder to Hatzfeldt, July 24, 1884, Gerhard Ebel (ed.), *Botschafter Graf Paul von Hatzfeldt: Nachgelassene Papiere 1838–1901*, vol. 1 (Boppard: Boldt, 1976), 440.
171. "Geographentag," *Verhandlungen der Gesellschaft für Erdkunde*, vol. 12 (Berlin 1885), 232. Koschitzky, *Colonialgeschichte*, vol. 2, 324. "West African Problems," *NYT*, January 21, 1885.
172. Brandenburg to Strauch, June 10, 1884, APR, Fonds Congo, File 116.
173. LII to Bleichröder, September 16, 1884, APR, Fonds Congo, File 117. Holstein to Herbert Bismarck, August 31, 1884, *Staatssekretär Graf Herbert von Bismarck: Aus seiner politischen Privatkorrespondenz*, ed. Walter Bussmann (Göttingen: Vandenhoeck & Ruprecht, 1964), 257.
174. Bismarck to LII, June 20, 1884, R1001 / 9044.
175. LII to Bleichröder, August 3, 1884, Bleichröder Papers, Box 34, Folder 1.

176. Bleichröder to LII, August 12, 1884; Bismarck to LII, Sep. 4, 1884, APR, Fonds Congo, Files 117–116. Compare Alvey A. Adee to Roosevelt, October 12, 1904, Theodore Roosevelt Papers, Reel 49, LOC.
177. LII to Bleichröder, August 8, 1884, APR, Fonds Congo, File 117.
178. Bleichröder to LII, August 11, 1884, APR, Fonds Congo, File 117.
179. René de Maximy and Marie-Christine Brugaillère, "Un roi-homme d'affaires, des géographes et le tracé des frontières de l'État indépendant du Congo (Zaïre)," in *Herodote* 41 (1986): 46.
180. But see John A. Kasson, "John A. Kasson, An Autobiography" *Annals of Iowa* 12 (1920): 355.
181. See Ludwig Bauer, *Leopold the Unloved: King of the Belgians and of Money* (Boston: Little, Brown, & Co., 1935), 106.
182. Courcel to Ferry, September 21, 1884, *DDF*, vol. 5, 422.
183. *Aus den Archiven*, 136.
184. Eugène Beyens's memo, July 1884, APR, Fonds Congo, File 2.
185. Crowe, 86. Adam Hochschild, *King Leopold's Ghost* (Boston: Houghton Mifflin, 1998), 83.
186. Stanley to Harold Frederic, July 24, 1885, STAN, #6961.
187. Bismarck to Hohenlohe-Schillingsfürst, August 29, 1884, *Staatsarchiv*, vol. 42 (Leipzig 1884), 254.
188. Sanford to Mackinnon, December 24, 1884, SAN, Box 127, Folder 10.
189. Gantier to Borchgrave, April 29, 1884, APR, Fonds Congo, File 56.
190. Ranieri, 25.
191. Bleichröder to LII, October 6, 1884, APR, Fonds Congo, File 117.
192. German convention with association in R1001 / 9047.
193. Borchgrave to Gantier, May 20, 1884 and Gantier to Borchgrave, May 24, 1884, APR, Fonds Congo, File 56.
194. "Congofrage," *Hamburgischer Correspondent*, May 12, 1884 and attached note, R1001 / 9041.
195. "Politischer Tagesbericht," *Norddeutsche Allgemeine Zeitung*, May 6 and May 10, 1884. "Kongo-Assoziation," *Norddeutsche Allgemeine Zeitung*, May 22, 1884.
196. Travers Twiss, "La Libre Navigation du Congo," *Revue de droit international*, vol. 15 (Brussels 1883), 551.
197. Bleichröder to Hatzfeldt, January 10, 1885, in Ebel, 445.
198. Bismarck to Münster, January 25, 1885, in *German Diplomatic Documents*, ed. E. T. S. Dugdale, vol. 2 (New York: Harper, 1929), 189.
199. Holstein to Herbert Bismarck, August 31, 1884, *Staatssekretär*, 250.
200. Malet to Granville, December 1, 1884, FO 403 / 48.
201. Compare Teobaldo Filesi, "Preludio alla Conferenza di Berlino: La Posizione Dell'Italia," *Rivista trimestrale di studi e documentazione dell'Istituto italiano per l'Africa e l'Oriente* 39 (1984): 554.
202. Hartmut Pogge von Strandmann, "Domestic Origins of Germany's Colonial Expansion under Bismarck," *Past and Present* 42 (1969): 140–159.

203. Paul Vasili, *La Société de Berlin* (Paris: Nouvelle revue, 1884), 30.
204. Hans Spellmeyer, *Deutsche Kolonialpolitik im Reichstag* (Stuttgart: Kohlhammer, 1931), 16.
205. "Dem Reichstage," *Norddeutsche Allgemeine Zeitung*, February 16, 1885. But compare Hans-Ulrich Wehler, *Bismarck und der Imperialismus* (Cologne: Kiepenheuer & Witsch, 1969), 479; Heinrich von Treitschke, "Die ersten Versuche deutscher Kolonialpolitik," in *Deutsche Kämpfe: Neue Folge: Schriften zur Tagespolitik* (Leipzig: Hirzel, 1896), 335.
206. Max Weber to Hermann Baumgarten, November 8, 1884, in Max Weber, *Jugendbriefe* (Tübingen: Mohr, 1936), 142.
207. Fritz Stern, *Gold and Iron: Bismarck, Bleichröder, and the Building of the German Empire* (New York: Knopf, 1977), 411.
208. Malet's report, December 1, 1884, Poschinger, *Bismarck und die Diplomaten*, 425. "Our Policy in South Africa," *The Times* (London), January 2, 1885.
209. Malet to Granville, December 6, 1884, FO 343 / 6.
210. M. de Pina de Saint-Didier to Ferry, October 19, 1884, AMAE 1CPC / 11.
211. Bismarck to Wilhelm I, December 21, 1884, in *Gesammelte Werke*, vol. 6 (Paderborn: Schöningh, 2011), 413.
212. Eduard von Knorr to Foreign Ministry, December 25, 1884, R1001 / 4205. Carl Scholl to his father, December 30, 1884, in Carl Scholl, *Nach Kamerun! Aus den hinterlassenen Papieren meines in Kamerun gestorbenen Sohnes* (Leipzig: Cavael, 1886), 38.
213. Hugo Zöller, *Die deutsche Colonie Kamerun*, vol. 2 (Berlin: Spemann, 1885), 172–207.
214. "Der Reichstag," *Berliner Börsenzeitung*, November 20, 1884. "Politischer Tagesbericht," *Norddeutsche Allgemeine Zeitung*, November 20, 1884.
215. Ernst Bieber's memo, September 25, 1884, R1001 / 4195.
216. Georg Arbogast von und zu Franckenstein and Franz August Schenk von Stauffenberg's speeches to Reichstag, in *Stenographische Berichte*, January 20, 1885, 743.
217. "Politische Nachrichten," *Berliner Börsenzeitung*, November 22, 1884. "Erklärung des Reichskanzlers," *Allgemeine Zeitung*, February 14, 1884.
218. "Die deutschen Schutzgebiete," *Die Grenzboten*, vol. 45 (Leipzig 1886), 256.
219. Devaux to Sanford, April 27, 1884, SAN, Box 25, Folder 19.
220. "War in Congo," *New York Times*, December 29, 1884.
221. Malet to Granville, February 16, 1885, FO 403 / 50.
222. Malet to Granville, December 15, 1884, FO 403 / 48.
223. Moritz Busch, *Tagebuchblätter*, vol. 3 (Leipzig: Grunow, 1899), 178.
224. M. d'Azincourt to Charles de Freycinet, April 23, 1885, AMAE 1CPC / 11.
225. Sanford to Gustav Nachtigal, May 13, 1884, Box 29, Folder 19, SAN.
226. Compare T. V. Lister's note, July 17, 1884, FO 403 / 39. Friedrich Fabri, "Kolonialpolitische Skizzen," *Deutsche Kolonialzeitung*, vol. 5 (Berlin 1888), 87.
227. Széchényi to Kálnoky, July 5, 1884, AT-OeStA / HHStA Diplomatie und Außenpolitik 1848–1918 GKA GsA Berlin 189-3.

228. *Neueste Mittheilungen,* June 26, 1884, ed. H. Klee (Berlin 1884), 4. This, *pace* Jörg Fisch, "Africa as terra nullius: The Berlin Conference and International Law," *BEA,* 352.
229. Schulte-Althoff, 109.
230. Woermann to Bismarck, October 28, 1884, R1001/4197. See Gordon Alexander Craig, *Germany, 1866–1945* (New York: Oxford University Press, 1978), 122.
231. Bieber to Bismarck, September 11 and 12, 1884, R1001/4195. See Jens Lauris Christensen, *Gegen unsere Kolonialpolitik: ein ruhiges Wort in bewegter Zeit* (Zürich: Verlags-Magazin, 1885).
232. Arthur J. Knoll, *Togo under Imperial Germany 1884–1914: A Case Study in Colonial Rule* (Stanford, CA: Hoover Institution Press, 1978), 20.
233. Otto Becker, *Bismarcks Ringen um Deutschlands Gestaltung* (Heidelberg: Quelle & Meyer, 1958), 116.
234. See Paul M. Kennedy, *The Samoan Tangle: A Study in Anglo-German-American Relations, 1878–1900* (Dublin: Irish University Press, 1974).
235. "Angra Pequeña," *Germania,* June 28, 1884. "In der 'Cap-Times,'" *Berliner Tageblatt,* November 7, 1884.
236. Eugen Richter's speech to Reichstag, *Stenographische Berichte,* February 4, 1885, 1083.
237. Holstein to Herbert Bismarck, August 17, 1884, *Staatssekretär,* 250. Friedrich Engels to August Bebel, October 11, 1884, *Briefe an Bebel* (Berlin: Dietz, 1958), 93. Ludwig von Pastor, *August Reichensperger, 1808–1895: Sein Leben und sein Wirken auf dem Gebiet der Politik, der Kunst und der Wissenschaft,* vol. 2 (Freiburg: Herder, 1899), 218. Stanley Zucker, *Ludwig Bamberger: German Liberal Politician and Social Critic, 1823–1899* (Pittsburgh: University of Pittsburgh Press, 1975), 190.
238. Wilhelm Liebknecht's speech to Reichstag, *Stenographische Berichte,* March 4, 1885, 1540. Wilhelm Liebknecht, "Parteien," *Der Sozialdemokrat,* January 29, 1885.
239. Anonymous memo, *Das Staatsarchiv,* vol. 43 (Leipzig 1885), 271. Syndicate to Bismarck, October 15, 1884, R1001/4203.
240. Bismarck's speech to Reichstag, *Stenographische Berichte,* November 28, 1885, 117.
241. Henry Shelton Sanford to Gertrude Sanford, November 24, 1884, SAN, Box 84, Folder 11.
242. Bieber to Bismarck, September 18, 1884, R1001/4196.
243. Erwin Wiskemann, *Hamburg und die Welthandelspolitik* (Hamburg: Friederichsen, 1929), 228. Heinrich von Poschinger, "Kusserow," *Deutsche Revue,* vol. 33 (Stuttgart 1908), 193. *Holstein Papers,* vol. 2, 272.
244. Eugen Richter to Reichstag, *Stenographische Berichte,* February 4, 1885, 1083.
245. Woermann to Bismarck, October 11, 1884, R1001/4196.
246. Woermann to Reichstag, *Stenographische Berichte,* February 4, 1885, 1083. Speech of Max Kayser, *Stenographische Berichte,* March 23, 1886, 1616.

247. Emil Schulze to Woermann, July 10, 1884, R1001 / 4202. Bismarck to Wilhelm I, September 14, 1884, R1001 / 4109. Max Buchner to Knorr, December 19, 1884, R1001 / 4025.
248. Schulze to Woermann and Bismarck to Caprivi, November 26, 1884, R1001 / 4198.
249. Max Buchner to Julius von Soden, July 1885, R1001 / 4213.
250. Baptist Missionary Society of England to Bismarck, March 1886, BMSA, Reel 31.
251. Woermann to Eduard Schmidt, May 6, 1884 and Schmidt to Woermann, July 29, 1884, R1001 / 4447.
252. Eduard Woermann, "Aus dem Tagebuch von Eduard Woermann," *Das deutsche Kolonialbuch,* ed. Hans Zache (Berlin: Andermann, 1925), 261. Bohner, 145.
253. Schmidt to Woermann, July 29, 1884, R1001 / 4447.
254. See Ulrike Hamann and Stefanie Michels, "From Disagreement to Dissension: African Perspectives on Germany," in *Racisms Made in Germany,* ed. Wolf D. Hund, Christian Koller, and Moshe Zimmermann (Berlin: LIT, 2011), 147.
255. Foreign Ministry to Justice Ministry, June 11, 1885, R3001 / 5246.
256. Gustav von Oertzen to Bismarck, September 1, 1885, R1001 / 2670.
257. Karl Heinrich von Boetticher to Hatzfeldt, September 23, 1884, R1001 / 9046. *Stenographische Berichte,* February 4, 1885, 1083. Knoll, 26.
258. Borchgrave to Stanley, November 27, 1885, STAN, #730.
259. John A. Kasson to Sanford, SAN, Box 25, Folder 4.
260. Stanley, *CFFS,* vol. 2, 399.
261. "Politische Nachrichten," *Berliner Börsenzeitung,* November 15, 1884. "Deutscher Kolonialverein," in *Deutsche Kolonialzeitung,* vol. 1 (Frankfurt 1885), 483.
262. "Kongogebiet," *Münchner Neueste Nachrichten,* September 27, 1884.
263. Sanford to Gertrude Sanford, November 15, SAN, Box 84, Folder 11. Stanley's notes, January 7, 1885, STAN, #4786.
264. "Stanley," *Export: Organ des Centralvereins für Handelsgeographie und Förderung deutscher Interessen im Auslande,* vol. 6 (Berlin: Pass, 1884), 774.
265. "Herr Stanley," *Deutsche Kolonialzeitung,* vol. 2, 62.
266. "Stanley," *Export,* 775.
267. Stanley, *CFFS,* vol. 2, 387.
268. Stanley to Joseph Hutton, December 13, 1884, in United States Senate Committee on Foreign Affairs, *Participation of the United States in the Congo Conference* (Washington, D.C.: Government Printing Office, 1885), 12.
269. Stanley to Sanford, January 3, 1885, SAN, Box 27, Folder 5.
270. Dorothy Tennant to Stanley, August 30, 1911, STAN, #6717.
271. Wilhelm Bismarck to Stanley, undated (November 1884), STAN, #3192.
272. Adolf Bastian, *Einige Blätter zur Kolonial-Frage* (Berlin: Dümmler, 1884), 40.

273. Woermann to Bismarck, October 11, 1884, R1001 / 4196. Woermann to Bismarck, October 15, 1884, R1001 / 4203.
274. Pierre Daye, *Stanley* (Paris: Grasset, 1936), 186. Compare "Founding of Congo State," *The Times* (London), May 26, 1885.
275. Heinrich von Poschinger, *Fürst Bismarck und die Parlamentarier,* vol. 1 (Breslau: Trewendt, 1894), 274.
276. M. de Pina de Saint-Didier to Ferry, November 14, 1884, AMAE 1CPC / 11.
277. Woermann to Wilhelm Bismarck, October 12, 1884, R1001 / 4203.
278. Bismarck to Hansemann, August 20, 1884, R1001 / 2790.
279. Bieber's memo, September 25, 1884. R1001 / 4195.
280. Compare Buchner's memo, April 17, 1885, R1001 / 4212. Knorr to Caprivi, December 25, 1884, German Federal Archive Freiburg (Bundesarchiv Militärarchiv Freiburg), RM 1 / 2725.
281. Hans-Peter Jaeck, "Die deutsche Annexion," *Kamerun unter deutscher Kolonialherrschaft,* ed. Helmuth Stoecker (Berlin: Rütten and Loening, 1960), 72.
282. Wilhelm Roscher, *Kolonien, Kolonialpolitik und Auswanderung* (Leipzig: Winter, 1885), 1, 251, 285, 400.
283. Charles Lowe, *Bismarck's Table-Talk* (London: Grevel, 1895), 259.
284. Compare Pierre Decharme, *Compagnies et sociétés coloniales allemandes* (Paris: Masson, 1903), 47.
285. Kasson to Frederick Frelinghuysen, November 15, 1884, *Correspondence in Relation to Affairs of Independent State* (Washington, D.C.: Government Printing Office, 1886), 23.
286. Ernst Jacob, *Deutsche Kolonialpolitik in Dokumenten: Gedanken und Gestalten aus den letzten 50 Jahren* (Leipzig: Dieterich, 1938), 136.
287. Münster to Granville, November 1, 1884, R1001 / 4113.
288. Gantier to Borchgrave, September 10, 1884, APR, Fonds Congo, File 56.
289. Baron Plessen to Granville, October 8, 1884, FO 84 / 1813.
290. See Henk Wesseling, *A Cape of Asia: Essays on European History* (Amsterdam: Leiden University Press, 2011), 54. Invitation to Sanford, January 27, 1885, SAN, Box 29, Folder 12.
291. Crowe, 192.
292. Compare Édouard Viard, *Explorations africaines: Au bas-Niger* (Paris: Guérin, 1885), i.
293. "Berliner-Konferenz," *Die National-Zeitung,* October 15, 1884.
294. "Anglo-German Policy in Africa," *Pall Mall Budget,* October 17, 1884. Credit for source to William Roger Louis, "The Berlin Congo Conference," in *France and Britain in Africa: Imperial Rivalry and Colonial Rule,* ed. Prosser Gifford and William Roger Louis (New Haven, CT: Yale University Press, 1971), 180.
295. William L. Langer, *European Alliances and Alignments, 1871–1890* (New York: Knopf, 1962), 303.

296. Hedley Bull, "European States and African Political Communities," in *The Expansion of International Society,* ed. Hedley Bull and Adam Watson (Oxford: Clarendon Press, 1984), 110.
297. Edmond Fitzmaurice, *The Life of Granville George Leveson Gower, Second Earl Granville,* vol. 2 (London: Longman, 1905), 375. Münster's telegram, November 12, 1884, and Wilhelm Koner to Bismarck, November 12, 1884, R1001 / 4142.
298. Granville to Malet, October 11, 1884, PAAA London 388.
299. Lardy to Welti, October 20, 1884, in *Documents diplomatiques suisses,* vol. 3 (Bern: Benteli, 1987), 577.
300. Lyons to Granville, October 17, 1884, in Thomas Wodehouse Legh, *Lord Lyons: A Record of British Diplomacy,* vol. 2 (London: Arnold, 1913), 334. Courcel to Ferry, December 3, 1884, AMAE 3md / 173.
301. Eber Carroll, *French Public Opinion and Foreign Affairs, 1870–1914* (New York: Century, 1931), 99.
302. Hans Lothar von Schweinitz, *Denkwürdigkeiten des Botschafters General v. Schweinitz,* vol. 2 (Berlin: Hobbing, 1927), 290.
303. The former point was argued by S. E. Crowe. For the latter, see Malet to Bismarck, November 14, 1884, R1001 / 4147.
304. Courcel to Ferry, November 22, 1884, *DDF,* vol. 5, 477.
305. Charles de Chavannes to Francis de Winton, November 12, 1884 and February 4, 1885; Édouard Destrain to Elliott, December 26, 1884, AMAE 1md / 93.
306. Sanford to Gertrude Sanford, November 13, 1884, SAN, Box 84, Folder 11.
307. Hatzfeldt to Bismarck, December 12, 1884, R1001 / 4169. Courcel to Ferry, November 23, 1884, AMAE 3md / 173. Bismarck to Crown Prince, December 22, 1884, R1001 / 9048.
308. Courcel to Ferry, November 22, 1884, *DDF,* vol. 5, 477.
309. Sanford's memo, December 1884, SAN, Box 29, Folder 3.
310. Courcel to Ferry, December 23, 1884, *DDF,* vol. 5, 519. LII to Bleichröder, November 29, 1884, Bleichröder Papers, Box 34, Folder 1.
311. Courcel to Ferry, December 12, 1884 and Ferry to French Ambassador at Portugal, December 13, 1884, *DDF,* vol. 5, 512.
312. Courcel to Ferry, December 11, 1884, AMAE 1md / 92.
313. LII to Sanford, January 22, 1885, unindexed personal note, SAN.
314. Courcel to Hatzfeldt, December 5, 1884, *DDF,* vol. 5, 506.
315. "Die Conferenz," *Berliner Börsenzeitung,* November 16, 1884. "The West African Conference," *The Times* (London), January 21, 1885. "Placement," February 26, 1885, R1001 / 4141.
316. Ranieri, 44.
317. Carl Schmitt, *The Nomos of the Earth: In the International Law of the Jus Publicum Europaeum* (New York: Telos, 2006), 216.
318. Sanford to Gertrude Sanford, November 22, 1884, SAN, Box 84, Folder 11.

319. Crown Princess to Lady Mary Elizabeth Ponsonby, October 17, 1884, *Letters of Empress Frederick,* ed. Frederick Ponsonby (London: Macmillan, 1928), 194.
320. Billy Gene Hahs, *Spain and the Scramble for Africa: The "Africanistas" and the Gulf of Guinea* (Albuquerque: University of New Mexico, 1980), 235.
321. November 2, 1884 entry, *Denkwürdigkeiten des Fürsten Chlodwig zu Hohenlohe-Schillingsfürst,* vol. 2, ed. Friedrich Curtius (Stuttgart: Deutsche Verlagsanstalt, 1907), 351.
322. Sanford to Gertrude Sanford, November 8, 1884, Box 84, Folder 11.
323. Sanford to Gertrude Sanford, February 16, 1885, SAN, Box 85, Folder 2.
324. Rennell Rodd, *Social and Diplomatic Memories, 1884–1893* (London: Arnold, 1922), 71.
325. December 27, 1884 entry, *Das Tagebuch der Baronin Spitzemberg,* ed. Rudolf Vierhaus (Göttingen: Vandenhoeck & Ruprecht, 1989), 212.
326. Crowe, 5.
327. See, for example, Francis H. Hinsley, *Power and the Pursuit of Peace* (Cambridge: Cambridge University Press, 1963), 256. See also Matthew Craven, "Between law and history: the Berlin Conference of 1884–1885 and the logic of free trade," *London Review of International Law* 3 (2015): 33.
328. Busch's memo, January 6, 1885, R1001 / 4153.
329. Stephen Lucius Gwynn, *The Life of the Rt. Hon. Sir Charles W. Dilke,* vol. 2 (London: Murray, 1917), 85.
330. Sanford to Gertrude Sanford, November 14, 1884, SAN, Box 84, Folder 11.
331. For more on the latter, see Mostafa Minawi, *The Ottoman Scramble for Africa: Empire and Diplomacy in the Sahara and the Hijaz* (Stanford, CA: Stanford University Press, 2016), 144.
332. Johann Kurzreiter, "Österreich-Ungarn und die Kongofrage 1884–1885," *Mitteilungen des Österreichischen Staatsarchivs* 46 (1998): 67.
333. Walter Sauer, "Habsburg Colonial: Austria-Hungary's Role in European Overseas Expansion," *Austrian Studies* 20 (2012): 20.
334. A. W. Thayer's report, January 24, 1882, *Reports from Consuls of United States on Commerce,* vol. 15 (Washington, D.C.: Government Printing Office, 1882), 537.
335. Foreign Ministry to Kálmán Tisza, October 25, 1884, AT-OeStA / HHStA Diplomatie und Außenpolitik 1848–1918 GKA GsA Berlin 189–3. Edouard Mambu ma Khenzu, *A Modern History of Monetary and Financial Systems of Congo, 1885–1995* (Lewiston: Edwin Mellen, 2006), 57.
336. Mancini to de Launay, c. November 15, 1884, *DDI,* 468.
337. Henk Wesseling, "The Netherlands and the Partition of Africa," *JAH* 22 (1981): 495. Compare Alvensleben to Bismarck, May 11, 1884, R1001 / 9041. Count van Bylandt to Dirk Arnold Willem van Tets van Goudriaan, November 5, 1882, in *Bescheiden betreffende,* part 2, vol. 3 (Gravenhage 1967), 308. Hahs, 237.

338. G. N. Sanderson, "The Nile Basin and the Eastern Horn, 1870–1908," in *The Cambridge History of Africa*, vol. 6, ed. R. O. Oliver and G. N. Sanderson (Cambridge: Cambridge University Press, 1985), 657. Jonathan A. Grant, *Rulers, Guns, and Money: The Global Arms Trade in the Age of Imperialism* (Cambridge, MA: Harvard University Press, 2007), 38.
339. "Die Conferenz," *Berliner Börsenzeitung*, November 16, 1884. Crowe, 11. Eric D. Weitz, "From the Vienna to the Paris System: International Politics and the Entangled Histories of Human Rights, Forced Deportations, and Civilizing Missions," *The American Historical Review* 113 (2008): 1313.
340. Courcel to Ferry, October 1, 1884, *DDF*, vol. 5, 435. Crowe, 221.
341. Count van Bylandt to Joseph van der Does de Willebois (attachments), October 17, 1884, *Bescheiden betreffende*, part 2, vol. 3, 716.
342. de Launay to Count Robilant, November 28, 1884, *DDI*, 520.
343. See M. Kuitenbrouwer, *The Netherlands and the Rise of Modern Imperialism: Colonies and Foreign Policy 1850–1902* (New York: Berg, 1991), 134.
344. Ranieri, 27. Selim Deringil, "Les ottomans et le Partage de l'Afrique," *Ottomans, the Turks and World Power Politics*, ed. Selim Deringil (Istanbul: Isis Press, 2000), 49. Hatzfeldt to Bülow, June 5, 1884, R1001 / 9043. Bismarck's memo, October 16, 1884, R1001 / 4111.
345. Chart for dinner of January 14, 1885, R1001 / 4144.
346. Sanford to Gertrude Sanford, November 18, 19, 24, and December 5, 1884, Box 84, Folder 12, SAN. See ball records in German Federal Archive, R1001 / 4143. "Kongo-Konferenz," *Münchner Neueste Nachrichten*, November 18, 1884.
347. Courcel to Ferry, October 1, 1884, *DDF*, vol. 5, 435. Hatzfeldt to Granville, November 2, 1884, PAAA London 388.
348. Kusserow's memo, November 11, 1884, R1001 / 4147.
349. Fabri, "Kolonialpolitische Skizzen," 85. Széchényi to Kálnoky, December 23, 1884, AT-OeStA / HHStA Diplomatie und Außenpolitik 1848–1918 GKA GsA Berlin 189-3.
350. Protocol of July 31, 1884, *Das Staatsarchiv*, vol. 46, 46. Ranieri, 27.
351. See George Louis Beer, *African Questions at the Paris Peace Conference* (New York: Macmillan, 1923), 280. Kasson to Sanford, October 30, 1884, Box 25, Folder 4, SAN.
352. "Wir sind in der Lage," *Norddeutsche Allgemeine Zeitung*, November 15, 1884.
353. December 1, 1884 entry, *Spitzemberg*, 211.
354. Sanford to Gertrude Sanford, November 18 and 22, 1884, Box 84, Folder 11, SAN. Ranieri, 34.
355. Copy of recognition letter in R1001 / 4120. Széchényi to Kálnoky, May 10, 1884, AT-OeStA / HHStA Diplomatie und Außenpolitik 1848–1918 GKA GsA Berlin 189-3.
356. "West African Conference," *The Times* (London), November 20, 1884. Ranieri, 29.
357. Sanford's memo, January 15, 1885, SAN, Box 29, Folder 2.

358. Jules Ferry had a role in the naming. Strauch to Sanford, undated, Box 31, Folder 3, SAN.
359. Sanford to LII, January 15, 1885, SAN, Box 29, Folder 2.
360. Jules Malou to Beernaert, October 26, 1884, *Léopold II et Beernaert,* vol. 1, 115.
361. Compare proposal by Association, February 1885, AMAE 1md / 92.
362. Memo for Alexandre Peyron, January 10, 1885, AMAE 1md / 92.
363. Grant Elliott to Jean-Marie Bayol, December 3, 1884, AMAE 1md / 93.
364. Sanford to Gertrude Sanford, November 26, 1884, Box 84, Folder 12, SAN.
365. "Politische Nachrichten," *Berliner Börsenzeitung,* November 22 and 23, 1884. Descamps, 31.
366. Crowe, 143.
367. Sanford to Gertrude Sanford, November 14, 1884. Széchényi to Kálnoky, December 6, 1884, AT-OeStA / HHStA Diplomatie und Außenpolitik 1848–1918 GKA GsA Berlin 189-3.
368. Sanford to Gertrude Sanford, November 24, 1884.
369. Émile Banning, *Mémoires politiques et diplomatiques* (Brussels: La Renaissance du livre, 1927), 15. Sanford to Gertrude Sanford, November 13 and 18, 1884. Strauch to Sanford, February 1, 1885, Box 27, Folder 13.
370. Compare General Appert to Ferry, November 30, 1884, AMAE 1md / 92.
371. Sanford to Gertrude Sanford, November 22, 1884, Box 84, Folder 11.
372. "Personal and General," *Huntsville Gazette,* November 22, 1884, 1.
373. Sanford to Gertrude Sanford, November 22, 1884. "Die Conferenz," *Berliner Börsenzeitung,* November 16, 1884. Records of maps, etc. can be found in German Federal Archive Berlin, R1001 / 4143.
374. Hohenlohe-Schillingsfürst to Bismarck, November 15, 1884, R1001 / 4142.
375. Sanford to Gertrude Sanford, November 15, 1884, SAN, Box 84, Folder 11; and February 17, 1885, SAN, Box 85, Folder 2.
376. Sanford to Gertrude Sanford, November 14, 1884.
377. Malet to Marquês de Penafiel, February 7, 1885, AMAE 1md / 92. Ranieri, 26.
378. J. Stuart to Granville, October 17, 1884, FO 403 / 39.
379. Courcel to Ferry, November 23, 1884, *DDF,* vol. 5, 482.
380. *Madras Mail,* January 10, 1885.
381. Lister's minute, November 19, 1884; Granville to Malet, November 25, 1884, FO 84 / 1815.
382. Lister's minute, November 19, 1884, FO 84 / 1815.
383. Lister's minute, July 17, 1884, FO 403 / 39.
384. Crowe, 127.
385. Granville's memo, December 1, 1884, PRO 30 / 29 / 144; Percy Anderson's memo, December 2, 1884, R1001 / 4149.
386. Lord Aberdare to Granville, February 28, 1883, CO 879 / 20.
387. Flegel, *Vom Niger-Benue* (Leipzig 1890), 93, 108. Various records on Flegel's activity in R1001 / 4201.

388. "Ueber die Begründung," *Berliner Börsenzeitung*, December 3, 1884.
389. Crowe, 101, 180.
390. "Des Afrika-Reisenden," *Berliner Tageblatt,*" October 4, 1884. "Deutscher Kolonialverein," *Deutsche Kolonialzeitung*, vol. 1 (1884), 437.
391. M. de Pina de Saint-Didier to Ferry, December 16, 1884, AMAE 1CPC / 11.
392. Boniface I. Obichere, "The African factor in the establishment of French authority in West Africa, 1880–1900," in *France and Britain in Africa*, ed. Prosser Gifford and William Roger Louis (New Haven, CT: Yale University Press, 1978), 449.
393. Undated notes on Flegel, FO 925 / 118. Hertslet's memo, November 10, 1884, FO 881 / 5026.
394. Malet's report, December 1, 1884, in Poschinger, *Bismarck und die Diplomaten*, 425. Bismarck's note, November 16, 1884, R1001 / 4197.
395. "Ueber die Begründung," *Berliner Börsenzeitung*, December 3, 1884.
396. "Robert Flegel," *Deutsche Kolonialzeitung*, May 1, 1885. "Stanley," *Export*, 774.
397. Stanley to Sanford, December 4, 1884, SAN, Box 27, Folder 4, SAN.
398. Sanford to Gertrude Sanford, December 5, 1884. See Andrew Fitzmaurice, "The Justification of King Leopold II's Congo Enterprise by Sir Travers Twiss," in Ian Hunter and Shaunnagh Dorsett (eds.), *Law and Politics in British Colonial Thought: Transpositions of Empire* (Basingstoke: Palgrave Macmillan, 2010), 109.
399. Mackinnon's memo, January 3, 1885, FO 403 / 49.
400. Pauncefote's memo, April 11, 1878, FO 12 / 53.
401. Granville to Malet, November 15, 1884, FO 84 / 1814. Strauch to Stanley, August 12, 1884, STAN, #970.
402. Strauch to Stanley, December 8, 1884, STAN, #970. Stanley to LII, December 12, 1884, #663.
403. Pauncefote's memo, December 2, 1884, FO 84 / 1815. Meeting protocol, June 9, 1883, AMAE 1md / 88.
404. Pauncefote to Herbert, June 24, 1884, FO 403 / 35.
405. John E. Flint, *Sir George Goldie and the Making of Nigeria* (London: Oxford University Press, 1960), 43.
406. Frelinghuysen to John Tyler Morgan, March 13, 1884, SAN, Box 24, Folder 11.
407. A. Hemming's memo, October 16, 1884, FO 84 / 1813. Pauncefote's memo, Nov. 20, 1884, FO 84 / 1815.
408. René Goblet to LII, April 27, 1883, APR, Fonds Congo, File 1. Devaux to Sanford, March 6, 1884, SAN, Box 25, Folder 19.
409. Napoléon Ney, *Conférences et lettres de P. Savorgnan de Brazza sur ses trois explorations dans l'ouest africain de 1875 à 1886* (Paris: Dreyfous, 1887), 267.
410. Granville's minute, December 1, 1884, PRO 30 / 29 / 144.
411. Granville to Malet, October 22, 1884, PAAA London 388.

412. Compare Granville's minute, December 1, 1884, PRO 30/29/144, with note of November 29, 1884, *Die große Politik,* vol. 3, 439.
413. Bismarck to Muenster, January 25, 1885, *Die große Politik,* vol. 4, 96.
414. Busch to Wolfram von Rotenhan, October 21, 1884, in *Gesammelte Werke,* vol. 6, 348. Taubman to Foreign Office, January 8, 1886, FO 84/1880.
415. Petition dated February 12, 1885, FO 403/71. Pauncefote to law officers, July 21, 1885, FO 403/72. Major L. Darwin, "British Expansion," *National Review,* vol. 33 (London 1899), 972.
416. Flint, *Goldie,* 43.
417. Pauncefote's memo, February 7, 1885, FO 84/1879.
418. Richard Koebner, "The Concept of Economic Imperialism," *Economic History Review,* vol. 2 (1949), 11. See Barrie M. Ratcliffe, "Commerce and Empire: Manchester Merchants and West Africa, 1873–1895," *The Journal of Imperial and Commonwealth History* 7 (1979): 293.
419. Ronald Robinson, "Imperial Problems in British Politics," in *The Cambridge History of the British Empire,* ed. E. A. Benians, James Butler, and C. E. Carrington, vol. 3 (Cambridge: Cambridge University Press, 1959), 164.
420. William Nevill Montgomerie Geary, *Nigeria under British Rule* (London: Methuen, 1927), 181.
421. Aberdare to Granville, October 1, 1884, PRO 30/29/148.
422. Lister's comment, January 30, 1885, FO 84/1879.
423. In January 1884, due in part to growing pressure from the British public, Prime Minister Gladstone's cabinet authorized Major General Charles Gordon to lead an expedition into the Sudan, which was in the throes of a war pitting Mahdist forces against Egyptian troops essentially under the command of Britain. With Egyptian forces about to pull out of the Sudan in accordance with the wishes of Gladstone, Gordon theoretically had orders to oversee an orderly evacuation. Instead, he took control of Khartoum and began to reform the administration of the city beginning in February 1884. A siege by the Mahdists soon followed, prompting a distressed Gordon to await a rescue by new expeditionary forces under his advocate, Adjutant General Garnet Wolseley. Wolseley did not arrive in time to prevent the fall of Khartoum or the killing of Gordon.
424. Edward Hertslet's memo, October 18, 1884, FO 403/46.
425. R. Popham Lobb, "British Influence in the Western Soudan: Its History and Results," *Imperial and Asiatic Quarterly* 6 (1898): 339.
426. Granville's minute, February 25, 1885, FO 84/1879. Granville to Aberdare, November 14, 1884, FO 84/1814.
427. Roundell Palmer's memo, March 4, 1885, FO 84/1879.
428. For examples of Niger treaties, see Edward Hertslet (ed.), *Map of Africa,* vol. 1 (London: Her Majesty's Stationery Office, 1894), 463.
429. Claude Maxwell MacDonald's memo, August 1, 1890, FO 84/2109.
430. I. Gunn, "Sir George Goldie and the Making of Nigeria," *African Affairs* 60 (1961): 546.

431. Percy Anderson's undated memo, in Colin W. Newbury (ed.), *British Policy towards West Africa: Select Documents, 1875–1914* (Oxford: Clarendon Press, 1971), 185.
432. Law officers to Granville, January 7, 1885, FO 403 / 49.
433. Bismarck to ambassadors, October 22, 1884, R1001 / 4112. John Bright to Edmond Fitzmaurice, November 11, 1884, FO 84 / 1814. Sanford to Gertrude Sanford, November 24 and 26, 1884, SAN, Box 84, Folder 12.
434. Ronald Robinson, "The Conference in Berlin and the Future of Africa, 1884–1885," *BEA*, 13.
435. Malet to Granville, December 5, 1884, FO 343 / 6.
436. Sanford to Gertrude Sanford, November 19, 1884, SAN, Box 84, Folder 11. "Politische Nachrichten," *Berliner Börsenzeitung,* November 21, 1884.
437. Mackinnon to Sanford, December 11, 1884, SAN, Box 127, Folder 5.
438. Stanley to Sanford, December 4, 1884, SAN, Box 27, Folder 4; Mackinnon to Sanford, December 15, 1884, SAN, Box 127, Folder 5.
439. de Launay to Mancini, December 4, 1884, *DDI,* 530.
440. W. T. Stead, "Character Sketch," *Review of Reviews,* vol. 27 (1903), 567. Sanford to Mackinnon, December 24, 1884, SAN, Box 127, Folder 10.
441. Poschinger, "Zur Geschichte," 342.
442. Nicholas Tarling, *Britain, the Brookes, and Brunei* (Kuala Lumpur: Oxford University Press, 1971), 255.
443. Herbert Arthur Smith, *Great Britain and the law of nations: a selection of documents illustrating the views of the government in the United Kingdom upon matters of international law,* vol. 2 (London: King, 1935), 41.
444. Graham Irwin, *Nineteenth-Century Borneo: a Study in Diplomatic Rivalry* (Singapore: D. Moore, 1955), 213.
445. Leigh R. Wright, "The Partition of Brunei," *Asian Studies* 5 (1967): 296.
446. Earl of Derby's memo, March 28, 1885, CO 144 / 60. Pauncefote's memo, January 13, 1887, FO 12 / 75.
447. Various documents attesting recognition in APR, Fonds Congo, File 132. Sanford to Gertrude Sanford, February 14, 1885, SAN, Box 85, Folder 2. de Launay to Robilant, November 28, 1884, *DDI,* 520.
448. de Launay to Mancini, December 11, 1884, *DDI,* 540.
449. Kuitenbrouwer, 142. Mancini to Italian ambassador at Lisbon, December 13, 1884, *DDI,* 547.
450. Schmidthals to Bismarck, February 24, 1885, PAAA London 388.
451. Sanford to Gertrude Sanford, February 13, 1885, SAN, Box 85, Folder 2.
452. Sanford to Gertrude Sanford, February 14, 1885, SAN, Box 85, Folder 2. Borchgrave to LII, June 9, 1885, APR, Fonds Congo, File 137. Montebello to van Eetvelde, July 9, 1886, in *Léopold II et Beernaert,* vol. 1, 115. Bismarck to Penafiel, February 7, 1885, AMAE 1md / 92.
453. Sanford to Gertrude Sanford, February 17, 1885, Box 85, Folder 2.
454. René Goblet to Ferry, May 13, 1885; Marine Ministry Memo, October 23, 1885, AMAE 1md / 93.

455. Copies of declarations in R1001 / 4141. Hatzfeldt to Bismarck, November 14, 1884, R1001 / 4147.
456. Stanley, *CFFS,* vol. 2, 396.
457. Mancini to Italian Consul-General at Cairo, December 20, 1884, *DDI,* 561; de Launay to Robilant, December 13, 1884, *DDI,* 550. Ranieri, 30.
458. Granville to A. Paget, June 8, 1880, FO 403 / 81A.
459. Rawson William Rawson, "Claims," *Proceedings of RGS,* vol. 7 (London 1885), 93.
460. Ranieri, 30.
461. Edward Hertslet, *The Map of Africa by Treaty,* vol. 2 (London: His Majesty's Stationery Office, 1909), 446.
462. "La Conférence du Congo," *Indépendance Belge,* November 5, 1884.
463. Ranieri, 26.
464. *The Economist,* November 15, 1884. Mustapha Assim Pasha's note, February 10, 1885, in *Recueil d'Actes Internationaux de l'Empire Ottoman,* vol. 4 (Paris 1903), 337. Mancini to Robilant, January 5, 1885, *DDI,* 588.
465. Ranieri, 28.
466. Henk Wesseling, "The Berlin Conference and the Expansion of Europe: A Conclusion," *BEA,* 528. Stanley to LII, December 29, 1884.
467. Undated note excusing Bismarck's absence, in R1001 / 4141.
468. Edward Marston to Stanley, June 6, 1885, STAN, #1591.
469. Bismarck to Münster, January 25, 1885, *Große Politik,* vol. 4, 96.
470. See the *Allgemeine Zeitung* from November 15, 1884 to March 1, 1885.
471. Fabri, "Kolonialpolitische Skizzen," 57.
472. Crown Princess of Germany to Mary Elizabeth Bulteel, October 17, 1884, 195.
473. "Kolonialliteratur," *Das Ausland,* vol. 57 (Stuttgart 1884), 576.
474. Joseph Jooris, "De l'Occupation," *RDI,* vol. 18 (Leipzig 1886), 238. Friedrich Fromhold Martens, "La Conférence," *RDI,* vol. 18 (Leipzig 1886), 279.
475. Rodd, 65.
476. Descamps, 41.
477. Széchényi to Kálnoky, February 25, 1885, AT-OeStA / HHStA Diplomatie und Außenpolitik 1848–1918 GKA GsA Berlin 189–3. Oscar II to Gillis Bildt, December 7, 1884, excerpted in David Nilsson, *Sweden-Norway at the Berlin Conference 1884–85* (Uppsala: Nordiska Afrikainstitutet, 2013), 34.
478. Richard Hall, *Stanley: An Adventurer Explored* (London: Collins, 1974), 239.
479. Walthère Frère-Orban's memo, February 26, 1885, in *Léopold II et le cabinet,* 374. Banning, *Mémoires,* xvii.
480. Frère-Orban to LII, March 17 and 30, 1885, *Léopold II et le cabinet,* 376.
481. Bismarck to Münster, December 17, 1876, *Gesammelte Werke,* vol. 2, 671. LII to Frère-Orban, March 31, 1885, in *Léopold II et le cabinet,* 378.
482. C. Loretz, *Le Congo-empire* (Brussels: Istace, 1885), 3.
483. L. Wils, " De regering-Malou opgeofferd voor Kongo," *Algemene Geschiedenis der Nederlanden,* vol. 13 (Haarlem 1978), 186.

484. *Aus den Archiven,* 64.
485. Various endorsements contained in R1001 / 4146. "Conférence du Congo," *Indépendance Belge,* November 5, 1884.
486. Exchange of declarations, February 23, 1885, R1001 / 4140.
487. van Eetvelde to Ferry, August 23, 1885, AMAE 1md / 93. Adee to Roosevelt, October 12, 1904, Theodore Roosevelt Papers, Reel 49, LOC.
488. Descamps, 32.
489. Széchényi to Kálnoky, December 2, 1884, AT-OeStA / HHStA Diplomatie und Außenpolitik 1848–1918 GKA GsA Berlin 189–3.
490. Jean Stengers, "Léopold II et le cabinet Malou," in *1884: un tournant politique en Belgique,* ed. Emiel Lamberts and Jacques Lory (Brussels: Publications des Facultés universitaires Saint-Louis, 1986), 171. *Life of Dilke,* vol. 2, 549.
491. George Washington Williams to President Benjamin Harrison, October 14, 1890, in George Washington Williams, *Report upon the Congo-State and the Country to the President of the Republic of the United States* (Loanda, 1890), 23.
492. Speech of Xavier Neujean in April 28, 1885 debate, *Annales Parlementaires: Chambre Representants* (Brussels 1885), 1027.
493. Louis, "Congo Conference," 196.
494. LII to Sanford, January 22, 1885, unindexed personal note, SAN.
495. van Eetvelde's memo, January 7, 1886, APR, Fonds Congo, File 144. Jean Stengers and Jan Vansina, "King Leopold's Congo, 1886–1908," *The Cambridge History of Africa,* vol. 4, ed. Roland Oliver and G. N. Sanderson (Cambridge: Cambridge University Press, 1985), 336.
496. Stanley to Sanford, March 4, 1885, SAN, Box 27, Folder 5.
497. État Indépendant du Congo, *Bulletin Officiel: Années 1885 et 1886* (Brussels: Weissenbruch, 1886), 213.
498. John Latrobe to Sanford, June 16, 1885, SAN, Box 25, Folder 9.
499. Sketch for transfer of sovereignty over Congo from AIC to LII, undated, APR, Fonds Congo. File 130. M. Cratheódory to Borchgrave, March 16 and 22, 1885, APR, Fonds Congo, File 143.
500. Sanford to LII, May 2, 1885, SAN, Box 29, Folder 12.
501. Stanley to Frederic, July 24, 1885, STAN, #6961.
502. LII to de Winton, May 26, 1884, in Luwel, *Sir Francis,* 222.
503. LII to Sanford, circa November 1884, SAN, Box 31, Folder 3.
504. "Proclamation de l'État," *L'Univers,* August 25, 1885.
505. "Neue Nachrichten," *Berliner Tageblatt,* August 21, 1885.
506. De Winton's proclamation, July 18, 1885, Madeleine van Grieken-Taverniers, *Inventaire des archives des affaires étrangéres de l'État indépendant du Congo et du Ministére des colonies, 1885–1914* (Brussels: Académie royale des sciences coloniales, 1955), 90.
507. "Aus Vivi," *Berliner Börsenzeitung,* May 14, 1885.
508. "Neue Nachrichten," *Berliner Tageblatt,* August 21, 1885.

509. Decree of July 1, 1885, Albert Thys, *Conférences sur le Congo* (Brussels: Société Belge des Ingénieurs, 1886), 42. Compare Lambert Petit (ed.), *Les codes du Congo, suivis des décrets, ordonnances et arrêtés complémentaires, mis en ordre et annotés d'après leur concordance avec les codes et les textes du droit belge utiles à leur interprétation, et précédés des traités et autres actes internationaux, ainsi que des lois et actes législatifs belges relatifs à l'État indépendant* (Brussels: Larcier, 1892).

510. L. Cuypers, "La Politique foncière de l'état indépendant du Congo à regard des missions catholiques," *Revue d'histoire ecclésiastique*, vol. 57 (Leuven: Katholieke Universiteit te Leuven, 1962), 53.

511. Khenzu, 60. See Bauer.

512. Quoted in J. F. Ade Ajayi, "Colonialism: An Episode in African History," *Colonialism in Africa, 1870–1960*, ed. L. H. Gann and Peter Duignan, vol. 1 (Cambridge: Cambridge University Press, 1969), 507.

513. G. G. Phillimore, "The Congo State: A Review of the International Position," *Law Magazine and Review*, vol. 29 (London 1904), 402.

514. See Adam Hochschild, *King Leopold's Ghost* (Boston: Houghton Mifflin, 1998). E. D. Morel, *Verbatim Report of the Five Days' Congo Debate in the Belgian House of Representatives* (Liverpool: Richardson, 1906), 7.

515. Tim Butcher, *Blood River* (New York: Grove Press, 2009), xv, 239.

516. See J. P. Daughton, *An Empire Divided: Religion, Republicanism, and the Making of French Colonialism, 1880–1914* (Oxford: Oxford University Press, 2006), 73.

517. Max Weber to Max Weber Sr., March 15, 1885, excerpted in Wolfgang J. Mommsen, *Max Weber und die deutsche Politik: 1890–1920* (Tübingen: Mohr, 2004), 8.

518. Charles Comte de Lalaing to Stanley, August 16, 1884, in Luwel, *Sir Francis*, 222.

519. Richter's speech to Reichstag, *Stenographische Berichte*, February 4, 1885, 1083.

520. Bismarck's speech, March 2, 1885, in Poschinger, *Fürst Bismarck*, 130.

521. Michelet von Frantzius's memo, February 23, 1885, R3001 / 5273. Roundell Palmer to Pauncefote, January 23, 1885, FO 84 / 1820.

522. See Hans-Georg Wolf, *English in Cameroon* (New York: de Gruyter, 2001), 51.

523. Hatzfeldt to Caprivi, October 27, 1884, RM 1 / 2436.

524. Hatzfeldt's note, May 11, 1886, FO 64 / 1152. Conrad Bornhak, "Die Anfänge des deutschen Kolonialstaatsrechts," *Archiv für öffentliches Recht*, vol. 2 (Freiburg: Mohr, 1887), 18. Georg Meyer, *Die staatsrechtliche Stellung der deutschen Schutzgebiete* (Leipzig: Duncker & Humblot, 1888), 174. Otto Köbner, "Deutsches Kolonialrecht," *Encyklopädie der Rechtswissenschaft in systematischer Bearbeitung*, vol. 2 (Leipzig: Duncker & Humblot, 1904), 1087. Franz Josef Sassen, *Das Gesetzgebungs- und Verordnungsrecht in den deutschen Kolonien* (Tübingen: Laupp, 1909), 13.

525. Jörg, *Historisch-Politische Blätter*, 443.
526. Eugen Richter to Reichstag, *Stenographische Berichte*, February 4, 1885, 1083.
527. Rudin, 128.
528. Edouard Rolin-Jaequemyns, "L'Annee 1888," *RDI* 21 (1889): 188.
529. Kusserow's memos, February 23 and 25, 1885, and Peters's memo, February 23, 1885, R1001 / 390. See separately Carl Peters, *Die Gründung von Deutsch-Ostafrika: Kolonialpolitische Erinnerungen und Betrachtungen* (Berlin: Schwetschke, 1906), 97.
530. Arne Perras, *Carl Peters and German Imperialism, 1856–1918: A Political Biography* (Oxford: Clarendon Press, 2004), 151.
531. Busch to Bismarck, September 30, 1884, R1001 / 390. Bismarck's conversation with Malet, November 28, 1884, in Poschinger, *Bismarck und die Diplomaten*, 425.
532. This from the treaty of December 4, 1884, in J. Wagner, *Deutsch-Ostafrika: Geschichte der Gesellschaft für deutsche Kolonisation* (Berlin: Engelhardt, 1886), 58.
533. See D. K. Fieldhouse, *Economics and Empire, 1830–1914* (Ithaca, NY: Cornell University Press, 1973), 374.
534. Barghash bin Said of Zanzibar to Bismarck, May 11, 1885, FO 403 / 94.
535. Maximilian von Berchem's protocol, July 18, 1886. R1001 / 360.
536. Perras, 63.
537. Edouard Whettnall to Borchgrave, May 29, 1885, APR, Fonds Congo, File 243. Parsons, 268.
538. See Susanna B. Hecht, *The Scramble for the Amazon* (Chicago: University of Chicago Press, 2013), 138.
539. J. M. Gray, "Zanzibar and the Coastal Belt, 1840–1848," in *History of East Africa*, vol. 1, ed. Roland Oliver and Gervase Mathew (Oxford: Clarendon Press, 1963), 212.
540. Kurt Büttner, *Die Anfänge der deutschen Kolonialpolitik in Ostafrika* (Berlin: Akademie-Verlag, 1959), 48.
541. Gustav von Brandenburg to Bismarck, November 11, 1885, PAAA Personalakten 8.384.
542. Günther Jantzen, *Ostafrika in der deutsch-englischen Politk* (Hamburg: Christian, 1934), 7.
543. Protection letter, February 27, 1885, R1001 / 9325. Notice of February 19, 1885, PAAA Personalakten 8.384.
544. Bismarck to Wilhem I, February 26, 1885, R1001 / 359.
545. Herbert Bismarck to Alfred de Rothschild, April 20, 1885, *Staatssekretär*, 275.
546. Rodd, 78.
547. Bismarck to Busch, August 30, 1884, *Große Politk*, vol. 3, 425.
548. Robert Morier to Granville, December 24, 1884, FO 403 / 48.

549. J. A. Betley, "Rogozinski," *Journal of Historical Society of Nigeria* 5 (1969): 101.
550. Alfred Henry Baynes to Granville, February 27, 1885, BMSA, Reel 31.
551. Peter Sebald, "Die Kolonialbestrebungen des Stephan Szolc-Rogozinski," *Wissenschaftliche Zeitschrift der Karl-Marx-Universität*, vol. 11 (Leipzig 1962), 503.
552. Treaty signed at Victoria, February 1885, BMSA, Reel 31.
553. G. Jantzen, "Ein deutscher Kolonialversuch im Mahinlande," *Koloniale Rundschau*, vol. 18 (Leipzig 1937), 89. Busch's memo, March 6, 1885, R1001 / 3410.
554. Wehler, 294, 331.
555. Compare Malet to Granville, February 26, 1885, Gerhard Ebel (ed.), *Botschafter Paul Graf von Hatzfeldt*, vol. 1 (Boppard: Boldt, 1976), 446.
556. See Bruno Kurtze, *Die Deutsch-Ostafrikanische Gesellschaft* (Jena: Fischer, 1913), 13.

Epilogue

1. Émile Banning, *La conférence africaine de Berlin et l'Association internationale du Congo* (Brussels: Muquardt, 1885), 7.
2. Bismarck's speech, November 28, 1885, *Stenographische Berichte*, 117.
3. John E. Flint, *Sir George Goldie and the Making of Nigeria* (London: Oxford University Press, 1960), 76. This, *pace* Hardinge Giffard's predecessor: Roundell Palmer's memo, March 4, 1885, FO 84 / 1879.
4. P. M. Olivier, "La British South Africa Chartered Company," *Bulletin de la Société d'Études coloniales*, vol. 3 (Brussels 1896), 60.
5. Hartmut Pogge von Strandmann, "The Purpose of German Colonialism, or the Long Shadow of Bismarck's Colonial Policy," in *German Colonialism: Race, the Holocaust, and Postwar Germany*, eds. Volker Langbehn and Mohammad Salama (New York: Columbia University Press, 2011), 202.
6. Anonymous, "Les Grandes Compagnies Coloniales," *Journal des Économistes*, vol. 49 (Paris 1902), 276.
7. U.S. Treasury, *Colonial administration, 1800–1900: Methods of government and development adopted by the principal colonizing nations in their control of tropical and other colonies and dependencies* (Washington, D.C.: Government Printing Office, 1903), 2845.
8. "Twelve Years' 'Land-Grabbing'," *The Times* (London), October 20, 1896.
9. George Washington Williams to President Benjamin Harrison, October 14, 1890, in George Washington Williams, *Report upon the Congo-State and the Country to the President of the Republic of the United States* (Loanda 1890), 23.
10. "Great Conspiracy," *New York Times*, July 2, 1894.
11. But see David Strang, "Contested Sovereignty: The Social Construction of Colonial Imperialism," *The Social Construction of State Sovereignty*, ed.

Thomas J. Biersteker and Cynthia Weber (Cambridge: Cambridge University Press, 1996), 35.

12. Muriel Evelyn Chamberlain, *The Scramble for Africa* (Hong Kong: Longman, 1974), 62.
13. L. C. A. Knowles, *The economic development of the British overseas empire* (London: Routledge, 1924), 21. A. E. Musson, "The Great Depression in Britain, 1873–1896: A Reappraisal," *Journal of Economic History* 19 (1959): 199.
14. Olivier, "La British South Africa Chartered Company," 61.
15. Charles Wentworth Dilke, *The British Empire* (London: Chatto, 1899), 118.
16. "Die Nachtigal-Gesellschaft," *Berliner Börsenzeitung*, March 29, 1888.
17. Albert-Lucien-Ernest Cabasse, *Les compagnies de colonisation: délégataires de l'exercice du pouvoir souverain dans la seconde moitié du XIXe siècle et au début XXe* (Nancy: Kreis, 1905), 88. Count van Bylandt to Joseph van der Does de Willebois (attachments), October 17, 1884, *Bescheiden betreffende*, part 2, vol. 3, 717.
18. Compare "Séance du 13 août 1885," *L'Association française pour l'avancement des sciences: Grenoble, 1885*, vol. 1 (Paris 1886), 230.
19. Edmond Cotteau, *Quelques notes sur Sarawak (Bornéo)* (Paris: Leroux, 1886), 3.
20. British North Borneo Chartered Company, *Handbook of British North Borneo* (London: Clowes, 1886), 7.
21. "Berlin, 7. Dec.," *Allgemeine Zeitung*, December 9, 1884.
22. Marquess of Salisbury's memo, October 24, 1885, FO 12/68.
23. V. L. Cameron, "Chartered Companies in Africa," *Journal of the Society of Arts*, vol. 39 (London: George Bell, 1891), 250. For similar sentiment: "Literary Gossip," *The Athenaeum: Journal of Literature, Science, the Fine Arts, Music, and the Drama*, part 2 (London: John Edward Francis, 1902), 256.
24. Mark Granovetter, "Threshold Models of Collective Behavior," *American Journal of Sociology* 83 (1978): 1420.
25. Henry Bruce to Earl Granville, May 18, 1885, FO 403/72.
26. Compare Kurt Büttner, *Die Anfänge der deutschen Kolonialpolitik in Ostafrika* (Berlin: Akademie, 1959), 24.
27. Harcourt to Granville, February 13, 1885, FO 403/71.
28. See Pauncefote to Taubman, May 22, 1885, FO 403/72.
29. Henry Bruce to Granville, May 18, 1885.
30. John Atkinson Hobson, *Imperialism: A Study* (New York: J. Pott, 1902), 243.
31. Walther Däbritz, *David Hansemann und Adolph von Hansemann* (Krefeld: Scherpe, 1954), 131.
32. "Niger Territories," *The Times* (London), December 21, 1888. Andrew M. Kamarck, *The Economics of African Development* (New York: Praeger, 1967), 190. But see Joseph C. Anene, *Southern Nigeria in Transition, 1885–1906: Theory and Practice in a Colonial Protectorate* (Cambridge: Cambridge University Press, 1966), 319.

33. M. d'Azincourt to Charles de Freycinet, April 23, 1885, AMAE 1CPC/11.
34. Albert Galloway Keller, "The Colonial Policy of the Germans," *Yale Review* (New Haven, CT: Tuttle, 1902), 394.
35. Paul Leroy-Beaulieu, *De la colonisation chez les peuples modernes* (Paris: Librairie Guillaumin et Cie, 1898), 809.
36. Latrobe to Sanford, June 2, 1885, SAN, Box 25, Folder 9.
37. John A. Kasson, "The Congo Conference and the President's Message," *North American Review* 142 (1886): 132.
38. Pierre Bonnassieux, *Les grandes compagnies de commerce* (Paris: Plon, 1892), 518.
39. "Séance du 6 Novembre," *Compte rendu des séances de la Société de géographie* (Paris 1885), 515. "Séance du 19 Février," *Comptes Rendus des Travaux de la Société des Agriculteurs,* vol. 15 (Paris 1884), 498.
40. Paul Édouard Didier Riant's letter, May 21, 1883, Conseil Municipal de Paris, *Année 1883: Rapports et Documents* (Paris 1884), 217. Lord Lyons to Earl Granville, April 7, 1882, FO 403/81C. See also files of miscellaneous failed proposals in German Federal Archive Berlin, R1001/2207.
41. For more on these plans, see UK National Archives, FO 99/262.
42. Leonard H. West, "British North Borneo," *Imperial and Asiatic Quarterly Review* 4 (1897): 331. "Delagoa Bay," *The Times* (London), December 16, 1887.
43. George Louis Beer, "Les grandes companies de Commerce," *Political Science Quarterly* 9 (1894): 138.
44. Bonnassieux, *Les grandes compagnies,* 520.
45. François Renault, *Lavigerie, l'esclavage africain, et l'Europe, 1868–1892,* vol. 1 (Paris: Boccard, 1971), 260. Cristina Della Coletta, *World's Fairs Italian Style: The Great Exhibitions in Turin and Their Narratives, 1860–1915* (Toronto: University of Toronto Press, 2006), 123.
46. "Another International Association?," *African Repository* 61 (1885): 115.
47. David Starr Jordan, *The Question of the Philippines: An Address Delivered before the Graduate Club of Leland Stanford Junior University, on February 14, 1899* (Palo Alto, CA: Valentine, 1899), 55.
48. Emily Sadka, *The Protected Malay States, 1874–1895* (Kuala Lumpur: University of Malaya Press, 1968), 107.
49. Herbert Jäckel, *Die Landgesellschaften in den deutschen Schutzgebieten: Denkschrift zur Kolonialen Landfrage* (Halle: Fischer, 1909), 18.
50. Julian Pauncefote to Law officers, July 9, 1888, FO 403/106.
51. See William L. Langer, *The Diplomacy of Imperialism* (New York: Knopf, 1951), 281.
52. Frederick Lugard, "Treaty Making," *Geographical Journal,* vol. 1 (London 1893), 54.
53. Compare with Franz Ansprenger, "African Perception of the new European Policies in Africa during the 1880s," in *Bismarck, Europe, and Africa: the Berlin Africa Conference 1884–1885 and the Onset of Partition* (hereafter

BEA), ed. Stig Förster, Ronald Robinson, Wolfgang J. Mommsen (Oxford: Oxford University Press, 1988), 516.

54. Paul Reichard, *Deutsch-Ostafrika* (Leipzig: Spamer, 1892), 9.
55. Lugard, "Treaty Making," 54.
56. Johann Karl Vietor, *Geschichtliche und kulturelle Entwicklung unserer Schutzgebiete* (Berlin: Reimer, 1913), 11.
57. *Deutsche Kolonialzeitung*, March 7, 1891, 36.
58. Adolph Woermann in *Stenographische Berichte*, February 4, 1885, 1083, 1086.
59. Jeffrey Herbst, "The creation and matintenance of national boundaries in Africa," *International Organization* 43 (1989): 674.
60. U.S. Treasury, *Colonial Administration*, 2679.
61. John S. Galbraith, *Crown and Charter: The Early Years of the British South Africa Company* (Berkeley: University of California Press, 1974), 107.
62. Oskar Marmorek, "Was ist eine Chartered-Gesellschaft?" *Die Welt: Zentralorgan der Zionistischen Bewegung* 5 (1901): 2.
63. Compare K. Wiese, "Konzessionsfrage," *Koloniale Zeitschrift* (1900), 240.
64. Rudolf Ibbeken, *Das außenpolitisiche Problem: Staat und Wirtschaft in der deutschen Reichspolitik, 1880–1914* (Schleswig: J. Ibbeken, 1928), 43. Maximilian von Hagen, *Bismarcks Kolonialpolitik* (Stuttgart: Perthes, 1923), 271.
65. P. L. McDermott, *British East Africa* (London: Chapman, 1893), 200. Büttner, 115.
66. Eugen Richter's speech to Reichstag, *Stenographische Berichte*, February 4, 1885, 1083.
67. Heinrich von Kusserow to Friedrich von Holstein, August 10, 1884, PAAA Personalakten 8.384.
68. Hans Schinz to Julie Schinz-Voegeli, March 13, 1885, in Dag Henrichsen (ed.), *Hans Schinz: Bruchstücke: Forschungsreisen in Deutsch-Südwestafrika* (Basel: Carl Schlettwein Stiftung, 2012), 41. Wilhelm Külz, *Die Selbstverwaltung für Deutsch-Südafrika* (Berlin: Süsserott, 1909), 187.
69. Carl Gotthilf Büttner to Bismarck, June 28, 1885, R1001 / 2152. Captain Willem Christiaan to Büttner, July 2, 1885, Namibian State Archives at Windhoek, NAW ZBU 2029, WIId18bd1, 7.
70. Karl von Stengel, "Die rechtliche Stellung der Eingebornen in den deutschen Schutzgebieten," *Deutsche Kolonialzeitung*, vol. 4 (Berlin 1887), 365.
71. Heinrich von Göring to Bismarck, September 15, 1887, R1001 / 1538.
72. Theodor Leutwein to Chlodwig, Prince of Hohenlohe-Schillingsfürst, October 29, 1895, R1001 / 1617.
73. Johann Kurzreiter, "Österreich-Ungarn und die Kongofrage 1884–1885," *Mitteilungen des österreichischen Staatsarchivs* 46 (1998): 80.
74. Hans Pehl, *Die deutsche Kolonialpolitik und das Zentrum* (Limburg: Vereinsdruckerei, 1934), 29.

75. German Foreign Ministry to German Colonial Society for Southwest Africa, December 2, 1887, R1001 / 1538.
76. Heinrich von Poschinger, "Kusserow," *Deutsche Revue*, vol. 33 (Stuttgart 1908), 191.
77. Bismarck to Lüderitz, August 15, 1884, R1001 / 1998.
78. *The Holstein Papers*, vol. 2, ed. Norman Rich and M.H. Fisher (Cambridge: Cambridge University Press, 1957), 159.
79. "Tages-Neuigkeiten," *Hamburgischer Korrespondent*, May 18, 1890; "Herr von Kusserow," *Berliner Tageblatt*, May 7, 1890, PAAA Personalakten 8.385.
80. Treaty between Germany and Frederiks, October 28, 1884, R1001 / 9325.
81. Schinz to Schinz-Voegeli, December 16, 1884, *Schinz*, 25.
82. Lüderitz to Richard Lesser, November 8, 1884, in Lüderitz, *Erschließung*, 102. Hubert Henoch, "Adolf Lüderitz," *Zeitschrift für Kolonialpolitik*, vol. 11 (Berlin 1908), 315. Schinz to Schinz-Voegeli, April 17, 1885, *Schinz*, 48.
83. Kusserow to Bismarck, January 19, 1890, R1001 / 1547.
84. Treaty between German Colonial Society for Southwest Africa and Lüderitz, dated April 3, 1885, Namibian State Archives at Windhoek, NAW ZBU 1853, UIVb1bd1, 93.
85. Edouard Rolin-Jaequemyns, "L'Annee 1888," *Revue de Droit International* (hereafter *RDI*) 21 (1889): 188.
86. Compare "Übersicht der politischen Ereignisse," *Luxemburger Wort*, March 5, 1885.
87. Decree of April 13, 1885, NAW ZBU 1853, UIVb1bd1, 58. See Bismarck's marginalia on Muenster to Bismarck, June 7, 1884, *Große Politik*, vol. 4, 64.
88. Hermann Hesse, *Die Landfrage und die Frage der Rechtsgültigkeit der Konzessionen in Südwestafrika*, vol. 1 (Jena: Costenobel, 1906), 83. Conrad Bornhak, "Die Anfänge des deutschen Kolonialstaatsrechts," *Archiv für öffentliches Recht*, vol. 2 (Freiburg: Mohr, 1887), 27.
89. Otto von Weber, "Die letzte Reise von Adolf Lüderitz," *Afrikanischer Heimatkalendar*, vol. 43 (Windhoek: Kirchenbundesrat, 1973), 57.
90. Woermann to Bismarck, October 15, 1885, R1001 / 4447.
91. Veit Simon, "Deutsche Kolonialgesellschaften: Rechtliche Erörterungen und Vorschläge," *Zeitschrift für das Gesamte Handelsrecht*, vol. 34 (Stuttgart: Enke, 1888), 136.
92. Eugen Richter to Reichstag, *Stenographische Berichte*, February 4, 1885, 1083.
93. Allan McPhee, *The Economic Revolution in British West Africa* (London: Routledge, 1926), 77.
94. Eugen Richter, *ABC-Buch für freisinnige Wähler: Ein Lexikon parlamentarischer Zeit- und Streitfragen*, vol. 5 (Berlin: Fortschritt Aktiengesellschaft, 1889), 132.
95. See Büttner, 115.

96. Bruno Kurtze, *Die Deutsch-Ostafrikanische Gesellschaft* (Jena: Fischer, 1913), 43.
97. Heinrich Helmut Kraft, *Chartergesellschaften als Mittel zur Erschließung kolonialer Gebiete* (Hamburg: Friederichsen, 1943), 147.
98. Eugen Richter to Reichstag, *Stenographische Berichte*, February 12, 1898, 996.
99. Kraft, 149.
100. Ruben Robertson and Eduard Hernsheim to Kusserow, August 8, 1885, R1001 / 2298.
101. Hans-Jürgen Ohff, *Empires of Enterprise: German and English Commercial Interests in East New Guinea 1884 to 1914* (Adelaide: The University of Adelaide, 2008), 77.
102. Eugene Staley, *War and the Private Investor; a Study in the Relations of International Politics and International Private Investment.* (New York: Doubleday, 1935), 311.
103. "Royal Niger Company," *The Times* (London), January 4, 1889. Compare Foreign Office to Colonial Office, November 21, 1889, FO 12 / 80.
104. G. L. Ryder's memo (undated, 1897), FO 881 / 6922. "Royal Niger Company," *Sierra Leone Weekly News*, July 8, 1893.
105. Flint, *Goldie*, 213.
106. Figure from Scott R. Pearson, "The Economic Imperialism of the Royal Niger Company," *Food Research Institute Studies* 10 (1971): 77. John Darwin, *The Empire Project: the Rise and Fall of the British World-system, 1830–1970* (Cambridge: Cambridge University Press, 2009), 127.
107. Foreign Office to Treasury, June 15, 1899, *British Documents on Foreign Affairs*, part 1, series G, vol. 21 (Frederick, Maryland: University Publications of America, 1996), 392. Credit for this source goes to Rebecca Ritchie, my former student.
108. See John S. Galbraith, *Mackinnon and East Africa 1878–1895: A Study in the 'New Imperialism'* (Cambridge: Cambridge University Press, 1972), Chapter 9.
109. T. O. Ranger, "African Reactions to the Imposition of Colonial Rule in East and Central Africa," *Colonialism in Africa, 1870–1960*, vol. 1, ed. L. H. Gann and Peter Duignan (Cambridge: Cambridge University Press, 1969), 295.
110. "Ostafrika," *Deutsche Kolonialzeitung*, September 7, 1895.
111. Joseph Thomson, "Downing Street versus Chartered Companies," *Fortnightly Review*, vol. 46 (London 1889), 173. D. J. M. Muffett, *Empire Builder Extraordinary: Sir George Goldie* (Isle of Man: Shearwater, 1978), 66.
112. Nicholas Tarling, *Britain, the Brookes, and Brunei* (Kuala Lumpur: Oxford University Press, 1971), 552.
113. Compare Joseph Chamberlain to Commons, February 13, 1896, in *Hansard*, vol. 37, 323. http://hansard.millbanksystems.com/commons/1896/feb/13/address-in-answer-to-her-majestys-most.

114. Auguste Beernaert to Belgian parliament, July 23, 1889, in *Léopold II et Beernaert: d'après leur correspondance inédite de 1884 à 1894*, ed. Édouard van der Smissen, vol. 1 (Brussels: Goemaere, 1920), 115.
115. "Die Borneo-Frage," *Allgemeine Zeitung*, June 21, 1878.
116. "The Congo," *Anti-Slavery Reporter*, vol. 5 (London 1885), 318.
117. Jean Stengers, "King Leopold's Imperialism," in *Studies in the Theory of Imperialism*, ed. R. Owen and R. Sutcliffe (London: Longman, 1972), 255, 259.
118. G. Kurgan-van Hentenrijk, "Léopold II et la question de l'Acre," *Bulletin des Séances, Académie Royale des Sciences d'Outre-Mer* (Brussels 1975), 339.
119. Rolin-Jaequemyns, 190.
120. Kurt Romberg, *Die rechtliche Natur der Konzessionen und Schutzbriefe in den deutschen Schutzgebieten* (Berlin: Süsserott, 1908), 4.
121. Pierre Bonnassieux, *Les grandes compagnies de commerce* (Paris: Plon, 1892), 520.
122. "Reigning Companies," *The Economist*, September 15, 1888.
123. Jules Ferry to Edmond van Eetvelde, July 21, 1885, AMAE 1md/93.
124. Charles Lardy to Adolf Deucher, June 15, 1886, *Documents Diplomatiques Suisses*, vol. 3, 652.
125. R. J. Cornet, "Rapport sur les dossiers," *Bulletin des Séances: Institut Royal Colonial*, vol. 25 (Brussels: Librairie Falk fils, 1954), 577.
126. Émile Louis Victor de Laveleye, "The Division of Africa," *The Forum*, vol. 10 (New York: Forum Publishing Co., 1891), 485.
127. G. S. H. Pearson's memo, April 1, 1903, *British Documents on Foreign Affairs*, part 1, Series F, vol. 5 (Frederick, MD: University Publications of America, 1987), 57. J. Forbes Munro, *Maritime Enterprise and Empire: Sir William Mackinnon and His Business Empire, 1823–1893* (Suffolk: Boydell, 2003), 454n8.
128. van Eetvelde to Albert Bourée, April 22, 1887, in *Affaires du Congo* (1890), 4.
129. Albert Thys, *L'Annexion du Congo* (Brussels: Cercle africain, 1895), 13. Max Schlagintweit, *Der Kongostaat und die Anklagen gegen denselben* (Munich: Buchdruckerei der Allgemeinen Zeitung 1905), 8, 17. E. D. Morel, *Verbatim Report of the Five Days' Congo Debate in the Belgian House of Representatives* (Liverpool: Richardson, 1906), 67.
130. Convention of July 1, 1890, *Archives diplomatiques*, 2nd series, vol. 30 (Paris 1890), 249, 261. Émile Banning, *Le partage politique de l'Afrique d'après les transactions internationales les plus récentes* (Brussels: Muquardt, 1888), 149. Edouard Mambu ma Khenzu, *A modern history of monetary and financial systems of Congo, 1885–1995* (Lewiston: Edwin Mellen, 2006), 63.
131. Cornet, 577.
132. Guy Vanthemsche, *Belgium and the Congo, 1885–1980* (Cambridge: Cambridge University Press, 2012), 151.
133. Louise de Belgique, *Succession de S. M. Léopold II* (Brussels: Lamberty, 1911), 27.

134. See Christopher Duggan, *Francesco Crispi, 1818–1901* (Oxford: Oxford University Press, 2002), 658.
135. Kraft, 76.
136. Barry Neil-Tomlinson, "The Nyassa Chartered Company: 1891–1929," *Journal of African History* (hereafter *JAH*) 18 (1977): 109; Leroy Vail, "Mozambique's Chartered Companies: The Rule of the Feeble," *JAH* 17 (1976): 389.
137. Robert Bulwer-Lytton to Marquess of Salisbury, February 23, 1889, FO 403 / 123.
138. See Gustave Moynier, *La question du Congo devant l'Institut de droit international* (Geneva: Schuchardt, 1883).
139. William Roger Louis, "The Berlin Congo Conference," in *France and Britain in Africa: Imperial Rivalry and Colonial Rule*, ed. Prosser Gifford and William Roger Louis (New Haven, CT: Yale University Press, 1971), 191.
140. Compare "The International Association," *The Times* (London), November 25, 1884.
141. Louis Delavaud, "La France et le Portugal au Congo," *Revue de Geographie* 12 (1883): 224.
142. Pasquale Fiore, *Nouveau droit international public suivant les besoins de la civilisation moderne*, vol. 2 (Paris: Durand, 1885), 154.
143. Henry Wack, *The Story of the Congo Free State: Social, Political, and Economic Aspects of the Belgian System of Government in Central Africa* (New York: Putnam's, 1905), 72. See "À propos du Congo," *Indépendance Belge*, November 10, 1883 and June 14, 1884.
144. See Casper Sylvest, "'Our Passion for Legality': International Law and Imperialism in Late Nineteenth-Century Britain," *Review of International Studies* 34 (2008): 403.
145. Travers Twiss, "La Libre Navigation du Congo," *Revue de droit international*, vol. 15 (Brussels 1883), 554.
146. Eugène Goblet d'Alviella to LII, April 27, 1883, APR, Fonds Congo, File 1. *Treaties and engagements affecting the Malay States and Borneo*, eds. William G. Maxwell and William S. Gibson (London: Truscott, 1924), 178, 194.
147. Émile Louis Victor de Laveleye, "Congo Neutralized," *Contemporary Review*, vol. 43 (London: Isbister, 1883), 780.
148. Charles Faure, *La Conférence africaine de Berlin* (Geneva: Schuchardt, 1885), 20. *Proceedings of RGS*, vol. 7 (London 1863), 73.
149. Henry Richard, *Papers on the reasonableness of international arbitration* (London: Hodder & Stoughton, 1887), 57.
150. Charles P. Daly, *The Commercial Importance of Central Africa and the Free Navigation of the Congo* (New York: Bessey, 1884), 14.
151. John Tyler Morgan to Henry Shelton Sanford, March 5, 1884, SAN, Box 26, Folder 5.
152. See Augustin Thys, *L'œuvre africaine du roi Leopold II* (Brussels: Monnom, 1911), 6.

153. Cornet, 559.
154. Morgan to Sanford, March 25, 1884, SAN, Box 26, Folder 5.
155. "Avis de M. Westlake Q. C. sur droits Domaniaux," APR, Fonds Congo, File 223.
156. Strauch to Sanford, December 31, 1883, SAN, Box 27, Folder 11; Arntz's memo, December 15, 1883, SAN, Box 30, Folder 9.
157. Stanley to Hermenegildo de Brito Capelo, June 4, 1884, FO 403 / 39.
158. "Arntz," *Belgique Judiciaire,* November 27, 1884, R10001 / 4143. "Congo-frage," *Linzer Tages-Post,* July 26, 1883. "Congo-Frage," *Allgemeine Zeitung,* July 13, 1884.
159. Bismarck to Wilhelm I, December 12, 1884, in *Gesammelte Werke,* vol. 6, 395.
160. See Judgment of October 26, 1880, *Entscheidungen des Reichsgerichts in Civilsachen,* vol. 2 (Leipzig: Veit & Comp., 1880), 109.
161. See Herbert Arthur Smith, *Great Britain and the Law of Nations,* vol. 1 (London: P.S. King, 1932), 399.
162. Georg Schuster, "Von 1878 bis zum Ausscheiden Bismarcks," *Gebhardts Handbuch der deutschen Geschichte,* ed. Bruno Gebhardt (Stuttgart: Union, 1890), 793.
163. Jules Devaux to Sanford, January 19, 1884, SAN, Box 25, Folder 9, SAN.
164. Compare Arnold Pann, *Das Recht der deutschen Schutzherrlichkeit: Eine Staats- und Völkerrechtliche Studie* (Vienna: Manz, 1887), 21. "Die Borneo-Frage," *Allgemeine Zeitung,* June 2, 1878.
165. Heinrich Zoepfl, *Grundsätze des gemeinen deutschen Staatsrechts,* vol. 1 (Leipzig: Winter, 1863), 555.
166. Compare Jesse S. Reeves, "The Origin of the Congo Free State, Considered from the Standpoint of International Law," *American Journal of International Law* 3 (1909): 116.
167. V. L. Cameron to Stafford Northcote, March 8, 1886, *Final Report of the Royal Commission appointed to Inquire into the Depression of Trade and Industry* (London: Her Majesty's Stationery Office, 1886), 73.
168. V. L. Cameron, "Chartered Companies in Africa," *National Review,* vol. 15 (London 1890), 478.
169. Mark F. Lindley, *The acquisition and government of backward territory in international law* (London: Longmans, 1926), 84. Gaston Jèze, *Étude théorique et pratique sur l'occupation comme mode d'acquérir les territoires en droit international* (Paris: Giard, 1896), 160, 382. Robert Phillimore, *Commentaries upon International Law,* vol. 1 (London: Butterworths, 1879), 24.
170. Laveleye, "Division of Africa," 482.
171. Quoted in Jean Stengers, "Léopold II et la fixation des frontières du Congo," *Le Flambeau* 46 (1963): 157.
172. Frantz Despagnet, *Cours de droit international public* (Paris: Librairie de la Société du Recueil Général des Lois et des Arrets, 1899), 432. Louis Delavaud, *Études sur les colonies espagnoles: Bornéo* (Toulouse, France: Imprimerie du Sud-Ouest, 1884), 7. Karl Heimburger, *Der Erwerb der Gebietshoheit*

(Karlsruhe: G. Braun, 1888), 61. Karl von Stengel, "Konzessionen," *Zeitschrift für Kolonialpolitik, Kolonialrecht und Kolonialwirtschaft*, vol. 6 (Berlin: Süsserott, 1904), 331. Georg Meyer, *Die staatsrechtliche Stellung der deutschen Schutzgebiete* (Leipzig: Duncker & Humblot, 1888), 152. Max Joël, "Gesetz betreffend die Rechtsverhältnisse der deutschen Schutzgebiete," *Annalen des Deutschen Reiches für Gesetzgebung, Verwaltung und Statistik* (Berlin: Stilke, 1887), 199. But see Paul Kayser's lecture in *Kolonial-Politische Korrespondenz*, vol. 3 (Berlin: Deutsch-Ostafrikanische Gesellschaft, 1887), 121.

173. Bornhak, 22.
174. Leroy-Beaulieu, *Colonisation*, 810.
175. John Westlake, *The collected papers of John Westlake on public international law* (Cambridge: Cambridge University Press, 1914), 153.
176. Antonin Deloume, *De Brazza, Stanley, Léopold II, roi des Belges: Le droit des gens dans l'Afrique équatoriale* (Toulouse: Durand, 1883), 65.
177. *Annuaire de l'Institut de Droit International*, vol. 8 (Brussels 1889), 346.
178. Charles G. Fenwick, *International Law* (New York: Appleton-Century-Crofts, 1948), 349.
179. Westlake, *Collected Papers*, 167. Liane Ranieri, *Les relations entre l'État indépendant du Congo et l'Italie* (Brussels: Académie royale des sciences coloniales, 1959), 30.
180. Henk Wesseling, "The Netherlands and the Partition of Africa," *JAH*, vol. 22 (1981), 504. Sanford to Frederick Frelinghuysen, undated, SAN, Box 29, Folder 9. Travers Twiss to Pauncefote, December 20, 1884, FO 84/1818.
181. Edward Malet to Granville, January 29, 1885, FO 84/1820.
182. Compare "Eine neue Berliner Konferenz," *National-Zeitung*, October 15, 1884. Malet to Granville, January 18, 1885, FO 84/1820. But see Sybil Eyre Crowe, *The Berlin West Africa Conference: 1884–1885* (London: Longmans, 1942), 182.
183. Protocol, April 19, 1886, PAAA London 388.
184. Martti Koskenniemi, *The Gentle Civilizer of Nations: The Rise and Fall of International Law 1870–1960* (Cambridge: Cambridge University Press, 2001), 124.
185. M. de Martitz, "Rapport de M. de Martitz," *Annuaire de l'Institut de Droit International*, vol. 9 (Brussels: Muquardt, 1888), 244. See Andrew Fitzmaurice, *Sovereignty, Property and Empire, 1500–2000* (Cambridge: Cambridge University Press, 2014), 271–302.
186. Compare Hans Böhme, *Die Erwerbung der deutschen Schutzgebiete* (Hamburg: Rougemont, 1902), 24.
187. Fitzmaurice, *Sovereignty*, 285.
188. Martitz, 247. See Antony Anghie, *Imperialism, Sovereignty, and the Making of International Law* (Cambridge: Cambridge University Press, 2007), 91.
189. R. J. Gavin and J. A. Betley (eds.), *The Scramble for Africa: Documents on the Berlin West African Conference and Related Subjects, 1884/1885* (Ibadan: Ibadan University Press, 1973), 170.

190. Baron Henri Solvyns to Gladstone, October 9, 1882, Papers of Prime Ministers, British Library, MS 44477.
191. Henry Richard Fox Bourne, *Civilisation in Congoland* (London: P. S. King, 1903), 57.
192. Walter Bell Scaife, "The Development of International Law as to Newly Discovered Territory," *Papers of American Historical Association*, vol. 4 (New York: Putnam's, 1890), 291.
193. *The Hendrik Witbooi Papers*, ed. Brigitte Lau (Windhoek: National Archives of Namibia, 1990), 109.
194. Julian Pauncefote's memo, July 28, 1886, FO 64/1152.
195. Wilhelm von Bismarck's note, May 29, 1884, *Gesammelte Werke*, vol. 6, 199. Bismarck's memo, August 15, 1884, R1001/1998.
196. Martitz, "Examen de la theorie," 247.
197. État Indépendant du Congo, *Bulletin Officiel: Années 1885 et 1886* (Brussels: Weissenbruch, 1886), 213.
198. "Extrait du procès-verbal de la séance plénière tenue par l'Institut, à Lausanne, le 7 septembre 1888," *Annuaire de l'Institut de Droit International*, vol. 10 (Brussels: Muquardt, 1889), 181. Alphonse Rivier, *Principes du droit des gens*, vol. 1 (Paris: Rousseau, 1896), 46.
199. Franz Florack, *Die Schutzgebiete* (Tübingen: Mohr, 1905), 10. Friedrich Schack, *Das deutsche Kolonialrecht in seiner Entwicklung bis zum Weltkriege* (Hamburg: Friederichsen, 1923), 97.
200. Friedrich Fabri, *Fünf Jahre deutscher Kolonialpolitik* (Gotha: Perthes, 1889), 20, 76.
201. Robert Adam, "Völkerrechtliche Okkupation und deutsches Kolonialstaatsrecht," *Archiv für öffentliches Recht*, vol. 6 (Freiburg 1891), 233.
202. Paul Laband, *Das Staatsrecht des deutschen Reiches*, vol. 2 (Tübingen: Mohr, 1911), 283. See Fitzmaurice, *Sovereignty*, 289.
203. Bornhak, 7.
204. Kurt Heinrich Johannes Fiege, *Der Gebietserwerb durch völkerrechtliche Okkupation* (Leipzig: Noske, 1908), 29.
205. Douglas A. Lorimer, *Science, Race Relations and Resistance: Britain, 1870–1914* (Manchester: Manchester University Press, 2013), 152.
206. See Lassa Oppenheim, *International Law: A Treatise*, vol. 1 (London: Longmans, 1920), 377.
207. Westlake, *Collected Papers*, 153.
208. Karl von Stengel, *Die Rechtsverhältnisse der deutschen Schutzgebiete* (Tübingen: Mohr, 1901), 8.
209. See Alice L. Conklin, *A Mission to Civilize: The Republican Idea of Empire in France and West Africa, 1895–1930* (Stanford, CA: Stanford University Press, 1997), 13.
210. Anonymous, "How Is Sovereignty Acquired?," *Law Notes*, vol. 7 (New York: Thompson, 1904), 4.

211. Jörg Fisch, "Africa as terra nullius: The Berlin Conference and International Law," *BEA*, 363.
212. Herward Sieberg, *Eugène Étienne und die französische Kolonialpolitik (1887–1904)* (Köln: Westdeutscher Verlag, 1968), 112, 154
213. Gustav Spiller (ed.), *Inter-racial Problems: Papers from the First Universal Races Congress held in London in 1911* (London: King, 1911), 407. See Fitzmaurice, *Sovereignty*, 298.
214. Emanuel von Ullmann, *Völkerrecht* (Tübingen: Mohr, 1908), 310.
215. Fiege, 30. See documents pertaining to Zanzibar in German Federal Archive at Berlin, R1001 / 4175. *Annuaire Diplomatique de la République Française pour 1877* (Paris: Berger-Levrault, 1877), 90.
216. Heinrich von Poschinger (ed.), *Die wirtschaftlichen Verträge Deutschlands*, vol. 1 (Berlin: Decker's, 1892), 102. Reichskanzler-Amt, *Central-Blatt für das Deutsche Reich*, vol. 2 (Berlin: Carl Heymann's, 1874), 176. Frederick V. Parsons, *The Origins of the Morocco Question, 1880–1900* (London: Duckworth, 1976), 57.
217. Hilary Richard Wright Johnson's speech to the legislature, December 4, 1884, *The Annual Messages of the Presidents of Liberia 1848–2010*, vol. 1, ed. D. Elwood Dunn (Göttingen: de Gruyter, 2011), 333.
218. Phares Mukasa Mutibwa, "Madagascar 1800–80," in *Africa in the Nineteenth Century until the 1880s*, ed. J. F. Ade Ajayi (Berkeley: University of California Press, 1989), 431.
219. See Annie Rey-Goldzeiguer, *Le royaume arabe: la politique algérienne de Napoléon III, 1861–1870* (Alger: Société nationale d'édition et de diffusion, 1977).
220. "Helena, Heslop Master, July 1st, 1801," *Reports of cases argued and determined in the High Court of Admiralty*, vol. 4 (London: Butterworth, 1804), 5. See Ivana Elbl, "Cross-Cultural Trade and Diplomacy: Portuguese Relations with West Africa, 1441–1521," *Journal of World History* 3 (1992): 165.
221. For example, see the treaty of August 6, 1861, in Edward Hertslet (ed.), *The Map of Africa by Treaty*, vol. 1 (London: Her Majesty's Stationery Office, 1894), 410. See also Charles Henry Alexandrowicz, *An introduction to the history of the law of nations in the East Indies* (Oxford: Clarendon Press, 1967), 107.
222. James Charles Ernest Parkes to Sir James Hay, February 4, 1891, CO 879 / 35. Convention of March 4, 1848, Baron Désiré de Garcia de la Vega (ed.), *Recueil des Traités et conventions concernant le Royaume de Belgique*, vol. 2 (Brussels: F. Parent, 1854), 103.
223. Werner von Melle, "Handels- und Schifffahrtsverträge," *Handbuch des Völkerrechts*, vol. 3, ed. Franz von Holtzendorff (Hamburg: Richter, 1887), 186.
224. E. F. G. Law, "International Rivalries in Central Africa," *Fortnightly Review*, vol. 35 (London: Chapman and Hall, 1884), 825.
225. Compare John Macdonell, "Occupation and Res Nullius," *Journal of the Society of Comparative Legislation* 1 (1899): 285.

226. John M. Francis to Frederick Frelinghuysen, May 2, 1884, USNA, RG 59, *Despatches from Portugal,* vol. 32. Compare Rawson William Rawson, "Claims," *Proceedings of RGS,* vol. 7 (London 1885), 115.
227. John Westlake, *Chapters on the Principles of International Law* (Cambridge: Cambridge University Press, 1894), 138.
228. "Conférence," *Indépendance Belge,* November 18, 1884.
229. Westlake, *Collected Papers,* 141. Roundell Palmer's memo, January 11, 1885, FO 84 / 1819.
230. See Lauren Benton and Benjamin Straumann, "Acquiring Empire by Law: From Roman Doctrine to Early Modern Europe," *Law and History Review* 28 (2010): 1.
231. Robert Travers, *Ideology and Empire in Eighteenth-Century India: The British in Bengal, 1757–93* (Cambridge: Cambridge University Press, 2007), 127.
232. Abel P. Upshur to Henry Stephen Fox, September 25, 1843, in Philip Slaughter, *The Virginian history of African colonization* (Richmond, VA: Macfarlane, 1855), 95. Upshur to Edward Everett, October 9, 1843, in Francis Wharton (ed.), *A Digest of the international law of the United States: taken from documents issued by presidents and secretaries of state, and from decisions of federal courts and opinions of attorneys-general,* vol. 1 (Washington, D.C.: Government Printing Office, 1887), 5. John Latrobe to Henry Shelton Sanford, April 3, 1884, SAN, Box 25, Folder 8.
233. Constantine Phipps to Archibald Primrose, June 21, 1893, FO 403 / 187; Cornelius Alfred Moloney to Adeyemi I Alowolodu (Alafin of Oyo), July 31, 1899, CO 879 / 33. Laband, 283.
234. Alexandrowicz, 96.
235. Martin Wight, *British Colonial Constitutions* (Oxford: Clarendon Press, 1952), 8.
236. G. L. Ryder's memo (undated, 1897), FO 881 / 6922. Edward Hertslet's memo, March 10, 1892, FO 881 / 6166.
237. Compare Ludwig Bendix, *Kolonialjuristische und -politische Studien* (Berlin: G. Meinecke, 1903), 9. Philip J. Stern, *The Company-State: Corporate Sovereignty and the Early Modern Foundations of the British Empire in India* (Oxford: Oxford University Press, 2011), 52, 59, 196.
238. Rolin-Jaequemyns, 185.
239. Paul S. Reinsch, *Colonial Administration* (New York: Macmillan, 1905), 345.
240. Ronald Robinson and John Gallagher, *Africa and the Victorians* (London: Macmillan, 1965), 183.
241. Arthur Berriedale Keith, *The Belgian Congo and the Berlin Act* (Oxford: Clarendon Press, 1919), 16.
242. See Khenzu, 66.
243. Denys P. Myers, *Non-Sovereign Representation in Public International Organs* (Brussels: Congrès mondial des associations internationales, 1913), 29.
244. Sanford's memo, c. May 1885, SAN, Box 29, Folder 8.
245. Compare Koskenniemi, 155.

246. C. Loretz, *Le Congo-Empire* (Brussels: Istace, 1885), 2.
247. Francis Jeune's memo, December 1890, Baptist Missionary Society Archives (hereafter BMSA), Reel 32. Cornet, 586.
248. Roger Anstey, *Britain and the Congo in the Nineteenth Century* (Oxford: Clarendon Press, 1962), 198. Elsabea Rohrmann, *Max von Schinkel: hanseatischer Bankmann im wilhelminischen Deutschland* (Hamburg: Weltarchiv, 1971), 178.
249. Hardinge Giffard to Edward Grey, May 11, 1906, in *Nouveau recueil général de traités et autres actes relatifs aux rapports de droit international,* vol. 35 (Leipzig 1908), 444.
250. "Declaration," *Anti-Slavery Reporter,* December 16, 1884.
251. LII to Sanford, February 16, 1885, SAN, unindexed personal note.
252. Twiss to Pauncefote, December 27, 1884, FO 403 / 48.
253. Compare Gerhard Rohlfs to Barghash bin Said of Zanzibar, June 19, 1885, FO 403 / 94.
254. "Report," *Congo Conference: Report of the Secretary of State and correspondence in relation to the Affairs of the Independent State of the Congo* (Washington, D.C.: Government Printing Office, 1886), 76.
255. See Daniel Laqua, *The Age of Internationalism and Belgium, 1880–1930: Peace, Progress and Prestige* (Manchester: Manchester University Press, 2013), 58.
256. Eric A. Posner and Jack L. Goldsmith, *The Limits of International Law* (Oxford: Oxford University Press, 2006), 185.
257. Kenneth Onwuka Dike, "The Development of European-West African Relations and the Partition of Africa," in *The Scramble for Africa: Causes and Dimensions of Empire,* ed. Raymond F. Betts (Lexington, MA: Heath, 1972), 133.
258. Westlake, *Collected Papers,* 145.
259. Compare Miguel Bandeira Jerónimo, *The "Civilising Mission" of Portuguese Colonialism, 1870–1930* (New York: Palgrave Macmillan, 2015), 15.
260. Hermann Hesse, *Die Schutzverträge in Südwestafrika: Ein Beitrag zur rechtsgeschichtlichen und politischen Entwicklung des Schutzgebietes* (Berlin: Süsserott, 1905), 159.
261. Henry Shelton Sanford, "Declaration by the International Association of the Congo," *The American Journal of International Law* 3 (1909): 5.
262. Stanley, *CFFS,* vol. 2, 379.
263. Hesse, *Die Landfrage,* 108.
264. Saadia Touval, "Treaties, Borders, and the Partition of Africa" *JAH* 7 (1966): 279.
265. Julius K. Nyerere, *The Second Scramble* (Dar es Salaam: Tanganyika Standard, 1962), 4.
266. Jean-Paul Sanderson, "Le Congo belge entre mythe et réalité: Une analyse du discours démographique colonial," *Population* 55 (2000): 331.
267. See Heinrich Jakob Waltz, *Das Konzessionswesen im belgischen Kongo* (Jena: Fischer, 1917).

268. Compare Jean Stengers, "Leopold II et la rivalité franco-anglaise en Afrique, 1882–1884," *Revue Belge de philologie et d'histoire* 47 (1969): 425.
269. Charles Dilke to Edward Grey, April 13, 1908, Dilke Papers, British Library, MS43897.
270. But see J. D. Hargreaves, "The Berlin Conference, West African Boundaries, and the Eventual Partition," *BEA*, 320.
271. David S. Landes, "Some Thoughts on the Nature of Economic Imperialism," *Journal of Economic History* 21 (1961): 496. Daniel R. Headrick, *The Tools of Empire: Technology and European Imperialism in the Nineteenth Century* (Oxford: Oxford University Press, 1981), 17–43, 58–129. David Eltis and Lawrence C. Jennings, "Trade between Western Africa and the Atlantic World in the Pre-Colonial Era," *American Historical Review* 93 (1988): 936.
272. Treaty of July 15, 1884, *Europäischer Geschichtskalendar*, ed. Heinrich Schulthess, vol. 25 (Nördlingen: Beck, 1885), 430.
273. Anonymous, "The Congo Question," *Quarterly Review*, vol. 204 (London: Murray, 1906), 48.
274. See Catherine Coquéry-Vidrovitch, *Le Congo au temps des grandes Compagnies concessionnaires, 1898–1930* (Paris: Mouton, 1972). See Henri Cuvillier-Fleury, *La mise en valeur du Congo français* (Paris: Larose, 1904).
275. Compare H. P. Merritt, "Bismarck and the German Interest in East Africa, 1884–1885," *The Historical Journal* 21 (1978): 97.
276. J. D. Hargreaves, *West Africa Partitioned*, vol. 1 (Madison: University of Wisconsin Press, 1974), 5. Compare Erik Gilbert, *Dhows & the colonial economy of Zanzibar: 1860–1970* (Athens: Ohio University Press, 2004).
277. Compare P. M. Holt, *The Mahdist State in the Sudan, 1881–1898* (Oxford: Clarendon Press, 1958), 148.
278. G. N. Sanderson, "Conflict and Co-Operation between Ethiopia and the Mahdist State, 1884–1898," *Sudan Notes and Records* 50 (1969): 15.
279. Enrico Levi Catellani, *Le colonie e la Conferenza di Berlino* (Turin: Unione tipografico-editrice, 1885), 556.
280. See Arno J. Mayer, *The persistence of the Old Regime: Europe to the Great War* (New York: Pantheon, 1981).
281. Édouard Descamps, *New Africa: an essay on government civilization in new countries, and on the foundation, organization and administration of the Congo Free State* (London: S. Low, 1903), 36, 27.
282. Alfred Zimmermann, "Der Kongo und der Kongostaat," *Preußische Jahrbücher*, vol. 60 (Berlin 1887), 309.

Acknowledgments

This book would not have been possible without my two graduate advisors, David Blackbourn and Charles Maier. Both offered a rigorous education, inimitable scholarly examples, and, not least, constructive critiques. Both were kind enough to take me on as an advisee when I arrived at their offices with few qualifications. Both have been kind enough to support me in my circuitous academic path. I consider myself lucky to have had such mentors, along with Alison Frank Johnson. Alison's support of my frequent, and frequently changing, ideas never flagged. Nor did her own work ever cease to inspire.

To Latif Nasser, Stephen Tardif, Ken Kimura, Martin Rempe, and David Weimer: thank you for your camaraderie and willingness to serve as interlocutors. To Erez Manela, J. R. McNeill, Aviel Roshwald, Hoi-eun Kim, Erika Rappaport, Tara Zahra, Jan Goldstein, Leora Auslander, Robert Richards, and others: thank you for your feedback and the opportunities you gave me to share my work. For various other intellectual exchanges I owe debts to Nicolas Tarling, James C. Scott, Timothy Parsons, David Armitage, Steffen Rimner, Marco Basille, Brett Carter, Joshua Walker, Shelby Grossman, and Niall Ferguson. Arjun Byju, a former student and all-around undergraduate dynamo, provided valuable assistance with obtaining material from the Sanford Archives in Florida.

For financial support, I wish to extend my gratitude above all to the Weatherhead Center for International Affairs at Harvard University. I consider it an honor to have been associated with this institution, and in particular with Clare Putnam, Steve Bloomfield, and the various graduate student associates. The Minda de Gunzburg Center for European Studies at Harvard, the Weatherhead Initiative on Global History, the Georgetown University International History Seminar, and Vanderbilt University also financed stages in my research.

At Harvard and Vanderbilt, postdoctoral fellowships afforded me space and time to complete final revisions of the manuscript. Both library systems were bountiful beyond my imagination, both in their own holdings and in their work to obtain rare works via interlibrary loan. In Nashville, I would like to thank Helmut Smith (my undergraduate advisor), Celia Applegate, Joel Harrington, Moses Ochonu, Paul Kramer, Marshall Eakin, Ari Joskowicz, Juliet Wagner, Alistair Sponsel, Lauren Benton, Carolyn Taratko, Pat Anthony, and Meike Werner. All provided valuable insights, as well as a warm intellectual community.

At Stanford University, where I had an opportunity to present my work in the fall of 2015, I would like to thank (in no particular order and inexhaustively) Jessica Riskin, Edith Sheffer, J. P. Daughton, Richard Roberts, Norman Naimark, James Campbell, Zephyr Frank, Robert Crews, Paula Findlen, Gordon Chang, Yumi Moon, Jun Uchida, Tom Mullaney, Allyson Hobbs, Jonathan Gienapp, Ben Hein, Mikael Wolfe, Paul Robinson, and Kären Wigen. Each member of this wonderful department took time to comment on my manuscript at a crucial stage in the revision process. Priya Satia's scrutiny of the manuscript, in particular, helped me to identify potential oversights and make final revisions.

At Harvard University Press, I would be remiss not to thank my editor, Andrew Kinney. Andrew and the entire staff at HUP have proven exceedingly generous and professional throughout the process of publication. Likewise the team at Westchester Publishing Group: Deborah Grahame-Smith, John Donohue, and Carol Noble. On a separate note, I would like to thank the referees for Harvard University Press, whose reports helped me to address certain infelicities and whose insights improved my final product immeasurably.

Quoted material from the Royal Archives is included by the permission of Her Majesty Queen Elizabeth II. For other permissions and facilitations I thank the Sanford Museum, Oregon University, the Baker Business Library at Harvard University, the Henry M. Stanley Archives at the Royal Museum for Central Africa, and the national archives of Namibia, Germany, Austria, France, Britain, and the United States, respectively.

Finally, a few words about my family, to whom this book is dedicated. My father, mother, stepfather, and brother have sustained me in various ways throughout my life. For this, no words of thanks could prove adequate. A similar sentiment applies to my wife, Miriam, a constant source of warmth, cheer, and keen perception.

Index